Worthy, by Faith

A

Bless Your Soul Publishing Novel

Written by

So surely you ought to stick to what you know is certain. All you have learned comes from people you know and trust because since childhood you have known the holy Scriptures, which enable you to be wise *and lead* to salvation through faith in Jesus the Anointed. All of Scripture is God-breathed; *in its* inspired *voice, we hear* useful teaching, rebuke, correction, *instruction, and* training for a life that is right that God's people may be up to the task ahead and have all they need to accomplish every good work.

2 Timothy 3:14-17

Dedication

All the glory belongs to you, God. I am in awe of the full completion you have bestowed upon my life. I am a precious Child of God. I acknowledge You as my Father and the bearer of all things. You are the One who kept me, carried me and most of all, you are the One who allowed me the pleasure of having this book poured out from the Holy Spirit onto these very pages. I am not a writer. I am an obedient stenographer of each word that flowed into me. I am a ready writer. He is my ink, heart, and my soul. I am simply the pen. Beyond mere words, I am so grateful for the honor. Through the creation of this novel, I learned, through trials and many tribulations, that I am worthy, by faith. I learned to give God full reign over my life. It was not an easy journey. Yet, through resting upon Romans 8:18, God cleansed me, mind, body, and soul. Whatever place in life you find yourself, as you read these pages, I pray that God will heal you, cleanse you, and I pray that you allow Him to move in and through you. This novel is a journey of love. This is my soul on these pages. Here in this novel, is purity.

Prologue

It must be him calling!

"Hey, Baby, are you running late?" Trinity moaned into the phone.

"Trinni, gurl, you can kill the sexy voice. I know you only put it on because you thought I was Grey calling. I'm impressed. You were really pulling out all the bells and whistles too!" Trinity's best friend, Jnana, teased.

Returning to her normal tone, Trinity replied, "Oh, Jnana, I'm so sorry. You're right. It distracted me, so I didn't bother checking the Caller ID before I answered the phone."

"No worries, Trin. Now, what time was he supposed to call you? Better yet, what time was Grey supposed to *be there*?"

"Jnana, Greysan was supposed to blow the horn for me to bring my luggage out to the car around nine this morning. As you already know, it's 3 p.m.!"

"Did you call him? Maybe he had an emergency or something. There's got to be some explanation for him not showing up at this point." Jnana breathed in deep then she asked, "He has never been a no-show before, right?"

"Nope…he has never done this before. And yes, I tried to call him, numerous times in fact." Trinity gulped hard. She hated lying to her best friend. "I just hope that he's okay."

"Trin, you want me to come over? We can pop some popcorn and have a girl's night-in like we used to."

Trinity smiled and savored the moment. Even as direct as she can be, Jnana has a heart of gold. "No, I'm good, I'll just wait on Grey."

"Ok. I'm sure Grey will be there. He's got to be crazy to stand you up on your birthday! That would be trifling with a capital T!"

"I'm sure he won't. You know that the economy is crap right now. And as the Director at Hextlers Bank, Grey must oversee a lot of the loans for homeowners trying to stop the foreclosure of their home. It's very stressful for him. Maybe, he got caught up in a meeting or something. He'll be here...I just know it." Trinity looked off into the room, melancholy and hopeful.

"Well, let me know either way. I cannot have my bestest friend in the whole wide world spending her birthday alone. Especially not the big 3-9!"

"Jnana, you know that I'll let you know. Thanks so much for thinking of me. Love ya, Lady!"

"Love Ya too, Birthday Lady. Oh, and Trin, enjoy this year because next year is the big 4-0! When you hit forty, your body acts like it's turning on you!"

"Yes, I remember. The big 4-0 hit you hard last year, and you haven't been the same since!" Trinity giggled softly.

"Oh, let's not get it twisted, Trin, I still look mighty sexy! Yes, even at my age." Jnana laughed out loud.

"I know! I see how that husband of yours looks at you. You must be swinging from the chandelier in that house. He just cannot keep his hands off you. Now, let me clear the line. Hopefully, Grey will call soon so I can show him how sexy I still am, even at 39 years old!"

"Sho you right, Trin! Have some birthday fun. I'll check on you later. Love you, my bestest friend."

"Love you too, my bestest friend. Don't worry about me. I will be alright. Believe me, I will be alright, with or without Grey."

They shared a hearty, familiar laugh and hung up without a goodbye. Over the years, their friendship had become as comfortable as an old recliner. Trinity was glad that the usually invasively inquisitive Jnana let her off easy. It was a special birthday gift; of this, she was sure. However, tomorrow would spell the return to realness, and the questions neglected today would be in full effect. For now, she hated lying to Jnana about Grey. She was sick of making excuses for the inexcusable and very foolish behavior of that man.

~1~
Souled Out

Then, because so many people were coming and
going that they did not even have a chance to eat, he
said to them, come with me by yourselves to a quiet
place and get some rest.
Mark 6:31
***

Trinity

Pacing back and forth in her condo, Trinity
wondered aloud about things a woman should never
have to ponder regarding a man she believes she is
monogamously committed to. Things like: *where is
this man? Why can't I reach him after trying for
hours? Why is he so darn selfish? And why does he
seem incapable of keeping his word to me...about
anything!?* But wonder she did.

She had been sitting in her condo half the
day. She looked out of the window as she
incessantly called her boyfriend's phone. He neither
showed up to her condo nor answered any of her
phone calls. Each call she made to him ended with
her getting more and more irritated when he did not
pick up. Each hope-filled walk to the window
disappointed her as she scanned the parking lot and
did not see his car. She was looking forward to
seeing her man. She felt as if she was in
love...deeply...so she was confused as to why she
was spending the day alone. Her birthday at that!

Greysan had often disrespected her and
shown her that he did not care about her time or her

personal boundaries. Still, hours later, Trinity refused to stop pacing and instead celebrate, alone. Alas, she became angrier and vehemently vowed to wait for him until he arrived. No matter how late. "I cannot believe he is choosing to ruin my day with this nonsense! You know, I must be the stupid one to think that he will be personally accountable, if even just this once. He has disappointed me since the beginning of this relationship! Each time he stood me up, he made up an excuse why he didn't show. Or the next time I saw him, he pretended that there were no specific plans made. Then, he would make me feel as if I am crazy and that I made it all up in my head.

"Then again, maybe I am crazy.

"Foolishly, I still hope that he will change. I love him blindly, and I give him complete control over me. Shame on me!"

Trinity took a sip of lemon water. She took a lemon piece out of the glass and ate the fruit before putting down the skin. Then, she angrily threw the glass across the room. She watched as the glass bounced off the wall and shattered into pieces. Her eyes were transfixed as the liquid cascaded down the wall. The artist in her found a beautiful picture in the mess on her wall. It was a quaint reflection of her mood. A stroke of red here and a few splashes of orange there, yes, that would be a lovely painting indeed, she reasoned. Peaceful for a few seconds as she admired the accidental piece of art, she smiled. Then as the distraction faded, her rage rose back to the surface with a vengeance.

Where is this darn man? In the four years of

this blatantly disrespectful nonsense, I have spent more time waiting for him than spending time with him. For some reason, I am still putting up with it. I have tried to stop seeing him, I really have. But then, the loneliness kicks in, and my mind betrays me by making all his wrongs seem right. I felt as if I miss him like crazy. Then, after a couple days of madness, I must call him. I must. It is as if I am under a hypnotic spell!

Trinity paced back and forth in the living room, creating a line of footprints on the carpet. With nervous energy guiding each step, her body slouched, and a frown appeared prominently across her forehead. This was yet another episode to remind her of her worthlessness. Still, why would he choose today to be a no-show? Yesterday or tomorrow would be perfectly good days for this nonsense. But not today!

She had been waiting for this ceremonious day all month. He had promised her he would take her to eat breakfast at her favorite greasy spoon restaurant, *Spoons,* and then take her shopping at Neiman Marcus until late afternoon. They were to see a locally produced play about love and relationships. He claimed to want to gain a better understanding of her issues as a woman. After the play, they were to drive to Philadelphia, in a rented Aston Martin. Upon arrival, they were to check into a hotel and sneak in a quick sex session before changing into party clothes. They planned to go listen to some poetry and afterward dance until the wee hours of the morning at the after-party. Then, to close out her birthday celebrations, they were to go back to the hotel to get all hot and sweaty while making love until the sun came up. If everything went as she planned, it could very well be the birthday of her dreams. In the four years they had been in a relationship, they had never spent the entire night together. If things went smoothly, maybe they would even become engaged!

And, she had every intention of getting him into an engaging state of mind.

In preparation, Trinity went out earlier in the week to get her nails, hair, and feet done. Last night, she got her eyebrows threaded and had been adventurous enough to get a Brazilian in the shape of a heart for the first time as a special surprise. Her hair grows so fast, so it just had to be freshly done. She also brought some provocative lingerie that was sure to be visually pleasing. She donned her sunglasses and big sunhat to go to a discrete pleasure shop that was quietly gossiped to be full of freak'em out paraphernalia. She did not want anyone she knew to know what kind of woman she was in the bedroom. Repeatedly, she had to close her own mouth from surprise at the shop's wide variety of pleasurable devices. Excitedly adventurous, she bought body paints, feathers, and other titillating things she never tried.

She had spent over an hour there, eyes wide and mouth open. Trinity believed that she was already an open-minded lover. However, she was, admittedly, tame compared to the possibilities the various products presented. Trinity mused that if she brought half the items they carried, she would elevate her freak status into the stratosphere. And, if things went well, she planned on making as many incognito trips back to the store as needed. Trinity looked forward to many nights of fun and experimentation with the products the store stocked. She refuses to have boring sex now that she knows that such sexual aids are on the market. You know that no one likes the same Ritz cracker the same way, every single time! Good, committed love needs variety and spice to keep loving passionately.

Deep in thought, the sound of the telephone ringing startled Trinity. The ringtone, *Can you Feel It* by Kem, echoed in the large, beautifully furnished condo. She rushed too fast to the phone and stubbed her toe on the big white leather wing chair. Hopping on one foot and writhing in pain, she tried to compose herself enough to answer the phone.

As Trinity's phone rang, this time, she looked at the Caller ID. When she smiled widely, her beautiful smile twinkled with small dimples. On the Caller ID pad, she saw that it was Grand Momma and Grand Poppa!

"Hey, Babea, Happy Birthday!" Grand Momma yelled sweetly into the phone.

"Sugarplum, Happy thirty-ninth Birthday!" Grand Poppa sang into the phone.

On separate phones in the house, they sang Stevie Wonder's version of Happy Birthday until Trinity cried softly into the phone. This is true love and acceptance. She wished that she could bottle it and wear it as cologne all her lonely days…if only.

"That was so sweet, Grand Poppa and Momma. That's my favorite birthday song. I appreciate you both for remembering how Momma used to sing it to me every single year."

She glanced at the clock. As with every single year, on her birthday, they called right on time.

"And I see that you two also remembered to call at the precise time that I was born."

Trinity harkened back to the days when Momma used to do little sweet things to commemorate her birthday. Over the years, no celebration was like the last. It was during those times that her mother would tell her how much she loved her, even though her father had left them. Her mother always reminded her that she was woman enough to be both mother and father. It was during those conversations that Trinity felt the happiest.

"Poppa, can you hang up the phone to give Trinity and me a moment, please?" Grand Momma asked.

"Sure, sweetie, anything for you." He answered.

"Thanks, Poppa. Can you run our bath, please? Not too hot and not too cold." Grand Momma moaned into the phone.

Trinity wanted to put down the phone. These two cannot still be…nah, not at their ages!

She cleared her throat, "Uhh, Poppa and Momma, I am still on the phone. This is more information than my ears can bear."

"Alright, I'm getting off here, you two. Love you, Sugarplum. Enjoy your birthday!" And with that, he hung up.

"Trinity," Grand Momma said, readying herself, "why are you still home? I thought your boyfriend, who we still have yet to meet…after four years…was taking you out?"

I cannot lie to her too! My heart cannot bear all these

fibs.

"Maybe he is running late…or something…because I haven't heard from him, and he was supposed to be here at nine o'clock this morning."

"Well, sweetie, in my day, we would call that stood up. Count yourself as without a date on your birthday, of all days! A respectful man wouldn't go these many hours and not even contact you."

Covering the phone with her hand, Trinity sighed loudly. I cannot deal with this!

"Yes, Ma'am." She finally spoke, respectfully, into the phone.

"Trinity, you know if your mom were here, she would tell you the same thing. God rest her soul."

"I know, Grand Momma, I know."

"Well, Baby, I have to go. Poppa has the bath ready, and you know how impatient he is. I love you, Babae. Enjoy the rest of your birthday."

"I will try, Grand Momma…I promise that I will try."

As Trinity continued to pace for a while longer, she eyed the many footprints embedded in her black plush carpet. Finally, she relaxed by going to check to see how her hair and make-up were holding up. She walked into her bedroom and stopped in front of her brass full-length mirror. She stood tall and forced a smile. She took in all her Queenliness. Five feet, nine inches tall, size fourteen, she is a vision of voluptuous beauty. She possessed warm light brown skin with a beautiful glow of grace and deep-set, almond-shaped brown eyes that complemented her small but defined nose and pouty, soft bee-stung full lips. Her physical features effortlessly bridged the gap between the ethnic features of her African-American mother and Caucasian father. She stood taller and poked out her chest. She assessed her average-sized 38C full breasts, which (thanks to an expensive silicon enhanced push-up bra) fit perfectly into her favorite teal colored sweater. It featured her favorite fashion styles: butterfly wing sleeves and sweetheart cut neck. Her thick thighs, wide hips, and full, round bottom fit snugly inside her cream-colored, wide-leg jeans. She smiled at the outfit that she had painstakingly picked out weeks ago. She enjoyed looking like a beautiful, free-spirited Bohemian Queen.

Her honey-blonde shoulder-length, naturally curly hair was flat ironed razor straight, making her appear much younger than thirty-nine years. Fidgeting nervously, she added a little more Nassie's Hope Cocoa Hair Butter around her hairline to tame the frizzes. Then, she flat ironed the back of her hair once more to assure that the style would last throughout the night. Some of her thick curls were already resisting the heat, and if left to its own devices, her thick, naturally curly hair would look like a wild lioness's mane.

She sighed, "Why do I have to be saddled with the most difficult hair to keep tamed?" It was a rhetorical question.

Trinity walked out of her bedroom and into the kitchen to make a turkey and Cooper Sharp sandwich with lettuce, tomatoes, onions, and mayo. She added a heaping pile of barbecue potato chips and grabbed a bottle of Sunkist Orange soda out of the refrigerator. She sat down with a pile of Oprah magazines to leaf through as she ate. Between bites, she cut out pages from the magazines and assembled a vision board that she would reflect upon throughout her upcoming new year of life. When she was happy that the vision board reflected all her plans and dreams, she hung it on the wall of her art studio. Bored again, she looked at the clock: it read seven o'clock. Yet still no call from Greysan.

Feeling herself coming undone, she drew some sketches that she later planned to put on canvas when she had more time. She signed onto her laptop and began an Audible audio recording of *Stillness Speaks* by Eckhart Tolle. Always on the go, she signed up for a membership with Audible so she could have literature, in audio form, playing at all times. It was the best investment she had purchased in a while.

After another hour, she was about to pick up her cell phone to call Greysan one…more…time, when the text message tone went off three times in succession. Gleefully, she reached for the phone, more birthday wishes, she was sure. All three of the texts were from her married ex-lovers. One sext even included a selfie of the man in his birthday suit holding a cupcake with a lit candle. The text attached read: "Wanna blow it out?"

Trinity pondered the question for a minute until the recollection of her last dealings with that man came flooding back. Wasn't *he* the man that acted like he did not know her when his wife walked into the restaurant where he and Trinity had a romantic rendezvous? Wasn't *he* the one that called her all types of trifling and disrespectful names to convince his wife and four crumb snatchers that *she* was a groupie trying to entrap him? Then, to add insult to injury, wasn't *he* the one that sat by and laughed as his wife beat *her* up and pulled out *her* entire weave? Hmm, how soon he forgets!

Trinity texted back, "No, I don't blow out trick candles anymore. I am grown up now. By the way, your number will be erased and blocked, so do not contact me ever again. If you do, I will forward the text messages, email messages, and this sext to show your crazy wife the real deal! I'm sick of protecting serial cheaters like you!"

He texted her back: "bet!"

To the other men, Trinity texted back her usual smiley face and promised to get back to them in the coming week to receive her birthday presents from them. They both texted back smiley faces. She smiled to herself, thirsty rich men with wives. This is too easy!

Honestly, Trinni was sick of dealing with married men. She wanted a man to want to look into her eyes and have his eyes dance lovingly. And in that glance, she believed that she would know that to him, she was the only woman in the world that mattered. She secretly longed for a spiritually enlightened man. One that would see past her outer beauty and desire to see the soul of her. In that quest, she had abruptly ended her arrangements with married men when she met Greysan. She was happy to be in a committed monogamous relationship with a single man. And it did not hurt that Greysan just happened to be a single, wealthy man.

Four years ago, she thought she had found her deepest desires alive in Greysan. He did not quite compare to the man of her dreams, but…at least he is single.

Trinity sat down on the couch to rest her aching feet. She looked at her cellphone, which was still charging. Surprise! Still no call from Greysan! She bit her lip and scratched her head. Where could he be? Why isn't he as excited to spend my birthday with me? It would be the first birthday he did.

Over their years together, each time he disappointed her and then made up for it was a temporary fix. It was a fix that would not repair her broken sense of self. Less and less money brought her to a place of self-acceptance. Less and less random sex satisfied her need to feel whole. Each diamond necklace and coveted Christian Louboutin, high heeled, shiny, red-lacquered sole pumps, which he brought as a consolation for his no-show behaviors, less than satisfied her need to feel true acceptance. Regardless of how badly he treated her, each time Trinity looked at him, she thought, *what woman could stay mad at Greysan Lobes? I should be happy that a man like him even wants a woman like me!*

Forty-eight-year-old Greysan is a six-foot, four inches tall, sexy drink of water. From his smooth mocha latte complexion and natural golden brown locs that rested sweetly upon his wide shoulders, he is handsome. His perfectly shaped-up beard and mustache, with speckles of gray interwoven throughout, complimented his soft, thick lips and sexy gray eyes. He had a smile that could light up the night sky with the beams of a thousand stars. His strong shoulders could hold the weight of the world (and Trinity, from time to time) upon them. He had a hairy chest with one nipple pierced, strong thick arms, a slight stomach, and well-defined pelvic muscles that lead down to the promise land of male pleasure. He was very easy on the eyes, dressed or undressed. Greysan was surely no stranger to mass sex appeal.

Trinity glanced at the wall clock again and shook her head. Dinner plans…*missed.* It is much too late now! To pass the time and clear away her rising angry thoughts, she logged onto her account on *Macys.com.* With meticulous intention, she scrolled through the fashions and filled her shopping cart with lots of merchandise that would serve as a temporary salve for her aching heart. She was sure that this no-show would amount to an extra monetary bonus. As she browsed online shopping sites, Trinity wondered how such a perfect initial meeting could have turned out to be such a disappointment.

   Trinity met Greysan at a networking event at a local church, The Glow up Church of Deliverance. Always the Dapper Don, he seemed to glide over to her side as she stretched her arm across the buffet to fill a platter of food. His short, freshly twisted baby locs were neatly laid down, and his beard appeared to be freshly trimmed. He looked as if he had walked off the cover of GQ magazine.

His expensive-looking olive-green slacks with a razor-sharp crease, crisp white dress shirt, olive green tie, and size twelve, black Stacy Adams shoes presented the well put-together image of a successful man. Trinity, a woman who loves a man with big shoe size and a taste for the finer things in life, was in awe of him. She observed his swag, the way he walked, how easily his words flowed, the size of his hands. They were big enough to easily touch and tease all of her. She remembers how she had salivated at the very thought of being the woman he would want in his bed. The mere physical presentation of Greysan presented Trinity with the perfect cerebral aphrodisiac.

That night, as Trinity reached out to pile more food atop her already full plate, Greysan gently grasped her wrist. The scent of his cologne smelled like a hit of Neroli Essential Oil. It filled the air like a fine mist, instantly intoxicating her. When she innocently looked at him, he looked into her eyes and smiled. She tried not to appear intimidated by his presence, so she closed her eyes and inhaled, slow and sure. She wanted to assure that she etched his scent into her memory banks for eternity. To Trinity, his was the scent of masculinity personified. She was moved to melt, but she was not going out like that. Not yet anyway. Still, she craved to see him naked.

When most women meet an attractive man, they usually sum up all his qualities to see if he would make a good husband and father of their children. Most women would ask pointed questions about a man's occupation, five-yearplan, and relationship status. Trinity's approach towards the opposite sex was different. When she saw an attractive man, she summed up his freak potential in less than five point six seconds. In her mind, when she saw a man, it was either: *yup*, potential freak'em candidate or *nope*, keep it moving, deactivated missile ahead. Detour.

That night at the buffet, Greysan had momentarily torn his eyes away from hers as he filled her plate with a sampling of the fattiest foods she had purposefully passed over. She tried to sound sexy as she said thank you, but hot, stinky breath flew out of her mouth, killing the vibe. Like a superhero of breath mints, Greysan produced a cinnamon breath mint from his breast pocket and slowly glided it into her mouth. His fingertips gently brushed her soft lips. She involuntarily kissed them, thanking the heavens for the pleasure.

Pretending not to feel her loving gesture, Greysan spoke softly, "You're welcome, sweetheart. Now, make sure you eat most, if not *all* this food. Wow, you are stunning. I wish that I could possess a beautifully voluptuous woman like you in my life."

Trinity thought she had heard the voice of an angel. It was husky, deep, and downright masculine. It reminded her of that sexy chocolate Allstate guy. *I just know I would be in good hands with Greysan,* Trinity thought. And, even with all this, Trinity still could not reply.

After a few moments of awkward silence, Greysan said, "Well, uh, have a great night. Eat up."

As if forgetting something, he doubled back to kiss her on the cheek. Avoiding eye contact, He rubbed her on the back before walking away. Lead-footed, he shook his head in defeat. Things didn't go as he had planned. He figured that he struck out. But, unbeknownst to him, his electric touch had sent shock waves through every single nerve ending in Trinity's body. She felt let down that he gave up so easily.

Rushing over, Jnana whispered, "Oh my gosh Trinni! I just know that wasn't Greysan talking to you. Gurl, he is all man! Didn't you notice? *Hello?!*" Jnana continued. "Is this thing on?" Jnana said as she pretended to bang on a microphone. "Trinni? And I just can't believe he made your plate for you. Girl, look, he gave you big servings of the sweet potato casserole, barbecued ribs, potato salad, and he even gave you a big piece of the three-layer chocolate cake. Hmm, I wonder what it means that he gave you lots of fatty foods. Anyway, you think that he is trying to insinuate that you need to fatten up? Humph, I can't see that. No offense, but Trinni, you are already thicker than a Chick-fil-a milkshake!" She shook Trinni by the shoulders and said, "Girl, snap out of it!"

Looking past her best friend, out of embarrassment, Trinity finally responded. "Jnana, you just don't understand. I was petrified!" Ignoring her friend's obvious discomfort, Jnana continued as if she were never interrupted, "Let me tell you when you shot him down, Greysan walked out with his head in his hands. All the ladies in the room, I included, watched the entire scene in total disbelief. All the men, understanding his embarrassment at having his manhood handed to him in such a public forum, gave him pounds in consolation as he walked out the door. What Greysan wants; he gets. That is until you. I just cannot believe that I witnessed something so wonderful. You, Trinity Marie Boussaint, shot down one of the finest men in this church. You made him work hard for your attention, yet you totally put him in his place. Good deal, my bestest friend in the world. That man needed to get knocked off his high horse. He really isn't all of that anyway. My Baby Shandon is way more of a man than Greysan will ever be."

Finally pulling herself together, Trinity replied, "Ah, Jnana, that was not an intentional diss. And it sure as heck wasn't wonderful for me! I stood in his face like a complete idiot, and to add insult to injury, I acted like I was mute. I waited months for him to notice me, and when he does, I flake. I know you think that Shandon is all that, but he is your husband! I need a man for me. I wanted that man to be Greysan, but I think I blew it. Honestly, Jnana, I wanted to speak, but my mouth was stuck like I had eaten an entire jar of peanut butter. And you will not believe this next part. Umm, Jnana, you know how I love to stop off at *Spoons* to get a double patty melt with extra onions, chili fries with extra cheese, and a triple thick strawberry-banana milkshake? Well, I forgot that I had eaten that meal before I came here, and I tried to talk to Greysan. When I opened my mouth to speak, my odorous breath was loud! Greysan had to give me a cinnamon breath mint to calm the raging hot storms of funk running wild in my mouth. Oh, Jnana, I was so embarrassed."

"Trinni, I am so sorry." Jnana giggled, "That must have really been a hot mess. I have been with you after you ate that meal, so I know how your breath can stink! I feel bad for Greysan's nose; his nose hairs must be all burnt out." Jnana laughed so hard her eyes watered, and she had to hold her stomach to compose herself.

"Alright now, comedian Jnana. You can stop trying to hone your comedic stand-up act on me. Listen to me closely when I say this - I was mortified! There stood Greysan, looking so fine and edible, in front of me, and yet I stood silent and embarrassed because my breath smelled like a sewer rat. How will I *ever* redeem myself?"

"Trinni, relax. This is a horribly embarrassing situation for you, but look on the bright side, he had empathy for you and passed you a breath mint. I mean, he could have played you out for real. You know that he must dig you, at all, to hook you up with some cinnamon breath help. That's a start, right?"

"Yeah, you're right, he helped me out. Then again, he almost seemed as if he felt sorry for me. Hold up, that's not good! I don't want him to feel sorry for me. I want him to want me, even one day, love me. Dammit, I really blew it!"

Jnana said, with her hands on her ample hips, "Trinni, you need to get it together. You are really coming undone over this. Not to mention, you got people staring over here, and you know that I cannot stand drama. So, calm down and get yourself together. Trin, look at you. You are a classic beauty, smart, and creative. You are a good woman too. You do realize all of this, right?"

"Yeah, Jnana, I do, "Trinni said, lowering her head. "It's just that you know I have never had a good track record with men, and Greysan is so wonderfully dreamy. I can't imagine what he wants with me, anyway."

"Trinni, you need to work on your self-esteem! You are a beautiful black queen. The last thing he better ask himself is: 'why didn't I stick around and chat up that stinky, double onion patty melt breath lady at the buffet?' You are worthy of that Trinni, ever so worthy! You said that he is dreamy, alright, he may be that in your eyes. But you are the one who needs to understand one thing: he should be pressed by you, not the other way around. So, what if he is dreamy! Is he saved? Does he even know God? Does he live with his Momma? Is he even gainfully employed? It's sad that you must ask nowadays, but does he have a criminal record or even been on the DL in jail. We have both seen Greysan around, and he seems like a well-put-together package, but do we really know him? No! Now, there are more important qualities in a man besides being dreamy. I swear, Trinni, you really need to stop settling with all these pretty boys that aren't worth your time! You are worthy of a good man that will treat you well. You deserve a man that will respect you and one that you can trust because of his words *and* actions. I know that you are a freak, so you need a man that will please you on the regular. You need a man who will put your spiritual, mental, and emotional needs in line with his. A man who is committed to only you, not one that only wants you around because your favor is easily attained. Trinni, please understand these things. You deserve a good man who is *all* yours."

"I will try to remember that Jnana." Trinity lied. It was her feeble attempt to stop the onslaught of further motivation she would get from Jnana if she disagreed. Her food was getting cold, and if she got Jnana started, she would never hear the end of it. The people would turn off the light and start locking up the church before she would stop her life coach's speech of inspiration. Trinity was not down for all that drama, not tonight!

Convinced her motivation worked, Jnana made a plate of sweets, and they both sat down laughing and chatting about Greysan and how perfect he would be for Trinity. Even before Trinity began a relationship with Greysan, she had images of him fitting into her life and being her man. In her mind, he was already hers. In her mind, Greysan was spooning her and whispering sweet nothings in her ear. He would be her sexual conquest. Greysan just did not know it yet.

Trinity smiled. Memories of her and Greysan's initial meeting pushed her back in time. The subsequent chasing he did to capture her was evident. She was his prey, and he was a focused predator. Trinity thought of how easily she and Jnana had sat down that night and planned her gloriously romantic relationship with Greysan. She thought of how Greysan had gotten her number and called her daily, how he had put on a full-court press from the very beginning, sending dozens of roses, boxes of See's chocolates, and how he had ordered her the best take-out food from any restaurant she had desired. She still gets heady thinking of their first time making love. How suave he looked when he had come over at midnight with a gallon of butter pecan ice cream, her favorite. She can still feel her legs shaking as he wore her out, again and again. He was a tiger, and she was his tigress. Afterward, they fell asleep. She remembered how he told her he could not hold her because he was too hot and sweaty. So instead, he had laid on one side of the bed, and she, on the edge of the other. Sadness gripped her as she fell asleep, hoping it was just nervousness that had him suddenly acting so cold. She had never felt more alone than when she had awakened hours later, ready for round three. She had looked around in those early morning hours hoping that he was simply in the kitchen making her a snack. *Love Jones*, all in her dreams of their love affair. She, Nia, and Greysan, Darius. Who knew what would happen when the love jones hit!

Instead of Greysan half-naked cooking her an omelet, she had found a note that he had left. To her surprise, accompanying the note was an envelope which contained one thousand dollars. His note said that he had to be at a big stockholder meeting. Save because it was only three a.m. on a Sunday morning. And save because it appeared to Trinity to be a weird excuse to leave so early in the morning, she was okay spreading out in her king-sized bed…alone. She sighed. No, it was not the way she had expected their first lovemakingsession to end. But as she had counted the money, she knew that he must be really digging her. She could see that he believed that she was valuable and important to him to leave her such a generous sum of money.

That morning, after she had showered and put her hair up in a towel, Trinity had signed onto her computer and, to the dime, planned all the things she would purchase with the money. She had thrown the money up in the air over her bed and rolled around in it. She smelled the sheets that he had laid on and touched herself softly, imagining every touch was his. She had fallen asleep thinking of how she could have been so lucky to have him pick her, out of all the other women in the world, to make love to.

It was during those early morning hours that she had created such a beautiful fantasy love affair in his arms and a life of passion and freedom for the first time in her life. From that day on, their relationship was based on a foundation of sex and money. There was an overflowing of both every time she had seen him. There was neither love, passion, nor freedom. But hey, Trinity figured, a girl cannot get all her dreams! Hence, she was sprung out: mind, body, and pocketbook.

Looking at the clock one last time, Trinity realized that it was ten o'clock. Too tired to pace any longer and after making the hundredth phone call to Greysan, Trinity changed into her brushed fleece footed pajamas and lit the thirty-nine candles on her chocolate buttercream birthday cake. She did not bother making a wish. Warm tears streamed down her face as she reflected in the dark condo filled to the brim with expensive findings. She thought of how cheaply she sold herself for the riches of the world. The Scripture her Grand Momma had once said came to mind…*what good is it to inherit the world yet lose your soul?* She blew out the candle as pain erupted in her heart. Without cutting the cake, she jammed a fork into the fluffy, very rich, layered delicacy.

While watching old Martin episodes on TV One, she ate half of the cake. Then, she dragged herself into the kitchen for some barbecue potato chips con queso dip and a two-liter Coca Cola soda. She ended the last few minutes of her thirty-ninth birthday melancholy, in forced solitude. She just knew that if Greysan would only cooperate with her fantasy, he could fulfill her deepest desires to feel worthy. In the core of her soul, she yearned to feel the peaceful warmth and love of the womb, just as she did her first seconds in the world. A new year of life…day one.

~ 2~

Intimacy

There's more to sex than mere skin on skin. Sex is as much spiritual mystery as physical fact. As written in Scripture, "The two become one." ...

Psalm 6:16

***

Jnana

Waking up next to my man is the high point of my day. It is beyond his physical presence. It is the ethereal sensuality that his spirit awakens in mine every time I look at him, this early in the morning. Daybreak thrusts forth with the sun reflecting lovingly upon our faces as he wakes me up by rubbing my scalp and kissing me on the neck. My Baby says that it soothes him. But the feeling of his fingers rubbing softly on my scalp and my spine tingling from his lips touching a sweet, sensitive spot on my neck is more than soothing to me. His intentional tenderness reinforces just how dedicated he is to be the most important man in my life. He knows I desire to be awakened with love and affection, not a lot of moving about or conversation. Every morning, just like today, as I slowly open my eyes, the most magnificent view greets me. My chocolate man stares into my eyes with such vulnerability as his dark eyes treat me to a journey into his soul. I am not going to lie; it is more than my heart can bear. His smile is my sunshine. His masculine scent is my enticing reason to begin a new day. His muscular legs and arms intertwined with my softness make me feel safe. Our

26 | P a g e

connection makes me so motivated to open my eyes and love all up on this sexy man just as he is doing to me. Each new day with Shandon teaches me that God loved me so much that he sent the perfect soothing balm for my heart. I may not always act like a lady, talk like a lady, or dress like a lady, but in my Baby's eyes, in this moment in time, so early in the morning, I am always his Lady.

When I open my eyes to find my man looking at me with his dark eyes, the world is a beautiful place. When he kisses my lips and tells me how honored he feels that I love him, he makes love to me cerebrally over and over. When he looks into my eyes and speaks to my spirit, it takes my thoughts to a transcendental level and reminds me of how spiritually connected we are. We are equally yoked in every way. I am the Ruth to his Boaz.

My husband, Shandon Donovan Roberts, and I have been married for eighteen years. We have loved each other through many happy years since I became Mrs. Jnana Jael Roberts. But do not get me wrong; our life isn't perfect. We argue and have had many disagreements over the years. Some arguments were bad. Those were full of pride, ego, and many regrets. However, the one thing that has made our love worth building upon is our easy forgiveness of each other. Since the beginning, our personalities have been complementary. He loves my outgoing, down-to-earth, strong, outspoken yet lovable personality. I love that he is laid back, calm, consistent, yet he is always ready with his sarcastic brand of humor to make me laugh.

In conversation, Shandon and I relate on

many topics. We know each other's strengths and weaknesses, plus we can both humble ourselves and cry freely in front of the other when we are hurt. We respect each other, implicitly, and we are both hard workers in our respective careers. We share a love of reading, listening to old jazz music, and spending the weekend watching old black and white movies snuggled up with an old tattered quilt.

We talk about anything and everything with an honesty that has stood the test of time. We have learned to communicate through even the harshest winters of our marriage. Each spring, we come closer and closer to being more in tune with each other, both physically, mentally, and spiritually.

Shandon is a spiritual man, first and foremost. When we met, he knew that I always desired a man that loved God more than he loves me. On our third date, he took me to church with him. I instantly fell in love when I saw the reverence and submission he has for God. Though we were still getting to know each other, he did not hesitate to raise his arms and praise God in front of me.

That day, I knew that my Baby's dedication to fulfilling God's purpose for his life would always be his driving force. With that knowledge, I knew that God's will would be done in our marriage. We do not judge each other. We provide complete support as we each grow into our best selves. That is why our love stays strong!

Another reason we are still so deeply in love is that my Baby spoils me. As we got out of bed, he kissed me on my forehead then hooked my bathrobe to the back of the door before he started my morning shower. When he finished, he went downstairs to prepare my breakfast. I showered in peace under the three heads. I imagined each warm droplet of water was a soft, sensual kiss from my husband. Oh, how that man stays in my head! The water stream felt so good that I did not want to get out. But I have employee issues to deal with in the coming day that I must finally meet head-on. I have procrastinated long enough. I wish I could take the longest shower in history, but I must get out, or my water bill will have to be delivered by Brinks! I stepped out of the shower and walked back into my adjoining bedroom.

My Baby was just walking into the room with a tray full of food and juice. This morning, he is treating me to breakfast in bed by serving me homemade Belgian waffles with strawberries and cream, orange juice, and my favorite Amish maple sausage. He also had an extra saucer of strawberries and whipped cream. I know that he had kept the remaining strawberries and cream for a specific purpose: to use on me. My husband put the tray down on the end table and got a towel. He bent down on his knees and dried my soaking wet body. When I was dry, he sat me gently upon the bed and fluffed up a pillow behind my back before covering me up. He smiled at me and climbed under the covers. While I ate my breakfast above the covers, he was down below having his breakfast, me - à la mode.

After I finished eating my breakfast, my Baby pulled the covers back and stood me before him. He took a warm washcloth out of the sitz bath that held warmed water. I could not stop the tears from falling as my lover washed me down until I wasn't sticky from his breakfast he had eaten on me. He used his tongue to clear away the stickiness in some of his favorite spots. I had to grasp his shoulders, not to lose balance. The feeling was so good! When he celebrated my womanhood with his tongue, two times, he quickly and deftly undressed. He kissed away my tears of joy, then we both smiled. I am so in love with this generous man. My husband's eyes flowed up and down my body. He sensually ran his firm hands through my brown and blonde highlighted, shoulder-length, bob cut hair, then down to the smooth caramel skin on my long thin neck. Then, he stood close and looked deeply into my eyes, before kissing my cute, small nose and heart-shaped lips. He cupped my chin and kissed me slow and sensually. His hands continued their heat-seeking mission all over my very satisfied body as our tongues danced a rhyme of desire. His passion has me mesmerized, so I gratefully allowed him to do as he pleased.

We got so energized from the kiss we fell on the bed. My lover kissed and caressed every inch of my body, and I passionately returned the pleasure. Our bodies moved in unison. Our rhythm so slow, deep, and intentional. We never lost eye contact. Our spirits connected deeply as we loved as husband and wife. There is nothing more satisfying than a love session that is mentally, physically, and spiritually fulfilling. This feeling of unbridled passion, so early in the morning, rose but never fell. Bliss called our names, and we answered several times.

When we were both spent, I pulled my Baby closer to me, and our foreheads touched. As I lay here looking into the eyes of my lifelong mate, his face still glowing from our lovemaking, I kiss him. I can still taste my sweetness upon his lips. I taste our love between our lips and smile. He is the man of my dreams, and, as I look at the love for me inside his eyes, I know that the feeling is mutual. I sigh as I hear our children outside of our door. That is our signal to finally get out of bed and begin our day.

Even though our morning releases have drained all our energy, we look at the clock on the end table and finally struggle to get out of bed. Then, I notice that my Baby is raring to go again. I watch him as he walks away from me. We are both walking around as naked as the day we were born. Walking with measured steps, we move to separate sides of the room. Finally, tired of teasing each other, we met face-to-face in the full-length mirror on our closets. Our eyes catch in the mirrors across the room from each other and assess each other. Turning to face one another, my eyes run up and down my husband's body. His construction body, thick, rough, and buff at the same time, is so enticing. His cute little round head with soulful black eyes, trimmed up goatee, thick, soft lips, and fade haircut, my breath catches. Oh, my! My Baby is gorgeous!

Shandon notices my introspection, and he runs his large hands over his body. He moves them slowly over his strong shoulders, short, thick neck, hairy chest, thick waist, small stomach, taut bottom, and thick thighs. I lick my lips when he dances for me. I was under his sexy hypnotic spellwhen we hear a knock on our bedroom door. I feel like ignoring the knock and instead crawl on my knees over to my husband, but he answers instead. *Shucks!* "Yes?" His voice cracks like someone caught off guard. Hmm, I guess he knew what I had in mind too.

"Mom," our daughter Liana asked sweetly, "did you sign the permission slip for the trip to the museum next week?"

I quickly signed it and glided it through a thin crack under our bedroom door. "Lili, are you keeping track of the time? We won't be chasing the bus down the street again."

She sighed that teenage sigh and said, "Yes, Mom. I'm about to go iron my clothes and flat iron my hair."

I quelled my attitude and said, "Okay, see you when we get downstairs. Love you."

She walked off without replying. Teenagers!

Shandon and I have two teenage children. A son, Ashton, 16, and our daughter, Liana, 13. We love our childrenand are good parents actively involved in their lives. I am an unapologetic, self-proclaimed helicopter parent. Shandon is an excellent father who has a laid-back parenting style. But he is a father who will not hesitate to come correct with his children if the need should arise. We have developed a system of parenting that works out great, despite our worlds apart parenting styles. He is rarely the disciplinarian but, on rare occasions, will do the harsh job of not sparing the rod.

For Shandon and me, we have intended to have a Christian marriage. One that is about the three beings within a marriage. As Ecclesiastes 4:12 reads, *a three-fold cord is not easily broken. Man, woman, and God, a three-corded rope is much stronger with God in the middle of two committed folks.*

We make it our business, with the realities of losing touch with one another, to be good parents to our children. But we are always a good friend, lover, and lifelong mate to each other. Shandon and I always make time for our children. We are purposeful about fostering our relationship with each other, so when our children are grown, the foundation of our relationship will still be solid. We have watched too many couples break up because they did not have each other's back or asked for God's assistance when the going got rough. Our children will be there for us to love unconditionally forever. But, in the best-case scenario, our children will want a life of their own, outside of our family home.

I turned back to my husband and was surprised to see that he was fully dressed. I put on my best smile and began getting dressed.

"So, my love, what's on tap for you today?" Shandon asked from inside his walk-in closet, loud enough for me to hear.

"Babe, I have to plan for an employee team-building meeting for the next month. But first, I must deal with a situation I have going on with Littia. I have a scheduled meeting with her today to discuss her job performance and reprimand her about her rude treatment of some of our customers. When I have been out and about in marketing in town, several customers have approached me to complain about Littia's lack of customer service. I am fed up with all the complaints she has been receiving, so I must talk to her so we can get some things straight. Babe, I've even called the store from a number other than my cell or home phone, and she has been rude *to me!* My customers are my foundation, and over the years, some of them have become like family to me. I cannot tell you how many people come in just to talk, receive inspiration, or simply get a book recommendation. My customers mean a lot to me, and I won't allow her to give my business a bad reputation."

"Jnana, I didn't want to say anything to you before, but she was even rude to me. I guess that she didn't recognize my voice when I called the store. Her tone was very stern, and she was very aggressive about finding out who I was. When I asked to speak with you, she asked all types of unnecessarily probing questions about why I was calling and what business I had with you. When I asked her what was up with all the questions, she must have recognized my voice because she hung up on me."

"Shandon stop playing! Littia hung up on you? When did this happen?"

"Jnana, it happened a couple of weeks ago. I didn't mention it because you told me she is going through some rough times with her health. I didn't want to add insult to injury."

"Babe, it doesn't matter what she is going through, health-wise. There will never be an excuse for disrespecting my customers, let alone my husband! I am so happy that you mentioned this. What you just shared makes this situation a more pressing matter for me."

"I'm sorry that you are in such a tough position, Baby. I know that it's hard when you are the employer, but you also know your employees personally. In this situation, I suspect that you have to remain impartial yet fair."

"Shandon, I know that you have your own employees to deal with. And you would deal with this with an iron fist. But you do not understand how difficult this is for me because Littia is a single mom! Working at Namaste is her primary income. Still, I have had numerous complaints about her. When I've sat back in my office, I have noticed on the cameras she is on the phone a lot. I assume she spends most of her time on the phones when I am out of the store as well. Several times, I called from my cell to see if there were messages. Shandon, there were several messages on the answering machine! I can only assume that she is not answering call waiting calls that come in while she is chatty on the main line. I had to open twice last week when it was her days to do it. Her excuse was that she was trying out some new medication for her depression. But I quickly found out the truth. She talks a lot, so she always tells on herself. She ended up telling a customer she had a rough night out partying at the contemporary dance club downtown until five in the morning."

"Oh, wow, busted! Jnana, so, what's your game plan?"

"Shandon, my first instinct is to fire her. I have thought of giving more responsibilities to Roshina, but I'm not sure she is up to the task of opening and cashing in and out the register. Rosh is a good employee, but she has only worked at the bookstore for three months. I don't want to give that kind of responsibility to her, just yet. After going over the pros and cons, I have drawn up a disciplinary warning letter for Littia to sign. I want to make sure I bring to her attention, in writing, the complaints I have received. I also want to bring to her attention that I realize that she doesn't get her work done because she is on the phone all day."

"Jnana, how do you think things will pan out?"

"Not good. She doesn't deal too well with me giving her direction. She acts as if Namaste is her bookstore. I opened Namaste to live out my dream and to fill the void of African American bookstores in the area. She hasn't been with me the entire time, so I'm not sure why she is acting like it's her store. Either way, I have a plan in mind, but judging from how my conversation with her goes, things may take a different turn. Hopefully not, but she can have a nasty attitude."

"I think you should just fire her after listening to what you just told me. But I know that you are considering the fact that she has children, so she needs the job. Am I right?"

"Yes, I would have let her go a long time ago if I didn't know her already shaky financial situation. I care about her, but she is taking advantage of me, and we are supposed to be friends, not only employer/employee. I will just have to be professional first and friends second."

"I agree. If you need someone to talk to, call me. I don't have many jobs to do today, so I should be done by two."

"What are you working on today?"

"I am rewiring an old Victorian-style house. The homeowners brought state-of-the-art appliances, and the circuits can't handle the load, so they contracted with me to update the circuits."

"It sounds like today will be a lucrative day for you. Rewiring entire houses costs a lot of money, right?"

"Yeah, I guess that it can be. However, I have a coupon posted on my company website to give loyal customers a fifteen percent discount."

That is another thing I love about my Baby. He is intelligent and business minded. He is knowledgeable, and he cuts corners in pricing to make his services affordable. He is a sexy nerd with business swag; you got to love him! Shandon had started his own electrical company named *Currents* when we first married. In this town, his name is synonymous with expertise, value, and safety. Today, my husband will do what he does best. He will serve his electrical customers by providing skilled electrical work that can be trusted yet still economically priced.

When we got dressed, we walked down the steps to begin our day with our children. I was about to sit down to a cup of Hazelnut and French Vanilla coffee when the phone rang. The Caller ID display read Trinity Boussiant, my best friend. I picked up the phone and walked into the living room. Getting a call from her always signaled drama. It is a good thing that I had already started my day perfectly with my husband. As I said hello to my bestest friend in the world, I breathed a sigh of relief; I am glad that drama does not live in my home.

~3~
Grey Skies

I'm speaking to you as dear friends. Don't be bluffed into silence or insincerity by the threats of religious bullies. True, they can kill you, but then what can they do? There's nothing they can do to your soul, your core being. Save your fear for God, who holds your entire life, body, and soul in his hands.

Luke 12:4-5

***

Trinity

"I'm married."

"Grey, what are you saying? You are not married. How can you be married when we have been in a committed relationship for four years?"

"Aww, come on, Trinni, listen to me. I *am* married. I have been for over ten years."

"You have got to be kidding! I mean really, Grey! Okay, you missed my birthday. Is it really that serious that you must make up such a ridiculous story? Baby, why are you lying to me like this? Of all the ridiculous excuses over the years, this one is the saddest excuse yet. What's next? What other preposterous lies are you going to tell me? Huh? Bring it on! After being stood up by you, on my birthday, I am ready for all your nonsense!"

"Trinity, look, I don't have to make this up. I didn't realize that yesterday was even your birthday. I didn't think about you at all yesterday. I had more important things on my mind. Right now, I need you to focus on what I'm saying. I am married. Not only am I married, but I love my wife very much. Let me ask you something since you need proof of what I am saying: have you ever met my parents? Huh, have you?"

"Grey, you told me they travel a lot since they retired. Remember?"

"Trinity, who travels non-stop for four years? Huh? You just can't be this naïve!"

"What do you mean that I can't be this naïve? I trusted you. In hindsight, I guess that I shouldn't have, but I did. Grey, I believed that you would introduce me to your family when you were ready to take our relationship to another level. I used to bring up how much I wanted to meet your family, but honestly, after a while, I mean it was like it didn't seem to matter. I had your love, so it didn't mean much to me. In the beginning, I told myself that maybe you didn't have a good relationship with your parents, and that was why I never met them."

"Oh, wow! You really are that naïve. Why wouldn't a man want his woman to meet his family? What kind of man wants a woman who doesn't even care to meet his family? Hold up, Trinity, what do you mean that after a while, it didn't mean much for you to meet my family? What the heck is that all about? My family means the world to me! Trust me, if I loved you, I mean *truly* loved you, not lied just to get sex, I would have taken you to meet my peoples, trust. My wife met my family in less than two months. I knew that she was from good stock when I first met her. She also proved herself to be classy and beautiful enough to present to my family with honor. They saw what I saw in her and loved her at first sight. Trinity, yes, you are a sweet person, but you are not classy or educated enough for me. You don't even come from money to make up for your lack of attractive qualities."

"Grey, why are you talking to me like this? You act as if I am an ugly bag of rocks. What did I do to make you so upset, and what can I do to make it better? Tell me, and I promise that I will do it."

"Trinity, you are not getting it, so I will put it plain so you can understand what I am saying. It…is…over! This charade of a relationship is through. To be brutally honest, it never began. You were never my woman. You will never be that lucky. Simply put, you were my jump-off!"

"*Jump-off!?*" Trinity exclaimed like someone had slapped hard in the face.

"Yes, you were my jump-off. A highly paid jump-off at that. Look around this condo. I furnished it with the best leather and art pieces. You have state-of-the-art kitchen appliances and a custom-made bedroom set. Even the heated marble floors are per your specifications. You and I had a business transaction. Don't act like this was more personal than it was. You were compensated, well, for your time and your services."

"Hold up, Grey! Yeah, you gave me all this stuff, that's a fact. But I am your woman. You are supposed to take care of me and buy me what I want. Why are you making our committed relationship sound as if I were just your prostitute?"

"Trinity, you were never my woman! Okay, I'll

relent; you were more than just a prostitute to me. You were good for laughs. In all honesty, you were someone that helped to take my mind off the seriousness of my marriage. Sometimes, you were even a hoot to hang out with. A court jester is fun to look and laugh at, but you sure don't make them your wife! Like I said, you are a good person, and you seem like you have a big heart. But tell me something, Trinity, didn't you realize that I never, in all four years, stayed the night? I always came over later, and I left early morning. Didn't that give you a clue I had obligations elsewhere?"

"Grey, I noticed that, but what's your point? I mean, yes, sometimes, I would have preferred that you stayed the night. You seemed to be happy with things, so I never needed to complain. I enjoy having you around and all, but you know how I like my own space."

"Yeah, Trinity," he sighed, "I know how you love your own space. I know how you like your things just so. But I also know that, from the beginning, it was all about the money for you, Trinity. You never cared that I didn't stay the night. You didn't care if I kissed you goodbye. All you cared about was the money-filled envelope I left on the nightstand for you. That showed me, early on, your true character. You are a cold-blooded gold-digger. But, even with all of this, you were still my jump-off, Trinity. I got some strange and freaky sex, and you were compensated accordingly. It was all about sex and money, albeit a boring and predictable sex life, after a while. But you were familiar, so I didn't want to go out into the street for satisfaction when you were here, always ready to satisfy my every need. No matter when I called or came by to see you, we had the perfect jump-off situation. I paid the mortgage and car note, and in exchange, you had sex with me how, when, and as often as I wanted. What a sweet deal! I searched my entire marriage for the perfect jump-off situation."

Afraid of what I would say next, Trinity frantically searched her mind for a subject change. "Grey, I don't understand what you are saying. This is all too much to take in at one time. Why don't we undress and talk about this another time? You have gotten yourself so worked up. Let us just relax and give this some time to sink in." Trinity arched her back and sashayed in front of Greysan before licking her lips seductively. He smacked her bottom hard as she walked up to him and sat on his lap. He ground his hardness against her softness, biting her neck hard. Then, he stopped suddenly. Trinity was unnerved; what is wrong? Realizing that she had not fed Greysan, she got up. She walked into the kitchen to search for something that she could microwave to eat. She never learned how to cook; it was the man's job to take her out. At least that is what she believed.

"Grey, are you hungry? May I make you something quick to eat?"

"Oh, alright. Fix me a plate of whatever you have while I turn on the television. Then we can get down to business. I don't have a lot of time, so let's get this show on the road. Our regular routine, of dinner and sex, is fine. I won't rock the boat tonight. After dinner, we can do our thing, and then I will leave, like usual."

Gotcha! The sudden calm turn elated Trinity. She was unprepared to deal with Greysan's revelation, and she was happy that he did not want to rock the boat tonight. Maybe he was just venting, and his hissy fit was simply a ploy to divert attention from him missing her birthday. At least she hoped. If this was all the truth, she was in trouble! As she searched for food, she smiled and kept things light. She hoped that their normal routine would smooth things over.

"I have some ravioli, Grey, is that okay? I can heat it up for you in a jiffy."

Shrugging his shoulders and shaking his head, he replied, "Trinity, that sounds good. While you do that, let me ask you one more question. Did you ever notice that I never took you to my place?"

Peeping out from the kitchen, Trinity smiled, "Yeah, but you told me that you keep a messy bachelor's pad. I even offered several times to clean it for you. Why do you ask?"

Scratching his head and smirking, Greysan said, "Well, you need to know, that too was a ruse. My wife keeps my home in immaculate shape. She even makes sure our children are spotless."

Walking into the living room with a plate piled high with ravioli, Trinity inquired, "What? Kids? You told me that you hated kids, that you didn't have the patience for them."

"Ahhh, Trinity, let me take that piping hot plate of food. Thanks. Well, uh, that was all a lie, too. I love kids. In fact, my wife is three months pregnant with our third child in five years. My wife was experiencing a difficult pregnancy when I met you. During that pregnancy, my sex life with her was mundane, routine, and very mechanical. In fact, in the last three months of her pregnancy, the sex was non-existent. She was on bed rest because of an elevated risk for preterm labor and had to monitor her contractions every hour. As you know, I have a high sex drive, so I needed a woman to take care of my sexual needs regularly. I searched awhile for the perfect woman to meet my needs and one who would willingly work within my time restraints. That night, when I saw you at the buffet, I smiled because I knew that I had struck pay dirt. I knew from the first time I saw you, how insecure you appeared, that you would do whatever it took to get and keep a good man like myself. It was obvious you suffered from low self-esteem and had poor self-awareness. Trinity, I knew you would be so flattered by my attention that you would stand on your head and be the freak that I desired just so I would never leave you. I nearly called off my plan because of the horrid onion breath you had that night. But I knew that I could get you to take better care of yourself, hygienically, even if I had to bring a box of Tic-tac with me, I knew that you would serve my purposes just fine. True to my initial estimation, you did an excellent job satisfying my requirements for a jump-off."

"Grey, I cannot believe that you're saying all these things to me. Was I just someone to fulfill your sexual needs? Do you really have children? With your wife?! Look, Greysan, I had two abortions, at your insistence, because you told me you didn't want any children. I was patient and waited for you to take our relationship to a deeper level, yet you were already married? To add insult to injury, all the while, you had a family with your wife. This is all ridiculous!"

"No, Trinity, *you* are ridiculous. Just look at you, how could I expect you, a woman who can't even control how often she raises a fork of food to her mouth, to raise my child? You are an out-of-control eater, too lazy to exercise, and an art college drop-out! You are not someone worthy of bearing my child. Your body is a cesspool for dysfunction. You are complacent and way too comfortable working that barely above minimum wage job at the department store. I need someone with ambition and someone who wants to do something with their life other than just getting by. How could you expect to deal with pregnancy and taking care of a baby? You can barely take care of yourself."

"Grey, please stop! Why are you so angry with me? What did I do to you? I'm not all those things that you are saying to me. Stop, please!"

"No, I won't stop. You started this, so I will finish it. You need to hear these things I am telling you. You are telling me to stop simply because you can't handle reality - the sick reality of who you really are. Your delusion is why you won't find anyone but me to deal with. You brought up your abortions! I didn't force you to kill your babies. You did that on your own, and it's a good thing too. I want more children, just not with you. How could I knowingly pass your family history of mental disease on to my children? I mean, your own Mom killed herself! What does that say about your mental stability? Your own father ran out on you. The outlook is bleak for your future. I know that much! You are obviously a product of your unstable and emotionally charged childhood."

"I said stop already! Why are you saying such hateful things to me? You met me at the buffet at the church, and now you complain about my weight and my eating? You have some nerve! I had abortions because every time I told you I was pregnant; you beat me up. You know that you would have made sure that I didn't carry to term. You better not even try to deny it either!"

"Trinni, wake up! I said and did what I thought I needed to get you to act and perform how I wanted you to. I was the adept puppeteer, and you were my eager-to-please marionette. Again, at the time I met you, my wife was pregnant and unable to satisfy me as I desired it. You were here and had low self-esteem, so I just took advantage of your weak mental condition. You let me do whatever I wanted to you. How weak! I lost respect for you a long time ago. I know how much you love painting, yet you even let me take you away from your painting. And you were great at it. How weak! I only did what you allowed me to do. But don't act like the victim! In return for your submission, you took advantage of my abundant cash flow. You have been living here and having me pay all your bills. As payment, I have been getting to smut you any way that I pleased. How I see things, this has been a win-win situation for both of us. Let's not act like

47 | P a g e

we caught feelings. This was purely a business transaction. Again, you were a highly compensated jump-off. There are weak-minded women hoeing around for free. You got paid more than all your wildest monetary dreams. Our transaction went well for over four years, so why are you acting like there is a problem now?"

"Look, I didn't want to be a jump-off. I thought we were in a relationship! I counted on the fact that you were single! I wanted to belong to you and only you. I was faithful to you, Grey. I thought you provided for me out of love, out of you being my man. You brought me this condo, I thought, because you were happy you could finally have me to yourself. And when my car broke down for the umpteenth time, you came through with a new car. You provided for me, I thought, because you wanted me to be happy. Why are you throwing all of this in my face? After four years, how can you treat me like this? You want me thinner? Fine, I will join the gym down the street and learn to eat better. You think I don't have class and I need more education? Well, those are easy fixes too. I will enroll back in college to finish my final two semesters to complete my arts degree. You don't have a complaint about my style; I make sure I buy the best fashions available. Look, Baby, I want to make this right. Tell me how to make things right. Whatever you want, I will do."

"Trinity, you just don't get it. You can't fix this. Just give it up!"

"You say that now but let me at least try to make things right. I know that I haven't been giving you all the extra attention you used to get. I'm sorry. I am really trying to be a makeshift manager, but they are making me jump through the hoops with my schedule. I want to keep you. I can't lose you, Grey. I just can't be alone again, please." Catching herself, Trinity cleared her throat, "I mean, I guess, umm, I can deal with the married thing too."

Disgusted, he tore into her even more. "Trinity, stop it! This scene you are causing is preposterous. Incessantly whining and insisting that you love me is cute, but it doesn't move me, not one bit. I don't love you. I never belonged to you! I was never a single man, so you can never lose me. You are someone that I care about as a human being. I mean, I am a good Christian man, so I have compassion. God teaches in His Word we are to love each other as we love Him. But that's it. I suppose that if anything happened to you, I would be sad for a second or two, but I would get over it quickly."

"Stop it, Greysan! Why? Tell me why you are saying these hateful things to me? Why?"

"Look, I am done with this conversation, so I will let you know my decision: I am tired of cheating with you. Simply put, I am bored. I need other conquests to satiate my hunger for sexual satisfaction. I am a predator, and I need new prey to conquer. Besides, my wife deserves better than this. She is so beautiful and thin. If she found out I was cheating, she could deal with it. But, wow, you look all out of shape and aren't as good looking as my wife. She would surely be disgusted and never let me touch her again. She would even take my kids and other things important to me, away. You aren't worthy of such huge sacrifices. To be brutally honest, Trinity, you aren't even worthy of me losing a ham and cheese sandwich!"

Feeling as if someone had punched her in the gut, Trinity questioned, "Why are you being so evil? I cannot believe that I dedicated the last four years of my life to you. I alienated my friends and family for you. They all told me to leave you alone, that you were no good, but I didn't listen. My own Grand Momma told me you weren't worth your weight in manure. I love painting, but I stopped because it took too much time away from you. I was even written up at my job because I took off so much time for you. I have one more time to get written up, and I am fired. After these sacrifices, you tell me this mess. You really are a piece of work, Greysan!"

"Look, Trinity, I didn't ask or tell you to do a single thing for me! Those are your problems, not mine. And you'd better watch your mouth. Don't make this a physical altercation you know that you don't want. We can talk about this, but you will not, I repeat, you *will not* disrespect me. Do you understand?!"

"Yes, Grey, I understand." Softening her tone, Trinity soothed, "It's just that you're acting so cold. Where has this side of you been all these years? I have seen the angry side of you, fact when you have hit me, but this evil side is new to me."

"Trinity, look, let's end this. I'm irritated by your simple-minded behavior. Let me state things real clear for you: you need to pack your stuff. On

50 | P a g e

Friday, in three days, I will change the locks. We will stop my payments on your car loan ASAP. If, in a rare occurrence, you want to keep everything, you can assume the payments. But then, we both know that your measly salary from the department store wouldn't cover a small portion of your condo mortgage, let alone the car note. As you just said, you might be fired soon."

"Grey, I can't just move out. I don't have anywhere else to go. I will be homeless. Have some compassion. *Please.*"

Gotcha! Greysan thought. "Alright, Trinity, if you crawl over here and give me what I want, I will give you three more days to find a place to move into. Deal?"

Without hesitation, I did what I was told. I needed those extra days to find a place to stay. Maybe if I performed well, he would even be kind enough to pay one more car note and mortgage payment. It is too cold to catch the bus and be homeless.

"And Trinity, make sure you watch your teeth this time. When you finish me, assume the position so I can watch you jiggle under my hand."

I did everything he asked, even the most disgusting and repulsive things. I tried to stop crying; I really did. But, as he pulled my hair hard and held my hips tight so he could dive deeper, I could not stop my tears from flowing. I had hit a perpetual rock bottom. I had to do everything that he asked. I just had to fulfill his most deviant sexual demands. I had nowhere else to go. I had no one who would pay my car note or condo mortgage and definitely no one who would put two thousand dollars of spending money in my bank account every month without fail. Greysan's wants were to be fulfilled, even if I had to cry through the entire thing. Oddly enough, the more I cried, the rougher he got, and the trashier his talk became. If his intentions were to make me feel like dirt, as he called me the vilest names, he accomplished his feat in grand fashion. When he finished destroying me mentally and physically, like never before, he climbed off me with no apologies. Robotically, he got up and jumped in the shower.

I was still lying in a crumpled mess on the floor, assessing rug burns all over my body, when he returned from the shower smirking. He tried his best to appear caring, but his devilish thoughts were spread across his face in a smirk.

"Trinity, you now have one month to get out. Maybe I should have threatened to cut you off months ago. You weren't boring this time."

"Thank you, Grey."

"Humph, you are welcome! I will say this; you proved once again that my wife is too honorable a woman to let me do the nasty things I could easily do to you. You truly are lower than dirt."

"I only did what you wanted because I only wish to make you happy, Grey."

He shook his head violently, anger rising again, "That's your problem! You lack self-esteem. I cannot tell you how unattractive that is!"

"You didn't care if I had self-esteem when you were messing me over, did you? So, don't tell me this mess now!"

He tucked in his shirt and buttoned his pants.

Without a word, he hauled off and slapped me across the face.

"Now that I have washed your filth off me, I am off to represent myself respectably with my wife and children. As I said before, Trinity, you have one month and not a day longer. Do you understand me?!"

"Yes, Greysan, I understand," I said as I looked up from my bleeding rug burns to find him sneering down at me.

"Aww, did I hurt you?" He quipped, not caring.

"Yes, but I will be okay. It's nothing some cotton balls and peroxide won't fix. Now, you run on home to your wife and kids."

"Okay. Now, be a good girl and crawl over here and kiss me goodbye."

I tried to stand up and walk over to him, but he violently pushed me back down on all fours.

"Uhh uhh…I want you to stay down there on all fours. I order you to crawl! I want you to stay the same way you were when you allowed me to do anything that I wanted to you. Act like the female dog you are and crawl. On all fours seems to be your favorite position." He backed up ten paces across the room!

Crawling on my raw knees and bloodied elbows, I did as he ordered me. After reaching his feet, I stood up to kiss him goodbye. I figured one kiss could get me more time to find a place to stay. To my horror, he turned away from my mouth at the last minute.

"Hmmm, I'll just take a handshake. I must kiss my wife with these lips. I already brushed my teeth and gargled repeatedly with mouthwash, but I still don't want to take a chance of carrying any nasty germs from you with me."

Obediently I responded, "Yes, Grey."

He patted me on top of my head and walked towards the door. He walked with a slightly slouched spine. His gait was slow and steady. He had his pimp walk on full display. As he walked out the door, he stopped and poked his head back in, "Trinity, don't call me. I will be in touch!"

Again, I responded, "Yes, Grey."

He turned and slammed the door without saying another word. I stood as still as a statue and watched the front door shake from the brunt of the door violently connecting with the frame. I rubbed the side of my face for the first time since he hit me. Oh yeah, that will leave a mark. Good thing I have makeup concealer from the last time Grey hit me that hard.

Beaten, broken, and corrupted, I cried until my face was ashen, and my head throbbed. I prayed for solace in the arms of Jesus. I cried out in this lonely place of sin and asked for forgiveness. I prayed to be cleansed from my head down to my toes. I know better than this! Yet again, in my quest to feel whole, I failed. Again, I sought in a man, something that would make me feel loved, but at the hands of a man who knew not my worth, I got hate. When am I going to learn that I will never feel completion from a man, especially from sex? I keep engaging in this internal war with myself. I know what would give me what I desire, but I keep doing things my way and not His way. I know what I need to do, but I am scared. This harsh treatment hurts but being alone hurts even more. Even God must understand that. Doesn't He?

Too mentally spent to even listen for the answer, I tiptoed to the window to see if Greysan's car had left the parking lot. Assured that he was not coming back with last orders, I fell to the floor and cried myself to sleep.

~4~
Double Hockey Stix

"I know how great this makes you feel, even though you have to put up with every kind of aggravation in the meantime. Pure gold put in the fire comes out of it proved pure; genuine faith put through this suffering comes out proved genuine. When Jesus wraps this all up, it's your faith, not your gold that God will have on display as evidence of his victory."

I Peter 1:6-7
***

Jnana & Trinity

I am so stupid for calling his office phone! I know this. I had been working on a new painting when I looked at the clock and realized that it was our regular lunchtime. I fought myself not to dial his digits. But, as if I were under a spell, I reached for the phone and allowed my fingers to dial. Even as I tried to remind myself of all the hateful things, he said to me, I could not stop myself. For the first time, I wondered, is it love or obsession?

Greysan's Secretary, Lisa, put me right into voice mail when she recognized my voice. Ol' Heffa! She and I used to be tight, or so I thought. We used to talk about all the sales my department store was having. I even let her use my discount, a time or two. Not too long ago, we even got our acrylic nails done on an outing that Greysan planned as 'Special persons in my life' day. It was his idea, not mine! I got to hold his credit card for the day, so I did not give a hoot whoever came along or what the occasion was. I was ready to spend, spend, and spend. I tried to call the office back, and this time, I disguised my voice. Lisa did not catch my voice, so she put me right through to Greysan. After a few bars of easy listening music, he picked up.

"Greysan speaking."

"Hey, Baby. How is your day going?"

Silence

"Baby, are you there? Can you hear me?"

Silence

"Grey, it is beautiful outside. The weather is nice, don't you think?" I interjected, grasping for any semblance of a conversation just to keep him on the line.

"Trinity, why are you calling me? I thought I made myself clear. Don't you remember, before I left you, I told you *I* would be in touch with *you*."

"Yeah, I noticed what you told me, Grey. I just wanted to say thank you for putting the money in the account. I had an enjoyable time shopping yesterday. I even bought something sexy to model for you with the extra reward."

"You are welcome. Is there anything else, Ms. Boussaint?"

"*Ms. Boussiant*? Why are you being so formal, Baby?"

"Come in." Greysan cleared his throat and sounded very business-like. "Look, I have someone here to take out to lunch, and I really can't talk right now. The next time you need to reach me, give my

Secretary Lisa a call so we can handle the closing of our deal. She will handle things from here on out, so there is no need to contact me directly. Have a good day."

"Grey? Greysan?"

I heard what appeared to be a click, then silence. *Oh no, he did not just hang up on me!? Who is there to take him to lunch? Lunch used to be our time to talk, but now someone is even taking that time away from me.*

I looked at the call counter on my cell phone. It was still running. I listened close. Hmm, he did not hang up on me, after all. I heard what sounded like things crashing to the floor. Oh, maybe he fell or something. I searched my mind for any medical condition that could make him pass out on the spot. Then, I heard a woman's voice.

"Oh, Grey." A woman moaned.

"Come on, let me get you out of these clothes. You know that we only have lunchtime. Did I tell you how beautiful you look today? That diet you're on seems to work. I love toned women. Just beautiful." I heard Greysan say. His voice was husky.

"Yes, Sir. I love it when you take charge."

"Hmm, I *am* the boss around here. Aren't I?"

Trinity screeched, "Oh my God! That cannot be his ol' snooty Secretary getting ready to please him at lunchtime, *my time!*"

"Sir, shall I take dictation?"

"Sure, I have a long briefing for you to take."

"Sir, just the way I like it."

Heartbroken and in shock, I cried. I cannot

believe that he is doing this to me. Believe me, I had my ugly cry face on! Grey did not waste any time replacing me. I was his woman just a few days ago. I would have even settled for being his jump-off to keep the money flowing. Now, he is giving that hussy my lunchtime.

I was pulled back into the goings-on with Greysan and Lisa. I heard many sounds I had only heard Grey make with me. Lisa sounded like she was very experienced in dictation. I could hear him motivating her with verbal applause about how good she was making him feel. Then, I heard Greysan's voice change as his voice cracked. I could picture his face just days ago; his head fell back, eyes rolled to the back of his head, totally engrossed in receiving satisfaction. I knew that was how he looked when his Lisa pleased him. Then, I heard him yell out. He was obviously finishing because the phone line was silent.
I heard a belt buckle hit the floor and a lot of rustling around.
"Oh no, they aren't about to do what I think! "I screamed so loud it echoed in the room.

Lisa's moans mixed in with his moans as bodies were slapping together. *How could he do this to me?* I wanted to hang up the phone, but my curiosity got the best of me. If curiosity killed the cat, then I was embalmed. I was downright intrigued. *Is he the same with her as he is with me?* Grey asked her many rhetorical questions, and she answered in the affirmative, stroking his ego. She made sounds I had never heard before, and her ecstasy-filled cries of pleasure seemed to motivate him to perform with more passion. After many minutes, I heard soft talking and kissing. He had gently made love to her. That was an experience that I never had with Grey. Even after four years. Jealousy filled my being.

I heard rustling around the phone like they were getting dressed, and then there was silence.

"Honey, you are so sensual. I am so glad that I hired you. I have never felt like that before. *Ever*."

"Why, thank you, Sir. I aim to please. May I get you a fresh cup of coffee?"

"Sure, two sugars. Hold the cream. I already had my cream for the day, thanks to you."

"Thank you for the lunch. I never had such an enjoyable time having lunch before. You are in great shape."

"You are something else, Lady. Come over here and give me a kiss. I just love the way you taste. Maybe tomorrow I can really find out how good. This session is worthy of a shopping spree. How about I take you out to dinner first, doesn't that sound nice? We can go to that little romantic restaurant you love with the Bananas Foster."

"That sounds great, Sir. I'll be right back; I really must go get cleaned up." Lisa's voice moved closer to the phone, taunting me. "Sir, you really had a lot backed up. I have got to take up the slack you get at home." I heard Greysan laugh, genuinely.

"Sir, I will be back soon."

"Okay, please don't take too long. I will miss you." Greysan sounded genuinely infatuated with her. I heard a door shut, then there was rustling around the phone.

"Trinity, are you still on the line?" Greysan asked me.

I was too embarrassed to speak and too stunned to hang up. I could not let him find out that I listened to it all.

"Look, Trinity, I know that you are there. The phone call counter is still running. You may as well talk. I know that you heard everything. You did, didn't you?"

"Yes, I am still here." I half-whispered. "Grey, how could you do that to me? And with your Secretary, Lisa?! It sounded like you made love to her! How dare you treat her better than me? I gave you four years of my life!"

He sighed, "Look, I told you I would be in touch. Since you invaded my space, I wanted you to get a taste of what I have been up to. How did you like it? Did it turn you on?"

"What? How dare you! Why would you ask me something like that? I love you, and it killed me to listen to you caressing someone else like that."

"Really? Trinity, you can't love me like you think. Here's a proposition: I will let you stay in the condo longer if you will take part with me and Lisa. What do you say? Huh? I will give you three thousand dollars a month to spend as you like and paying all your bills."

I had to think...hard. That was a good deal. I must admit that as hurt as I am, I am still turned on by the prospect of all that money. The spring line at the store is coming out soon. Maybe I should at least try it before I turned it down. Maybe he misses me, after all. Maybe this is Grey's sick way of telling me he misses me. Maybe. Hopefully. "Greysan, I will think about it." It was all I could muster.

"Fine," He said, and then the phone line really went dead this time.

I tried to call back, but the answering machine picked up. When I tried again, an hour later, Lisa picked up. She immediately put me into voice mail. When I called back, I tried every voice impression I could think of. I did that until it was late afternoon. Finally, I took a break to do some painting. Creating always helps me to destress. I am usually in creating mode, so I never critique my paintings. But today, I inspected my paintings.

Over the years, I have gotten meticulous in my process of creating. Over the years, just as Jnana told me, and amazingly, Greysan, I am good. I wish that I had given more time to painting than I gave Greysan. Painting makes me feel full, where Grey empties me. Still, I cannot be alone again. And I have no avenue to make a living from my painting. So, I cleaned up my supplies and tried to call Greysan again. To my surprise, it was almost three o'clock. I must have gotten lost in my art. Robotically, I tried calling back again. The call went right to voice mail. There was a new recording on the line explaining that they were closing the office early. I could just guess what Lisa and Greysan were doing while the office was supposedly closed.

Pulling myself out of stalker mode, I glanced at the wall clock. My heart dropped.

"Oh my God, it cannot be four o'clock! I am supposed to be meeting with Jnana for our bi-weekly get-together. Already late, I threw on some sweats and put my hair into a ponytail. I hope that I don't see anyone while I'm out looking a mess."

****

When I finally arrived at Namaste, Jnana was waiting for me. She already turned the closed sign around. I knew that she was probably inside, livid, that I was late for our meeting, yet again. Perfect Jnana is always punctual. Perfect Jnana never sees that other people have valid reasons for being late. She is on time, so it does not matter. Still, she is my best friend, and I love her! I knocked on the door, and Jnana quickly opened the door with a smile. Wow, maybe she is not upset. Still, to cover all bases, I apologized right away. And I brought a peace offering just in case that did not work.

"Hey, girl! I'm so sorry for being late. But I stopped off for some Krispy Kreme on the way. This carrot cake donut is allathat!"

"Trin, no need for apologies and definitely no need to try to manipulate me with high fat but incredibly delicious donuts! You had me at donuts."

She smiled, and I let released the nervous energy from my body. Now, we can get down to some spicy girl talk. I made a plate of the food that Jnana had prepared. I piled my plate high with her signature seafood salad, Hawaiian Rolls, and spinach salad with Italian dressing. I made myself comfortable and dug in. After filling my stomach so much I had to roll down the top of my sweatpants, I dished my dirt.

"Jnana, you won't believe what happened!"

I quickly filled her in on my messiness and the added messiness of Greysan. She took it all in and maintained her silence. This cannot be good! She usually cannot help herself before interrupting me. My old friend, nervous energy filled my being yet again. Then, she opened her mouth.

"Okay, uh, let me get this straight. That no-good negro had the nerve to lead you on for four years!? Trinni, you just can't be serious! Greysan is married?" Jnana asked in dismay.

"Jnana, I already told you the story three times. Why are you still asking me all these questions? Can't you see that I am embarrassed enough?"

"And how were you getting in touch with him all these years, if he is so married, Trinni?"

"Don't yell at me or anything, but I have been calling his office phone."

"What the double hockey sticks? Okay, I will take a breath before I ask more stupid questions, I already know the answer to. But how's that workin' out for yah? Seriously though, Trin! This is ridiculous, even for you! So, what hours does he work if you could only reach him on his office phone?"

"Well, he is a Director at the big bank downtown, so he worked banking hours. Typical nine to five. Why?"

Jnana was incredulous, "Trinni, again, what the double hockey sticks?! Are you trying to tell me that you only had his office phone number? The entire four years? No cell phone, home number, secret Bat Cave phone? Nothing?!"

"No, Jnana. I was only allowed to talk to him during office hours. I rarely called him, so it was understood that he would call me on his lunch hour. That way, we were in touch once a day. He often worked on Saturdays, so I talked to him around noon that day too. Sunday was the day Greysan and I had taken a breather from each other."

"Wow, all this is a mess, Trinni. You have been messed over by men in the past, but this right here…wow, you really struck oil! You let this man get all up in your head and ruin your life; all the while, he was married."

"Thanks, Jnana. All your summations are making me feel so much better. Thanks for the compassion."

"You're welcome. Look, girl, I love you like a sister but, you were being played like a flute the entire four years you were with Greysan. The signs were all there. I don't know how you missed them. Get your eyes checked. Everyone saw them; many even pointed some of the most obvious ones out to you. Yet, you didn't seem to have a clue at all. You have all your family thinking that you have found Mr. Right when he is already someone else's husband. And did I hear you say that he has kids too?"

"Yes, Jnana, I did, three times in fact. I also told you that his wife, of ten years, is now pregnant with their third child in five years."

"Trinity, you were talking earlier about taking a break on Sundays. It seems like he and his wife haven't taken a so-called breather in a minute. I mean, they must have spent most of that time in bed. They are having babies so quickly. And what the heck is that anyway? If you love someone, you will call them on all days, The Lord's Day. I guess you realize that Sunday was a family day for him, his wife, and his being pushed out faster than rabbits' children. Right? You realize that don't you?"

"Yeah, Jnana, I realize all of that. I had so much to think about after he left. Even with how he treated me last night and learning all this mess, it still hurts."

"Okay, hold up, hold up! My head is spinning from all this craziness. Trinni, you are intelligent. You are a talented artist with mad skills, which I don't think you use. You work as a Manager at that big ole department store downtown. You were almost done college until you dropped out to be with yet another loser guy. But with all of this, where the double hockey stick is your common sense? You must not have been born any because none of this makes sense. None!"

"*Your* head is spinning? Dang, Jnana, how do you think I am feeling? My world revolved around this man, and all this time, he has been manipulating me. I seriously cannot believe all of this either. I thought that I had found a dream man that was single, fine as wine, and had enough money to make me happy for a lifetime. But now, it is a joke. He is married, and worse yet, he is cutting off my money supply."

Trinity got emotional thinking about her last shopping spree. The arrangement she and Greysan had was solid. And the stress-free money Grey gave her was attractive too. Addictive even.

Ignoring Trinity's obvious greed, Jnana shook her head. Money is truly the root of all evil! Even with this huge revelation, all Trinni could think about is shopping. Her horns are really sprouting!

Wavering between anger and compassion, Jnana continued, "Oh, Trinni, I am so sorry. I know this hurt. Please, don't cry. I am sorry for being so hard on you. But you know how I get down, real talk, all day, every day. Come here and let me give you a hug."

Drying her tears and crossing her arms, Trinity managed a few words, "Jnana, I don't need a hug. It's okay. I know that you are just being you. But sometimes your brutal honesty is brutal."

"I deal in tough love; you know that. You have a poor track record with guys that you let run all over you and leave you like a sack of potatoes. You need someone that will be honest with you about your messy, drama-filled life. Aren't you tired of that endless cycle, Trinni? Aren't you tired of letting men track muddy footprints in and out of your life? Aren't you? Aren't you tired of being someone's side joint or sexual fill-in while the guy truly wants or has another woman? Aren't you? You keep letting these men jump in and out of your body and play with your mind, but they always leave an empty place in your soul, time and time again. Aren't you tired of that dysfunctional cycle, Trinni? As you like to say, aren't you tired of all that unnecessary mental violence?"

"Look, yes, I am. But most of what Grey said to me was true. I am weak. I am not worthy of him or any other man wanting to make me his wife or even his girlfriend. I am one thing: a body. I have no worth other than what I can give a man *sexually*. They never want to have a deep conversation with me. They only want sex with me. What does that say about who I am and what I show to the world?"

"Girl, that's a load of crap! You are wonderful, and I'm not saying so because you are my best friend. You have always had a heart of gold. But you are a tad…no, a whole lot weaker for a man with, shall I say big feet and big money flow."

"Big feet and bigger money…flow? You make me sound like the women I despise. Those weak women sit around and let men do and say whatever they want, just to have a man and some money. Those are sad, stupid gold-digging women. Jnana, I'm not that kind of woman!" Looking at the look upon her best friend's face, Trinity asked pensively, "Am I?"

"I know this will hurt, so let me just rip the Band-Aid off fast! Yes, sweetie, you are! You have this man giving you money on the regular. He pays your bills and brought you a brand-new car. He appeared to care about you and liked to take good care of your finances. Yet, amazingly enough, you have gone nowhere in public together, you have never met his peoples, and he never stayed the night at your place, nor you, his. He even leaves you money on the nightstand like he is your John. Adding all this information together, you do realize that the writing was on the mirror in red lipstick. He wasn't really your man. I hate to say this, but Greysan was right. At two thousand dollars per month plus more and he paid all your bills, you really can't complain too much. Honestly, he paid you well for your time. I mean, it's not like you saw him every day."

"Jnana, paid me well? You sound just like Grey. What is this, some kind of conspiracy? Am I being pranked or something? I never thought I would live to see the day that you agree with any of the ignorance that Greysan says. What gives?"

"Look, Trinity, I can tell you I am very uncomfortable agreeing with Grey, but hey, the truth is the truth. You were too busy feeding your vicious shopping addiction to notice. I lost count of how many times you stalked that bank just to see when he deposited money for you. You even stopped working as hard at your job. Correct me if I'm wrong, but didn't you sign your check back over to them because you were too busy buying merchandise right off the truck? You have a shopping addiction. But, more seriously, you have a bigger problem with being attracted to men who are useless. You keep allowing these men to buy your self-esteem, cheaply at that! Sweetie, is it all sinking in now? You were supposed to be his queen, but you turned out to be his pawn, and now he has you in a state of check-mate."

"Yeah, it is sinking in, so you can stop with the chess analogies. I have been selling my soul to one man after another. See, I get it, a little. But he called me a high-priced jump-off, Jnana. I am not a prostitute. Not me!"

"Alright, I will keep it real. He wasn't far from the truth. Now, some men think if a woman takes his money and material things, he owns her. Trin, you told me he stood you up on his whim, talked to you any kind of way, and even roughed you up a few times. You just spent your birthday by yourself. Grey told you he forgot? After four years? It's obvious the only thing holding you two together is the money he gives you and the sex you give him in exchange for that money. Trinity, as much as you want to deny the truth, you were a kept woman."

"Jnana, I'm leaving now. When I get home, I'm going to run myself a bath and soak these rug burns. I hope it doesn't sting too badly. Maybe, I'll light some candles and have a glass of white wine to relax my thoughts."

"Rug burns? Oh wow! He breaks up with you and tells you he's married, yet you still had sex with him. Are you crazy?!"

"Jnana, you don't understand. He gave me a brief time to get my stuff packed and move out of the condo. He even told me he was not paying another car payment. What else was I to do? I had to buy some time, so I gave him what he wanted."

"You could have kicked his scandalous behind out! *That* is what you could have done! It's a stretch, Trin, but you could have maintained a shred of dignity. For the moment, that's still your condo."

"Jnana, not for long. You just don't get it! It's not as simple as you keep making it."

"It *is* that simple. Don't you see that you keep giving him and many other men your power? You really need to work on your self-esteem. This is ridiculous! It's not that simple? Gurl, please!"

"Why are you getting so angry at me? This is my life, not yours! Remember? We both know your life is perfect. So, you can stop yelling at me like I did something to you."

"Trin, ooh gurl, I *will* stop yelling at you, but I will make my point, first. How many times have you called me to tell me about all these trifling men? Huh? How many nights did you wake me up from a good sleep to cry on the phone about one man or another? How many times did you interrupt our drama-free conversation to talk about one man or another checking you out or wanting to get to know you better? How many? As much of your business as you tell me, you might as well say it *is* my business too! Now that we got that straight, answer this, how long are you going to sell your soul to this or that man for a new handbag here or a pair of heels there? Huh? Is your soul that cheaply bought? Is your self-esteem that low? Huh? Come on, Trinity, snap out of it. You can't be this weak!"

"Okay, I see where this is going, Jnana. As if Greysan didn't abuse me enough, you want to finish the job. Well, go on ahead! First, I'm a prostitute. Now, I'm weak too. Really?"

"I'm not taking back one single thing I have said, Trin. Not one single word! You will not get an apology. Not one! As I have told you before, you hold the power. You control how you let a man treat you. You show a man you are a woman to be respected, no exceptions. Don't act like this is all new. I have been telling you this for years. You know this, so stop playing."

"I know, Jnana, I do. But it's so hard. I am so afraid of being alone."

"Look, Trin, deal with it! Stop being weak! You are still alone with these trifling men! They are only using your body! Don't you value yourself? You are a rose. But every time you get into a dysfunctional relationship with a married man, you get your heart stomped on. You keep up this pattern, and one day, your heart will turn cold, and people won't see the beautiful person that you are. One day they will see a thorn."

"Sheesh, whose side are you on? First, Grey, now you. You are my friend, but you are acting more like my enemy."

"Really? So, a true friend would coddle you and let you continue with this nonsense? Is that what you think a friend would do? I have never been a *yes* person, and I won't start today. You are a hot mess, Trin. You are better than this. So, what you are afraid of being alone. Again, get over it! You must learn your worth. When you are afraid, do it anyway. God won't always take you out of circumstances, but He will always lead you through them. You have heard that scripture before, right? Now tell me, how did Grey abuse you? Did he hit you?!"

"Yes, I have heard that before, Jnana. There is one problem. I don't have any worth. To answer your other question, yes, he pulled my hair so hard that I found my hair all on the carpet after he left. Plus, he made me perform the vilest sexual acts. He said I would work off all the money he gave me. When he said that, let me tell you, he made sure that I was his sex slave for a couple of hours. He made me swallow fluids and lick hidden orifices on his body. His deviant fantasies were all fulfilled, trust me."

"Aww, Trinni, I am so sorry. I know that you are a platinum card-carrying, certified freak, so if you say that he was a sexual deviant, he must have really gone hard with it."

"Exactly. He had the nerve to tell me that he didn't want to kiss me goodbye because I was full of germs. What the heck was that all about?"

"Girl, you were the one swallowing fluids and licking hidden body orifices. So, you tell me. Maybe you needed to disinfect yourself by gargling with some acid or something to kill the bodily germs. I don't know."

"Alright, that does it, Jnana! It is way overdue for me to leave."

I opened the front door of Namaste to leave.

"Okay, okay, I know when I've said too much. Call me later, k?"

"I will think about it, Jnana. For now, I just need some fresh air! And honestly, some space away from you!"

"Fine, but I still got mad love for you, girl. Best friends?"

I smiled, "Best friends. Work on that brutal honesty, girl. It is razor-sharp today."

"I will if you promise me you will work on your self-esteem. Call me later if you want to talk."

"I will. Love you, my best friend."

Jnana reached out and embraced her best friend. It was a hug that said...I am not sorry for being so truthful, so get it together.

Trinity's hug was more of a hug that said…I know, but still. Uncomfortable is still all I have until something better comes.

They stood back and smiled awkwardly at each other.

"I love you too, Trinni, my bestest friend in the whole wide world."

Jnana stood at the door, and Trinity walked out. They said their goodbyes.

"Namaste"

"Om Shanti"

~5~
Double Dutch Jump off

And this, my best friend betrayed his best friends,
his life betrayed his word. All my life, I've been
charmed by his speech, never dreaming he'd turn
on me. His words, which were music to my ears,
turned to daggers in my heart.
Psalm 55:20-21
***

Trinity

I meditated on scripture all day and all night
then back around again. In-between, I put on some
gospel music, and I cried. I threw my hands in the
air and had church right here in my condo. *Now
Behold the Lamb's* lyrics keep moving through my
spirit. The lyrics always cut me deep. I know that I
broke Jesus' heart, *often* with my bad choices. Still,
no matter how lost I get in the world, my thoughts
always return to my Grand Momma reading the
Bible to me when I was a little girl. She would tell
me that no matter how rough things got, Jesus was
always there to rescue me as He did Peter on that
boat. All I need is to trust Him. All I need is to
trust? That seems to be my huge issue. I trust in
men to hurt me. I trust in money. I trust in sex to
give me love. Why is trusting in God to heal me
and deliver me from sin so hard?

In the stillness of my bedroom, I heard
Greysan's angry voice in my head, and I felt my
brutally honest best friend's words weighing

heavily upon my spirit. What I did not hear was my common sense telling me I should have known better. Somewhere along the way, I guess I made an impasse in teaching Greysan how to treat me.

During moments of clarity, I often wonder if I had inadvertently taught Greysan it was okay to disrespect me and continue disappointing me if he paid me well, afterward. Sadly, I wonder if I put more emphasis on money instead of respect. Respecting and loving me were, honestly, often not even on Greysan's list of priorities. And I never required them to be.

I will admit; initially, Grey's outward beauty and caring nature overtook me. However, after further assessment, neither of those things turned out to mean very much. His narcissistic tendencies replaced his suave demeanor. That caring man became someone obsessed with possessing me.

The moment money came into the picture, things changed. The moment I slept with him, things got out of focus. He and I were on our paths, each with separate agendas, neither sharing it with the other. The smile that I previously loved so much, the one that turned up into a smirk as he spoke such angry and demeaning things to me, has lost its luster. His true nature, an evil, ugly-spirited person, is now front and foremost in my mind. No longer am I under any kind of delusion about who he really is. Still, I cannot lie. Throughout the four years that we were together, I thought he was my man. I believed he gave me what I showed him I needed. He made me believe I was his one and only woman. And he did it in grand style. But, in retrospect, I can see that Greysan only gave me what I greedily assumed was without strings. I allowed myself to be manipulated with material things the entire four years. I was so caught up in the fame of belonging to someone of his societal position I did not see all the signs that our relationship was a lie. I can never get those years back because I was so foolish. I was ignorant and never saw his habit of never being available to me after five o'clock could signal he was committed to someone else. It never ran through my mind that he was married.

Foolishly, I trusted that everything he told me was the truth. It hurt he did not feel like all I had given him was good enough. I gave him my soul. With all I willfully gave him, he treats me as if I am unimportant in his life. How he spoke to me the other day shows his utter disrespect for me. As I run Greysan's words and actions back through my mind, he never told me that he loved me. Never! Not even close.

After our second year together, I finally told him that I loved him. I expected reciprocity; however, he sent me flowers the next day with a diamond necklace from Tiffany. Whenever I talked to him about spending more time with me or talking longer on the phone, he brought me gifts. When I was needy, he was freer with his money. When I needed comfort, he gave me his credit card to go shopping. I took those gestures to mean that he

77 | P a g e

loved me and wanted me happy. What I question is this: when did I begin to use shopping as a salve to heal my aching, needy heart? Someone once told me that a man shows where his heart is by where he spends his money. I took those words to heart and thought Greysan was in love with me by how much money he spent on me. Ironically, his money means less to him than I do.

Now, I have cheated with a man who was committed or married before. My only requirement is the wife or girlfriend cannot be pregnant during our affair. I mean, I do have some self-respect. See, in my mind, it is better for me. I was respectful enough not to cheat with someone else's man while they were pregnant. If I did, I would be a homewrecker. When I went into an *arrangement* with a married man or a man with a girlfriend, all I did was simply scratch an itch. I was a woman who likes to please and be pleased. Even if the man was in a relationship with another woman, that is their issue. No harm, no foul. If I go into a cheating situation, knowing all the pertinent facts, I am fine. I mean, if a man wants to cheat with me, it is not my fault. It is not my fault those men had a woman who wasn't satisfying them well enough. All I can say is those women should be glad I helped them out by servicing their men while they got their nails and hair done or tended to their spoiled children. The wives were too prudish to even get their knees dirty, let alone satisfy any need their men had besides the missionary position. See, I am a good person. An unlicensed sex therapist if you will. I gave unselfishly of myself to save so many relationships. I never wanted nor expected any of the men to leave home. In fact, after each of those relationships ended, each of the men seemed to have more dedication to their relationship than they had before they met me.

Last I heard, all those relationships were still going strong. I know this because every so often, one or two of the men I cheated with will call me hoping for some catch up on old times sex. When I inquired into their relationship status, each time, they told me they were still with the same woman they were with when they cheated with me. I respect those men, to a point. I mean, hey, they are cheaters, I cannot trust them completely! But, because they were at least honest about their relationship status, I deal with them. They did not hide a thing. Now, either I was good for their relationship, or they were not unhappy.

Even though I deal with cheaters, I am not a cheater. I am strictly a one-man woman. I was faithful to Greysan for four years, so I expected him to be honest with me! Since his pretty and thin wife is not satisfying him, I will gladly take him back and, yes, continue to be faithful to him. I know you think a mistress being faithful to a married man is ridiculous, but hey, do not you dare judge me! I am a Christian. So that means that I must forgive him! Greysan is the biggest fish I could have ever imagined having on my fishing line. *Judge lest ye be judged.* When I got my chance with him, I turned him out and reeled him in. Dating a rich married man beats dating a single broke man, any ol' day! Trust!

Forget what Jnana had to say. Blah, blah, blah, she does not know what is going on in the real world. She has a good man. One who waits on her hand and foot and is dedicated to her. She does not know what I go through as a single woman. She is pretty and successful in her own right. With her bookstore and various other side money-making ventures, she has a full life. But it sure gets lonely for me. If she could be a fly on the wall of my life, she would see how much I cry myself to sleep at night with a bowl of ice cream and my remote to keep me company. She does not have a clue how badly I wish that I had what she has with her husband and kids. If she could get out of her idealistic world and try on my deeply embedded shoes for a moment, then she would understand.

Look, I know I am settling for the disrespectful behaviors from Greysan because of how I feel about myself. To add insult to injury, Greysan often called me hateful, disrespectful names and even hit me a time or two, all in the name of motivation. When he was angry, cranky, or otherwise needed a whipping post, he would tell me he was disgusted with my weight. Still, I feel like I need a man to be happy, to feel valued. I am fed up with Greysan's disrespect! But I am afraid of being alone. I do not want to go back to struggling to pay my bills. I do not want to go back to feeling unwanted.

With all the hurtful words that Grey said to

me, what really hurts is he has children. The fact his wife was pregnant when he met me and is pregnant yet again when he broke up with me, turns my stomach. My frustration with Grey is that he purposefully kept his marital status and the fact that he had kids from me. I still cannot get it through my head that Greysan was having kids with his wife of ten years, during which I had had two abortions for him. Each time I missed my monthly cycle, I was excited. I ordered out for food and prepared a romantic night during which I would share the wonderful news I was pregnant. However, each time I told him that I was pregnant, he would push cash into my hand to pay for the abortion procedures. He would rush through eating the meal I had set out, and then he would have sex with me before going home. I hate he wanted me to get rid of my babies, yet he was readily creating a new life every nine months with his wife. Well, if Grey knows what is good for him, he better keeps our little arrangement, or I will go talk to his thin and pretty wife. Maybe I will show her the rug burns from her man. Yeah, he does not know who he is messing with. Not at all!

I will bet he won't think I am weak then, will he? I bet not. He does not know me! I will blow up his spot for real. When he is broke from paying child support, I know that he will have no choice but run back to me, begging for satisfaction. When he needs me, I will ask him, who is the trashy jump-off now!?

I turned down the lights in my bedroom to clear my head. Even though I know I should not be seeking revenge and that the Bible speaks against it, I can't help myself. My mind keeps rewinding back to all the hurt and pain from past relationships with men. The tape recorder in my mind was stuck on repeat. Grey will pay for all the scars he and other men have caused me. I prayed for forgiveness because I know that when my mind wanders like this…it is a losing battle. I am a slave to my mind. I make no excuses for my lack of strength.

When I got up from my nap as if on autopilot, I showered then sat down on my bed. I called my bank to see if Greysan had put money into the bank account. The Customer Service Rep. confirmed that there was more than enough in my joint account with Greysan. I must have performed well because he had deposited an extra five hundred dollars over the normal two thousand dollars.

I took out my bills tablet and added all my bills. My condo mortgage is fifteen hundred dollars, my car note is six hundred dollars, and my credit card payment for the month is two hundred dollars. For a moment, I thought about paying my bills while I still had some money to mess around with. I figured I would be able to pay my monthly bills and still play with two hundred dollars of stress relief money. Adding my bills two more times, I remembered a big blow-out sale at the shoe store. I logged onto my online account and found some sexy shoes I had on my wish list. I checked my email and viewed an email that reminded me an outfit I was watching was for sale. My paycheck would be deposited next week, so I nixed the idea of paying my bills ahead of time in favor of going shopping. I am stressed out!

Paying my bills will not get me de-stressed. Only shopping will do at a time like this. I got dressed in my breast-framing, baby blue cashmere sweater, black wiggle hip-hugging skirt, calf-defining black five-inch-high heels, mid-length black mink, and grabbed my keys to my brand-new BMW. In no time, I was looking sexy and ready for some retail therapy. I will get Greysan back, but for now, there are some cute shoes calling my name. After shopping half the day and spending darn near every dime of the twenty-five hundred dollars, I poured the bags onto my bed. I assessed the delectable new purchases and smiled. I had purchased a pair of red and a pair of black four-inch heels, two sets of brass bracelets, one chocolate brown silk top, one red stretch taffeta dress, a small handmade yellow purse, a new tongue ring, and a pair of high-priced stylish sunglasses. I also brought some sexy lingerie to wear once I get Grey back. I also filled up the gas tank, got the car detailed, and treated myself to lunch at Spoons. After undressing, I brushed the things off my bed and stretched out. I looked up into the mirror on my ceiling and looked right into my own eyes. Nothing…there was nothing there other than tears. Shopping did not make me feel better! Seriously, I felt empty. Even after spending well-earned money Greysan gave me, I did not feel better about his angry words or Jnana's insistence I had low self-esteem. I have gone on many shopping trips, but this has never happened before. I changed into my pajamas and sighed. Today was not a good day.

Hopefully, tomorrow will be better.

~6~

Out of Balance

Brothers, if anyone is caught in transgression, you who are spiritual should restore him in a spirit of gentleness. Keep watch on yourself, lest you too be tempted.

Galatians 6:1

***

Jnana

I pulled up to Namaste and looked to the front of my store. Book deliveries were sitting out front of the store. Angrily, I put my car in park and gathered my things. Today is not starting out too well! I put my stuff back down and rubbed some lavender essential oil on my temples to calm my thoughts. Slouching down into my seat, I took long sips of my black coffee. I let the warm liquid flow down my throat, and a moan escaped. I love me some Wawa coffee! Before I go into the store, I will create a peaceful mindset of relaxation. If I keep my peace, I will be okay…even in chaos. I opened my eyes, and the sight before me enraged me, yet again. Those cannot be my keys dangling in the door! I am not in the mood for this mess today. It is ten o'clock, and my bookstore is *still* not open! This has got to be a joke! My store always opens at nine o'clock sharp! Why did I walk up to my front door, and not only are the keys hanging in the lock, but the music is blasting like it is a dance club? I do not even play rap music! What the heck is going on? Am I in the twilight zone or what?

"Is anyone here?" I yelled. I got no immediate response. I walked to the stereo and turned the music off. Calming music is my idea of peaceful music. I put in a thunderstorms CD and breathed deeply. Relax, relate, release.

I cautiously placed my things on the counter before proceeding into the store. I took the keys out of the door and brought the book deliveries inside. I picked up a large hand-whittled wooden cane and tiptoed further into the store. I saw the office light was on, and I heard jubilant laughter. Either some criminal stole my keys and had a conversation on my off-limits office phone, or Littia was in there. The heifer had the nerve to be on the phone *again*! I peeped into the office and was astounded by the sight before me. She had her bare feet propped up on my desk and was leaning back in my high-backed, special order office chair! This hussy was chatting it up between bites of a banana nut muffin we sell. She had the nerve to have a Dunkin Donuts cup of coffee too. She was supposed to brew fresh coffee as part of her store opening duties, but I sure do not smell coffee brewing inside the store. I put down the cane and burst into my office.

"Good Morning!" I sang loudly, with more glee than I was feeling.

"Morning," she said. Then she went back to her conversation! "So, as I was saying…"

That hussy did not get to finish her sentence before I ripped the phone from her ear and violently rested it in the cradle. She has some nerve!

"Excu…"

"No, excuse me! Littia, are you out of your mind?"

Before I reached out to put hands on her, I caught myself. I must have caught her by surprise because she fell out of the chair onto the floor. I wanted to do a wrestling move and pretend that I was on the high rope and slam down hard on her, but I held myself back. *Two strikes*, she will not be so lucky on try number three. I will not lie; it was hard restraining myself. If there is one thing I cannot stand, it's blatant disrespect! Here she was in my office, hanging out on my office phone while my keys were hanging in the front door. She had not opened the store, and to add insult to injury, she was on the phone, chatting it up like she was home. She did not have the decency to pretend as if she was doing her job when I arrived unexpectedly. She knows on Thursdays, I am usually out marketing until early afternoon. I know I surprised her, but she is acting recklessly right now! I must set her straight, once and for all. I had another plan in mind. However, she has tied my hands with this little fiasco.

"Littia, pack your things up. This is your last day. You are fired."

"Huh?" She struggled to get on her feet, her arms raised in submission. She must have looked at my eyes and saw I was not my normally balanced self. The winds of change were blowing up in the place, and I was surely on the verge of reverting to my pre-saved days.

"You are fired! I came in here today to have a meeting with you, nicely. I only planned on writing you up for being disrespectful and not providing optimal customer service. I wanted to let you know

I wanted you to remain an employee here because I value what you have contributed to Namaste."

She sucked her teeth, "So, how did you get from a write-up to fired so quickly?"

Is she dense?!

"You know you can't just fire me like this. I have given this place my all. I have carried this place on my back and helped it to thrive."

"Let's get one thing straight…*I* financed this place, not you. *I* opened these doors many years before *I* hired *you* as an employee…not an owner! Yes, your services have been invaluable, but as Janet Jackson asked, *what have you done for me lately*?!"

Under normal circumstances, she and I would have burst out in stitches from my old school corniness but, not today! I will not allow her to distract me from my mission. A mission she set into motion! *Choo-choo*, the train is about to leave the station. First stop, unemployment office!

"Jnana, look, I have bills to pay and kids to feed. How are you just going to fire me like this? I thought we were friends."

Oh, no, she didn't!

"Littia, I too thought we were friends. But what kind of friend would I be to let you try to run my business into the ground? What kind of friend would I be to let you disrespect my customers and my *husband*? What kind of friend would I be to let you treat me like a chump?"

She was trying to sit back in my chair and put her needing-a-sander-and-a-nail-clipper-really-badly feet back up on my desk when she said, "Excuse me if I don't speak to all the customers. I do not have time to be listening to their endless stories and stupid questions about books. I am only as respectful as I know how to be. I mean, look, I cannot be you, coming in here smiling all the time like things are so great. I am a *real* sistah. I have *real* problems. No worries, it's a black thang, you wouldn't understand."

Lord, guide my hands, so I don't slap this heifer right in the mouth!

"You're a real sistah? I wouldn't understand?! Who, what, when, and where is that supposed to mean?"

"Look, forget what I said. I need this job."

"No, I won't forget what you said! Explain."

"Well, Jnana, you walk around this bookstore floating on air, like you have no problems. You give advice and pray with customers. You walk around, acting all spiritual. Like you're so perfect. As your friend, I know that you aren't as perfect as you want people to believe that you are."

"Littia, I may not be perfect, but I still have a job. You may leave now. Oh, and you better be glad I don't call the police on you for stealing from the cash register. Ms. Imperfect!"

She started gathering her things much quicker.

"What are you talking about? You think I'm stealing? If you want to fire me, fine. But don't think that I'm going to let you call me a thief."

"You want to look at the security tape? *Huh?*"

"Uhh, nowadays, people can do anything with photo editing. You could have doctored up the video to make it look like me."

"Do you think because you only steal small

amounts that it isn't stealing? Don't answer; it is! If you will steal insignificant amounts, I can only imagine what important things you have taken around here."

"I only took those amounts because I needed to get my kids on the bus to go home. I work here and travel all the way across town. You know that I am on the bus line, you don't offer a ride. You owe me that money. All the hours I work overtime, twenty minutes here, and five minutes there."

"Oh, you are tripping! Every single minute you work, I pay you for. Don't be silly, Littia. I have paid you *well* over the years for your employment. You are the only one that gets a holiday bonus! You are the only one that gets to bring your kids to work with you. Remember that snow day when the schools were closed? Did I *not* let you bring the kids here? *Didn't I?!*"

"Yeah, you did, Jnana. Look, things are getting out of hand. I apologize."

"Littia, we have been friends for years. I trusted you. How could you do this to me? I was your friend before you started working here. Let's stop all the nonsense and really talk."

Littia and I walked out of the office and sat down in the big comfy chairs. Facing each other, we had a better chance of being real with each other. Bull aside, we needed to deal with things head-on.

"Look, Jnana, you have been a good friend. But somehow, our friendship got pushed to the side for an employer and employee relationship. I have been going through some serious things lately, and I feel you haven't been a friend to me. You have been worried about your business."

"Littia, I have had some serious stuff going on with me too. You never once asked about the kids or Shandon. Even when you heard it in my voice, I was exhausted, you didn't pitch in. You just got on the phone. I counted on you to manage the other employees for day shift. But I had to hire Roshina to cover a lot of your duties."

"It seems like we have both had some things we needed to talk about. I'm sorry, Jnana."

"Me too, Littia."

The wind chimes rang out, and we looked at the door. *Sheesh,* I had forgotten about the children's book reading scheduled for eleven this morning. In shuffled the cutest little four-year-old children. I looked at the clock; it is ten-thirty, and I am not set up for the group. Sending them back to the daycare is not an option. It is time to shift into hyper-drive.

"Good Morning, Twinkle Feet Daycare. How are you all today? I hope that everyone is excited about the story for today. I am. It's *Nassie's Garden of Hope*, my favorite book."

I talked to the instructors and explained story time procedure. Since they were early, I told them each of the four students could pick out a storybook to take home with them. I looked at Littia and told her I would be busy opening the store. Without a word, Littia and I dried our tears and hugged each other. I turned on the rest of the lights, put on some children's music, and made coffee. Good thing I had stopped off to get cookies and milk on the way here. I set up a cute little *Dora the Explorer* tray of refreshments. Then, I went back to my office to unpack the book deliveries as she set up the book reading. Littia and I would finish our discussion after the children left. I will still let her go. Preserving our friendship is more important. Our conversation up until now has reminded me being out of balance, in any relationship in life, causes ripple tides that are often hard, if left to waver long enough, to rein in. Choices need to be made to let go or hold on tighter. I am letting go of Littia, the employee. However, I am holding tighter to the one relationship that means more to me, which is her friendship.

After the book reading, I helped Littia pack up her stuff, and we finished our conversation. I gave her the funds that she earned up until today so that she did not have to wait until payday next Friday. I know that she has bills, stealing and disrespect aside. I cannot get what she said to me out of my head. It was interesting. *I think that I am so perfect, and I am so judgmental.* If I couple Littia's words of *I think that I am perfect*, with Trinity's words of, *my honesty is brutal* and my family's words, *you know how you get*, it would appear as if I am far from perfect in the eyes of those that I value. It would appear as if I am out of balance. I made an intention to try to get back into balance when I get a quiet moment.

Finally completing the store opening procedures, I opened the cash register and counted one hundred fifty dollars in change. Then, I sat down and thought about the last year of my life. Before I knew it, tears were running down my face. I quickly dried my face when I heard the wind chimes sound out. Roshina is so great to come in early to cover Littia's shift.

I let Roshina get settled in before I gave her instructions on day shift procedures. I lit some sage and cleansed the entire store. Then, I took extra time to cleanse the negative energy inside my office space. Once inside, I silently made an intention to get back into spiritual balance. I need to start at the one place that seems to have thrown me off the most, which is my office. I lit a lavender tart that I made at home last night and turned out the light. I sat down on my meditation mat and crossed my legs in lotus pose. Holding the Bible up to the candle, it fell open to Isaiah twenty-six. My eyes scanned the chapter as I asked the Holy Spirit where to lay my eyes. He guided me to meditate on verses three and four. I thanked the Holy Spirit for such a timely Rhema Word. This scripture is exactly what I need. I pressed my palms together as I closed my eyes and said the scriptures over and over. *'You will keep in perfect peace, all who trust in you, all whose thoughts are fixed on you! Trust in the Lord always, for the Lord God is the eternal Rock.'*

I said this scripture until peace rose inside me like a tidal wave. The peace washed away all the pent-up anger and all the negative energy that had been consuming me. The peace felt lovely, and I rested in the stillness. Breathing deeply, in and out, I sat still for twenty minutes. I felt my thoughts rise and fall from the pain of being misunderstood back to joy at having so many people who care about me. I spoke neti, neti to those hurtful thoughts that did not serve me in my journey to getting back to balance. Bliss found me, and I reintroduced myself to her. We hugged and smiled a smile of recognition. We reclaimed a connection that I will work harder to keep. It is a wondrous thing to find harmony in self.

I opened my eyes and got up to turn on the lights. As I looked around my vast office, I know one thing for sure: there is always a light in darkness; we just must reach out our hands for it. There, in that embrace, lives spiritual balance.

~7~
Mind Pixilation

Then hangman's noose was tight at my throat; devil waters rushed over me. Hell's ropes cinched me tight; death traps barred every exit. A hostile world! I call to God; I cry to God to help me. From his palace, he hears my call; my cry brings me right into his presence - a private audience.

Psalm 18:5-6

***

Trinity

I have been off work. The stress from Greysan breaking up with me has taken me under, fast. I do not know how to act without him. I figured that he would want me back in his bed by now. He has not even called. Every time I looked at my phone, I cried until my eyes burned, and I stained my skin with dry, white tear marks. I did not do my hair, brush my teeth, or eat. He wanted me thin, then so be it.

In the past, under his pressure, I had previously tried everything to lose weight. My only motivation now was that I wanted to compete with Lisa. The good part was that Lisa was barely a size smaller than me. Still, I had to be thinner than her at all costs. I cannot believe that after all these years of struggling with up and down weight, I am back to this low point, yet again!

In my thirty-nine years, I had tried everything to be thin. I danced, ate cabbage soup, and on several occasions, I took dangerous amphetamines to drop pounds. Since the age of seven, I had been dubbed as chubby. I had gotten so used to the nickname, Chubbs, that I timidly embraced it as my unofficial middle name. The bullying went on until the age of twelve when puberty set in, and I developed into a young woman. Back then, baby fat had moved to other places as I developed breasts, hips, booty, and thighs. Still, I could only see the ugly, chubby little girl in the mirror. Much to my dismay, in the sight of the boys at school, they considered me sexy and thick. I was so happy when I graduated from high school, so I did not have to deal with the daily judgment of my peers.

In the years since high school, my weight continued to fluctuate. At twenty, I finally got tired of being identified as the chubby girl, or the girl too cooled out to be someone other than a friend, so I acted. I stopped thinking of a temporary fix. I began to think about changing my lifestyle. I exercised and spent a lot of my minimum-wage earnings on personal trainers in my quest to be fit. I desperately needed the acceptance of a man...any man. For most of my life, the soul-deep feeling of self-acceptance has been a mirage that seemed to disappear as quickly as it felt as if I had reached it.

I must get thin! This time, I must get thin, and it must stick. I must get Grey back. I have put in years of work manufacturing this image. I have even taken dangerous diet pills to lose weight. I buy the best name brand fashions and keep my face beat with the best make-up brands. I have a nice body shaper, so my body is snatched all the time. How could it all have failed me, especially now?! I thought I found myself a rich single man, and that even turned out to be a lie. If this didn't hurt so badly, honestly, this would be funny. But alas, thus is my life. And there isn't anything laughable about this feeling of emptiness!

I know that getting Grey back will force me to make some allowances. I will not share him with Lisa. Or any other woman…well, I will at least share him with his wife. She had him before I did. I am not greedy. I'll share with her. But sharing with Lisa, no, it is not an option. So, she was the cream in his coffee now? Well, we will see about that. I planned on staying in this condo until there was room in my pants. That mission was accomplished after three days of starving myself. I only drank water and ate saltine crackers. I was so hungry and tired, but I was a size thinner, so I was elated. In and out of sleep, all I did was utilize my dialing finger to call Greysan's office. They must have Caller ID now because that heffa answers the phone saying my name before she puts me through to voice mail. She is such an evil person. She has created a compartmentalized message box just for me. The outgoing message is a personalized message from Greysan. To make it worse, it was recorded in Lisa's voice.

Talk about digging in the knife and twisting it. I am still determined to hold out until I reach him. If need be, I will stalk him at the bank and follow him home. I am miserable and lonely, so, if he forces my hand, I will mess up his home life and make him miserable too. If his wife leaves him, I will make sure that he is not lonely for long. I will take pity on him and take him back. That way, we will both be happy together. If my plan works out, maybe he will appreciate me more. As Jnana said, I must gain back my control. I know that she did not mean it like this but give me a break! I am getting desperate, and I know it. It is like I'm in an alternate universe. I have never had a broken heart that hurt this badly. I cannot concentrate, and I can't think about anything but Greysan. He broke my heart. My head is throbbing, and my heart hurts even worse. I have no appetite, and I cry all day and night.

I woke up in the middle of the night. I was terrified of a nightmare that shook me out of my sleep. In the nightmare, Greysan had my heart in his hands. He was twisting and turning it until all the blood poured out. He had kicked it into a trash container in the corner of my bedroom. Then, he began putting all my beautiful, expensive designer clothes and shoes in a huge shredder. Balls of colored fabric and leather flew into the air like snow. I could hear myself screaming out for him to stop. How could he be so hateful? How could he destroy my things? I must have been running in my dream because I woke up in a pool of sweat.

When I woke up, I was so angry that I Googled his name. I even tried to do a background check on him to find out his address. Neither worked out because in the four years we were together, he was careful not to tell me very much about himself or his family. He had his game wrapped tight. But I knew that there was a loophole somewhere. I just had to keep looking. Greysan will not beat me at a game that I had honed my skills in, for years, before I met him.

In the meantime, I cried incessantly. I drained my tear ducts until it seemed as if I cried dust from the reservoir of my soul. I blew my nose endless times until I thought my heartstrings were coming out of my nostrils. I cannot believe that I am here again! Through all my foolishness, I let these men hurt me, again and again. I shook away the thought of me taking responsibility for my predicament and cried some more. I forced myself to eat my near liquid diet and slept off and on while crying. I slept when reality seemed to be too much. I cried when my heartbeat for yet another worthless man that I allowed to treat me as less than dirt. I may not act like it, but honestly, I know better! How many times can I come across the same type of man and let him do the same thing to me and expect a different outcome?

The definition of insanity is doing the same thing over and over yet expecting a different result. Based on my present condition, I am on the fringes of insanity downward spiral.

For hours at a time, I lived under the covers blocking out the reality that I was still alive. I sure wanted to die. It seemed as if I was dying from the inside out. Misery was taking over my body, and like a flesh-eating disease, it was overtaking me fast. My heart was beating so loud it hurt my ears to breathe. Why? I kept asking myself, why am I here yet again?! Why?!

Four days in, I finally peeped out of my covers. I looked around, and my place was in severe disarray. The dishes piled up from days ago. Fruit flies were buzzing in my ears and were official squatters. My floors need to be vacuumed, and my television played on mute. For days, I did not leave the inside of my bedroom. The days flew by; the sun rose and set. Between my curtains, I did not even see a shooting star to wish upon as the moon grazed the indigo night sky.

I had lost count of how many times I picked up my phone to check for a dial tone. I even called my cell phone company to make sure there was not an outage in the area. Hey, you never know! I obsessively looked at the pictures of Grey on the bank's website. I learned more about him from his bio than he ever shared with me in four years. Surprisingly, he is not as accomplished as I thought! In fact, he is only the acting director. Who does he know that got him that job? I see that he has skeletons in his closet too. Interesting.

During these days of struggles, I thought little about shopping. I wanted to call to check the balance on my bank account, but I was not motivated much to do that. All I did was look around my dirty bedroom. My comforter was laden with used tissue and many empty bottles of water. The empty saltine packages had spilled crumbs all over my bed. I was officially a heartbroken victim. It stunk horribly in my room from days of endlessly avoiding brushing my teeth and washing my butt. My hair was even jacked up. My curls were a frizzy mess. So much so I looked like Side Show Bob on the Simpsons! I look and smell pathetic!

In a desperate attempt at gaining some mental bearing, I figured that watching other people's misery would make me feel better. So, I turned the channel on the television. Yes, I was that desperate for relief from my mental torture. I needed a mood change, badly. I watched show after show of dysfunctional women that did not know who their baby's daddy was, and court shows where some people had the nerve to sue their own Mommas and ex-lovers. I yelled at the television when one show came on about a woman whose man was so doggish that he slept with her mother *and* sister. He drained her bank account of their savings, and he was even trifling enough to empty out the kids' college funds. As a result, she is on welfare. That man was a sad sack, but the stupid heifer was on television, begging him to take her back. I cannot believe this nonsense. She is truly lost. The guy ended up flirting with an audience member most of the show.

My plan worked perfectly, and I am feeling better. It was a clever idea to watch other people's misery. Then my favorite talk show came on. I love everything about the host. She is classy, beautiful, and not afraid to be goofy and down to earth. Today's show is about true beauty. I got to blubbering as I watched the women's stories of survival through the tough times in life. I was so inspired by their stories that I could not help but analyze my life to see if I am a true beauty.

Yes, I cleaned up good, and I could rock

some heels with my long shapely legs. But am I truly a beauty from the inside out? I was quiet and listened for an answer. As if it was call and response, I heard it…I felt it clear as day, n*ot yet you must look within and stop looking outside of yourself to find love.* The reality of that answer got me to crying hard all over again. I turned off the television then threw the remote at it. Stupid talk show! I found myself even worse off than before. I cried and laid in my filth for the rest of the day. I laid there and cried because I cannot be wrong about another man! I counted how many men I allowed into my body and let them rule my mind. The number embarrassed me. From the first time that I had sex, I was never without a boyfriend for more than a week. I did not have sex with all those boys, but I had emotional situations with all of them. I had little affairs with the ones who tried to play games with my heart. The hardcore boys, I let them get further. There is something about a man with an edge to his personality! Unfortunately, most of the men I have known went over the edge. I heard Oprah once quote Maya Angelou on her TV show, "If someone shows you who they are, believe them." Well, I have been told so many lies that I can no longer discern head from tails. All I know is that I have given up too much head and tail to worthless men. Yet the part of me that needs attention is deeper than any man has ever cared to look. My soul desperately needs caressing. I need rebuilding. Resurrecting.

****

I must be in a twilight zone because I keep

hearing my cell phone ring. After the sixth hang-up call, I figured it was Jnana calling to check on me. I bet that she is blowing up my work phone. I had missed our bi-weekly girls' night in session. I love Jnana; she is my best friend. I wanted to call her, but her brand of truth would send me off the edge of a bridge today. I turned my ringer mode to silent with lights only. I cannot bear the sound of the phone ringing one second longer.

Despite the phone calls, I feel alone. No one knows how badly this hurt. It is like the walls are closing in on me, and I won't survive even as I climbed the walls in my self-imposed padded cell. I do not think that anyone has ever had their hearts broken so callously. I am full of anger and pain. I laid in this misery for a full day, and I planned Greysan's demise. I laid in my funk for another day before I ate or drank anything. Every time I woke up, I snuggled back up to sleep some more. I was in and out all day in a depressed mental coma.

The next morning, I got up the nerve to look at my cell phone. I curiously checked to see how many calls and voice mails I received. Did anybody truly give a darn about me? I smiled when I realized I had twenty missed calls. I rationalized that most were from Jnana. Out of twenty calls, there were only six voice mails. Seriously?! As I investigated my call log further, I realized Greysan had called twice. Hmm, that changes my mood a bit. Pensively, I dialed my voice mail and smiled. I consoled myself by thinking he found I was hard to replace. I was eager to see what gift he had for me that would get me back. I was not going back that easily with all the nonsense he said. However, if the gift were glistening enough, I guess he could wrangle me back. Who am I fooling? The way I am feeling right now, if he has a Cracker Jack prize, it's back on and popping! The devil I know is better than being alone.

I propped myself up in my bed before I played my voice mail. I put it on speaker so that I could hear him beg me to be with him again, in stereo. The voice mail machine began, *you have six unheard messages. If you would like to listen to your messages, please press one.* I excitedly pressed one.

The first unheard message, "Trinni, it's me, Jnana. Girl, I am so sorry for all the things I said. In retrospect, they were harsh, true, but still harsh. You need to stop letting guys take advantage of your gullible nature. Even Shandon sees it. And his friends have mentioned how desperate you appear when they have met you. Call me, girl. *"Beep Delete!*

"I cannot believe this. My first message, and this is what I must listen to? I don't care what Shandon has to say about me. And I'll be damned - did she say that she was asking his friends for advice about me? Wow. I should be happy about this advice, why? As If! Darn, I hope the other messages are of some consolation. Yup, had I talked to her days ago, my body would be crab food at the bottom of somebody of water. Some save you, but some just unwittingly push you off the bridge. Alright, let's see what else is here."

The second unheard message, "Ms. Boussiant, this

is Mr. Arbour from the Hextlers National Bank. We would like to notify you that there is an overdrawn balance on your checking account. Please give us a call as soon as possible. We need to remedy this situation ASAP! Mr. Lobes is also on this account, and I know he would devastate him to learn his account is overdrawn since he *is* the Banking Director here. It just would not look good if it got out that you are causing this bank any embarrassment. Call me back at extension 302. I am sure that you know the phone number by heart! *"Beep.*

It floored me. Overdrawn? How could it be? My paycheck was deposited already, and I know it was a decent amount. Then I realized, dammit, I had signed a paper at work for them to take my entire check this pay period. I just had to have the new spring collection. I forgot I had spent over eight hundred dollars on the pieces right off the truck. It was worth it. I will look amazing in those pieces. Once the weather breaks and the temperature is at least thirty degrees warmer.

Delete!

The third unheard message, "Trinni, girl, it's me again. Now, I have called you ten times already..."

Delete

"I love you, Jnana, but right now, I cannot deal with this!"

The fourth unheard message, "Trinni, this is Greysan. I don't know why you keep calling my office, but it is really pissing Lisa off. I had to give her full use of my credit card so she wouldn't quit. I need this girl to work here in the worse way. Stop

105 | P a g e

causing problems. And oh, I cleared up your little issue with the account. I will not allow you to embarrass me at my place of business. Now, I said I would be in touch with you. Stop calling here! You're making a fool of yourself. I asked you about joining me and Lisa in sessions, none of your messages have been regarding that. So, call me, I mean, us, when you have an answer in the affirmative and only the affirmative! *"Beep. Delete! Delete! Delete!*

"I have no words. Just plain ol' disrespectful behaviors. No words!"

The fifth unheard message, "Honey Bear, it's Grand Momma. Young lady call me. I haven't heard from you all week. Your Grand Dad sends his love.

"Beep.

Delete.

"Yeah, Grand Momma, *as if* I will call you when I am down and out. You and Pop-Pop are in the same boat as Jnana. You two have too much reality for me to deal with right now. How can I ask advice about trying to feel better when all I'll get is worse news? So, what your hip gave out again? So, what Pop-Pop can't deal with the rising costs of his medications? So, what his bowels are backed up again, and you might just have to give him an enema. I don't even want to hear how cancer and heart disease are running so rampant throughout my family I should stop eating pork and high-fat foods. I don't want to hear how beneficial fiber is and how it should be my best friend so I can stop being so fat. Negative, negative, negative! They would have me driving to the gun store, waiting three days in

106 | P a g e

the parking lot for the gun permit, then driving to an unknown hotel room and ending it all. Nope, they won't be getting a call back until I am fully recovered from heartbreak. Love you both, but not today. And the way I'm feeling, it doesn't seem like tomorrow either."

The sixth unheard message, "Trinity, this is Lisa. Yeah, I know you saw the phone number from Grey's office and figured that it was him. Well, gotcha! Now, don't get all upset and think that he doesn't know that I'm calling you because he does.

Hello Trinity, it's Greysan. I want to let you know I am looking forward to hearing your voice say yes. I miss you, sorry Lisa, but I do. So, how about it, will you join me and Lisa? Trinity, as you can see from the time, it's noon, lunchtime. If you were here, we three could be having a good ol' time together then when I am satisfied, I would take you both shopping. Come on, Trin, doesn't that sound good? I know that you miss me. We've been together four years; you can't be over me that fast. Now, I didn't realize Lisa isn't really into the sharing thing, but she will come around. I'm sure of it. I will offer you three thousand, two hundred dollars a month for you to join us. How does that sound?

"Baby, are you serious? Are you offering her more money to share you? Why? Am I not good enough for you anymore? I don't want that fat girl on my man. Give me that money. I don't want to share you, anyway.

"Lisa, the voice mail is still running, sheesh! I am

trying to make this deal with Trinni, now hush. She was here before you, and she knows how to shut up on cue. Get on your dictation so you can learn when to use your mouth. I'm talking to Trinity! Now, you want to share or have none of this? Huh? Just be quiet. I'm trying to leave a message, and you are messing it up. Yeah, see don't you feel better now? This is what you're good for, dictation—not spouting off your mouth on my message! Now, Trinni, as I was saying...damn girl, that feels so good. Alright, Trin, call us. Oh, my...Lisa! *"Beep.*
Delete!
There are no new messages. Main menu if you would like to hear your messages again.

I disconnected the call. I had heard enough. I cannot believe that those were my messages. Greysan gets more and more disrespectful with every call. What did I find attractive about him in the first place? That just drove the knife deeper. I am hurt because I cared for him, despite it all. And this is how he rips my heart straight out of my chest.

I had enough. My world is too much to take. I searched my medicine cabinet. I need to find a way to end this crazy life of mine. All I found were over-the-counter meds. I searched in my medicine cabinet, under my bathroom sink, in the kitchen, and in my junk drawer.

"I wonder if I can overdose on too much of the pink stomach diarrhea medication. Maybe even some allergy stuff. Oh, hold up, this might work, oh no,

it's just some out-of-date anti-vomit medication.
Maybe?"

I laughed at my feeble and insincere attempt
at planning my suicide. Am I truly that depressed?
Over Greysan?! I am depressed, yes, but to end my
life over a man, especially one of his calibers, is
ridiculousness personified. I am going hard with it;
I know. I closed the medicine cabinet door and
faced my other horror. I looked a crazy, hot mess.
My hair was matted, lying to the right, all weird.
My lips were cracked and crusty. My eyes were full
of sleep. My face was ashen. I usually had to look
close to see the melanin in my skin, but after a week
in my bedroom, I look like a Halloween ghost. My
eyes were puffy and bloodshot. My face was a
mess. My nose was red and raw from wiping it so
much. I was truly nasty looking.

This is stupid. Just plain ol' stupid! I am giving
Greysan all my power. Hmm…I think that is what
Jnana told me. I need to get revenge, yes, that
always makes me feel powerful. But how can I do
it? I smiled with cracked, nasty lips and thought,
*What can I send to the office that will bother Grey
even a smidgen of how he has messed with my
head?* I got it! I got my credit card, and I checked
the balance online. To my surprise, it was not
totally maxed out. I had one hundred and fifty
dollars left, so I ordered a dozen of black roses and
a fish head off the internet and had it sent to their
office for delivery first thing in the morning. It
costed me seventy-five dollars but imagining the
look on Lisa's face was priceless! I feel better
already. It is five in the morning, and I am alive.

Blessed and hopeful for a new happier day. I am alive! I looked to the skies and thanked God for holding me when I needed to be held. It could only be He that saved a wretch like me. I turned on iHeartRadio and created a gospel station. I sang along with one of my favorites, *King Jesus,* and then returned the call to my Grand Momma and Pop-Pop. They prayed over me, and I felt in my right mind again. Father God loves me still. My God loves me despite my recent and past messiness. My God is the best healer and spirit cleaner. I feel full just thinking about how forgiving God is. He has given an unapologetic sinner like me a new lease on life. I feel so blessed to be so loved. Now, I need to exercise some spiritual fortitude and stay this course of positivity. I cannot ask the Holy Spirit to help me if I do not first help myself.

As I sat polishing my nails, I felt sad again. I do not know how to act. Seriously, I know I need to change, but I am afraid. For the first time in my life, since about the age of sixteen, I do not have a man to call my own. I am sitting here, smiling at how crazy it sounds out in the universe. I do not have a man, hmm, it sounds less crazy saying it this time. What do women without a man do? Do they take themselves to the movies? Do they sit like lonely heifers in the middle of a restaurant like being alone is the most natural thing in the world? I giggled at that thought. Nah, no woman can be that comfortable or desperately sad to go out alone. The Pastor on the online Christian station once said, *"that a man who finds a wife, finds himself a good thing."*

Am I a *good thing?*

And when I find the man for me, will my karma of years creeping with someone else's man come back and bite me in the butt? I desperately need spiritual peace and emotional clarity. I did something that I had not done quite as frequently as I should. I prayed.

"God,

I don't know what to do right now. I don't have a man. You know that I'm not used to being alone, and it's scary. I have heard people say it is good to love yourself. But I don't know how to do that. I have always counted on a man to do that for me. Ironically enough, God, you know no man has ever really loved me. No disrespect, God, but all they ever loved was my body and the things I could do with it. I know you created me to be more than someone who is used and abused by a man - at least I pray you have. I want to be who you desire me to be. I want to live like the women at church. They're the ones who have that, 'I have the look of I know I am beautiful' upon their faces. Lord, I don't want to be conceited, as if I could ever love me that much, I just want to love myself. Grand Momma says God loves us unconditionally. The only one that ever loved me like that was Momma. You know she is with you now. So, who do I have left? My father walked out on me. God, I am coming to you; I submit myself to you. Make me, mold me, as you please. Please help me live as you purposed me. Until I get my true love, I will be abstinent. I am not saying it is going to be easy, God. You know my heart. I am struggling with even saying that "c" word. But, please, help me keep my word to you. Oh, this is Trinity Marie Boussiant.

In Jesus' name, I pray. Amen."

I didn't immediately feel any different. But I know I am supposed to just wait, wait on the Lord for an answer to my prayers. I know in the future I want to be a follower of God. I do not want to be a fan anymore. I will be in high pursuit of my Lord and Savior. No longer will money be my god. Now, I do not know how this works, but for the first time, yes, another first, I will not push myself onto a man. When the right man comes along, it will be beautiful. He will court me and make me feel special. All of this will happen way before he touches my body. I will not go out like that ever again. Pray for me and with me y'all.

I reflected upon how easily I was about to end my life, and I sighed. God has a plan for me. I am not sure if he wants me to be abstinent. But I figured if I try something different, I might get different results. I had free will, but ultimately it was his voice that rang in my head. Live. You are born to live. Live. Be patient. Live. Be honorable, live. Love yourself first. Live.

I got up off my knees, and I picked out an outfit for work. I had been out for seven days. I searched and searched for an outfit that would best show off my recent weight loss. I found it in my black high-waist stretch pants, ruffled red silk shirt, black three-inch heels, and black plush baby-doll midriff sweater. I will look mighty fly. I am done crying and feeling sorry for myself. I ironed my clothes, made myself a cup of Kona coffee with hazelnut and vanilla creamer, and looked around my nasty condo. Even though it was thirty degrees outside, I opened the windows in my bedroom then cleaned like the health board was coming to inspect. I lit some Wood Wick Candles because it is eye-watering funky. In no time at all, my place smelled lovely! Done cleaning, I sat down to a decent meal of strawberry ice cream and chocolate chip cookies.

I finished around seven. I got into the shower for the first time in seven days.   After showering, extra-long, I did my hair. I was excited to get out and begin living life to the fullest, so I put some mousse into my hair and put it in a bun. I do not have time for the regular hour-long hair styling I normally do.

After getting dressed, I am ready for the world. I drove to *Spoons* and got my patty melt combo. I turned up my car radio and sang along to Leona Lewis' *Better in Time*. Yes, my day is looking up already. I am strong enough to talk to Jnana today. I will surprise her by dropping by on my break.

~8~

Bliss…Interrupt…Us

An excellent wife who can find? She is far more precious than jewels. The heart of her husband trusts in her, and he will have no lack of gain. She does him good, and not harm, all the days of her life.

Proverbs 31:10-12

***

Jnana

"Good Morning, Shandon, my love. Whew, I can't believe I was so exhausted I fell asleep in Liana's bed last night. Your daughter talked to me until I fell asleep. I could hear her talking as I drifted off to sleep."

"Yes, she can talk. I know you've seen our cell phone bill. We really must upgrade to unlimited talk and text plans."

We shared a laugh, and I went back to reading my newspaper while Shandon fixed his breakfast plate. Jnana asked, "Shandon, did Trinity call last night? I haven't heard from her in a while."

Between bites of turkey sausage, Shandon replied, "Baby, no, she didn't. You know how long she takes to get over heartbreak. You would think that as long as it takes her to get over heartbreak, she would be more selective about the men she gets involved with."

Smirking, Jnana said, "Baby, there you go busting on my best friend. She just wants to be loved. She may have issues with men, but she really is a good person with a warm heart."

"Yes, I guess that Trinity is a good person. I mean, she watches the kids when we need alone time. Point one for Trinni. But how can you still be friends with a woman that systematically goes after married men? Huh? It's morally wrong. I have been wondering about that for a minute."

"Uh, well…how do I even answer that? I mean, Trinity is my best friend. While I don't agree with what she does or how she does it, I love her unconditionally. I guess that I never really thought about it because it wasn't my situation she was encroaching upon. I mean, she doesn't even like you," Jnana said, trying to hide her smile.

"There must be a mistake because I am attractive, sexy even," Shandon said, anxiously awaiting further discussion on the subject.

"Baby, relax." Jnana walked behind her husband and rubbed his back, trying desperately to soothe him. As much as she loves him, she knows his insecurity periodically comes out. "You are handsome. Everyone can see that. But she just isn't into your type of man." Jnana said, regretting that he has taken her joke to heart.

"What kind of man is that Baby? Hmm, tell."

"Well," Jnana rubbed his chest, "you are sexy, chocolate, and a sensual mix of nerd and brawn," Jnana said as she rubbed his firm bottom.

"Oh, that type. The strong backed if you will. I understand men like me are hard to find and even harder when it's time to get hard. Huh, Baby?" Rubbing the front of his pajamas, she moaned, "Yes, Baby, sho nuff!"

"Speaking of alone time, I haven't seen my sexy wife's form in a minute. How about we make some time in our busy schedules for quality time? Doesn't that sound exciting?"

"Baby, it sure does. When though? We both have to go to work."

"How about we play hooky from work today? We've been too busy to even focus on each other. You know that's what has kept us together all these years. You put me first, and I do the same for you."

Feeling a pang of guilt at being too busy for my husband, I relented, "You're right, Baby. We need to take special time away from the world just for us. We have been slipping. How about this? I just bought a nice long silk scarf last week. I would wear it to work today, but I would rather tie you up with it. Are you down?"

"I missed your sexy body next to me last night. So, I'm down for whatever fantasy you want to be fulfilled. I will do anything and everything to reconnect with my beautiful wife."

Shandon walked behind me and pulled me to standing. The chair fell at our feet as he kissed my neck. He wrapped his strong arms around my waist, and I blushed. He turned me around and bent me over the sink while pulling up my nightgown.

They heard their children running down the steps, and they both quickly fixed their clothes and started pretending to be making a cup of coffee. As their children sat down at the kitchen table, husband and wife shared a sly smile and mouthed, whew! Shandon stood behind his wife as she sat back down at the table. He politely pushed her chair

117 | P a g e

under the table and kissed her on her neck. She smiled widely and hugged him tightly.

"Eww," Liana and Ashton mocked. "Mom and Dad!"

"Hush!" Shandon said and smiled at his teenagers. "How do you two think you got here?"

Their teenagers made a face at the realization of what their Dad was implying. Then ewww was exaggerated this time. As Shandon placed a plate of food in front of each of his children, he and Jnana mouthed sensual messages back and forth across the kitchen. This foreplay was commonplace for the couple. They were a passionate couple, and even if time kept them from consummating their passion for each other, they often left sexy little notes around the bedroom. When they were feeling extra wild, they even videotaped themselves and left the evidence for the other to watch. It was all fodder for the things that would take place when they did finally find some alone time. After making plates and cleaning up a little, Shandon sat down with his family to talk about the day ahead of all of them. They blew kisses and licked their lips at each other across the table. Jnana ate her food sensually, and Shandon blew on his breakfast, even though it was already lukewarm.

"So, how is your reading class going, Liana?" Shandon asked.

"Daddy, I'm in the sixth grade. It's called English now. Sheesh, keep up with the times." She giggled.

"Yeah, I forgot they changed that title last year." Shandon shrugged. Fail!

Jnana chuckled at his lackluster attempt at getting

her sexy moves off his mind. As if! Looking across the table at his son, he realized Ashton wasn't eating. He's sixteen, so that's very suspect. Teenage boys are always within a growth spurt, so for him to not eat, something had to be terribly wrong.

"Ashton, what's on your mind? You aren't eating, and you aren't cracking jokes on your sister either, what's up?" Shandon asked with his brow furled up.

Hesitating before he replied, he said, "Dad, it's girl stuff. Can we talk about this another time? You know, without Mom and Sissy present?"

Looking across the table, Shandon could see Jnana was hurt and about to open her mouth to say something. To assure his wife he could handle things alone, he blurted.

"Uh, okay. How about I make some time for you when you get out of school? I can pick you up instead of you riding with Mr. Jenkins after school. We can take a drive to look at some toolboxes. How does that sound?"

"Great!" Ashton replied gleefully, a weight lifted. "I feel better already. My construction teacher keeps reminding me I need to get a toolbox before he takes points off my grade. He is giving me until next Monday."

"So, we need to get this done today. Mr. Jenkins just pulled up in front of the house. Let him know that I appreciate him carpooling you to and from school. Tell Celeste that I said good morning. Have a wonderful day, son."

"Bye, Dad. I'll see you after school. Moms, I love you, and I will text you later on to see how your day is going." Then, he hugged his little sister. They were very close, despite their age difference.

As Ashton left, Jnana mouthed, one down. Shandon responded by flicking his tongue at her, nice and slow.

"Umm, so, Liana, how is your reading class going?" Jnana asked, fully distracted by her husband.

"Mom, ask Dad!" Liana screamed as she ran out of the kitchen, shaking her head. "Parents!"

Shandon and Jnana laughed hard. When Shandon walked over to help his wife out of her chair, their eyes locked, and they kissed so passionately that steam could have risen from the floorboards. Their bodies were enraptured with each other when the screech of the school bus brakes sounded, interrupting them.

"Liana! Your bus is here. Hurry up; you *cannot* miss it today!" Jnana screamed and winked at Shandon.

Jnana stood in the doorway in her bathrobe to assure the bus stayed in place so Liana could get safely off to school. Liana ran past her mother and blew a kiss. After watching the bus drive down the street and turn a corner, Jnana practically jogged back into the kitchen, only to find her husband gone. As she walked into the living room, she saw her husband's clothes in a path leading upstairs. She could hear the water for the jacuzzi running, and she smiled. She realizes that she has a good man, and she isn't losing him to anyone, like her friend, Trinni. She loved her best friend, but as a happily married woman, she did not respect her friend's hustle. Trinity took advantage of the lulls in people's marriages. That's why Jnana was ever so motivated to make sure she didn't have many of them in hers. She had a rock-solid marriage, and at the center of it was sensually fulfilling her husband's *and* her fantasies. Unselfish devotion lived strong in her marriage.

Jnana walked upstairs to find a trail of yellow rose petals leading to the bathroom. She tiptoed in to find her husband in the jacuzzi, surrounded by bubbles. She made eye contact with him, then let her bathrobe fall gently to the ground. She could tell by Shandon's smile her voluptuous form pleased him. He reached his hand out to help her into the jacuzzi.

Jnana and Shandon bathed each other with sensual sudsy touches. They kept eye contact as they kissed with promises of more to come when they got out of the jacuzzi. The bathroom rarely featured any other activity besides foreplay. Shandon always said he needed to have his woman spread out so that he could enjoy touching every part of her body. However, when the mood to get rowdy hit them, the bathtub provided lots of lubricating motion that often led to most of the water ending up on the floor and walls. They were exercising patience.

When they were done in the tub, Shandon dried his wife off. He took great care to touch every part of her. He kissed each part too. He had a foot fetish, and that part of her got special attention. He allowed his woman to dry him off just as slowly and passionately. She enjoyed her favorite part of him by drying him off with long, slow strokes that had Shandon leaning on the wall for support.

After they oiled each other down, they near ran to the bedroom. Then, Jnana tied Shandon up with her scarf, just as he desired. She left him tied to the bed while she went downstairs to prepare some goodies for their love session. Once back upstairs, Jnana strutted around in her red five-inch heels and poured them both a glass of sparkling water. Focused on her mission to turn Shandon out, she stepped onto the bed and stood over his body like his Mistress Jnana. She intended to take full advantage of a rare moment when Shandon allowed her to tie him up and do whatever she pleased with him. Fully apprised of the many options available to her, her imagination would be the only detriment to their pleasure. As Jnana stood over Shandon's tied-up body, she rocked back and forth. She provided him all the visual effects that drove him up the wall. Her frame, five feet three, her beautiful face, down to her round bottom, was glistening from the massage oil Shandon had moisturized her bodies with. In her right hand, she held warm, melted chocolate sauce. Shandon lay spread-eagle under her, in awe of her adventurous nature. His thick five nine, dark as midnight form trembled in excitement. His soft thick lips, he licked, expecting his favorite pastime.

In his words, he has an eating addiction. To heighten the thrill, Shandon struggled to get loose. But she moved away each time he tried to reach for her. He thrashed around, trying to loosen the knots she no doubt learned to tie from her years in the

Girls Scouts. Jnana waited for her sweetheart to calm down before she raised her hand slowly over her head. She tipped the container over her perky mounds and poured warm chocolate sauce down onto her body. She continued to pour it down her body as it drizzled onto her husband, who held his breath in anticipation of what she would do next. She was super creative, so anything could happen next. His wife was still so sexy to him. Even after all the years they had been together, so sexy was she that he wanted to suck every drop of chocolate off her body. From her head on down to toes, especially her toes!

Jnana sat on Shandon's thighs and got comfortable. She looked him deep in his eyes.

"Baby, you like that? Huh?" Jnana asked seductively, enjoying being in control of their session.

"Yes, yes, I do. Baby, you are so sexy! Oh, my gosh! Jnana, I cannot control myself, untie me, please?" Leaning down, she brushed her body seductively across his face. He tried to open his mouth and catch a taste, but she pulled back up just in time. A bit of chocolate dripped down onto his lips as she pulled away. He lapped it up in excitement. She put her finger to his lips then she slid it into his mouth. He flicked his tongue lightly onto her finger, then, surprising her, he sucked the tip of her finger deep into his mouth. Jnana smiled, knowing that her plan to drive her husband to the edge of ecstasy he had never experienced was working out better than she had expected. But she had one more show in store for him.

"Baby, why are you doing this to me? Why? You know that I can't get my hands loose to touch you. Loosen the knots a little bit. Baby, please, have mercy on me. Please?"

"No, I am not untying you, Shandon. Not yet. So, tell me, do you like what you see, huh?"

"You know darn well that I do. Untie me so I can show you, my love."

"Not yet, Baby, not yet" Jnana whispered in his ear. "Relax, Shandon, let me show you my appreciation for you. Just look at you…you sexy chocolate man, I just want to eat you up. I am so proud that you're mine. Come on, Baby, relax. Well, some parts of you may relax." She smiled, looking at his thick body, her mouth, watering.

Jnana sat back, and she rocked her body back and forth. As she sat on him, she caused him to tremor too. Jnana relaxed and tensed up just enough to raise the temperature in the room, then fell forward onto her husband's chest. The heat between their bodies was causing sweat to bead up. Jnana was getting heady and couldn't hold back any longer. She kissed him sensually. They stayed in that position for what seemed like forever. Their passion was at an all-time high! Shandon was about to take charge when the phone rang. Disturbing the virtual silence in the room, the ringtone seemed to echo. When the phone wasn't answered, the caller called back five more times. After the fifth call, Trinity's voice came blaring through the answering machine. Their bodies froze in reaction.

"Jnana, hey, it's me, Trinni. I know that you've been trying to contact me, but I'm fine. Jnana? Girl pick up. I know that you're home. I'm parked out front. Open up. I only have thirty minutes for my break, and I used up five driving over here." The banging on the front door began. "Open up this door, girl!"

Jnana slowly climbed off her husband and put on his bathrobe. She looked at him and mouthed sorry in consolation. She was enjoying quality time with her husband, but she was eager to find out what her friend had been up to. She walked out of the room when Shandon said, "Jnana? Are you just going to leave me like this? I mean, we *were* in the middle of something."

"Oh…yeah…Baby, I know that we were in the middle of something. I'm sorry. But you know that she is my best friend."

"And?! Jnana, here we go again! We get closer when she disappears on you when she finds a new man. But, when she comes back, I get pushed aside like week-old trash. Ask yourself this: who was here all week when you were worried about her, and she was selfishly ignoring your calls? Now, all she has to do is show up, and you run to her aid?" He cleared his throat, and his tone softened, "What about me? Don't I matter? At all?"

"Baby, don't be like that. Please. I should make sure she is okay. She is my best friend. You know that I have been trying to reach her all week."

"Jnana, don't be like what? I am your husband. Forsake all others for me? Isn't that what our vows said? So?"

Painfully recognizing the vacant look in his wife's eyes, he knew that he was fighting a losing

125 | P a g e

battle. With Trinity, Jnana was loyal, often to a fault. Watching his wife, again, head towards the door, he sighed. Not again!

With her hand on the doorknob, he asked, "So are you going to untie me or what?!"

Jnana said, walking over to the side of the bed, "Baby, I'm sorry, I forgot." She methodically untied him, purposefully ignoring the pained look in his eyes. She rationalized he is mad now, but he is her husband. He will eventually get over it. He's easy like that.

"So, it's like that, Jnana?"

"Shandon, what more do you want? I said that I am sorry. I forgot. Ok?"

Shandon tried to will Jnana's eyes towards his. She was so beautiful with chocolate all on her. And he loves to see her in his bathrobe. He was trying to be understanding, but he was losing the battle with her lack of consideration for his feelings. He thanked her for untying him before a fire rose in his belly.

"You forgot? Oh, of course, you did! Before you tout Trinity as being your best friend, remember I am your husband. That should be more important, don't you think?"

When he got no response, Shandon stomped to the shower a sticky, irritated, and sexually frustrated hot mess.

"I was so close. So darn close. Trinni strikes again!" He slammed the bathroom door and hopped into the shower.

Jnana ran down the steps, holding her breath. She hoped that her best friend was okay. As soon as the door opened, Jnana and Trinity hugged and kissed each other on the cheek. Then, they stepped back to assess each other.

"Umm, Jnana, you have chocolate on your cheek." Trinity smirked then asked, "What's up with that?"

"Well, it's a long…uhh hard…umm story."

"Don't lie, Jnana, I see Shandon's truck parked in the driveway. I may not have any kids, but I can only imagine how you two get your groove on when the kids aren't here. I already called the bookstore, and they told me you're playing hooky today. Could it be that you had an appointment with Dr. Shandon for a well body checkup?"

Ignoring her friend's attempt at prying, Jnana asked, "So, Trinity, what's been up with you? I have been trying to reach you all week. What were you ducking me or something?"

Jnana attempted to change the direction of Trinity's conversation. She wasn't willing to share any inside information about her marriage with her best friend. Not today.

"There was nothing much going on with me. On the other hand, it appears that a lot has been up in…I mean up with you."

Jnana cleared her throat and smoothed down her messy hair. She felt some dried chocolate in it and discretely tried to smooth it out. "Trinni, how about some hot chocolate? Yeah? Now, do you want hazelnut or French vanilla creamer with that?"

"Alright, hot chocolate sounds great. But what will you put in it? I see that you have already found a use for some *hot* chocolate." Trinity giggled as she pointed to some more dried chocolate in Jnana's hair.

127 | P a g e

"Stop minding married folks' business!" Jnana rushed into the kitchen and made the hot chocolate as quickly as possible. When she peeped out into the living room, Trinity was smiling while listening to Shandon stomping around upstairs. When Jnana finally made her way back into the living room, she said, "Trinity, you only have a few minutes left before you have to go, so tell me, what has been up with you?"

"Okay, since you insist on keeping me out of your *married* business, I'll tell you what has been going on with me and my *single* business. My heart was broken. I was going through! Grey broke things off with me, and he has moved on to his secretary. He said that if I join them, he will increase my monthly rewards to thirty-two hundred dollars of spending money, plus he will still pay all of my bills indefinitely."

Jnana was stunned. She knew from the stories that Trinni had shared over the years they have been friends that Trinni is a grade-A board-certified freak. But this latest escapade might escalate that status into the stratosphere.

Assessing her friend's face first, she asked, "So?"

A sly grin moved across Trinni's face, "So what? Oh, you want to know if I said yes. Huh? Is that it?"

"Yeah, girl, don't play with me! Give me the sordid details like only you can. I just left my husband hot and bothered upstairs, so I know that he is beyond upset. It may be awhile before he touches me again. At least allow me to live vicariously through you. You aren't shy, Trinni, so stop playing. Spit it out and tell me what you told him."

"Well, all I really said was that I would think about it."

"And? Have you, thought about it, I mean."

"Yes, I have. As much as I miss him, you know darn well that I have. I have been thinking hard about what I could do with all that money. Sometimes, I think that I would do anything to get him back. I know it seems as if I didn't care about him, but I do. Foolishly, I thought he cared about me too."

"Trinni, girl, I know that the truth must have really hurt you. I am so sorry."

"The truth hurts, but I would rather know now than after wasting more time on him. I would have given him time to miss me. I thought what we shared was special. That this was another one of our breakup-to-makeup episodes, that is until he did something so unforgivable."

"Trinity, what's worse than him cheating on you, his mistress, with another woman?"

"Jnana, hold your breath! He told me not to call him, he would be in touch, but I missed him so much. I called him anyway. I thought he had hung up the phone, but the counter on my phone was still rolling. I heard him having relations with his secretary, Lisa. And when I say relations, hmmm, let me tell you, they were relating on a level exciting enough to release to the mass market for sale. He was *really* getting it in…in the office at the bank!"

"Trinni, are you serious? Gurl, they were getting it in like that? How did it sound? Wild or lame?"

Looking at Trinni's face full of hurt and pain, Jnana

apologized, "I am so sorry. That was very insensitive of me. Will you forgive me?"

"Yes, Jnana, I will. I do. To answer your question, it wasn't loud or tame. Honestly, he sounded like he made love to her. It was tender and sounded very sensual. Afterward, he told her he had never felt that way before. That hurt to hear. In my mind, that was the day he ended things with me. He couldn't really have loved me or even gave a darn about me to act so flagrantly. When he picked the phone up, after she left the office, Greysan asked if I enjoyed listening to them going at it."

"Well, I'm sorry that Greysan's actions have hurt you, Trinni. He has always been a jerk. Haven't I always told you that? Huh?"

"Yes, you sure have. All the times you called him a jerk used to irk me. But you are right. He has always lived down to your expectations of him."

"Trin, I am here for you. But the next time you plan on disappearing, let a sistah know. I thought Shandon and I would have to bust all up in that condo with guns drawn. You know how me and my Baby get down. We be Delaware gangstas all day running!" Jnana said animatedly like she'd seen acted out in many gangster movies.

Laughing hard enough to need to hold her stomach, Trinni said, "Aww, Lord. Bless your heart. Thank you, Jnana, I really needed that laugh. It has been rough for me. I laid up in that condo for days, and it felt as if I was dying from the inside out. These men are trying to kill me slowly. I'm tired of hurting like this. I am so worn down. Anyways, thank you for the hospitality, but it's time for me to get back to

130 | P a g e

work. I stayed much longer than I expected. I am already on probation. I have one more write up before they fire me. Without Greysan's money, I need this job more than ever. Especially in this lackluster economy. My job is all that I have."

"Girl shut your mouth! You have me and Shandon if you need anyone to lean on. Plus, the kids love their Auntie Trinni. Okay, get on out of here. I have a good man waiting, no doubt, impatiently, upstairs for me. I have to go make this banana split."

"Aight, gurl. Go handle your married business and keep yours tight. You wouldn't want that fine man of yours to get it in his head to go outside of your marriage to find what may lack with you."

Snapping her neck back, Jnana grabbed Trinity's arm then exclaimed, "What?!"

Trying to pull her arms loose from her best friend's tightening grip, Trinity whispered, "Nothing, Jnana, I was just playing. You know I meant nothing by it. Come on, let me go. I have to get back to work."

Squeezing Trinni's arm tighter, Jnana said through clenched teeth, "Look, Trinity, I love you like a sister. But woo gurl, don't you ever come out of your neck at me like that again! Am I clear?! My marriage or anything that has to do with it is none of your damnbusiness unless I share it with you. Understood? I'm not playing with you, Trinni, not one bit!" Jnana said, her nose flaring in rising anger.

"Jnana, yes, I understand. Okay, I will admit that I was out of line. I'm sorry. I love you, girl." Trinity could finally pull her arm loose. Trying to placate an angry Jnana, she then tried to hug her best friend.

Jnana crossed her arms over her chest.

"Love you too. Now, get going." Jnana pushed Trinity towards the door.

"Uh, okay. Geez, Jnana, you don't have to push me out the door. I said that I am sorry."

Jnana didn't reply, but when Trinity stepped out onto the threshold to leave, Jnana couldn't hold herself back. She slammed the door so hard the wall shook, and it sounded like a car backfiring.

Sowing Seeds of Deceit

He must correct his opponents with courtesy and
gentleness, in the hope that God may grant that they
will repent and come to know the Truth {that they
will perceive and recognize and become accurately
acquainted with and acknowledge it}
2 Timothy 2:25
***

Trinity

     I barely made it back to work on time, even
though I had mostly green lights on my way back.
Since I only have one more write up before I get
fired, they were a definite blessing. I must be on my
best behavior more than ever today because the
secret shoppers are here in full force. I got that
secret tip from my work best friend, Montoya. I'm
already on thin ice, so I can't risk being reported for
anything negative.

     I'm glad that I had stopped by to see Jnana
instead of calling her. I truly missed my best friend.
She always kept it real and always had my back,
unconditionally. Despite the way our visit ended, it
was still a decent visit. I know Jnana is probably
mad at me. In fact, I am sure of it. I said what I did
to her before I left because I was being hateful. I
make no excuses for my negative behavior. When
she slammed the door as I walked away, it scared
the heck out of me! I have never seen her so angry.
For a moment, I regretted what I said. By the way
she slammed that door, I would not turn around,

knock on the door, and apologize. I am not a coward, so I was not going out like that to make her feel better. Jnana needs to know how truth feels, if only once!

She can dish it out, but I see now she can't take it. I love my best friend, really, I do. I just wish that Jnana could understand where I am coming from. I love her so, but deep down, I despise her. I mean, I really have a bit of envy built up for her. I know there are many characters in the Bible that show me jealousy and envy are sins. Still, for as long as our friendship has existed, Jnana has had it all. She is successful, beautiful, and in shape. Although she is not what people have traditionally considered to be thin, she is beautifully proportioned. Her skin is always so smooth and moisturized. She loves her family with her all. She is giving and very loyal. Essentially, she is a wonderful woman. She finished high school in the top five, got a full-ride scholarship to college, and found Shandon when she wasn't even looking for a man. Things always work out for Jnana. It seems like everything she touches turns to gold. Even her children are perfect.

The real reason why I feel my soul harden towards her every time she talks about her happy life is that she has a good man. I try to act like I don't like him, but Shandon is an amazing man. He is a hard-working entrepreneur with, it seems, endless drive. He is intelligent and industrious with a touch of a roughneck. Even his dedication to his family is commendable. He isn't what I consider to be a pretty boy, but he has a distinct attractiveness that isn't too often found in a faithful man. See, I don't want Jnana's husband. I just want what she has. I would give my last breath to live her fairytale life. I don't know why I only get married men who want to be in a relationship with me. Single men don't even look at me anymore. I'm not down on myself. I have just realized what my limitations are in the dating arena. So, I work with the types of men that are approaching me.

Because of Jnana's attitude, I didn't stay nearly as long as I wanted. She always had my back, but today she had been out for self. Even as she listened to what I had been up to during my absence, I could see that she was listening closely to Shandon moving around upstairs. She was clearly more interested in what her husband was doing than me, her *best friend*. One more episode like this and I would seriously have to re-evaluate my friendship with her. I was more of a friend, especially today, than she had been to me.

I upset her, but honestly, I feel like I have more of a reason to be mad at her. I hadn't answered her calls in a week, and she has the nerve to come to the door with chocolate sauce on her cheek. She even had the audacity to flaunt her freak session in my face by answering the door in her robe. She knew that it would hurt me to know that she has a good man that satisfies her on the regular. Even after I told her what Greysan had done to me, she flaunts her solid relationship in my face. She was being selfish by not getting dressed before she opened the door. She even smelled like sex. Ugh, I was upset, and admittedly very jealous. I got even angrier when she tried to play coy with me by telling me to get out of married folks' business. How dare she insinuate that I couldn't have anything to add to the discussion because she's married, to a good man, and I'm just a jump-off! I hate that Jnana is so together. I hate that she has it all. I hate how she seems to look down on my cheating lifestyle with married men. Hmmm, does my attitude towards her makes me a bad friend feeling this way? If it does, oh well, I have a right to be upset right now. Don't judge me unless you have walked in my shoes…Manolo Blahnik shoes!

As sure as I stand here at work, I know that right now, Jnana is probably back to fulfilling her husband's sexual fantasies. That thought was overtaking my brain. I know that I am so jealous of my best friend. How dare she get everything that she wants so easily! I stood silent, and I realize that I was coming undone. I was beyond jealous of Jnana. I am going down the road to hysterical hate, and I must get focused. Quick! Jnana is my friend, not my enemy! I yawned and cleared away the negative energy. I have got to gain control over my negative thoughts, especially when they have to do with my jealousy of Jnana.

To redirect my wayward thoughts, I pulled out the to-do list the store manager had written for me. Between the two of us, we want to get my department tight. Because I was so organized and fashion-minded, I had won several in-store contests. Once, we received a visual arts award from a local art college when I set up the display at the beginning of the mall. Other store employees and customers alike often gushed about the color schemes and the clothes I displayed. We usually sold out of every item I used in the displays. There were even two times we had to sell the display clothes. Unfortunately, we can't sell the display items anymore. A new general manager has made the store tighten its budget on overtime. Still, in my mind, I think to derail my creative efforts at selling seriously overpriced clothes. They complained it cost too much money to keep paying me to repeat the same display. They worded the policy to assure anyone, besides me, our job was being made easier. To heck with the haters, I must keep the accolades coming. Fashion is who I am!

The entire week I was gone, healing my broken heart, the fill-in department manager only completed two things on the to-do list of twenty things. Sadly, and to my utter dismay, those two things also had to be redone. I can't stand working with lazy, unmotivated, and trifling people. This employee is always half stepping around the store, but she is still making more money than I am. I wonder who she is servicing in the head office because she sure as heck isn't earning her pay the traditional way.

I had spent the last three hours working through the to-do list and had finally gotten to the last five items when I noticed that three women were taking over my department. They were boisterous and appeared to be ghetto. They were talking and laughing loudly amongst themselves. For a second, I was ashamed to be half black. The shocked white people were stopping, staring, and pointing. The bravest ones gossiped loudly amongst themselves and shook their heads. The three women were dressed in designer clothes; however, they had an edgy essence that was very apparent. I have seen women like this before. They dress up in high-priced fashion and think because they have money, they can buy class. Class is born; it cannot be earned, no matter how much someone is worth. Major fail!

I tapped my favorite coworker, Zelelia, for this type of scene. I begged her, "Please handle them. I don't have the patience today."
Looking the three of them up and down, she replied with a shake of her head, "Nah, I'll pass. This isn't the first time they've shopped here. I have dealt with them before, and I received a disciplinary write up because of them. I am *not* the one, not today. Besides, I just realized I must go potty. Deuces!"
I am furious! How dare she desert me like this. I can't bear to get another write up. I pray that these heifers know what they want and made a quick business of finding it so they can get out of my department.
I finished my to-do list, and these three were still here. It has been two hours already. Every twenty minutes or so, the thinnest and prettiest one interrupted me by asking for darn near every piece of black lingerie we have in the department. She quickly nixed each one until I brought her a tiny cream-colored lace midriff and thong set made delicately in silk. It was gorgeous. If I were her size, I would have purchased it and modeled it for

Greysan months ago. But I was at least ten sizes bigger than she was. She was about five feet, ten inches tall with long honey blonde hair, which was perfectly crinkle curled. Her rich brown eyes were beautiful and Asiatic shaped. She had the smoothest satiny caramel skin; I wanted to touch it because she looked like a painting come to life. Her teeth were straight, and her lips were very full, probably full of Botox. She had Naomi Campbell chic and an attitude to match. Perfect smoky eyes and natural mineral makeup framed her high cheekbones. She was a size four, but she had thick girl hips and butt. Her thirty-four B breasts were smaller than mine and even more firm and supple. I'm not having a girl crush moment, but she is enticingly hypnotic.

I had to stop looking at her while I rang up her ghetto friend. This woman was so beautiful, but I had to stop looking at her; it was mesmerizing. Conversely, her friend has a weave that needs to be redone. Her hairstyle is way past its expiration date. The tracks are showing, and so is the black glue. Her skin is broken out, and her face is too heavily made up to allow her pores to breathe. Her body is okay, but she seems to insist on shopping in the junior department when she needs to be shopping in the women's department. Her dialect is horrible. The Bomquisha attitude and 'ya know what I mean' is wearing thin with me. I want to yell: No! I don't know what you mean, and I don't even care. Now, go on back to that ghetto in your mind. Speak English like the rest of us humans before you have conversations with intelligent, well-read folks!

This hussy had two arms full of clearance items,

which were at least one size too small. I took the clothes off the hangers, folded them, and rang up the items. She wanted to pay with her debit card, which I recognize as one of those prepaid debit cards. Hmm, interesting, the card got declined. I watched in glee as she looked around in shame. Her light face turning red with embarrassment. I wanted to laugh in her face so bad, but I had to maintain professionalism, especially with the secret shoppers lurking around. I made a mental note to have a good laugh in her honor later. Mos Def!

"Tineta, girl you knew your debit card wouldn't go through. You don't have any money. Stop playing with that cashier. She has other things to do besides mess with your broke behind. Miss, please put those things aside, I will purchase them when I pay for mine." The prettiest one named Quintaria said.

"Aww, Quin, thanks. You know I got you next time." Bomquisha chick gushed.

Shaking her head at her friend, Quintaria stated, "Sure girl, like always, you got me."

The Bomquisha chick slid her rejected prepaid card back into her knock-off Dolce bag. Sheesh, who does she think she's fooling? Not me. I can spot a bootleg version from a mile away. As I was still trying not to burst out laughing in her face, she had the nerve to roll her eyes at me and turn her James Evans nose up at me. I quickly gave her the screw face then changed back to my professional mode. Ole heffa better ask somebody before I remind her, she doesn't have class because she hung out with friends with money.

"She got this like you heard her say." She spat at

140 | P a g e

me. "You better put my things aside and don't play with me and put them back on the racks when I'm not looking. I already got that other girl written up, don't make me put you on my list too." Apparently done putting me in my place, she slinked away in her nasty attitude puff of green funk.

"Yes, Ma'am," I said with a smile as fake as her purse.

I hate saying that to low life women like her. She was gum beneath my feet. With Greysan's money, I can buy and sell her. Even with my limited cash flow, I can afford the five-dollar baby shirts she tried to purchase with her declined prepaid card. She had better fall back, or she would see the anger in my eyes since I couldn't possibly say what I was really feeling and expect to stay gainfully employed. I was on thin ice already, and my reason for being fired would not be put in her hands. I am not going out like that. I was piling her clothes in a neat pile when I was summoned.

"Miss, miss, can you come over here and clean this three-way mirror? It's smudged with little fat fingers. I cannot possibly be subjected to using such a dirty mirror. Clean it now! I have to make sure that I look good, and I can't be assured of my fabulousness if this mirror is so dirty."

I rushed around looking for the glass cleaner and paper towels. When I found them, I quickly cleaned the mirror and all the others on the wall just in case she wanted to use them too.

"Yes, Ma'am, right away." I didn't mind saying that to her. She is classy, thin, and beautiful. I wish that I could be her for a day. She exuded so much style. I wonder what she was doing hanging out with her Bomquisha friend. In their friendship, opposites truly attracted.

I cleaned off the mirror and discretely watched Quintaria and her two friends in awe. When it appeared as if I was being too obvious, I busied myself while I listened to the three women talk.

"Quin, girl, you are rocking that one right there. Yeah, you should get that one. Your man's eyes will bug right out of his head if you model that one for him." The Bomquisha chick said.

"Well, I may get this one. It is my size, and I do look great in it." She modeled the lingerie with pride and never took her eyes off herself. Maybe she was as in awe of herself as I was.

"Tineta, do I look like I am three months pregnant? My husband isn't turned on when my stomach gets bigger and I look pregnant." An insecure Quintaria inquired.

I was stunned. This heffa is three months pregnant? Isn't that a trip! And she is insecure to boot!

"Quin stop asking that stupid question. Sis, you look fabulous." The quiet one finally spoke.

"Vonnie, but is it sexy enough? I really want to look good on our anniversary. You know how much I love this man. Despite all his faults."

"Despite all his faults?! Quin stop complaining! You got yourself a good man, plus he is gorgeous and rich! I wish that he had a brother so I can get some of his family DNA all up in me." Bomquisha chick added.

Quintaria sucked her teeth, "Tineta, why do you have to be so crass all the time. You're using bedroom language in a department store. Get it together."

"Sorry, Quin. I was just joking with you." Bomquisha chick said, and she looked down to the floor, ashamed that her true feelings had slipped out.

"Yeah, you are always joking. But I bet if you were alone with my *good man*, you would be one of his conquests too. I can see you now feigning after his money and mediocre bedroom skills. Do you think I haven't noticed how you make eyes at my man on the sly? I see how you always seem to find a reason to bend over to show your oversized butt whenever he is around. And don't think I haven't noticed how he likes the teasing you do with him. You really irk me! Go get me all the colors in this style. I need a break from your nonsense. But don't take too long, my baby is hungry."

Being obedient, Bomquisha chick submitted, "Aight Quin, I will be right back. I really am sorry." She walked around the department looking in the wrong areas. I didn't even bother to tell her. Finally, she gave up and walked out of the store altogether. Quintaria ignored her friend's hollow apology. "Vonnie, tell me again why we let her hang with us? She is so droll sometimes. It seems like it gets worse every time we take her out. Did you see that she didn't even try to defend herself? She really would come on to my man if he gave her the chance!"

"Quin, relax. As whorish as your man is, he would never stoop to the low levels of messing with Tineta. Now, let's focus on how great you look in your lingerie. You will blow your husband away, I promise."

I watched how classy these sisters were. I was wrong about these two, but that Bomquisha chick, aww yeah, I was dead-on right about her.

"Aww, Sis, thank you so much." She reached out and hugged her sister. "I love you."

"Sis, you know that I love you too, but you need to get yourself going. We have been in here for a long time, and my feet are killing me."

"Alright. I am hungry too. While I change back into my clothes, can you please call the house and check on the kids?" She offered as she walked toward the dressing room.

"Sure, Quin."

She was halfway to the dressing room before she turned and yelled back to her sister, "Thank you, Vonnie. Do you want to use my cell, or did you remember to bring yours?"

"Ha Ha Ha Quin...no, I didn't lose it while I had it on vibrate again. I have it right here. You go on back there and change while I check up on the kids."

"See, that's what I like about you, Sis, you don't take yourself so seriously. But you must admit how funny it was when you tore your house up trying to find that expensive cell phone and it was right in your back pants pocket. I sure enjoyed watching you searching high and low for it. With that big booty of yours, I can see why you couldn't feel that it was on your person."

"Again, Quin, hahaha, you're just hating that you got less of the sistah shape than I did. Now, go on back there and get changed already."

"Alright, don't forget to call the kids. There's no telling what that husband of mine has up his sleeve since he knows I'll be gone most of the day."

I watched as Quintaria walked back into the dressing room. She is three months pregnant! She is in better shape than I am, not pregnant. Just amazing.

I shifted my focus back to Vonnie because she was having a heated conversation with someone on the phone. This is better than any talk show.

"Hey, we are out at the store. Yeah, Quin wanted me to call and check up on the kids. How are they? What? Are you taking them to your Mom's again? Why? Come on. I know you aren't really going to work. It's Saturday! Now, you can tell my sister all types of bull, but we both know that you have been stepping out on her *again*!"

Oh, heck yeah, this is the most excitement my department has ever seen!

"What? Oh, you sure got a slick mouth for someone that doesn't have a pot to piss in. I have only been gone a few hours, and you are trying to pawn the kids off on someone else. You are sad for that. What? Hmm, let me say this since you want to play with me. I will call all four of my brothers if I ever find proof that you are cheating on my sister again. I would do it the last two times, but Quin loves you, so she talked me out of it. This time is different. There is nothing she can say to stop me from making that phone call. Especially now since she is pregnant with your baby *again*. And when I make that phone call, I will make sure that my brothers beat that booty like a Mexican piñata! They will also kick you out of that house. Huh? What do you have to say now? Oh, you're quiet now. You better have my niece and nephew at home, with you, when we get there, or I will make that call. Understood? Yeah? I thought so. Goodbye!"

This is better than a talk show. Vonnie was classy, but in defense of her family, she can sure pull sistah gurl out of her back pocket in a flash. Good for her! I wish that I had a brother that I could call to beat Greysan up for using and abusing me. If only!

I walked to the register to appear busy when she noticed I was eavesdropping on her phone conversation. Trying to find something to do, I cleaned up the register area and hung up some clothes. I realized their Bomquisha friend Tineta never made it back to the department. I hope she made her way to the store in the mall named Attitude Adjustment because I am so over her! Quintaria and Vonnie made their way to the register for me to ring them out. Things seemed to progress as usual as they began their order.

"Ladies, did you find everything you needed today?" I asked as I took the clothes off the hanger, folded them, then rang them up.

"Yes, you have been very helpful. Thank you." Quintaria answered.

Vonnie added, "Yes, we've had a good time today so far." Turning to her sister, she said, "Quin, I called that husband of yours. You will not believe this, but he was trying to drop the kids off at his mother's house."

Quickly turning to face her sister, Quintaria asked, "What? We haven't even been gone that long, and he is trying to ditch them already? Here we go again." Her voice began cracking with emotion. Rubbing Quintaria's back to console her, Vonnie continued, "Yeah, he said that he has to work. Sis, you better check that man. I think he is stepping out on you again. And yet you keep popping his babies out like it's nothing. I told you a long time ago, in fact, after the first one was born, you cannot save a shaky marriage by adding children to the mix. Not even a baby will save a marriage to a man like your husband."

Dang, Vonnie seems to be a real talk fan like Jnana! Real talk, every day, all day!

"How are you paying today? I asked, totally engrossed in their conversation, but I had to maintain professionalism even though I was hanging on their every syllable. The things I hear at work, I could write a book.

Vonnie nudged her sister, "Quin, snap out of it. The cashier is asking you a question. Quin!"

"What?" Quintaria screamed, much louder than she had intended. Her anger was rising by the minute.

"Miss, how will you be paying today?" I asked with measured caution.

Trying to clear her mind, she began, "How am I paying today? Oh, I'm sorry. I will pay by credit card. Please excuse me. I have a lot on my mind right now." She said as she dug into her genuine Dolce bag.

"Ma'am, I understand. No worries." I tried to make her feel better, but I knew how it felt to have someone cheat on you, even if Greysan was someone else's husband.

Quintaria finally offered, "Vonnie, can you please deal with this for a minute. I need to get myself together. I am out in public acting so uncouth. I'll be right back."

I looked at Vonnie, who shrugged her shoulders and tried to occupy her time by looking at the jewelry on the counter. She added a few of the pieces after browsing. Quintaria walked back into a dressing room. She wailed something terrible for about sixty seconds. It sounded like a wild animal in pain, then she called someone on the phone and cursed them out. Sistah gurl could really get it on. I didn't recognize some of those curse words because she was shooting them off so quickly. Then, there was an ominous silence. You could hear a pin drop! Everyone in the department waited for what would come next. It was like a soap opera up in here. Then Quintaria composed herself and walked back to my register as if nothing happened. The others in the department looked away as she made eye contact. They didn't want to risk getting some drama thrown their way. Quintaria stood back next to her sister, who gave her sistah gurl dap of the utmost respect for her method of setting things straight in her household.

"Good for you, Quin. You better check him when you get home too. Daddy got him that job, and with just one word, he will most definitely fire him too. The position at the bank has truly gone to his head. He needs to be reminded whose money he keeps spending like water."

Quintaria is loaded with money, yet she has a whorish, no good man that's freeloading off her money. Wow, I wonder who this man is. I hope he isn't cheating with a woman that thinks his money is really his and not his wife's. That would be tragic.

"I will, Vonnie, I will. Let's just get these things rang up so we can go eat. I'm famished."

"Okay, I will lay off, but you really need to remind that man he would be a penniless fool without you. He has no right to spend your trust fund money like this. I am only looking out for you and the kids. Now, where is that girl at? You sent her to get the lingerie a long time ago."

"She called me while I was back in the dressing room. She told me she got sick in the mall and needed to go home." Quintaria consoled.

"Well, I hope that she gets well soon. I'll call her when we get home." Following her sister's eyes to me, Vonnie asked, "Quin, are you okay?"

I looked up to find her staring me down. She looked away at the last second.

"Uh, what's your name?" Quintaria asked with her eyes squinted like she needs glasses.

"Trinity, why do you ask?" I was curious. I sure hope that she isn't one of my ex-lover's wives.

"I was trying to figure out where I know you from. I would say something earlier, but I wanted to look at you a little while longer to be sure. At first, I thought I knew you from my gym, but looking at you, hmm, you couldn't possibly belong to a gym. But I know you from somewhere, I just can't place you. But since you don't belong to a gym, here is

149 | P a g e

my personal trainer's card. Call him. He does fabulous work. You have a pretty face, but you will look so much better if you lose some weight."

Wow! I find haters everywhere. Nah, she isn't so pretty.

"Miss, thank you, but I won't need the personal trainer's number. I don't think I need to lose weight, but again, thank you."

Vonnie interjected, "Miss, please excuse my sister. Sometimes she gets diarrhea of the mouth. She means nothing by it."

I shrugged my shoulders this time. "It's okay. Now, which credit card will you be using?" I was ready to ring them up and get them out of my face.

"Here, you can use this one. I know that I was being a little rude earlier, but seriously, I noticed that you don't have a ring on your finger, and that might be because you need to get yourself in shape. I will leave his card anyway. You never know, you may change your mind."

She is irking my entire soul! How dare she assume that I don't know what I need to get a man! How dare she assume that I don't already have a man! I will not let a stranger get me all upset about my body image. Not today. I had been nothing but nice to this heffa, and she is coming at my neck like this. She better back on up.

"Ma'am, while I appreciate the gesture, I don't need the business card. Now, your credit card has been declined. Is there another means of payment that you would like to use?" I was so flustered that I busied myself by looking down at her card while she looked in her wallet for another one. I noticed

the name on the card and almost screamed.
Quintaria Lobes, as in Greysan Lobes? What the heck is going on here?

Quintaria looked around, hoping that no one noticed her issue. Her sister had stepped away to go find the bathroom so she couldn't provide a quaint distraction.

"Hold up. Let me give you my husband's store credit card. He doesn't even like this store, so it should go through without question."

I was tickled pink. Now, it's time to seal the deal. I slyly looked at the name on the second card. Yes, it was Greysan Lobes all right. I wanted to blast her and tell her how I had blown that card up on many an occasion, but now is not the time. I need more information.

I quickly thought of a lie so I could get more information on her and Greysan. "Ma'am, we are giving out random customer surveys. If you will fill out this form with your name, address, phone number, and other pertinent information about today's visit, you will receive a fifteen percent discount. Would you like to fill it out?" It was really a return slip, but she doesn't need to know that.

When she smiled, I knew I had her.

"Sure."

She filled it out while I ran her credit card.

Her sister came back to the register just as the card went through.

"Ma'am, this card went through. And I gave you credit for the fifteen percent off."

"Quin, what is she talking about *this* card? One of your credit cards was declined?"

"Yes, Sis, my credit card was declined. I don't really know what's up, but Greysan and I have some things to discuss because I always keep at least one thousand dollars on this card. "Again, handle that, Sis. Now, let's get out of here. I'm tired and hungry now."

When Quintaria and Vonnie walked away, Quintaria left her personal trainer's card right on my register. I don't know what I did to upset her, but either way, I have her personal information. I will see who is so smug when I blow up her spot! By the time I get done with her pompous behind, she will be so fat from eating butter pecan ice cream right out the container. With any luck, she will be so heartbroken and out of shape she will need to keep her personal trainer's number on speed dial after she has her b

~10~
Shadow Dancing

Wives, understand and support your husbands in
ways that show your support for Christ. The
husband provides leadership to his wife the way
Christ does his church, not by domineering but by
cherishing. So, just as the church submits to Christ
as he exercises his leadership, wives should
likewise submit to their husbands.
Ephesians 5:22-23
***

Jnana

"Baby, wake up." I nudged my husband and
whispered.
"Jnana, I'm trying to sleep. Leave me alone.
Please."
I was not taking no for an answer because we have
unfinished business, "Come on, Baby. I'll do that
dance that you love. The kids won't be home for a
little while longer. How about I put on *Til the Cops
Come Knocking* by Maxwell? Doesn't that sound
nice? Baby?" Shandon was playing hard to get. All
I wanted him to do was get hard.
He wasn't even biting when I turned on some music
and gyrated in front of the mirror. He usually loves
this scene. He was either exhausted or angry at me.
I know that I left him excited when Trinity came
over, but I was worried about her. Shandon never
understood why I am friends with a woman like her,
because we are so different. I told him that's the
precise reason we are friends. I don't like the drama

she creates, unnecessarily, in her life. But hey, I am her friend. I am not a morality police officer. She is a good person and has a big heart. She just needs to learn to love herself. I try to explain this to Shandon, but he doesn't buy my explanation one bit.

There has only been one major issue in my marriage since I had met Trinni. That issue started the day I met her. I met Trinity when I went back to take a few classes to advance in my job at an accounting firm I worked at. Trinity was going to college to be exposed to educated men whom she hoped could advance her wealth of, shall I say, things other than purely textbook knowledge. The first day of class, we did an activity together, and we found out we got along well. Then, we helped each other with assignments and tests. Not really one to have female friends, I took a chance on trusting Trinity. She, too, had issues with female friends. Based on that one premise: our shared bad experiences with female friends, we tried hard to be the best female friend we always wanted. Over time, it appeared as if she told me her secrets, and I told her mine. We bonded instantly, and I watched her, over the years, go from one man to another.

Within each situation, it appeared as if she put those men before herself. Then, she smoothly flipped the script on them as they found themselves heavily caught up in her web of sex and intrigue. I watched in awe as she turned our instructor's life upside down. Within a month of arriving at the college, she had our Civics Professor solidly wrapped around her well-manicured finger. He let her use his employee credit card, and she was even driving his state-owned vehicle, albeit without a valid driver's license. Yes, she was a pro, even back then. Men always seemed to fall head over behind for her. Sadly, for them, she got bored with them as quickly as milk spoils in the heat of the summer sun. She seemed to know exactly what they yearned to hear. Even back then, she knew how to stroke a man's ego, so he easily dropped his pants and even more quickly opened his wallet. She sharpened her teeth on each bone that was thrown her way. Until Grey, that is. No, he was clearly different. He was the one that got *her* sprung out so fast. The stone-cold tigress got caught in her own trap. She told me that she loved Greysan, but I don't think so. I think she is in love with what he gives her, money. The money has a strong pull over her. She is used to driving around in the best car and rocking the newest high fashion styles. Without Greysan financing her extravagant lifestyle, she will be Buster Browning it all over again. Her foolish pride won't allow her to go out like that. Her ego has already taken a hit since he has replaced her, seemingly without a thought. Karma, karma, karma!

Although I don't respect her hustle, I have to respect she takes life by the horns and is determined to march to the beat of her own drum.

Determined to get my Baby out of his foul mood, I said, "Shandon! Come on, Baby. I'm still in the mood. How about you? Shandon? Baby?" Although I was speaking to him with measured assertiveness, I was jumping on the bed like a kid trying to get his attention.

"Jnana, I said to leave me alone! You dropped me like a hot potato when your *best friend* came over. How do you think that made me feel? Oh, so now that your *best friend* Trinity is found to have been okay, now you find it convenient to remember that you have a husband?"

Ouch! "Shandon, that's not fair. You know I had been trying to reach her all week. I was just worried about her. Don't be like that." I laid down next to him and rubbed his face. "Baby, please don't be like this. Please."

He sucked his teeth at me, then rolled over to the other side of the bed. "Jnana, you are my wife. I expect to be put before her, or anyone else. I am not being unreasonable. I know you would agree. I have supported your friendship, but this is where I draw the line. Trinity should not come first before your family, especially not your husband. She should even be second to our kids. I put my friends behind you and my kids. When are you going to do that? Huh?"

Sheesh, he has a point. But, as stubborn as I am, I'm not ready to give up the fight. "Shandon, I need you to understand something. I am all she has. She says her grandparents don't understand her, and neither do all the men she has in her life. I think I understand her."

"Okay, now have you ever thought that maybe, just maybe, her grandparents don't like the reputation Trinity has developed in this town. You say you are her friend, but how can you honestly hold your head up high when most of the men in this town have been sexual with Trinity? I asked you this before, but I wonder why I never got an answer. It is seriously ironic."

"I didn't know that you felt like this. I always thought that was just an inside joke between us. I mean, this thing with Trinity is really ripping us apart."

"Nah, she isn't ripping us apart. She is *your* friend, not mine. I know the damage having a woman like her can do to a relationship—even a strong one. My aunt and uncle broke up because my uncle's best friend messed around with my aunt. They tried to keep things together for my cousins, but it was too devastating. At one time, we even thought that my younger cousin Ezekiel was his."

"Oh my gosh! Baby, I didn't know that. Look, if it will make you feel better, I can tell you I don't share our innermost private matters with Trinity. Whatever takes place between us, stays between us."

"Okay, that makes me feel a little better."

"Baby, please understand. I am only being a good friend. I don't want us to be like this. I love you. Please, let me touch you, please."

"Jnana, it's not that easy. I want to touch you. I want to make love to you, my beautiful wife. But I need your assurance this will never happen again. I need you to promise me I will be put first."

Shandon put his hands on my face and looked into my eyes. His eyes begged me to promise something I couldn't easily promise. He is my husband, but she is my best friend. He kissed my lips, and I gave in. He is my life mate. Any sacrifice is worth

157 | P a g e

keeping him happy.

"I promise, my handsome husband. From now on, you are my priority."

He released my face and pulled open my bathrobe. Our eyes met, and I got caught up in the deep emotion. The white-hot desire I have for my husband is getting stronger. I love this man, I really do.

I put on Jill Scott's *Crown Royal on Ice* and danced for my husband. He watched me and patiently awaited the moment when we touched. I didn't make him wait long. I lit a vanilla candle, turned out the lights, and waited for my Baby to invite me into his arms.

He reached out his arms and guided me onto the bed, "Come over here, my sexy wife. I want to get back to watching the banana split!"

"Alright, but Baby, wait a moment. I am turning off the ringer and the answering machine. If the cell phone goes off, I will only answer it if it's the kids' ringtone. Otherwise, all other calls can be returned when I'm done spending time with my husband. From now on, you will always come first."

"Nah, Jnana, you are my woman. I always want to make you sing out first and second before I even think about coming close. It's always about pleasing you, my love."

"Hold up, Shandon, you know I'm a pleaser too. How about we both sing out together?"

"Deal. Let's get this sixty-nine plus two on and popping."

~11~
Charge it to My Soul

You'll need buckets for tears when the crash comes
upon you. Your money is corrupt, and your fine
clothes stink. Your greedy luxuries are a cancer in
your gut, destroying your life from within. You
thought you were piling up wealth. What you've
piled up is judgment.

James 5:1-3

***

Trinity

My last day at the department store began
normally. As I took off my coat, my nasty attitude
co-manager of my department, Elvira, came
walking into the employee break room. She smiled
at me with that nasty yuck mouth of hers and spat,
"Morning Trinity. You sure look happy so far this
morning. Did you just roll out from under
someone's husband?"
I figured she was baiting me, so I smiled back and
replied, "I'm blessed, and my private affairs are
none of your business."

That took her by surprise. She thought I was
a heathen, but I do know from where my blessings
flow. I just don't wear my spirituality on my sleeve.
Admittedly, nor do I always act like I know God. I
can be an unapologetic sinner, but she doesn't need
to know that.
"Well, I would like for you to meet me upstairs in
the main office in ten minutes. Before you join me
upstairs, clean out your employee locker. And
159 | P a g e

Trinity, make sure not to leave any shred of evidence that you ever worked here. I have been waiting for this day for so long; I just cannot believe it has finally arrived. I'm so giddy! I am having a hard time containing my joy. Since this is your last day, this is the perfect time for me to tell you what I really think of you. No holds barred! Trinity, you are a lost, small-minded little girl who tries to live out caviar delusions on a food stamp budget. The other day, I was the one who took the complaint from one of our favorite customers. Mrs. Lobes was appalled you showed such unprofessional behavior when serving her and her friend. You appeared all too happy that her friend's debit card was denied, and Trinity, I just cannot tell you how important it is to have some decorum when dealing with our high-end customers. However, it's neither here nor there. Today, you will end your employment here. So, I will leave you alone to get your stuff together. Oh, and bring *your* God with you. I'm sure you will need him."

"Hold up, since you say this is my last day, I have some things to get off my chest too. First off, I never liked your nasty yuck mouth behind. You are, by far, the laziest human being on the face of this planet. I despise who you are, and I was the one that left that bar of soap in your locker last year. You stink so badly; you're like a dirty onion, you make my eyes water. When was the last time you bathed? When Noah built the Ark? Are you sitting here trying to fire me? How dare you think you would have such an honor! I am tired of doing all the work around here while you run off to the bathroom to hide in a stall to sleep away your entire shift. You said I am a lost little girl? Well, I am more woman than you will ever be. I may have a taste for the finer things in life, and I will date whatever married man I need to attain those things. I deserve everything I receive. At least I can get a man! Yes, I will meet you upstairs in five minutes, but understand that I am taking you with me. I have videos of your lazy behind sleeping in the employee bathroom. See you upstairs!"

For the first time, she was silent. I guess she thought that she had me good and fired. I know it shocked her to learn I had her strung up in the same net she thought she had me trapped in. Check! Mate!

I cleared out my locker and even took a few lunches from the refrigerator that belonged to other employees before I went upstairs. Yeah, so what? I'm hungry. Do you have a problem with that? Yeah, I didn't think so!

I walked up the stairs one step at a time. I felt like I was walking my last mile. When I reached the office, the secretary had an ominous look upon her face. Was it really that bad? She didn't even maintain eye contact for long. I guess it is! I had never had a good feeling when I came up to the office. Even when I came to pick up my department award, I was nervous. But, as I thought about the last time Greysan deposited money in my account, I realized I was about to be fired, and I am officially broke! I had no money to pay the mortgage and no money to put gas in my car. I thought about calling him to talk to him, but I didn't feel like kissing his ashy booty. Not when he had Lisa's hands on it now. Oh no, I am not going to swallow my pride, or anything else, and beg him for anything.

I sat out in the lobby for what seemed like an eternity. When I was finally called into the office, all three of the store managers were sitting around the conference table. There was a makeshift television security set up at the head of the table. Oh, my gosh! This *was* more serious than I thought. I figured they would hand me the proverbial pink slip, and I would go do my walk of shame out of the store. This was considerably different from what I thought.

"Good Morning, Trinity. How are you today?" Mr. Paulson asked.

I don't understand why folks always ask that stupid question when they really don't give a darn about the answer. I'm not sure just what they have on me, so I answer politely.

"I'm fine. Thanks for asking. May I ask why I am here today?"

He leafed through his papers and slid one over to me. I read it and realized not only was I getting fired from Greysan's wife's bogus complaint, but I was also being accused of using her credit card information, on several occasions, after the sale at my register. They presented to me sales receipts which were signed with my name, but looking closely at the signature, I knew darn well it was not my signature. All the people present in the room should know that it wasn't my signature since I signed many daily department time management

162 | P a g e

sheets. But the haters were all delighted to finally get my behind out of here.

He showed me all the evidence they believed proved I was the one stealing Greysan's wife's identity. I carefully looked at all three of the receipts and realized they were all for purchases made while I was at work. It appeared I stole their credit card information, including the three-digit security code on the back. I had never been an avid online shopper, but someone went hard with it because they made purchases to the grand total of one thousand dollars. I was about to denounce these as being my purchases because I was at work during the times someone used the credit card on various internet sites when two State Police Officers walked into the room. When they sat down on each side of me, Mr. Paulson played a videotape. We all watched in silence. They watched me as I watched myself. They were convinced they had me nailed while I knew this was a big mistake, and it amazed me I was even here.

The video showed the transaction between me and the Bomquisha chick. It even showed me lurking around watching Vonnie and Quintaria as if I were plotting something. I was eavesdropping, but on the videotape, my behavior looked very suspicious. They slowed down the video during the transaction between me and Quintaria. It showed I began the transaction just as they trained me. However, when I asked her for her personal information, I gave her a discount for it. That was against company policy to give customers any unapproved discounts. When she handed me the card for the purchase, I slyly wrote down the card number and three-digit code from the back when she turned to talk to her sister. After she left, I pretended to get a piece of gum out of my pocketbook so I wouldn't draw attention to me putting the credit card information in it. If Greysan ever got back with me, I planned on blackmailing him into giving me much more money by telling him I have his home address and phone. But as I sit here, in this hot mess, all that doesn't make much sense, at all!

Looking at the video, from this angle, it appeared as if I was stealing her credit card information, but I wasn't. But, I couldn't exactly tell Mr. Paulson and the State Police I was having an affair with a man I realized was Quintaria's husband and how I hashed the plot to blow up their spot. So, I relented. From the video, yes, it appeared as if I had broken the law and company policy. Defeated, I allowed the State Police to arrest me without trying to persuade them otherwise. I was caught up in my web of greed and lust with yet another married man. In my right mind, I knew that was crime enough. I knew right from wrong; I did whatever I wanted, and I would now have to suffer from making bad decisions.

As I was read my Miranda rights, I started to cry. I've never been arrested before, and it seems ironic that this would be my first trip downtown. I loved my job, Greysan, and from the money he gave me, I birthed a new love for shopping. Yet, right this moment, as the cold steel of the handcuffs snapped around my wrists and sent a chill through my bones, it all seemed irrelevant. None of it mattered because the managers at my job, whom I thought had my back, turned me into the law like a common criminal. Greysan had used me up like a well-paid jump-off, and the things I whored myself for were soon to be lost to me. It seems, my freedom. No, it all didn't seem worth all this drama. I always joked I was too cute to go to jail. As they tightened the handcuffs, so tight I could feel the steel cutting into my wrists and the blood rushing into the area, I didn't feel so cute. All I felt was stupid. The pain of my arms locked behind my back sent shocks down my back. Spasms rose and went down my arms.

One officer, Officer Micah, grabbed onto my forearm and escorted me out of the boardroom. My eyes moved throughout the room, and they rested uneasily upon Mr. Paulson, who kept his head down in shame. Yuck mouth was smiling and blinding me with her yellow teeth. The other staff were looking at me with sadness in their eyes. All I could do was lower my eyes too. I was embarrassed; not only was I fired and had let down my co-workers, but now I was being escorted through the store and the mall.

As they escorted me through the store, all the customers in the store stopped and watched me being paraded past them. A few even recognized me and tried to walk towards me to ask if I was okay. Officer Micah's partner stopped and put his hand on his gun to signal them not to approach a step closer. They quickly obeyed his nonverbal threat. I ventured a smile to let them know I would be okay. I heard snickers and whispers about the reason for my arrest. As they aimed cellphone cameras my way, to memorize the worse day of my life, I also knew in less than ten minutes of the meeting's end that yuck mouth would be spreading the sordid details of my liaisons like wildfire. Some of my former co-workers would understand my plight, yet I was sure some would pass harsh judgment on me and be happy I was gone.

When the police walked me out of the mall, I broke down crying. I had never been so humiliated in my life. Where was my soul leading me? I am saddened to pronounce, straight to hell!

I Miss the Bliss

So clean house! Make a clean sweep of malice and pretense, envy, and hurtful talk. You've had a taste of God. Now, like infants at the breast, drink deep of God's pure kindness. Then, you'll grow up mature and whole in God.

I Peter 2:1

***

Jnana

"Trinni did it again!" I yelled into the vast universe.

I was worried about her before she came over, but now I'm worried about myself. Shandon hasn't talked to me in days. He talks at me for the sake of our children, but that's all the interaction I get. He makes sure the kids are asleep before he sneaks down the stairs to sleep on the couch. He is really fed up with me over the whole Trinni episode. I have so much pent up sexual energy! I haven't gotten near enough to Shandon to even smell him in days. I dislike this drought crap. I need some physical nourishment. My body is in full withdraw. I shake and drool just thinking about how gorgeous my husband is and how sexy he looked tied to the headboard, chocolate sauce dripping down his…whew! I have got to shake these thoughts out of my head.

After Trinity left, Shandon and I made love, and I thought we were back on the same page. Since the children were gone, we made love loud and wild like we used to. It was amazing! The next day, Trinity called at three in the morning, and I got out of bed to talk to her. She was having a crisis and needed someone to talk to. When I got back in bed, my husband was gone. He was sleeping on the couch! Since then, his routine has been to sleep on the couch but get up early enough, so our children don't find out. I thought I would get back to the hot steamy loving. But, just that quick, things went from the pot to the frying pan. I've got to stop this madness, or I will be in my private drawer taking out my battery-operated friend, Tarelle. You know what? To heck with it all! I will dust off Tarelle and get some tuning up done. I can hold out just if Shandon can. Sheesh, who am I fooling? Feeling Tarelle is alright, but he doesn't compare to Shandon's tender loving touch. Oh, I can get so heady from our intimate moments together. Just his loving arms around me is enough for me to feel fulfilled as his wife. But, he won't let me near him. I hope my marriage isn't falling apart. Sadness overwhelming me, I pushed that thought away. For now, I will lock myself in the bathroom, take me a nice warm bath and knock the cobwebs off with Tarelle.

I have some serious making up to do with my husband. But I will not do it with so much pressure built up. If I did, I would agree to anything because I would look at his lips and imagine what they would feel like on me. Before I know it, I would babble about anything just to get him to touch me and tease me. I will get my man back in my bed before the week is over. But I will not be focused if I am in this weakened state. This hot

Momma is cooling down to be dangerously low temperatures. I must do something, quick! That is after my private session with Tarelle. It has been too long anyway—time to get reacquainted with my battery-operated lover.

****

It has been an easier couple of days since I have been meeting with Tarelle several times a day. Sheesh, I even took him to work with me a couple of times. Don't tell anyone, but I used him on the way to work a few days ago. Trust me, morning traffic was a pleasurable experience. Tarelle and my slow jams smoothed out all the kinks. Yup, I had a fulfilled smile on my face all the way to work. Then it happened: the crash! Things started out well with my daily visits with Tarelle, but for the rest of the week, I struggled. No matter how enamored I was getting with Tarelle, he is not my husband. All the sexual aids in the world don't take the place of a warm, loving body. I need to kick my plan into high gear. Being complacent is making me a dull girl. *I ain't neva that!*

Thank God it's Friday. After they got home from school, I packed Lili and Ashton up and dropped them off with my Mom and Dad at my childhood home. They are my best example of black love. From watching them, while growing up, I learned that true love endures all. It supports, keeps it real, and through it all, the eyes are always on God, first. I watched the way my parents interacted and realized that was what I wanted out of life. Even as I dreamed of having a career, I also dreamed of a chocolaty black man that would love me through it all, just like my Dad did with my Mom.

I drove with more focus than in a long time as I dropped my babies off with my parents. I tried to run in and out of the house, but my Mom stopped me. She hugged her grandkids, and I knew this weekend would be one of spoiling to the max. As I walked to the door, determined to get all I had in mind accomplished before Shandon got home, she called me back.

"Jnana, can we talk?"

Le Sigh, "Ahh, Mom, I really have to get back on the road. It took me twice as long to get here with the traffic jam."

Not taking no for an answer, as usual, she cut me a piece of Edwards Key Lime Pie and made me a cup of coffee.

"Come join me for a snack. I know you can't resist the sweets." Dang, blackmail! Through the tangy tartness of the key lime pie, I smelled a setup.

I sat down and dug into the creamy, succulent slice of pie. The coffee was even fresh. Yes, this is a setup, all right. Daddy hasn't come running into the kitchen to hug me and tell me how beautiful I am yet. That's unusual. Hmmm, what's up?

"Jnana, I love how caring you are. I even love the fire you have in your spirit. You sure are a firecracker. You get that from your Dad's side of the family. But I have been hearing some things from the children about you and Shandon arguing a lot more than usual."

"Ma, I don't really want to get into this. I only stayed for something sweet."

"Well, as I was saying…"

She doesn't even hear me refusing to discuss my marriage. Who does that remind me of? She is just so bullheaded! I get up, push my chair back under the table, and was careful to speak respectfully, "Ma, I have got to go. I do not want to discuss my marriage. I don't know what Lili and Ashton have been telling you, but it's nothing I can't handle." I kissed her on the cheek and walked towards the door.

"Jnana, now Baby, I love you. If you ever need to talk, I am here. Just promise me that."

I turned back around and held back my tears, "Ma, I have got to go. I love you."

I walked as fast as I could to the car. Then, the tears started falling. I sure wish I could talk to my Ma about this, but she would find a way to give me old-fashioned advice that wouldn't apply during these days. She and my Dad have been together most of their lives she doesn't even have to work at making her marriage work anymore. She wouldn't understand. I dried my tears and headed out to run my errands. I put the key in the ignition, back out the driveway, and quickly got back on the road. I need to have lots of time to get my hair done, shop for some sexy apparel with some latex, maybe even a whip, prepare a delicious meal, and decorate the house with candles…all before Shandon walked in the door. Yea, good luck with that.

When I arrived back home, I put on some sensual Sade and turned out all the lights after I lit the candles. Then, I soaked my feet. Shandon has a serious foot fetish, and I love that about him.

Sometimes he will even polish my toenails for me. Now, that's what being treated like a Queen feels like.

I took a nice long bath then I spritzed my entire body, especially my feet, with his favorite body oil, Jasmine. Shandon was due in at seven since he has a busy schedule on Fridays. At about six forty, I started getting nervous. What would I do if he plays me out after I did all of this for him? My first instinct would be to yell and throw things, but I quickly reminded myself that it is all about my man. I imagined that he would walk in the door and see the love in my eyes. With such a sight, my Baby would never play me out. My man is a good man. He is someone with a forgiving heart.

I had the massage oils warming with his favorite calming scent of Ylang Ylang. Tonight, I will massage him from head to toe. I love pleasuring my man in every way. After all the times he has had my back, I want him to know I still have his. I have been against dealing with his feet, but tonight, I will even attempt to suck on them. Maybe.

Yes, we had issues in our marriage before Trinity. But, more and more, my friendship with her had become an issue in my marriage, and that made me very uncomfortable. I took my vows before God and my husband. Those two are the most important beings in my life. It's time I set things straight and made it clear to my husband. Convincing him will take some work, I concede. However, he is my man, and I'm ready to do anything to please him. Anything.

As soon as Shandon came through the door,

he stopped. I got nervous butterflies in my stomach. Even after working all day, my man is *fine*. From his feet in his boots all up to his hat on his head, he is my ideal man. Just the way he speaks my name sends me to heaven. There is something unspoken between us. It's like there are spiritual vibrations flowing between us in the sound of African drums. As my husband stands in the doorway to our home, a home in which I loved building my family with this man, the vibration of African drums is sounding in the key to love. Still trying to maintain his apparent vow not to forgive me so easily, Shandon visibly poked out his chest and spoke arrogantly, "Jnana, what is all of this? Why is it so dark in here, and where are my kids? Kids? Daddy's home! What is going on around here?"

I smiled, but not so confidently. I knew I had his attention when he looked me up and down in my see-through black camisole and thong set. He licked his lips and smiled. I purposely walked away from him before sitting in my recliner. His eyes never left me.

I answered, "Shandon, I took the kids to Mama and Papa's house. I think we need some time alone. Don't you agree?"

"Uh, well…"

I put my finger in my mouth and sucked on it. His mouth fell open. He loves it when I do this. I had him, lock stock and barrel. Then, I crossed my legs back and forth.

"So? Do you agree or not, Shandon? You didn't finish your sentence, Baby."

"Uh, well Jnana, I really am hungry, what is that

173 | P a g e

that I smell? Uh, it really, umm…"

I picked up a strawberry from the glass with whipped cream in it. Then I dipped the strawberry into the chocolate. He finally put down his lunch box and locked the door when I put it into my mouth and took a slow bite. We sat silently in the dimly lit room as I finished the strawberry. His eyes were stuck on me; a soft smile graced his handsome face. He was hungry for me. Still, we both sat and looked deeply into each other's eyes. The love was ablaze. I could hear the drums playing and the spiritual vibration rising. And…the drums played.

"Jnana, Baby, what's this all about?"

"Shandon, Baby, you know what this is all about. I miss you, my bliss. I miss the way we used to be, the way we were a week ago. Tell me you forgive me, please? I am so sorry for putting you and our marriage aside for Trinity. I didn't mean to hurt you."

"Jnana, Baby, I love you. I forgave you days ago. I have been waiting for you to give me a sincere apology. I love you too much to lose this marriage because you haven't set boundaries with your friendship with Trinity. I have missed you too, my love."

"Aww, Baby, it's good to have you back. Now, would you like to have some dinner? I have been planning this all day."

"Sure, woman, what did you prepare?"

"Well, my handsome man, I prepared your favorites: Meatloaf, buttered potatoes, steamed broccoli, and, for dessert, your favorite, strawberry trifle."

"Wow, my love, the menu sounds amazing. Lady, when you want to, you treat me so good. How did I get to be so blessed? Huh?"

"Well, you are hardworking, respectful, sexy, educated, industrious, caring, and a wonderfully sensual black man. That's how."

"Are you sure I am all of that to you, Baby? I mean, I have been feeling like you take me for granted."

"Baby, I am so sorry. I never meant to take you for granted. I value you! You are Shandon. You are all that, and so much more. Now, come over here and let me feed you your dessert. As you can see, I have prepared some strawberries, cream, and chocolate for you."

"My love, I can't wait to put the sweet fruit in my mouth."

I treated Shandon like a King all night long, and he treated me like a Queen well into the morning hours. We fulfilled each other like no one's business. That's why I will not tell you all the details. Well into the early morning hours, we both fell out in exhaustion. Our bodies were still wrapped into each other's when the phone rang. It jarred us awake, both of us looking at the clock at the same time. What the heck? It is after four in the morning. It must be an emergency for someone to call this early in the morning!

Neither one of us reached for the phone. We waited to hear who was calling and what the emergency could be. Then Trinity's voice came blaring through the answering machine, I was reaching for the phone when Shandon got up to unplug the phone and answering machine. He threw them both in the bathroom and shut the door. Then, he slid under the covers and licked me from head to toe before becoming one with me. He made sensual love to me so good I cried. We romanced each other and made promises through passionate kisses. We finished with a fulfilled smile upon our faces. He was still lying on top of me when I realized he was already snoring. I got comfortable under my husband and fell asleep. Trinity will not ruin my marriage a second longer. Whatever she was calling about was probably of her own making. I will let her deal with it…for now.

~13~
Uppity Down to Hell

A person who gets rich dishonestly is like a
partridge that hatches eggs it did not lay. During his
lifetime, he will lose his wealth. In the end, he will
be a godless fool."
Jeremiah 17:11
***

Trinity

They escorted me through the mall, and when I
stepped outside of the door, I was immediately
greeted by television crews and cameras. Stragglers
with cell phone cameras ready were also waiting
around to see what all the media coverage was
about. It seemed as if my life was now newsworthy.
I was at my lowest point, and to add insult to injury,
this episode was being memorialized for all to see. I
tried to keep my head down like I had seen
criminals do on the news because I just knew my
foundation was smeared, and because of my crying,
my mascara was a runny black mess. I was partly
embarrassed about my physical appearance, but I
was more worried about what my family would
think when they saw me on the news. When I
looked up for a second and noticed the news van of
my grandparents' favorite news station, I cringed. I
could imagine their disappointment as they sat side-
by-side in their recliners, sipping on coffee and
eating dinner on their tray. I am sure their eyes
would bug out at the sight of me on the nightly
news. Grand Momma and Pop-Pop would surely be

disappointed in me when they heard the nasty truth; I had had an affair with a married man, and I was also foolish enough to believe ill-gotten money came without karma. I know my Mom is probably rolling over in her grave. Like her, money, and the sexual things I did to earn it, was ruining my life.

I was put into the car with Officer Micah's hand on the top of my head when someone called my name from behind. Turning to see who it was, I hit my head on the door panel. Officer Micah instinctively pushed me hard into the car, so I could be on my way to jail. No doubt, he thought that I had no feelings of guilt or conscience.

The cold-molded plastic of the back seat was uncomfortable, and I squirmed around, trying to get comfortable. My arms were still cuffed, and I was seat belted in. I tried moving from one side to the other, but I was quickly ordered to stay still. I felt like a caged animal. I cried again. This is too much! I cannot believe that I am inside of a cop car on the way to jail. I finally tried to get my mind off this mess by enjoying the scenery. The weather had finally changed to spring, and the trees were showing green leaves and bulbs sprouted with flowers. When I looked up and met the unfriendly eyes of Officer Micah, I tried to look away, but I couldn't. He kept looking into the mirror at me. He squinted his eyes in hate, and his icy gaze froze me. Still, his Milky Way brown skin, six feet one-inch tall, deep-set black eyes, close-cropped hair, model cheekbones, thin mustache, and thick brown lips, were very attractive to me. However, to him, I was just a disgusting criminal trying to steal a rich woman's identity. I was just a roach to be crunched under his spit-polished policeman shoe. I had to fight my unnatural attraction to this man that was arresting me. His harsh gaze but sexy looks will not confuse nor intimidate me. How dare his fine behind judge me!

Officer Micah's partner, Officer Lorenzo, turned to me and spoke in an unusually soft tone.

"So, you were trying to take someone's identity, huh? You look too classy to be doing something so low class and stupid. Do you want to tell me and my partner what the real issue is? I mean, as incriminating as the videotape and receipts were, there still seems to be some pieces missing from this puzzle. Do you feel like sharing what they are? You know that if you help me, I can help you." His hand reached out to touch my leg.

I didn't want to talk to either of them, let alone allow this cop to touch me inappropriately, so I ignored him and moved my leg away from his touch.

Trigger fast, his tone changed! He pulled his hand back and smirked, "Oh, so you think you are too good to talk to me? You are on the way to jail for identity theft, and you think you are too arrogant to talk to us." Then, he laughed eerily. "Just wait and see how that attitude of yours serves you in women's prison. Oh yeah, those girls will love a thick, darn near white skinned sistah like you. You do know some incarcerated women would love a sexy milkshake like you, right?"

I looked at him and shook my head. Yet another man that only sees me as a sex object!

Predictable. Why can't I ever be a whole woman with a heart and soul, not just a body? I guess that will be the question of my life. Hopefully, one day I will learn the answer.

His lecherous eyes ran from my thighs on up to my breasts and stopped. He licked his lips perversely and smiled. I stared him deep in his eyes. Then, I saw it, right behind his eyes. He was a prime mark. I knew under different circumstances I could easily have his paycheck. Five feet ten inches tall, willowy build, blonde hair with a military cut, green/blue eyes, and a sinister smile, I knew that he had never had a woman like me. He was the type of man that secretly craved a woman like me. To him, I was a voluptuous woman, ready and eager to please his every need. He probably believed the long-standing stereotype that all black women were wild and adventurous women in bed. I looked at his hand upon the top of his seat. He is married. He would be ready to jump my bones if given a chance. Even with me handcuffed, I could feel the heat coming from his body. He wanted me bad. Officer Micah looked over at him, then nudged him. He gave one last wink before he turned back around. This time when I looked into the rearview mirror, Officer Micah had a look of contempt. He didn't seem to appreciate his partner's overt and unprofessional attraction to me. Hey, I don't like my attraction to his brown-skinned sexiness, so we are even.

We finally pulled into the police station parking lot. Officer Micah got out first to get me out of the car. I could smell his cologne, and I wanted to taste him so bad. When he pulled me out of the car, I was too busy being distracted by his intoxicating scent that I bumped my head. I don't know what his problem was, but I was not feeling all the hostility. He halfway dragged me up towards the police station while his partner walked behind me. I could feel his hot eyes upon my body. When we got up to the door, we stopped so that Officer Micah could be buzzed in. Officer Lorenzo took advantage of his partner's distraction and stopped very close to me. His hands ran up and down my body as he breathed his hot breath heavily upon my neck. I was so uncomfortable, yet to my dismay, defenseless. Officer Micah finally got the door opened and pushed me in front of him, so he was between me and his partner. I tried to make eye contact to say thank you, but he wasn't having that. So, I just smiled. They walked me into a room of police officers sitting at their desks, and others were milling around the station. They slammed me down into a chair next to a vacant desk. I asked the officers for a cold cup of water or some coffee, and both officers chuckled at me before walking away.

"Don't move!" Officer Micah barked at me.

I did as I was told and stayed still. I looked at the pictures on the desk and realized it belonged to Officer Micah. He had several pictures of him and two children. The boy looked like he was around six, and the girl appeared to be around ten. They were cutie pies. Then I spied a picture in a white frame that appeared to be from a wedding. He was so handsome in his tuxedo. His smile was magnetic. The side where the wife and her bride's maids were supposed to be was cut off. I guess his marriage didn't work out. How sad. Maybe his wife got tired of trying to figure out how someone so handsome can ruin his looks by scowling all the time. Maybe.

Officer Micah came back to his desk after a short time and caught me looking at his pictures. I was deep in thought about how wonderful it would be for me to be on the other side of that picture with him. I bet he is a caring and tender lover. Hardcore men always are. Lovemaking is the one time they let down their guards. That's if a woman had enough patience to work through the brick wall around their heart. I wish that I weren't his prisoner because I am just the woman built for bringing the softness out of Officer Micah. I would love to be his woman. I cannot explain it, but there is something about his eyes. Behind the contempt, there is such a beautiful softness. His eyes speak to me spiritually. That's a feeling I've never experienced before. It had me curious yet put off. He cleared his throat, hoping to pull my eyes away from his pictures. Then he did it again.

"Oh, I'm sorry. I was bored, and you have such lovely pictures. I got distracted."

"No problem. Now, let's get going so we can begin processing."

I was caught up in his deep voice. He sounded like Barry White. He took me by the arm to a small room with two women officers in it. One of them took my arm and moved me over to her. Then, Officer Micah left. He didn't even bother to say goodbye. How rude!

The woman, Officer Shelby, took the cuffs off me.

Not even to be ignorant, but sheesh, I felt like an emancipated slave.

"Come over here and stretch your fingers out like this. I want you to pretend as if you are trying to separate each finger from the other. Now, I will take your fingerprints, and when we are done, I will take your mug shot. Your fingers are too stiff. I need you to let your fingers relax a little. Let me do the work. I will guide them as I roll each finger to make sure I get a good print of all your fingers. Do you understand?"

I sighed, "Yes."

I cooperated throughout the fingerprinting process. Then, the officer gave me a wet napkin to wipe the ink off my fingers. As much as I rubbed and rubbed, I still couldn't get the ink completely off my fingers. It was as if I was already branded a criminal. The ink stains, the evidence of a crime committed. It appeared to me as if I were guilty until proven innocent. Then, they took me into the mug shot room.

"Do I get to go clean myself up and straighten out my hair and makeup before you take the mug shot?" I asked so seriously.

She and the other officer looked at each other and had a good hearty laugh.

"Uh…Ma'am…No, you won't. This is not a professional photo studio; it is a police station." One of them answered snidely.

As I looked around the stark room, I noticed it was not a professional photo studio. It was as comforting and personal as a morgue. As the officer set up the camera, he ordered me to stand with my back to a white panel on the wall with height markers. First, they photographed me facing the camera, then they took two side shots, one on the right and the other on the left. They put my handcuffs back on me and took me back to the holding cell.

As soon as I heard the clank of the metal meeting metal of the big cell gate, I knew I was in throngs of hell. The nasty smell of the dirty cell made me sick to my stomach. My stomach churned, and my head pulsed in pain. I am not strong enough to handle this reality. However, the gray walls and unsanitary gloom had to be my temporary home away from home. I looked around and spied five women. Two of them looked like prostitutes. They were sleazily dressed in four-inch heels, black, too short miniskirts, white fishnet stockings, and too much makeup. It is a surprise that any man was desperate enough to pay a dollar for them. And this is what Greysan said that I act like. Hmm. One woman looked like a housewife. In fact, she still had on her matronly smock and old fashion clothes and shoes. The other two appeared to be hood rats. One woman was thugged out in black jeans, purple flannel shirt buttoned all the way up, expensive sneakers, and her dyed bright purple hair was pulled back into a ponytail. The other looked like she shouldn't even be in this cell. She was dressed in a high-priced black suit with brown Stacy Adams dress shoes, braided back, jet black hair which hung all the way to the middle of her back. I was in a cell with five women, so diverse, yet still, women caught up in the drama of illegal activity.

Over the course of the night, the housewife went before the judge and got bailed out. She was in here for assaulting her husband after she caught him cheating on her. He was the one that bailed her out in hopes of reconciling with her, not very smart. The two hookers were bailed out by their pimp after going before the judge. I guess he was getting them out early enough to make his money back while they lay on their backs and scuffed up their knees.

By early morning, I was left in the cell with the two hoodrats. I tried to get comfortable in one corner of the cell. I was so exhausted that I nodded off, hoping to get in a long nap. I didn't care that I rested my head against the dirty wall. I just let my heavy eyelids fall. It felt so good. At least in my dreams, I could be anywhere else besides here.

When I woke up, the hood rats were sitting on the other side of the cell, kissing each other. I was astounded. I had heard that this sort of thing happens in jail, but I never wanted to witness it. When they noticed me watching, they walked over to me, and each of them sat on one side of me. They kept scooting over until they had me boxed in. I tried to get up, but the one dressed like a man pulled me back down by my hair. I was so scared that I screamed. The officer came running to the cell to see what was happening. I ran towards her and told her what was going down. She looked behind me, and the two hood rats had moved to different sides of the cell. For the rest of the night, I cemented my body to the jail door. I stayed there so that I was within earshot of the officer on duty. The two women continually tried to intimidate me with their eyes, so I turned my eyes away. They let in a new prisoner, and they immediately started bothering her. Better her than me.

They finally called me before the judge for a video arraignment. I was so nervous; I felt like I would puke right there. I held my right hand in the air to proclaim I would tell the truth and nothing but the truth, so help me, God. The judge read from his court papers before he addressed me.

"Trinity Boussiant, how do you plead?"

"Not guilty."

The Judge ruled they should give me fifty thousand dollars unsecured bail. I overheard the other women talking about a bail bondsman would only require ten percent of that down for me to be released. As much as I hated to, I called the one person who had that kind of money. I called Jnana, repeatedly! It was four a.m., but I just knew that when I called her, she would move heaven and earth to come bail me out. I was wrong. She didn't answer the phone.

Because my bail wasn't posted by the next morning, they took me to the women's prison to await my hearing on all the charges since the judge at my arraignment found there was sufficient evidence to support the charges brought against me. After being transported to the women's prison in a van with the other women that didn't post bail, they took me into a room and ordered to undress. I took off all my clothes, leaving on my bra and panties. The correction officer came in and saw that I had my underwear on and ordered me to undress totally. As I stood in my birthday suit, I was chilled to the bone. I stood in a line of naked women. All of us all different shapes, sizes, and complexions. First, she ordered us to open our mouths wide. Then she ordered us to raise our hands above our heads. Embarrassingly, we were ordered to lift our breasts and open our legs. Over the speaker, she ordered us to turn our backs to her and bend over. Then spread our butt cheeks. I have never felt so humiliated. When we were done, we were lined up and were given our prison wear. My outfit was too big and wrinkled. I can't wear this mess! I asked for a different outfit, preferably one that was pressed, and I was yelled at. The other women looked at me and shook their heads. I was instantly branded as goody two shoes and ostracized.

They took me to my cell. Oh, my gosh! It was as small as my bathroom at my condo. Minus the jacuzzi. I instantly felt claustrophobic. I am at a loss as to how to deal with this low point in my life, but I do the one thing that Grand Momma always said got her through things: I got down on my knees and prayed. I figured if I could use God at any time, this was it. I didn't feel any instant relief, but I remember Grand Momma telling me that God doesn't work in my time. He works in His. I'm not usually the most patient person, but right now, I don't have any choice. I let go and let God.

I met my cellmate. She was a pretty woman, about six feet tall with a nice smile. She looked just like me, a random person that just got caught up in some illegal activity. I was instantly happy we could be friends. She wasn't anything like the stereotypes I had heard about women in prison. She offered me any bunk that I wanted. I picked the one that wasn't taken. I was not trying to make trouble and make things harder than they already were being locked up. The first day went well. I and my cellmate bonded and played homemade cards. I enjoyed myself for the first time in my ordeal. The second day, we were on lockdown for twenty-three hours out of the day. It went as well as the first. My cellmate, Peggy, made me some prison oodles of noodles with hot dogs and listened to me talk for hours. She hung on every word like she wanted to be my friend. She even got me a phone call. I called Jnana three times, back-to-back. She still didn't pick up.

On the third day, with trepidation, I went into the general population. I had been in the cell with Peggy for two days. Now, it was time for me to really throw myself into the prison culture, as temporary as I planned this stay to be. As they walked me around the pod, I saw a few of the women who were in processing with me. They rolled their eyes and pointed me out to their friends. I tried to sit with them at lunch, but I quickly learned that I was in the wrong seat. Before I knew it, a mocha latte' skinned woman with her mousy brown hair in a ponytail pulled me out of the seat by my hair and started punching me in my face. I tried to fight back, but her friends kicked and punched at me too. It seemed like forever before anyone came to my rescue. The correction officers were milling around, taking their sweet time getting to me. When I was finally pulled up from the ground, it was Peggy who saved me. She walked me back to the cell but stopped before we went up the stairs. I could have sworn she winked at one of my batterers. She helped clean the blood off me with a washcloth and watched over me for the rest of the night. I fell asleep in pain, but I felt safe with her. The next morning, I woke up to find her watching me sleep. She was rubbing my hair. I didn't know how to feel about the severe invasion of my personal space, so I closed my eyes and rolled over, facing the wall. I pretended to go back to sleep. She kissed me on the top of my head and got up off the floor.

When I woke up, she was gone, and I was all alone. I went to a Corrections Officer to ask for phone privileges. I had to get out of here. I called Jnana several times at the house, and I finally got a hold of her at the bookstore. She said she would bail me out today. I thanked God for answering my prayers. I stayed in my cell most of the day. It was midafternoon when the three women from the cafeteria came into my cell while Peggy was gone. At first, they tried to make small talk. I was not having it. Suddenly, two of them tried to hold me down and pull down my pants. Thank God they didn't make much progress! I fought like crazy when one tried to rip off my shirt while the other tried to hold me still. This was not going down like this! I was flailing around on the floor when Peggy came to my rescue by pulling them off me. She stood with power and boldness, and they looked at her in fear. Without a word, they left my cell. What the heck? Why did she let them go so easily? They tried to take my prison virginity. I thought that she and I had become friends so she could at least beat them up before letting them just run past her. I fixed my clothes and adjusted my bra. As I smoothed my hair down, I looked up to find Peggy staring me down. For the first time, I saw lust in her eyes. She licked her lips and moved towards me. I quickly pretended to be fixing my clothes and my hair again. Talk about awkward! Peggy sat down on the bottom bunk and patted the bed beside her. I was afraid of her for the first time since I arrived. It didn't appear as if being my friend is good enough for her.

"Look, Trinity, I protected you from those girls twice. Do you remember when I pulled you up off the floor when they were jumping you in the cafeteria? Huh?" She paused for me to answer.

"Yes, but..."

She held up her hand to pause my response. "Hold up."

I saw the fire in her eyes, and I obediently stopped talking.

"As I was saying before you interrupted, I pulled them off you in the cafeteria, and now they are trying to rape you in my cell. Do you know how this makes me look? I have been in here for ten years, and no one has ever disrespected my cell. You must have invited them in here for this. Am I right, Trinity?"

I shook my head. I didn't invite those crazy rapists in here.

"No, they just came up in here. I just woke up a little while ago. I don't find girls attractive. Trust me, I'm straight...as an arrow. I don't change my sexual orientation, even in jail."

She licked her lips and moved closer to me. She rubbed my hand and told me to listen closely. I did as I was told.

"Look around here. I have a reputation to uphold. Every cellmate that has lived up in here has become my woman. Don't feel bad. I will treat you good. I won't let anyone hurt you or rape you. You will only belong to me."

I cried. I didn't want to be anyone's woman, but a man. This has got to be a joke, a sick one at that! She reached out to dry my tears, but I moved away from her.

Her voice became sympathetic, "The same thing happened to me when I got locked up. I was straight too; I even had a boyfriend. When I was sentenced to fifteen years for assault with a deadly weapon, I tried to fight every woman that came on to me. But after three months, it seemed as if I was fighting the entire pod. I got tired of fighting after a while. I got lonely, and I knew I couldn't spend the rest of my sentence alone. I went about looking for someone to belong to. I stopped fighting, and I was quickly claimed as someone's woman. She told me I would belong to just her, but she lied to me. I was passed around to a few other women to buy my cellie drugs. I won't lie to you like she lied to me. You will only belong to me. One reason why I protected you is you are my cellmate. I can't have anyone disrespecting my cell. I also protected you because you are now my woman. Understand?"

"No, I don't understand! Are you kidding me? I thought we were friends. How or why would I be your woman? I am not a lesbian. Not under any circumstances! I won't even be a jailhouse lesbian, no matter how lonely I may get! Besides, I didn't ask you to protect me. You helped me because you were my friend, or so I thought!" I was aggressive, and I knew I had to show her I was a strong woman that wouldn't easily be controlled or manipulated. She was testing me, and I knew this was my time to show her my character. No matter what goes down, I was not going down easily.

"Trinity, you are my woman because I claim you! You can either fight half the pod or you can voluntarily be with me. I can tell you can't fight by the way those girls whooped your behind. So, tonight you will start doing your wifely duties. Do you understand?"

I didn't answer her. I didn't want to upset her, but I wasn't doing any wifely duties; I don't get down like that.

She pulled my ponytail hard and asked again, "Trinity, do you understand?!"

I nodded yes.

"Now, I have some business to tend to. Those three had no business up in my cell messing with my property. This cell is dirty; clean it up for me now! Lights out is soon. Be ready for me. Understand?"

I nodded yes. But, as soon as she walked out of the cell, I cried. I was claimed as someone's wife, against my will, and tonight I must perform for her. I sure hope Jnana bails me out before lights out! I have faith this isn't how things are supposed to go down. The devil is a lie! I got down on my knees and prayed harder than I ever have.

~14~
Cry Freedom

Fear nothing in the things you're about to suffer—
but stay on guard! Fear nothing! The Devil is about
to throw you in jail for a time of testing—ten days.
It won't last forever. "Don't quit, even if it costs
you your life. Stay there believing. I have a Life-
Crown sized and ready for you.
Revelation 2:10
***

Jnana & Trinity

Thank God Jnana bailed me out of jail before lights out! When she picked me up, I was ecstatic. I wanted to hug her so tight and tell her just how close I came to being jailhouse currency. But I can't share my misfortune because she wouldn't understand. I wanted to tell Jnana all I had been through, but I knew she would only judge me. I even wanted to tell her about the gorgeous police officer Micah. I wanted to tell her how easily his eyes had shown me a feeling I had only dreamed of. But she would just shake her head at me like what in the heck would he want with a woman like you. A woman he was arresting no less! I couldn't disagree with her on that point. I mean, I *was* being arrested by him, not meeting for a date. But still…just the thought of that man makes my heart race. If only I had met him under different circumstances. If only.

Jnana leads a simple life, and other than watching Scandal and The First 48 hours, she doesn't know much about the seedy side of life. She sees life through totally different eyes than I do. Her life is so different, and things like my crazy jail ordeal are foreign to her. Before my bogus arrest, it was foreign to me too! Jail is somewhere we never thought about because it wasn't our reality. I never wanted it to be my reality, either!

As I walked out of the prison gate, Jnana took one look at me, how dirty I looked and how nasty and matted my hair was, and she cringed. I was free of makeup, and even the clothes I had on had a dirty tinge to them. I was a wrinkled hot mess. I was embarrassed for her to see me like this, but there was nothing I could do about my appearance. In all the years we've been friends, she has never seen me so broken down. All the way to her house, we were silent. That was fine with me. I didn't want to talk because I still had my jail ordeal on my mind. I still can't believe Peggy wasn't my friend. She was only trying to win my trust so she could claim me as her jail wife. I'm still feeling scarred from the experience. But I need to put it all behind me and try my best to prove my innocence, so I don't find myself back in prison.

After nearly four days in jail, I was so tired I could sleep for days. They demoralized me in jail from the second I stepped foot in there. They called me horrid names and beat me up. The jailhouse outfit was too baggy, and it was not up to my name brand standards. But I had no other choice than to deal with it all. They tried to sexually assault me, but I fought hard to maintain my jail virginity. The guards tried to intimidate me, but I had dealt with an evil man like Greysan, so they were amateurs. For days, I didn't know who would bail me out. I was so desperate I even tried to call Greysan at the office. But once Lisa heard the collect call recording, she hung up. Ultimately, the only friend I had in there was God. He listened and dried my tears when I cried. He answered my prayers and sent Jnana to bail me out. He loves me, unconditionally. Yes, He does. Even at my lowest point, God met me right where I was. I wish I could find the time in my busy day to spend more time with Him. Maybe one day.

When we arrived at Jnana's house, I saw she had picked up my car from the mall as I asked her to do. At least I still have my car. Jnana gave me some clothes I had left there once and a towel with a new bar of soap. She wanted me to soak in the bath to get that jailhouse crud off me before I spent any time in her house. I agreed. I don't want the kids to see me like this anyway. As I soaked in the tub, I tried to scrub my skin off. I needed to erase the last four days as well. An hour later, as I walked out of the bathroom, Jnana motioned for me to get dressed in the guest room. After I put on some luxuriously scented lotion, that I missed, I got dressed. I combed out my freshly washed and conditioned hair and put it up in a ponytail. Jnana told me to come downstairs to the basement. I thought we would watch a movie and catch up, but I was wrong. When I got down to the basement, Jnana handed me a plate of steak and onion with a baked potato and broccoli. She also handed me a glass of chilled white wine. When she saw I was comfortable, she talked to me.

"Trinity, what was this whole jail episode about? I had to pay five thousand dollars to bail you out. Shandon is heated beyond words right now!"

"Huh? What do you mean what was it all about? Do you really think I did this mess on purpose? Well, I didn't! Greysan's wife must have looked through her credit card statements. Apparently, she confronted him about the women's purchases that she didn't make, and he lied. He said someone must have stolen her card and went on a shopping spree, several ones on different days. Maybe she searched her mind and remembered the last time she tried to use her card, which was at my register when it got declined. From that situation, she accused me of using it. Greysan saw it as a perfect opportunity to burn me and get his wife off his back, so he framed me. When she called the store with her concerns, they viewed the videotape of the transaction between her and I. They showed it to me before they arrested me. Honestly, it does make it look as if I was acting suspiciously."

I rambled on. I added in my vast assumptions, reflecting, and trying to figure things out as I talked. I couldn't possibly tell Jnana it was simply one word, karma! I know in my heart it is retribution for all the dirt I have done. This incident is payment for all the dollars I earned on my back and my knees. I know this is a wake-up call. Until I figure out a way to fix things in my spirit, I can't share anything with anyone but God. He will be my nonjudgmental confidant. I love Jnana, but right this moment, I can't even deal with her tone and judgment. I just can't!

"Trinity, what do you mean 'acting suspiciously?' What were you doing during the transaction that caused them to think that her concerns were valid?"

"Well, I uh, I realized who she was, Grey's wife, when I saw his name on the credit card she was trying to use to make her purchases."

"Okay, and? It sounds like you are leaving something out here. Continue."

"I was just trying to get her personal information, so I could frame Greysan into continuing to pay my bills and give me more money. So, I made up a discount so she could give me her name, address, and phone number. After she filled out a survey of her shopping trip experience, I gave her a fifteen percent discount. After she turned to talk to her sister, I wrote her credit card number and three-digit security code off the back of the card."

"Why, Trinity, why would you do that? Didn't you realize that security was probably watching you do that? Huh? Why would you be so foolish?"

"Honestly, I was so tickled to have Greysan's personal data that I was too busy planning how I would enjoy spending his money once I blackmailed him. I didn't even remember the cameras until I was sitting in the boardroom getting fired and about to be arrested."

"Trinity, this all sounds so sick and depraved. What you did is illegal! You know this, yet you still did it. Now, you took her information and did what with it? Writing down her information is not going to get you put in jail. You know that it should get you rightfully fired, but tell me, what happened next."

"Jnana, I did nothing yet. What I would do is to use the phone number to harass him, and then I would blackmail him for money and other stuff."

"I don't understand, so how did they charge you with identity theft then?"

"Here's the tricky part. Lisa, Greysan's secretary and new mistress, has apparently been blowing up that credit card and signing my name to get me nailed if anyone ever found out. So, when Greysan's wife found out about the charges, she asked the credit card company for copies of the receipts, which were signed with my name. Lisa even created a home shopping channel account with my name on it. She put her address on the account so she could receive the packages. Greysan's wife must have put my weird behavior together with the receipts and alerted the department store and the State Police. They turned me over to the Feds since identity theft is a federal crime here."

"So, let me get this straight, this is all about Lisa framing you and Greysan trying to cover his behind once the truth came out. So, your married lover threw you under the bus?"

"Yeah, but there's more. I used that card frequently before too. That's why it was so easy for them to pin everything on me."

"No, Trinity! Please tell me you're lying, oh my gosh, please!"

"Well, Jnana, I can't. I was Grey's mistress before Lisa was. That's the card that he gave me to go shopping with. It's the same one he now lets Lisa shop with. Look, I know I am in a lot of trouble.

That's not even the half of it."

"Oh Lord, Trinni, there's more? Do tell!"

"Well, to start, I am probably homeless. I assume since she found out about the credit card, she also knows about the condo as well. If so, I can't get my things. I'm sure she didn't waste any time having someone change the locks. All the money I spent on those things, and now she'll lock them away from me. I deserve all that stuff. I worked hard for them. How dare she do that to me! I did nothing to her. If she has anger, she might as well take it out on her husband, not me. That's what's wrong with women; their man cheats, and they want to fight the jump-off, how foolish!"

"Trinity, you have got to be kidding me! This entire scenario is full of ignorance. You have got to stop this gold-digging madness. You are ruining your life, as well as the lives of others. Each one of your ex-lovers had a family. Why won't you go out and get your own man? That way, you can begin to live a life of joy. You are stifling your own happiness with this mess. Stop already!"

"I *am* happy, Jnana," I lied. "Every time I shop, it's joyous. Whenever I have sex with a married man, it's joyous. They could cheat with anyone, but they choose me. That's a heady rush for me. Someone else's man wants me. Nothing compares to that feeling of being singularly pursued. Every time I walk out the house and a man finds me attractive, it's joyous. See? I am happy!"

"Trinity, I keep holding my tongue, so I don't hurt your feelings. This stuff you are talking is ridiculous. You have got to hear yourself. If a man wants to wet your behind, that doesn't mean he finds you attractive or that you are better than his wife. He is just okay with stepping out with you because you are easy. You need to stop putting your self-esteem in the hands of some lost man who only wants you temporarily. Now, as I said, I am holding my tongue, so don't keep pushing me!"

"Push you to do what, Jnana? So, now you don't want to hurt my feelings? Oh, that's funny! You do that every time you tell me how I don't have common sense or how I'm not living my life how God created me to. Reality check, Jnana, I am not you. You have a good life with a good man who loves you. Even your kids are perfect. What do I have? Huh? Near to nothing! Yes, I have a thick body that men love to have sex with, but other than that, I have nothing good in my life. I am not you, so stop pushing your high standards off on me. I'm not you!"

"Trinity, okay, since you didn't get the hint when I tried to warn you, here's the truth. I hope that you can handle it."

"Bring it on, Jnana! I've been waiting to see how you really feel about me. Let the truth set you free."

"Alright, Trinity! Now, as far as my perfect marriage to a perfect man, well, the reality is it isn't perfect. Perfection takes a lot of work, and after all the years Shandon and I have been together, we have never attained perfection. Still, he and I are very much in love, and the joy builds every day. Yes, my kids are treasures. However, they are far from perfect. They are teenagers, and that comes with a lot of imperfect behaviors. You believe that my family is perfect because that's all you want to see. I stopped telling you my problems a long time ago. You never listened. It was all about your mess and your men of the moment. I got tired of competing with you to have a conversation. Now, I love you like a sister, but you are a selfish, one-track mind money-hungry hussy. You give good women a bad name. You are a needy woman, but you have the nerve to be picky. I have heard you complain about the men who have approached you in the past. Good, hard-working men that take each breath seriously. But you don't see them for who they are. All you say is, 'Oh, no, that construction worker didn't think that he could approach me.' You get all uppity like you are above them. I have been with you when good looking men in their company uniforms have approached you with serious interest and seen your reaction.

Trinity, you looked at them and got your screw face on. You straight-up dissed them! And to their faces, no less. Most of the women I know will work with a man, especially if he has dreams and aspirations. We will support a man who knows how to work towards making them a reality. Most women I know are hard-working, dedicated women who, though we are strong, we are not pressed to love a good man. We know how to make that money, but we don't ever make our man feel less than if he makes less than we do. But you, oh, you are a different type of woman. You are lazy to a fault and want a man to carry you! You don't know how to be a good woman to him. Oh, hell, naw! All you want to do is put your foot on his back and make him feel like he owes you something. A hard-working man is not what you want. Nope. You would rather settle. Let a woman-hating man, who is wearing an overpriced suit, approach you, and right away, you assume he is rolling in cash. Let him give you a business card, a business card that anyone can cheaply create and buy online, and you open your legs as wide as the Grand Canyon. I guess the potential of money turns you on, huh?"

"Wow, really! Is it that serious? The Grand Canyon Jnana? Are you really saying this to me? Are you? Because those are fighting words, and I really don't want to let this wrath loose on you!"

"Look, Trinity, we can throw down, we really can. You can even try to unleash the wrath, as you call it, on me. But I hoped we could be honest for a change. Our friendship has been superficial for so long, and I hoped we could get things out on the table for once. We have known each other so long, too long, to have this impasse in our friendship and not try to repair it."

"Fine, Jnana. Well, since we are being honest here, I have some honesty for you too. You talk about me being selfish, but how do you think I felt listening to how wonderful your man is, and I can't even find a man who wants anything from me besides my body? Well, it hurts…a lot! Why are you always so lucky in love? What do you have that I don't? I would kill to have a man like Shandon."

"Trinity, are you saying what I think that you're saying? Do you want my husband?!"

"Naw, Jnana, I would never want your man. That's nasty. What I want is a good man like him. You know, a caring black man who doesn't want to buy

202 | P a g e

my time like I'm a prostitute. I want to feel worthy of that. I don't want you or Nana or Poppy to tell me I am. I want to feel it in my core. I know I have flaws, but I don't know how to fix myself. I feel so alone, even in a room full of people. I want what you have. Theoretically, I want your man. If that makes sense."

"Trinity, yeah, it does make sense. I'm glad you cleared it up because when you first said it, we were going to have a huge problem. But see, you don't get it. You won't be me or have a man like Shandon until you stop expecting to use your body to get what you want. A respectable black man, any man, will rarely marry you, let alone take you home to his family if you have slept with him within five days. He will rarely respect you if he feels as if he has just purchased a prostitute and has to leave money for you for services rendered."

"I get that now, Jnana. Okay? But I don't know how to get a man without doing that. I don't know how to entice a man with anything other than my body. I see it like this, why give up my goodies for free. Why not get something from the deal?"

"It is that exact thinking that has you right where you are! You just put all that mess out into the universe. Why would you do something like that? Huh?"

"Jnana, I am being honest with you. I watched my Mom being pimped by my Stepdad for years. She and I had rough times before she met him, but we did okay, and we had each other. Six months after my Mom met my Stepdad, they married. Because my Dad had never been around, my Stepdad took on the father figure role for me when he married my Mom. Soon after their wedding, he introduced my Mom to the grimy side of street life. He told her since she was built like a brick house, she might as well use her body to make some money. He convinced her she shouldn't have to struggle to take care of me if she could make some quick money on the streets to get us out of poverty. She worked the streets hard with him as her security guard while she took care of her johns. She even did some drug runs for people my Stepdad knew. But ultimately, she took care of business by laying on her back. We started to live better, for a while. But she got beat up by her Johns because my Stepdad was too lazy to go out with her at night. She wasn't supposed to go out alone, but since she was the only breadwinner in the house and we needed food on the table, she only did what she grew to know as the normal way to make quick money. Things were good when she came home with money for my Stepdad. But when she got beat up and robbed, he beat her up again. Then, he beat me up because my Mom was a whore who allowed a John to take the goods without paying for them. I developed a strong heart from seeing her being misused. Things went on like that for years. Until he left us when my Mom got addicted to crack. I saw my Mom hurting after he left, and that hurt me bad. She was used and abused for so many years, but she couldn't take it when he left. I don't believe she was sad over him. She was hurt another man had left her like my Dad had. None of the men my Mom got involved with ever measured up to my Dad in her eyes. Still, she settled, over and over. She never forgot my Dad and the love he gave her. She talked about my Dad all the time. My Dad was her lost love, and she tried to find men to measure up to her memory of him. I'm sad to say every man she got was worse than the one before him. When I was sixteen, she overdosed on heroin. I don't think that it was the drugs that killed her. I think it was the pain of heartbreak that did her in. She never got over my Dad leaving. Jnana, my Mom died in my arms one night. She was heartbroken. That night, I didn't shed one tear. All I did was pray to God she has a better life in Heaven than she did on Earth. She could finally stop settling for rotten men that meant her no good.

After the funeral, my Stepdad came back to take custody of me. That first night in his home, he tried to rape me. He said I was a whore, just like my Mom. I fought him off and ran away. I moved in with my Grandparents and lived with them until I finished school. After that, I went to college, where I honed my skills of manipulating men for money. Since then, I promised myself I would never let a man pimp me. I would pimp them before they ever got it in their head to pimp me."

Jnana was upset. She knew none of this about Trinity. How could they have had a friendship that spanned many years, and she never heard this story before? *Maybe I'm not as good of a friend to Trinni as I thought since she never felt like she could trust me with this. I have got to do better by my friend.*

"Trinni, I am so sorry. This is all news to me. Why didn't you tell me this before?"

"Jnana, because it didn't matter. It doesn't matter

what happened between my Mom and Stepdad. It doesn't matter my Dad abandoned me and my Mom. It doesn't matter she never recovered from the heartbreak and how I hated not having a father who loved me enough to stick around. I am in control of my destiny, and all I know how to do is to sex men for money. That's all I ever knew how to do. Nothing that you say or do will change that. So, stop trying... just stop trying!"

****

I ran out of the house and drove away. I don't know where I will go or how I will live, but I must survive. Where is my happily ever after? Fate can't be this cruel to shortchange me. It just can't be! I'm not giving up that easily. If I must sleep with a married man to live, then so be it. Then that's what I will do. But I will not die over one. No way! I am not my Mom. I will get them way before they got a chance to pimp me. Trust!

~15~
Damage Control

"It is not an enemy who taunts me—I could bear that. It is not my foes who so arrogantly insult me—I could have hidden from them. Instead, it is you—my equal, my companion and close friend. What good fellowship we once enjoyed as we walked together to the house of God. Let death stalk my enemies; let the grave swallow them alive, for evil makes its home within them."
Psalm 55:12-15
***

Jnana

I cannot believe our confrontation went down like this. It was like World War III when Trinity told me off then left. Oh, how the tables had turned. Not only had I kept it real with her, she kept it real with me. When she told me a story of her childhood that I never heard before, I was dumbfounded. But it explained so much to me. Trinity watched her Mom pimped out by a man that she loved. No wonder it's like second nature to her. My heart aches for Trinity.

As much as I love her and am worried about her, I have issues of my own. I took almost every dime of our emergency fund out of the bank to bail Trinity out of jail. Shandon is so upset with me. I must fix things before I am without a man and lonely, just like my best friend. It pains me to say I must fix things in my marriage because of Trinity. Again. I am telling myself good luck with that! I just promised Shandon I would never be in this situation again with Trinity. Yet, I gave up bail money for something she had done, not me. I am in serious mental distress. Before I realized it, I was crying, and I am not a crier. Not one bit! I am just so beside myself. How did I get here when my marriage is one so many would dream of having? I want to be a good friend to Trinity, but ultimately, I want to remain committed to my best friend, my husband, Shandon. I love him more than anyone. I am at a loss for words. I need him to stay here with me. I can't lose my family.

I didn't know what I would do when Shandon walked down the basement stairs. We looked at each other, and I cried some more. I don't want to lose my husband. He is all I ever dreamed of. He surprised me when he came over and hugged me. He held me so tight I held my breath. He held me while I cried tears of defeat. He listened and held me tighter. He was so compassionate while I told him what happened with Trinity. My Baby kissed my lips softly, then he told me he stands behind my decision to bail Trinity out. We both know she is not built for prison. She is not one for the stringent boundaries and hanging out with a bunch of women, day in and day out. She is a free spirit that must fly and spread her wings.

Shandon stated hearing some of Trinity's past explains a lot of her present. I was on the fence with his thought process. But he is always the voice of reason. He reminded me of how old he was when his mother and father deserted him. He told me how bad it hurt him that the man of the house was gone, how he felt like he had to be the man of the house at the tender age of eight. He was a son, the man of the house, and emotional support to his mother. He knew nothing about how to be the man of the house, but he did the best he could. Hence, his relationship with his mother is incredibly loving and supportive, to this day.

I remember how afraid he was when I told him I was pregnant with our first child. Back then, he told me he could never be a good father because his father left him. Shandon believes watching me give birth to our son irrevocably changed his soul and his thoughts about his potential to be a good father. A fatherless son turned into an amazing father. He struggled with his father issues, but he overcame his past. Just as Trinity can overcome her past issues. With time and patience, and lots of prayers, anything is possible. Shandon and I bowed our heads and said a prayer for Trinity. We prayed for spiritual fortitude during her trial. *She can do all things through Christ that strengthens her.* Anything.

Shandon and I talked openly. We opened the floodgates to communicating about many things we were battling separately with. That night, we forged a bridge between us that was stronger than ever. For this, I have Trinity to thank. One day, maybe, I will thank her.

"Jnana, I know you're close to Trinity, I really do. And I respect you for maintaining a friendship with someone that's so different from you. But I will no longer stand in silence while a wedge is driven through our relationship. I love you too much to lose what we have. It's too special."

"Shandon, I agree. What we have is so hard to find. In fact, Trinni said earlier that she envies what we have. She even told me how she would love to find a man like you to love her."

"Really now? Where did that revelation come from? All of a sudden, I am a good man? I work hard for all that we have, but I'm just, according to her, a lowly electrician. Remember? I work with my hands, and I know how she feels about men that don't wear a suit to work. How did she go from being disgusted by my trade to respecting it?"

"Well, suddenly is accurate. I guess a married or spoken-for man with a credit card is bad news to her now. She doesn't know how many times she could have been in this situation where the wife was financing her little shopping sprees. You know she has dealt exclusively with married men or men with girlfriends since I met her. I guess a man she can tell earns his pay is a better catch for her now. She knows she needs to change her way of thinking. She just doesn't know how."

"I understand, Baby, I really do. But, Jnana, have you ever thought that maybe the unconditional love you give her is inappropriate? Like you are enabling her nonsense? Right now, she needs tough love. Not someone patting her on the back saying it will be alright. It may not be alright if she gets convicted and this mess doesn't get cleared up."

"Shandon, I don't baby Trinni. Trust me, I tell her how I feel, raw and uncut. You know I am a real talk fan, all day, every day. However, I may tread lighter since I now know what has spearheaded her dysfunctional behaviors. I can't forget I know about her childhood. Now more than ever, she needs a tender hand. Real talk might be too much for her. I know how emotionally fragile she is, and I would never forgive myself if what I did or said made her kill herself. She may kill herself like her Mom did."

"Hold up, Jnana! You didn't tell me that part. What happened with her Mom? She killed herself?"

"Shandon, her Mom committed suicide by purposefully overdosing on drugs when Trinni was only sixteen. I left that out because I was afraid you would tell me it was no wonder she acted like a nut case half the time."

"Jnana, suicide is nothing to joke about. You know that I joke about Trinity's bad choices, but you think I am that cruel?"

"I'm sorry, Baby, you aren't the least bit cruel."

"Her mother's suicide is another reason she might need to invest in her spirituality. She needs God. I believe that she knows of God, but she doesn't appear to know Him intimately. A psychiatrist can treat her mind, but God will rebuild her from the spirit level." Shandon said.

"I wholeheartedly believe she needs to take a personal assessment of how she has lived her life up until now. I believe that she is during a spiritual test. I've been Trinity's friend for years, and I don't know how she will endure it. She seems so broken."

"I agree. I just think she went with what they normalized in her mind. The problem with personal assessment is you need to be prepared for what you find out about yourself. For some people, it's a hard truth to see the person they truly are. The person they are at the core. Trinity is not ready for that, not the Trinity that was here tonight."

"For Trinity, it was so easy to use her love of money to hide her broken spirit. She thought she could have all the finer things in life, given to her by someone else and there would be no negative repercussions. That was her misstep. Greed led her every move, and now she has to repair the damage she has done to her soul."

"So, so true, Baby. I only hope she knows how strong she really is. The sad thing is she hasn't even tapped into her true potential. Just think of the creative mind she possesses. I love the painting she created so much I encouraged you to hang it in our home. I think if she would follow that path, she could find so much more happiness in the living she earns for herself."

"Now, we have been discussing Trinity for a long time. How about we change the subject?"

"Not yet, we have to discuss the bail money first."

"We can deal with the bail when Trinity shows up to court to face these charges. Then, we will get our ten percent back from the bail bondsman."

"Okay, I know she is happy to finally be out of jail."

"Of course, she is. I think this episode has possibly scared her straight. I will say this, I hope she doesn't break that no-contact order and go over their house to try to make this right. She needs to let the courts handle this."

"True, but knowing Trinity, she is probably headed over there now. Especially since her clothes and belongings are locked in the condo, no doubt, she'll want to march over there and demand her stuff. I hope we are wrong, though. She has too much living left to do without Greysan in her life."

"Babe, let's focus on us now. How about we put in a movie, turn down the lights, and invite the kids down for movie night?"

"Aww, that sounds so nice. But I doubt our teenagers want to hang out with their uncool parents."

"Well, how about we have horror movie night? That would get them down here fast."

"Shandon, you know I'm scared of horror movies."

"Well, how about I wrap you tightly in my arms to protect you?"

"Deal!"

"Alright, I will gather the kids and pop the popcorn then make some fruit juice."

"And I will set up the movie."

"I love you, Babe. Thank you for loving me so completely."

"I love you more. Thank you for stretching me and challenging me to be a better wife, lover, and friend."

Flat Lined

Again, my loved ones, do not seek revenge; instead,
allow God's wrath to make sure justice is served.
Turn it over to Him. For the Scriptures say,
"Revenge is Mine. I will settle all scores."
Romans 12:19

***

Trinity

I drove to a fast-food joint to eat after I left Jnana's
house. I should have cooled my jets and at least
eaten a decent home-cooked meal before I stormed
out. Jnana can put her foot in some food. I am so
hungry for some non-prison food I ordered every
item on the dollar menu at the Golden Arches. Now
that Greysan has cut me off, had me fired, and put
me in jail, I must live off my savings. I figure I have
almost fifty dollars in my joint account with
Greysan. After ordering, I drove up to the payment
window and gave the attendant my debit card. I
impatiently waited for her to open the window to
give me my debit card and food.

"Ma'am, your card came back as declined." She
said, pensively handing back my card.

Declined? There has got to be a mistake!

I looked at her closely. Is she possibly on drugs?
My order only came to ten dollars. I know I have at
least that much in my account.

"Please run the card again. There has to be a
mistake. I know I have enough on it to cover the
total."

She rolled her minimum wage eyes at me and smirked. "Okay." Then she closed the tinted slide window. The next time she opened the window, she wasn't alone. It seemed as if half of her shift was peeping out to see who was having issues with their declined card.

"Ma'am, your card got declined again."

"That can't be, run it again!" When I am hungry, I am cranky. Sue me!

She grits her teeth at me and says, "Look, Ma'am, this is dinner rush, and you have six cards lined up behind you. We all took up a collection, and we have enough money to pay for your food."

I looked up from digging in my purse for some spare change. The peepers were all up in my face, nearly hanging out the take-out window. What is their issue? I was so embarrassed I grabbed the bag from her hand and sped off. How dare they think I'm a charity case. Did they not notice I was driving a brand spanking new BMW? They better recognize! I'm sure it must be a bank error. I parked in the back of the parking lot and ate most of the food. More like devoured it. I saved the remaining food for breakfast and hope it was still edible since I didn't have a way to heat it up later.

After I stuffed my face, I unbuttoned the top button of my jeans as I called the bank to find out if my debit card got compromised, hence the little issue at the fast-food joint. If it was their issue, I am getting a huge apology. I dialed the number I knew by heart and pressed the appropriate numbers when prompted to bypass the computer so I could talk to a human being. Technology is good for some things, but when I'm dealing with my money, I have to speak to a human being and get some answers! I didn't have long to wait before customer service came on the line.

"Hextlers Bank, Andrea speaking. Customer number K56L3. How may I help you?"

"Hi, my name is Trinity Boussiant. I am an account holder at Hextlers Bank. I just tried to use my debit card, and they declined the transaction. Can you please check out what's going on?"

"Sure, Ma'am, may I have your account number?"

I gave her my account number and smiled. I was in that account so much I had it memorized.

"Thank you, Ma'am. Can you please verify some information for me first? Then I can look into your account."

I verified all the usual information, then there was silence on the line for about thirty seconds.

"Is there a problem, Miss?" I asked with attitude. I don't have a place to live, and I was just bailed out of jail, but she had better hurry up with my account information. Nobody messes with my money, especially since I'm on my last few dollars.

"Trinity, it appears…"

"Trinity? Did I give you permission to address me by my first name? Please, if you will, I would like to be addressed as Ms. Boussiant."

"I am sorry, *Ms. Boussiant,*" she cleared her throat tersely. "It appears this account was closed out earlier today. It was closed out by the other party on this account, hmmm, it appears to be a…a Mr. Greysan Lobes. He also took the remaining money out when he closed the account."

"How can he take all of my money without my consent?"

"Well, Ms. Boussiant, it appears as if Mr. Lobes has been depositing substantial amounts into this account every month without fail. You, on the other hand, were the one decreasing the balance, practically as soon as it was deposited. Hmm, so the money that remained belonged to Mr. Lobes…not you. I see your payroll checks were deposited also. But, again, you seemed to have spent them just as quickly as they were deposited. Ms. Boussiant, has Mr. Lobes informed you we, here at Hextlers Bank, have a program for people interested in debt relief and developing plans for spending smarter?"

I can't believe this hot mess, "Excuse me, I don't mean to be rude, but may I please speak with your manager? It appears as if you are looking at the wrong information. Not to mention you are beyond rude and unprofessional. Why would you assume you could tell me I need to spend smarter and reduce debt? Are you looking at the correct account?!"

"Ms. Boussiant, is the name of the other person who was on the account Greysan Lobes? Was this account opened four years ago? Do you live at Sicamore Lane? Do you have direct deposit every other Thursday?"

"Yes, to all of those questions. So, what exactly is your point?"

"Well, *Ms. Boussiant*, I just verified this is, in fact, the account in question. Now, my Manager will tell you the same thing I have. Your account is closed and, per the notes on this account, you will have to contact Mr. Lobes for further information. Have a good night, *Ms. Boussiant*."

Then, she hung up on me.

I am livid! Greysan has locked me out of my account. How dare he treat me so coldly! My clothes, furniture, and personal items are locked up in the condo. Now, my account is closed, and I have no money left. I am so ready to blow up Greysan *and* Quintaria's spot! I will set my plan into motion. Trust me; I'm determined to bring everything to the table! It is paramount I clear my name.

****

I'm ready to blow up Greysan and his wife's spot. I used GPS to find Greysan's house and was surprised. Based on the map provided, he didn't even live in town. He lived so far out it would be like driving to another state. On the drive there, I turned on my gospel music and even tried to sing along with a couple of my favorite songs. But there was something so wrong about singing gospel songs on the way to commit a sin. A sin I know better than committing. But I'm willfully going through with it anyway. I turned to a morning radio station filled with music that allowed my mind to stay in the land of sin. The beats and raunchy lyrics reinforced my thought process that Greysan needed to be taught a lesson, once and for all. Hopefully, after I blow up his spot, he will know how to treat a good woman.

I arrived at Greysan's house at five

a.m…prepared to wait here all day. I had enough of this nonsense. I must teach him and his wife a lesson. She thought she could forge a false complaint against me and get away with it? She got me all the way messed up! Yes, I have a no-contact order against contacting Greysan or his wife. I'm not allowed to visit his place of work. But the court order didn't say a thing about his home. I guess they forgot I already had that information.

I sat silently while the Nanny took the kids for a walk in a stroller. The kids were beautiful. They had their Dad's gray eyes and Quintaria's beauty. I had no beef with the kids or the Nanny. I slouched down when I saw a car driving out of one garage. It was Greysan. He was leaving so early. I bet he was meeting Lisa for some breakfast and coffee. Greysan was driving a brand-new Jaguar. Oh yeah, he is enjoying his wife's fortune, the smug jerk. He used to be so handsome to me, but now all he looks like is a snake.

As I sat outside of Grey's house, I was in awe. I had never seen a house so beautiful. I was looking around for Robin Leach because this house could have been featured on *The Lifestyles of the Rich and Famous* television show. The stone front made it look like an international villa. The five-car garage, four-level house stood amid lots of trees and hundreds of acres of land. It was so dense I could hide in my car here without being detected. Quintaria's family must be rolling in the dough. And to think Grey had me believing it was he that was running things financially at his home. Sadly, it has come to light I was, in fact, spending the heck out of his wife's money. No wonder he let me spend it like water. I keep wondering how Grey caught me in his web of deceit. Yes, I was impressed his rap game was tight, and the sex game was good too. But the reality is he was a less than an honorable man. He lacked integrity and he had me believing I was a kept woman when he was the kept one. Now he has stopped giving me money, I was broke as a joke! Not to mention, as I sat outside of my married ex-lover's home, I was toddling along on my tightrope of being morally bankrupt. Still, it only seems right Greysan should pay for his indiscretions. It only seems right he should give me at least fifty percent of my soul back. I sure sold it to him at a discount!

After today, maybe I can feel whole again. Maybe after I get this little misunderstanding cleared up, I can forgive myself. I need to let Quintaria know it wasn't me using her card illegally. She needs to know the times I did use her card were always with Grey's expressed permission. I want to tell her Lisa is spending her family money now, not me. And I'm going to show her proof to back up my case.

My mind freely danced in the land of sin; I allowed my mind to wonder about whether I was more hurt in my heart, or if my ego is bruised. To be honest, it was a bruised ego. My heart will heal; it always has, but my ego was bruised because I allowed myself to care for a man whose entire existence was a facade. The entire affair was a masterpiece in minimalism. I fell for it, lock stock and barrel. Fool me once, shame on you. Fool me twice, shame on me. I am determined not to be the fool for a married man ever again. So, why was I here to settle the score instead of just moving on? Because it is overdue for Greysan to meet his karma face-to-face!

I think back to everything Greysan gave me over the last four years: The car, condo, shopping sprees, numerous scrumptious take-out meals, blacked eyes, bruised skin, and admittedly, when he wasn't taking my body by force, even good sex. I assessed the total value of my wardrobe was more than ten thousand dollars. The twenty pounds I had gained because of his preference for me to only eat high-fat calorie-laden foods was even well paid for. The condo, which I thought was supposedly mine, cost over two hundred thousand dollars. The condo was my temporary solace, but in retrospect, it was simply my concubine's den. The new car, which is valued at approximately seventy thousand dollars, served me well as I drove it to the biggest and best sales. Things I brought with money I earned by devaluing every bit of my soul never made me feel complete. With all the material things I gained, even temporarily, I still felt morally bankrupt.

I sat here outside the home of a pregnant woman whose husband is a snake. My master plan was to get into the house and convince Quintaria I was not the one making the fraudulent charges she is accusing me of making. Part of my plan was to prove to her she was to blame her husband's *current* mistress, Lisa, not me, the old one. Pause! *What in the heck is wrong with me? Have I come undone?!*

All at once, it hit me, why…why was I here? Why was I trying to make a statement now?

And for the likes of Greysan! Why was I trying to make a point with this cheater? Why now? I shook off the uneasy feeling in my bones and focused on the task at hand. Maybe I would find an answer to that unnerving question another time. Who knew…why? Did I normally need a rhyme or a reason to sin? In the past, I never cared much about the men who cheated with me. Nor did I give too much weight to how much they took from me. I took just as much from them. What was going on with me? Why was I feeling convicted in my spirit now? Could God really be in this moment?

Why was I at this married man's home? Can you believe this? In my mind, I thought Greysan's wife would invite me in for tea so we could compare credit card receipts of my approved purchases. I would help her compare my purchases against the ones gained illegally by Lisa. I, the old mistress, who was a partner in a long-term affair with her husband, would be willing to help her bust up the present infidelity of her husband.

After all this, I expected her to simply dismiss the charges against me. I expected her to gratefully forgive me for the charges I made on the credit card because her cheating husband approved the purchases as part of compensation for companionship and sex. Oh yeah, that plan would have worked out perfectly. What a lame-brained scheme I hatched! I must have lost my darn mind. In all the years I was a mistress, I always made a solemn vow to never show up at a man's house bearing honesty about our affair. We were both adults when we committed our sins. I never wanted to hurt an innocent woman with the truth about her man. If I held this vow, I kept it. Yet, there I was, breaking that vow, for a low life man like Greysan. It didn't quite seem worth it. I never broke my vow to myself, and I will not start today.

How was I to know what Quintaria would do to me when I started telling her about my affair with her husband? Judging from the time I overheard her cursing Greysan out, she had hood tendencies. I totally forgot about the Bomquisha chick. I'm sure she would love to beat me down right about now too. Oh, and Quintaria's quiet, but you gotta watch the quiet ones. Sister Vonnie and her four brothers were probably hoping I got up the nerve to drive out here and confront her. As bad as I pretend to be, I will not take a chance and go out like that. I will not foolishly risk my safety by blowing the whistle on a serial cheater like Greysan.

With my pride tucked neatly in my back pocket, I drove away from the house. I ducked down when a cop car drove towards the house. No way I was risking going back to jail, especially not for someone as unworthy of me as Grey. As their house got smaller and smaller in the rear-view mirror, I felt boundless. This was one step towards me getting back to my free-spirited self. I was broke, homeless, and manless, but I am alive. I wish Jnana could see how strong I was. She would be so proud of me. I deserved better! I did! Now, it was time for me to do better.

As Tasha Cobbs' gospel song, *For Your Glory*, played on my Sirius Radio player, I sang out loud to each lyric. Tears streamed down my face. My Spirit was convicting me, more and more. I knew better than this sin. I knew better than to let my flesh rule me like this. Christ is in my heart. But I drove past that exit a long time ago. Haven't I? Is it too late to make a U-turn? I pulled over on the road and bowed down on my knees. I raised my hands to the air and cried out for solace. I felt my rage for Greysan and Quintaria leaving me. In its place, there was a peace only Jesus could give. All the glory belongs to Him, who has given me victory during my testing. Maybe it's not too late to make that U-turn back to the road of righteousness, after all. Maybe.

~17~

Protect Yourself

The sins of some people are obvious, going ahead
of them to judgment. The sins of others follow them
there. In the same way, the good things that people
do are obvious, and those that aren't obvious can't
remain hidden.

I Timothy 5:24-25

***

Jnana

I tried calling Trinni again.

The last time we talked wasn't a good
episode in our friendship, but we have been through
too much to let silence scream aloud in our
friendship. I still love her like a sister. I cannot
stand not being able to talk this out. I tried calling
her cell phone three more times. Each time, the
answering machine kicked right on. It's like her
phone battery was dead by the way it went right to
voice mail. Each time I got her machine, I sighed
and left another message. I haven't heard from
Trinity in a week. I could have sworn I told her how
I felt about her little disappearing acts before. I
didn't know if she was still alive or just still upset
with me. Maybe she took her own life like her
Mom had. The last option scared me. I loved
Trinity and hoped she was doing okay. Yes, we had
a deep talk that night, and I knew my real talk, as
she puts it, was harsh. But I said what was on my
mind. I will not apologize for being honest with my
friend. That's what's wrong with a lot of people;

they have so many yes folks around them they don't know how to deal with folks that tell them the truth. Well, the truth was she was weak-minded when it came to men, and she was stronger than she realized. I smiled. I forgot another option. Maybe Trinity was lying up with some fine man living the high life, gold digger style. Even though I didn't respect her hustle, I couldn't go around telling a grown woman how to live her life and expect her to listen to logic when she just wanted to have fun. I am a married woman with a good man, and she is a gold-digging single woman trying to find the next married victim. We are most definitely different women with different agendas. Still, I love her and want to keep our friendship from being crushed under pride's feet. Still, when we reconnect, I must maintain some boundaries for the sake of my marriage.

After I got tired of calling Trinity's cell phone and talking aimlessly to her answering machine, I began my day. Today was a rare day for me to relax. I had some me time planned, laundry to do, and I had to clean the kids' rooms because they were a mess. So, I guess my day was going to be part relaxation and part maid duties for my two children. What else is new?

My bookstore, Namaste, was closed for the day. I stayed home to rejuvenate my spirit. Every month, I designated the same day of the month to close for the same reason. My customers got used to the idea, and some even took a day off from work, on the same day, as a pledge of solidarity. This was more than just a small business. This is my calling. Many of my customers became extensions of my family. I loved it!

I was doing my yearly inventory the last couple of weeks, and I was exhausted. While going through my literary inventory, I had to smile at how many wonderfully creative and talented African American writers there are. All too often, non-writers take reading a published novel for granted. It takes a great mind to use their imagination to birth a story from one idea and make it interesting enough for others to want to read it. Writers seemed to weave a web of words like a spider and pull in one more reader each time they spin their tales of love, drama, and adversity. Yes, I was impressed with writers. I was my dream job because I get to educate my customers about the vast variety of African American Literature. I loved literature, and I respected writers more than any other group of people. As I was thinking, I had an idea.

"Hmm, writer appreciation day. But could it go over with readers? I could get a few of my customers' favorite local authors and have them come in for a book signing and appreciation party. Yes, that's a plan." I thought aloud.

I wrote what I thought about because I have so many things on my mind, I often forget quick thoughts like this. I finished off my tea and started dinner before I got too comfortable. I prepared barbecued beef ribs, macaroni and cheese, mixed veggies, and cornbread, all my family's favorites. When I was done with cooking, I was tired and sweaty. I took a bath then laid down for a few to rest my body.

I ran my bath water extra hot with lots of bubbles, just the way I loved it. I lit some vanilla candles all around the bathroom and turned out the light. The Boney James CD played on low volume, and I became instantly relaxed. After getting undressed, I got into the tub. I just loved the feeling of being surrounded by warm water. I washed my body with an exfoliating lavender body scrub and let the soothing scent engulf my senses. I just loved the smell and feel of lavender. My body felt so soft and moisturized, which Shandon loves. My mind flowed into a spiritual place of joy. I was about to wash my hair when the phone rang. I used the remote to turn off the music. I was only answering the phone for four people this morning: Shandon, my two children Liana and Ashton, and my missing-in-action, best friend, Trinity. Anyone else could wait until I woke up from my nap. I stopped washing and listened closely. I was shocked when Trinity's voice came through the machine.

"Hey, Jnana. Yeah, it's me, Trinni. I called the bookstore, and the machine said you were closed for your special day of rejuvenation. Well, uh, I guess I will catch up to you later. By the way, I'm okay. I am sleeping in the car for now. Love you, Jnana, my bestest friend in the world."

Beep

Now I know Trinni was okay, I washed my hair with Nassie's Hope Lemongrass Shampoo and Honey Hair Conditioner. When I was done, I rested my head on my bath pillow and closed my eyes to think. I tried to think calming thoughts, but the last time I spoke to Trinity kept rushing back. I sure miss my best friend very much. One day I pray we will work this out. For now, I am truly glad to hear that she is okay.

When I got out of the bath, I looked at the phone to get the number that Trinity had called from. It came up as unknown. There is no way for me to get in touch with her. In the meantime, I will love my best friend from afar and hope doing things her way does her spirit some good. Although I questioned why she was sleeping in her car when she has a bed to sleep in here, I smiled at the realization that maybe she is finally taking responsibility for herself and this was her way of doing it. Maybe time apart will help us both to heal ourselves and this friendship I still value very much.

I moisturized my body with Nassie's Hope Matcha Green Tea Moisturizer and used Nassie's Hope Lavender Hair Oil for my hair, putting the oil from root to tip. Then, I wrapped my hair in a scarf so it could air dry. I laid down for a couple of hours and woke up refreshed. As I have gotten older, I realize the essential benefit of taking daily cat naps in the middle of the day. They are life extenders!

After I woke up, I was energized and well-rested. I started taking my children's hampers down to the basement to wash clothes. I sighed. My children were way too old for me to be coming behind them like they were two.

I started in my daughter Liana's room. She kept her room neat, but I had to check her closet and under her bed, because those were her favorite spots to put things when I told her to clean her room. And she didn't disappoint. There were dirty clothes in both places, and I found a D-graded paper in her pants pocket. I will talk with her when she gets home from school. I went into my son's room. Now, this child keeps his room just like a pig's sty. I stepped over clothes, dirty plates, and cups, and even schoolbooks. Interestingly, I guess he doesn't need his schoolbooks at school. I checked the pockets of his pants pockets and was stunned by what I found. A condom! My son is sixteen, but I never thought for a second, he was sexually active. Let alone have access to condoms. I pushed the stuff off his bed and laid down. This was enough to make me lightheaded. I could not believe it! My son, my eldest child, was sexually active! I felt like I could be knocked down with a feather. Where did I go wrong as a parent, and why wasn't I consulted about this sex issue? I also wanted to know how and when he had time to have sex. It seemed to me he is always here at home or at the Jenkins' house. I am shocked. The thought of my son being naked with some fast tail girl enticing him with her goodies didn't sit well with me. I was so angry I screamed so loud the walls shook. What the heck is going on with my son? And why don't I know the answer to this question?

I know I am a good Mom. I even thought I had a close relationship with my children, especially my son. I am very involved in their lives, but I didn't know anything about this. How? This was disheartening. Where did I lose touch with my son? I thought back to the day when Ashton was acting weird at the breakfast table. Shandon said they were going to take a ride so they could talk. That's it! I called my husband. He is the one who would more than likely have all the answers to my questions.

I waited impatiently for the call to connect.

He answered, "Hello, Shandon speaking. How may I help you?"

I tried to keep my composure, "Shandon! Want to guess what I found in your son's pant pocket?"

"Oh, hey, Baby. What's going on with the guess what game? Spit it out, what did you find?" Shandon asked calmly.

His calm voice infuriated me more. "A frigging condom! Shandon, Ashton is sexually active. Did you know this?"

I waited while Shandon mulled over his answer.

"Well, I did know about the sex issue. But I'm not exactly sure if he is, in fact, sexually active."

I am blindsided. "What?! Not sure? Okay, how long have you known about Ashton thinking about sex, and why didn't you tell me?"

"Jnana, you know how you get sometimes. Ashton wanted this to be between him and me, so he didn't catch any drama from you. He was both too embarrassed and scared to talk to you."

"Oh, really now. *How do I get*? My son thinks he is ready for something as serious as sex, and my husband keeps this kind of secret from me? Wow! This is just amazing. What about the abstinence promise of purity pledge he made last year? Hmm, no wonder he doesn't even wear the bracelet anymore. Things are becoming clearer. I am almost too scared to ask you one more question, but I must. Shandon, did you give Ashton the condoms?"

My husband was silent again, and I was getting extremely irate.

"Yes."

"Oh my gosh! Oh…my…gosh! Shandon, please tell me that you're lying to me…please."

"Jnana, Baby, do you remember the day at the breakfast table when he was acting oddly? Well, he was thinking of asking for my help long before that day. He has been going with Celeste for six months now, and they wanted to take their relationship to the next level. They love each other, so they wanted to consummate the relationship."

"Shandon, stop! Please. This was sounding bad before, but now it sounds much worse. Do you condone this type of behavior from your son? We are Christians. Is this the type of behavior we have read about in the Bible?"

"Yes, Jnana, I do. I know what the Bible says, but Jnana, if I didn't get him condoms, he wouldn't have protected himself. This is not the Bible days. The world is losing children every day to incurable sexually transmitted diseases. I wanted our son to protect himself from all the sexually transmitted diseases like HIV, HPV, and AIDS. I also wanted our son to take responsibility for the sexual health of the young girl that he loves. Jnana, why are you tripping? We haven't been to church in a long time. We aren't even active members at one specific church anymore! So, I didn't have a Pastor to consult. I took our son's health into my own hands. I mean, you act like I gave him a box of condoms and simply patted him on the back. Ashton and I went driving that day, and we had a father-son talk about girls and sex. He told me how he felt about Celeste and how he wanted to have sex for the first time with her. We drove to the pharmacy and talked, at length, with the Pharmacist about what prophylactic was best. We even went to a clinic to get information on the proper options for preventing sexually transmitted diseases. Jnana, I didn't make this decision lightly. Ashton and I educated ourselves. However, even after hearing all the facts about teen HIV transmission rates, Ashton was still set on consummating his relationship with Celeste. Seeing he was going to do it, whether I supported him or not, I purchased some condoms for him."

"Look, Shandon, I respect how you went about educating him and assuring he had protection. You are his Father, and you love him. I even felt the hit below the belt about us not having a home church. I get it. We will talk more deeply about that another time. But let me ask you a question: what would be your answer if our daughter, Liana, asked the same thing of you Ashton did?"

"That isn't the least bit funny, Jnana! Lili better keep her legs closed…tight! And if I find out some boy is sniffing around; I'm going to hunt him down like a dog!"

"Shandon! Do you hear yourself? You are so foul. Your son tells you he wants to have sex and asks for condoms, and you give them to him. Your daughter isn't even old enough, nor is she sexually active, and you get angry with me for even asking the question. You are truly sexist, Shandon. Did you forget that Celeste is a girl too?"

"Look, I am only being honest. Celeste isn't my

233 | P a g e

responsibility. Her father better worry about protecting his daughter's virtue. The fact you even take the time to call me sexist doesn't hurt me. Liana is daddy's little girl, and Ashton is a boy growing into a man with testosterone and desires. There is a difference, you know."

"Shandon, I need to get off the phone with you right now. I really don't recognize the man on the other end of this phone. Not only did you keep this from me, but you don't seem to have any regrets. Your nonchalant attitude is just priceless."

Shandon sighed heavily. "Okay, I will see you at home. Babe, I love you."

I am irked with Shandon because he truly has some mess with him. But I do love my man, even when he is short-sighted and sexist. "You too."

I hung up the phone and stayed in my son's bed. Darn if time isn't really flying. Just yesterday, it seemed as if Ashton was learning to walk without falling on his tail. Now, it seems as if he was chasing Celeste's tail. He had condoms, courtesy of his father, and was ready to have sex. I must do something to prevent him from making this mistake. He is too young to be having sex. What if he got caught up in the moment with Celeste and didn't use the condoms anyway? I am too darn young to be a grandmother. And I refuse to sit around while he tries to derail his life because of some girl. I liked Celeste before, but now she looks like a girl trying to mind meld my son with her little teenage body. I must do something to stop this! I just don't know what to do. However, as I look around my son's dirty room, I realize that he couldn't possibly be thinking about sex when he couldn't even pick his dirty drawers up off the floor! Yeah, this must be a huge misunderstanding. Either way, I will call a family meeting after dinner so I can get to the bottom of this mess. Hmm, Shandon is talking about how I get? Well, we'll see how I get tonight!

Back Draft

So, submit yourselves to the one true God and fight
against the devil and his schemes. If you do, he will
run away in failure. Come close to the one true
God, and He will draw close to you. Wash your
hands; you have dirtied them in sin. Cleanse your
heart, because your mind is split down the middle,
your love for God on one side and selfish pursuits
on the other. Since the beginning, our loving
Creator has been pursuing us, drawing us closer to
Him. He invites us to move closer to Him so we can
be fully His. Now is the time to lament, to grieve,
and to cry. Dissolve your laughter into sobbing and
exchange your joy for depression. Lay yourself
bare, face down to the ground, in humility before
the Lord; and He will lift your head so you can
stand tall.
James 4:7-10
***

Trinity

After the revelation from the bank, I don't know
what I will do. I have no money and my bank
account is closed. I also have no real home and no
job. I am officially poor, again. I wonder where I
went wrong. Why am I back to square one? This
time, with this man, I thought I struck gold.
Greysan was my money bank like no man ever was.
He gave me money, and he seemed to care for me. I
guess in their own ways, all my lovers had made me
feel as if they cared for me. To be totally

transparent, all I ever wanted was to be loved. The closeness of a man's body, his masculine scent upon my soft feminine scent, was all I ever needed. When I was in the company of a man, even someone else's man, the way they held me and talked so sweetly to me made me feel so special. When I didn't have a man, there was something in my being that was missing. It was as if I could feel the wind blowing through the gaping hole in my heart. If I didn't belong to someone, even if it was a lie, I didn't matter. I could walk down the streets with my head held high and a sway in my hips and many men would look at me, lustfully. But, if a day went by and no man looked at me, not even one, I was depressed. In desperation, the next day I would be near naked just trying to entice a man, any man to look my way. I figured if my aura didn't snag them, my sexuality would. After all the men I let have sex with me, today, I am alone. None of the married men wanted to make me a permanent part of their lives. They left my life after my need for more of their time became apparent. I can tell myself it was my desperation that smothered man after man. But, if I am completely honest with myself, I know they used me to their capacity. I served a purpose in their life and they were ready to move on. Period. In a way, everyone I ever cared about left me. My own Momma found it necessary to leave me. She chose the pain from a man over the love of her daughter. If I weren't good enough for my Momma to live, if I wasn't even precious enough for my Dad to stay in my life, how could I expect a man to want to live for me?

Ultimately, I must deal with the harsh reality of my life: Greysan turned the tables on me and now my money flow had ceased. I never felt so alone in my life. Even the week I mourned my relationship with Greysan doesn't even come close to this. At least back then the money held me over while I went shopping. That week I kept coming up with question after question. What am I missing? What is wrong with me? And why has God failed me? Why hasn't God sent me a real man that would love me? All of me. I want to be loved, completely. God knows the heart of me, He knows what I desire. I need this like I need a new soul because my soul tank is on empty. I need a heart transplant because this one is broken. It seems like it has been since my Mom died.

I think back to the last time my Mom held me in her arms and how safe and loved I felt. It was that time in the past I tried to recreate in my present, time and time again. The security and joy I felt when I was accepted has been hard to replicate. Even when I had sex, I very rarely felt safe or loved. I felt satisfaction, but that was physical and temporary, neither mental nor spiritual. I yearn to feel a genuine dose of love. Sadly, the things I did previously didn't work to heal me. The truth is they damaged me even more. I need to find a way to fill my empty spiritual tank.

I drove around for another hour, by this time it was dark out. Lonesome for home, I drove through the parking lot of the condo and parked in my old parking space. I sat in silence wondering what I was going to do without a roof over my head. I know I took my lifestyle for granted. I know I took for granted I would always have a place to rest my head. I even took for granted Greysan's money flow would always be there to provide my needs.

I sat outside of the condo and watched my old neighbors coming home from work. I missed living here. Here was home. Here, I felt some semblance of normalcy and I was happy in my own space. Space where I believed Greysan when he told me he put my name on the mortgage note. I have been bamboozled again. Fool me once, shame on you. Fool me five times, shame on me.

I got brave and got out of the car to go see if my old home is still locked. As I walked up to the door, I looked around to make sure no one I knew saw me. When the coast was clear, I put my security code in the main door and miraculously, it still worked. I tip toed up the steps and was happy no one was outside in the hall. I was shocked and appalled at what I saw. To my surprise, there was now a different lock on the door. There was also a note on the door. I can't believe Greysan's wife has gone this far! This was my home! My solace! I earned all the things I had. How dare she so easily dismiss me and my hard work! Heck, the least she should do is to call us even.

Quintaria wanted to make sure my name was dirt in this town. She added a no trespassing sign in neon orange, and she had posted a copy of the police report of my arrest for identity theft. This hussy even hung a letter explaining how much of a whore I was to earn the condo and its contents. She posted she would sell my things at a one-dollar garage sale on an upcoming Saturday. I cannot believe she went hard with it. I knew she had hood tendencies, and this proves it. She has gone stark raving mad!

I was so consumed with reading the papers on the door I didn't realize that a couple of my neighbors had gathered behind me. When I turned around, I saw it was a pair of the hating females in the building. They had the nerve to come out here with rollers in their hair with faded, wrinkled pajama on. Did they get dressed today or what?!

"So, Ms. Uppity," as she moved into my personal space, "was earning this condo the old fashion way huh Porsha?" My old neighbor, Pamela, who lived down the hall, asked her peer pressure, susceptible friend.

"Yeah, gurl, I always knew those knees looked a little rough and dry!" Porsha said.

These heffas high fived!

I am homeless and broke, but I'm not taking crap from either of these two. Oh no, not today!

I snickered animatedly, "Ha ha! Oh, you two got jokes now huh? Well, guess what Porsha. I was earning the milk money when your man paid me a visit too. Maybe if you were doing your job, he wouldn't have come by here every two weeks on payday. Yes, I am a pro! A well-paid pro at getting your neglected man's hard-earned cash. Crazy huh?" I lied to bait her.

"Oh no she didn't Porsha. Oh wow, I am at a loss for words. You gonna let her talk to you like that? Gurl, it could not be me, trust!"

"Trinity, gurl, I'm not going to beat you down. Nope. I can see you are already going through a lot of rough stuff. I saw your name and mug shot in the paper last week. You looked real model like with the runny mascara and blood shot eyes. Judging from that bruise you have under your eye, the girls in jail really beat you down."

I was fit to be a tired, ole heifer, "You know what? I will go before I catch another case. By the way, tell Jeff to holler. I may need some gas for my ride soon. I know how he loves when I swirl my hips for him. Cackle on ladies. Especially you Porsha, looking like a Pinto!"

I switched my hips as Pamela tried to hold Porsha back. I wish she would mess with me today. My hair is messed up anyway and I have some, wanting to beat Quintaria's behind, anger built up. I wanted her to be the one to bring the noise. Tonight, I am not the one!

I walked out of the building and a couple of other residents walking up the sidewalk looked past me but took a second look. Right on time, Jeff walked up the sidewalk. Yeah, he tried to kick it to me. I took down his new cell phone number and promised to call him soon. Porsha doesn't know who she's messing with. I was only joking with her to make her mad. I never let Jeff touch me. I only stroked his fragile ego when I passed him in the hall. Too bad for him he must deal with my lies when he gets in the building. As much as she hates me, I bet my life she will take my word as bond against her man. I'm sure they will be arguing half the night over my lies. Foolish woman!

I was so hurt my neighbors knew all my sordid business. I thought I led a quiet existence here and now they all know that a married man financed my lifestyle. Quintaria had no right to post that sign on the door. If she would have satisfied her husband, he wouldn't have come to me. She pushed her husband into the arms of a band of lovers and she is mad. Amazing.

As I walked out to the parking lot, a tow truck driver drove close to my car then looped to the back of the parking lot. Then he quickly drove back towards it. I was irritated because he looked like he came awfully close to hitting the back of my car and now he appears to be returning to the same place for a second try. This nonsense is just another sign that it's time for me to leave. This is no longer my home or peaceful solace.

I got into my car and drove off just as the tow truck driver was looping back by. He looked like a mad man, so I drove out of the parking lot and cut off another car just to get away from him. I'm not sure what the tow truck driver's issue was but I'm not trying to make it mine. The truck followed me out onto the road when the way was clear. I thought he was following me, so I put the pedal to the floor trying to lose him. When I got a mile up the road, I looked in my rear-view mirror. I didn't see the tow truck anymore. Maybe I was just paranoid.

I was going to stay parked in the condo parking lot for the night because I'm tired, but I found a safer place to park. I drove around looking for a safe place to park my car aka my homeless sweet home. I finally came to the front of a church. It was a regal looking church. The kind that looks like it can hold hundreds of people and the Pastor has wide screen televisions on the walls because the folks in the back cannot see the pulpit from their seats. The parking lot was empty, all but one car. It appeared there were lights on inside. Who would be at a church this late? I looked around at my surroundings. It appeared to be a decent enough neighborhood, so I parked. This parking spot will be my home address tonight. My BMW didn't have the comforts of home, but it was my safe haven from the outdoors.

I slept in the cramped car all night. Thank gosh the windows are tinted so no one could see me up in here. I slept twisted up like a pretzel but seriously, my spirit was so calm I slept peacefully all night. It is amazing what peace of mind can provide in terms of comfort.

I was roused awake by the sound of doors opening and closing. I realized it was morning as the sun shined through the car. Dang, I was so tired I had slept through the entire night. I woke up smiling from the restful night but then I remembered \ I don't have anywhere to go today. My stomach barked at me and I realized \ I had to decide where I was going to eat. All I know is it won't be at Jnana's house. I want her to be proud of me. I don't want to be a burden on her.

I sat up and peeped out the window. I must have been very sleepy because the previously near empty parking lot was now filling up with cars. There were cars parked all around me. I tried to look at my cell phone, but the battery was dead. I looked at the car clock and it read Sunday at nine thirty. I completely forgot today was Sunday, the Lord's day. Sunday was the same day I previously took a break from Greysan. Or was it the other way around?

I was about to turn the ignition on to drive off when someone banged on my window, hard. I was so scared to roll down the window, but they kept banging. Then they yelled they could see my shadow inside the car. I looked around at the church goers and I was less afraid. Who would hurt someone in front of a church with these witnesses? Besides, they too were investigating who could be causing such a commotion for a crime to be committed. I was afraid, but I carefully opened my door. It was a burly man that looked like a mountain man. He was the same man from the parking lot at the condo! Behind my car was a tow truck. In his hand was the reason why the banging was so loud, a flashlight. Oh no, he is not who I think that he is. He cannot be…nah…not the repo man!

"Ma'am, I am from Hextlers Bank. I have a court order to take possession of this here vehicle. Would you like to see the court order?"

"Yes," was all I could muster. I looked at the paperwork and it appeared to be legitimate. It had Quintaria's name all over it! I looked up from the papers and was shocked to realize just how many church goers stopped walking from their cars. Much to my dismay, some were even filing out of the church to catch a glimpse of my vehicle repossession. I was mortified.

"Ma'am, I will give you five minutes to clear your personal belongings out of the vehicle. After the vehicle is repossessed you won't be able to retrieve them without paying a forty-dollar processing fee. With that in mind, is there anything that you would like to get out of here?"

I nodded yes. He handed me a thirty-gallon plastic trash bag and I put everything I owned in it. How ridiculous is it that everything I own fit into half the size of a thirty-gallon trash bag? Let me save you the thought. Very!

I held my bag tightly as I stood on the curb watching him hitch my car, aka my homeless sweet homeless, onto the tow truck. I don't know what I am going to do. As the sky opened and rain began to fall, I cried. I think I cried so hard my tears became one with the rain drops. I looked up towards the sky and asked God why. I could have sworn the clouds opened and bigger rain drops fell the harder I cried. Eventually, several of the church goers came over with an umbrella and walked me into the church. I stood in the middle of the street as my makeshift home was wheeled down the street and turned the corner. My 'allpd4' vanity license plate shifted off center. How perfect!

Once inside of the church, I sat at the back of the church. I was drenched. As if my hair wasn't jacked up enough, now it was officially ruined. I moved my hand over my hair and tried to press the rain out of it. Enough water fell out to fill a bucket. I was tore up from the floor up. I was so embarrassed when the Usher came by for collection and all I could do was a nod. I couldn't even spare the lint inside my soaking wet pant pocket.

After the time of tithes and offering was complete, I relaxed. I got comfortable in the wooden pew and listened intently. I must say the sermon was moving. As I watched the Preacher dancing around the pulpit, his voice rising and falling with every other word, I took in his use language and diction. He was eloquent and practically a poetic. He taught scriptural lessons with ease and expertise. As learned as he appeared to be in the things of purity, I couldn't help but wonder what his sin journal looked like. I knew mine was filled to the brim. He was dressed in the finest designer suit and tie. He even had on nice shoes, but at this point in my life, I wondered what he was really like, not as a Preacher, but as a man. I was fixated by his smooth eloquence as was the entire congregation. I shook off thoughts of insecurity that were overriding my brain. It appeared I should have taken more time to look past the exterior of the man and look deeper into his soul before this moment. Is it possible my assumption of Officer Micah's inner beauty had already begun this thought transformation? One can only hope.

I was drawn back into his sermon when he paused and began speaking in tongues. It surprised me. Gone was his eloquence. Instead what remained was a man totally engulfed in the flow of the Spirit. It was beautiful. Not one for church gatherings and still deeply ingrained with bad memories of church folk, I am surprised this vision before me was reaching my cold heart. I felt the

Spirit in that place. As quickly as the Preacher was in the flow, he came back to his sermon. I was on the edge of my seat. I really must get back to church more often. I pray God is not done with me yet. I want to feel the Spirit too. I want to be engulfed in the flow too. I want to be healed and whole too. I was hopeless until the Preacher began speaking directly to my soul.

"Let's refer to Romans 8:10, *And if Christ is in you, the body is dead because of sin; but the spirit is life because of righteousness. As sinners, we must come to God Almighty for covering. We must submit to His Will, leaning not to our own understanding.* As we refer to this scripture, I want us to ask ourselves just how many of us have shot out in the dark on our own. The mistakes we made and sin we committed allowed us to believe we were in control of our lives and we were grown. Until we come to God, through Jesus' name, we are but babes. The first step to becoming spiritually mature is to get in the Word of God. Through study and time invested in intimate time alone with God, we can begin to live the Word. We show our Word knowledge in our actions and in what we spend our time on. As Matthew 15:8 states: *What people say with their mouths comes from the way they think; these are the things that make people unclean.* What are you allowing to consume your time? What words are you speaking? Are you speaking of sin? Is your life run by thoughts of impurity? Ask yourself these things and you have the condition of your heart. You will easily see the passion for Christ or the attention to things of the world. Remember that you need to answer these questions honestly. I cannot see into your soul. As Psalms 44:21 says, *God knows the secrets of the heart.* But be careful, for self-righteousness and pride keep us from our destiny. There is a difference between being self-assured as opposed to self-righteous. Can I get an Amen? Now in loving Jesus, we learn to give our life over to a God who cares for our direction in life. When we care about our purpose in His kingdom, we begin to focus inside instead of outside. When this shift begins, we fulfill our life's plan. Can I get an Amen?"

In my present state of mind, I needed to hear all his words. I felt something inside me shaking loose. I even wept most of the sermon. When they called for all visitors to stand, I'm not going to lie, I didn't even attempt to stand. I was too embarrassed to let these people see me like this. I knew I didn't know any of those people from a can of paint, but I had an image to uphold. I looked like a hot mess. I would be so embarrassed if someone told someone else they saw me, Trinity Boussaint, in church, looking like a wet dog. I would be laughed out of this state. Even with all the people at the condo knowing about my lascivious tales with married men, at least it could've been said I looked good while I was hoeing around. This is not my most stellar moment, by far. I was so against going up to the front I did not stand even when an Usher tapped me on my shoulder. I looked up from my shame to realize the entire church was turned around facing in my direction. The Preacher Man was motioning for me to come up. His soft smile and extended arms seemed to say, we welcome you. I didn't want to disappoint all those strangers, so I relented. I slowly started my way up to standing when *Amen* erupted throughout the church. I looked like a wet poodle, yet they were clapping for me. Go figure! Maybe they were surprised the ceiling hadn't come crashing down when I walked in the door. Maybe they are just as surprised as I am. See I know God, but I don't *know* Him.

The Preacher smiled widely then said, "Come join us Child of God. Please don't give one care to the onlookers. You need to be worried about *your* salvation. Time to get right with your Father! Just as Romans 12:12 says, *do not be conformed to this world, but be transformed by the renewal of the mind, that by testing you may discern what is the will of God, what is good and acceptable and perfect."*

The Usher held my trembling hand as I walked up to the front of the church. Initially, my footsteps felt heavy, each step felt like cement. Like a soft spiritual magnet, the more words he spoke, the quicker I moved. My steps began to feel less heavy. My steps got softer and easier, each one seemed feather light the closer I got to the pulpit. The weight upon my heart seemed to lighten too. The gaping hole in my soul closed just a little more. I finally reached the pulpit and the Preacher still had his hands out to receive me. I was truly amazed by how welcoming the prayer team made me feel. There were other lost souls walking up to the front of the altar, but the Spirit made me feel as if I mattered for being brave enough to be obedient to

249 | P a g e

the call. It was as if, I was finally accepted for the first time in my life. Those people were dressed so beautifully in their Sunday's best, but there I stood in my soaking wet, wrinkled, and dirty clothes. My hair was drying in a curly but fast turning frizz ball. Having my car repossessed so early, I didn't get to brush my teeth this morning. You could only imagine how wretched my morning breath smelled. It was said 'you can come the way that you are' to God's house but this was the first time I truly believed I was accepted in the church. I could come as I was, no matter what I wore or how spiritually broken I was. Their humility didn't make me feel ashamed or make me feel as if I was out of place. How humbling.

The Usher gently placed my hand into the Preacher's awaiting hand. When I touched his hand, I felt the undeniable energy. My body was lighter. Then I fell to my knees. My tears flowed harder and I wailed loudly. I could feel the echo in my soul. Jesus' love instantly filled my being and I was alone with Him. I laid my burdens at his feet. All my past sins and even the sins I already planned on committing were laid in submission before him. I could feel my sordid past becoming less and less important. I was being restored. The hole in my heart closed even more. I could feel Jesus' arms around me, his peace and tranquility so overwhelming and deep in my soul. I held Him tight and let my being fill up to the brim with His love. I finally felt free. I heard about what it felt like when Jesus moved into your life. But, before this moment, I never thought I was worthy. Now, I realized God knows I am worthy, that's why He sent Jesus. I caressed the presence of Jesus' peace. I laid my weary head upon His shoulders and He held me tighter. My soul sang in the key to His love. I was moved by His forgiving embrace and His unconditional love for me. Even though my life was wroth with sin, in His arms, His amazing grace was sufficient…it was increasingly healing me by the second.

Wrapping my being around Him even more, I looked over His shoulder and saw a being standing there smiling. It…no… it couldn't be. Momma?! She was here with Jesus. She looked just as beautiful as I remember. Her shoulder length thick brown hair was flipped in a page boy and her smile was as bright as the sun. Her soft brown eyes twinkled when she saw me and just like that, I was an innocent little girl all over again. I was as pure as the driven snow. My Momma was still my Momma, as alive as she seemed to be. I looked at my Momma and smiled lovingly at her. Oh, how I missed her. As if all at once, Jesus moved aside, and Momma moved to the forefront. I dried my tears and reached for Momma. She looked into my eyes and smiled. I heard her say she loved me a thousand times. For the first time in a long time, I smiled a genuine smile. Suddenly, I realized I was the mirror image of my Momma. I don't know why I never noticed it before. The smile she smiled was mine, mine was hers. My Momma pulled me towards her, our embrace, eons long. The motherly embrace I missed was here…this moment all I ever wanted. I looked from Jesus to my Momma. The two beings that loved me first and best were here with me on the hardest day of my life. Even in my dysfunction, Jesus and Momma still loved me, unconditionally. I know I let them both down, repeatedly, by allowing the sins of the flesh and my unnatural love of material thing to rule my life. I felt sad and embarrassed, so I lowered my head in shame. Momma reached out and lifted my chin. She told me I am flawless, and I need not be ashamed ever again. Something in their eyes told me they forgave me. That all will be ok. This pure and loving feeling is the one I had craved all my life. Its name…acceptance.

Once I had it, I soaked it up for as long as I could. As my Momma held me in her arms, she told me how sorry she was she left me. She told me she missed me so. Then she told me she always knew I was stronger than I realized. As I melted in my Momma's loving arms, I didn't feel strong, I felt so weak. I missed my Mommy so much! I miss her hugs! Though she loved me, being with Jesus, who loved her, was her desire. One day, I will reunite with my Momma, but as she held me, she whispered to me I had to live. She told me I had to be stronger than she had ever been. She said though I was in uncharted waters I had to push through my fear of not being good enough because I am perfect as I am. I needed to feel these words in my spirit so badly. As I looked deeply into my Momma's eyes, I felt the words moving inside my soul. Here with Jesus and my Momma was where I want to be. I needed to feel this love, this joy. But I knew I must live. I held my Momma tight as she lovingly hugged me tightly too.

Suddenly, the Pastor touched my arms and pulled me to standing. Instantly, I was back on the pulpit. I wanted to scream so loud. No! Instead, I closed my eyes over and over to try to get back to Jesus and Momma. I reached out to them, but Jesus was guiding Momma gently back with Him. They were gradually leaving my view. My heart was being painfully tugged. I held tightly to the peace I felt. Physically, they were gone but, in my heart, I felt them close. I cried, and the Preacher held me tightly. Within his embrace, I forgave Momma for leaving me. I cried in his arms and finally cried the tears I never cried when Momma killed herself with drugs. I cried at the beauty of finally realizing I held worth in the eyes of Jesus, my Savior. I released all the energy I had pent up into the universe and it made me feel better. I released all my pain and self-destructive ways. I broke my alabaster box at Jesus' feet and repented from a lengthy list of sins. I was ready to submit to Jesus. I released all my wrong assumptions about God into the universe. That way they could no longer be a burden upon my soul. I broke the chains around my feet. I was ready to praise!

I could stay on the stage until I got myself together. A Deacon was called up to say a final prayer. The dismissal was announced. When I finally felt together enough to walk off the stage, I sat in the front pew. I stayed at the front of the church until I stopped crying. As the congregation left their seats, many of them came up to embrace me and pray for me. I always had an issue with church folk, but I easily allowed these caring people to pray with me. I composed myself as everyone filed out of the church. I sat back down in the front pew and sighed heavily. It was such a beautiful service, so much so I forgot I had no car to live in. I watched the people leave and I was jealous. I had no home to go to. I was jealous of something that just two weeks ago was taken for granted. I was nodding my head and humming to the tune that was playing in the sanctuary. The lyrics for Jekalyn Carr's *Bigger* were up on the big screen. The lyrics spoke directly to my soul. Could it be the Spirit within me is working already? Without even trying, my eyes closed, and my body relaxed. Even at my lowest point, Jesus washed away my iniquity and cleansed me through and through. I thanked Jesus for His healing touch, then I was tapped on my shoulder.

She asked, "Ma'am, are you ready to go now?"

I asked, "Huh?"

"My name is Ms. Mabel. I saw your car rolling down the street after the tow truck guy repossessed it. Do you need a ride home?"

I shook my head no.

"Where do you live little girl?" She asked me, firmly like a mother.

I lowered my eyes and shook my head before whispering, "I don't have anywhere to go."

"You don't have a home either?" Ms. Mabel asked. Her brow frowned in confusion.

I didn't want these people to know all of my business, but she had such trusting eyes, "No, I don't have a place to stay. I was living in my car."

"Oh, I am so sorry, uh, what's your name, little girl?"

"Trinity, Trinity Boussiant. You can call me Trinni if you like."

"Okay, Trinity. So, are you coming with me or not?" She turned and walked away. Her wide body moved from side-to-side like a teeter totter.

I shrugged. I didn't know where I was going, but if it had a roof and four walls, I was in like Flynn.

I got up as if slowly still mesmerized by the service I just experienced.

Ms. Mabel said, "Good, I know you need to get a hot shower and get out of those dirty clothes. And I figure you are due for a good hot meal too. You can get that where we are going."

She started to grow on me. Let her say I had a comfortable bed to lay my weary head down and I was moving in! Lock stock and barrel.

"Yes, Ma'am, I do need a bath and some tasty food to eat. I had fast food early last night, but I haven't eaten since then."

"Good, then we have just what you need. Now give me a minute while I round up the other girls. I believe they all walked outside. Meet me at the green van outside in the parking lot."

Wait? What? I am ready to go now. Still, on my last hope, I put on my patient smile then thought, My God, is awesome! He will provide all my needs…*it's happening already*?!

I practically ran out to the green van. My jog slowed when I spotted the lettering on the side of the van. Redeeming Hope was written in blue Old English lettering. I didn't know what Redeeming

Hope was, but I wanted some hot food and a hotter shower, quick. When all the women were rounded up outside the van, I looked from one face to the other. These women were from all ethnicities, shapes, and sizes. What is Redeeming Hope, United Nations, or something? Ms. Mabel motioned for me to sit up front with her. A couple of girls sighed and rolled their eyes at me. See, this is why I don't get along with women, besides Jnana, too well. Most women are perpetual haters and consummately catty. I wasn't feeling this arrangement anymore. But then my tummy rumbled, so I obediently got into the front seat. One of the haters kicked the back of my seat when she sat down behind me. Ole heffa! I genuinely changed from seeing my Momma and Jesus but dealing with hating women brought me too much drama to change that part of me, just yet. Don't judge me. I'm a work in progression!

We put on our seat belts and hit the road. Almost immediately, one of the nosy women began twenty questions.

"So, who you? Miss repossessed BMW, what's your story?"

I ignored her. English…please, darn it!

Then Ms. Mabel asked me politely, "What's going on with you Trinity? Tell me why you ended up homeless in front of our church this morning."

I shrugged my shoulders, then she gave me that serious Mom look. No matter how old I got, that look always set a fear into my bones.

"Well, my condo got locked on me and then I lost my job. You all saw my car get repossessed, which is where I lived when I was homeless, so here I am.

256 | P a g e

By the way, where am I going?"

Ms. Mabel said, "Redeeming Hope is a women's homeless shelter, Trinity. Have you ever lived in a shelter before?"

Before I realized it, I yelled, "No! I would never let myself get into this mess twice."

All the women in the back grumbled. Sheesh, haters are gonna hate!

Then the improper English speaker spoke again, "You know for someone that's homeless, carless, brainless and jobless you appear to be an awfully snotty woman. Do you think we chose to be in a homeless shelter, on purpose? Huh?!"

Wow, she can speak proper English. I cannot stand when people think they are bilingual because they speak Ebonics and English! Choose one and stick with it. Now she was giving me attitude. This is getting to be way too much drama. "Well, I guess not," I said, "But then again, some of you may like having the state take care of you. I'm not that weak, I am just hitting a rough spot in my life right now. I'm going to be back on my feet in a week or two, tops."

The women in the back, and surprisingly Ms. Mabel, said in unison, "Uh huh."

I wasn't sure about anything I was saying but it sounded good. I will not let these miserable homeless women knock me off my hustle. I will never mess around with another married man, but I had to do something before I spent too much time with these women. No, I was not like them. I was just having a rough time. I guess I was the only one in the van who thought my being there was a

257 | P a g e

temporary situation. I was determined to prove it to them. Game on! We were only riding in the van ten minutes before we pulled up to a big house. I looked around for the shelter because this huge house couldn't be a homeless shelter.

I asked Ms. Mabel, "Uh, is this the shelter? Cause all I see is a mansion."

Ms. Mabel giggled, "Yeah, I guess someone like you would think this was a mansion. It used to be, in fact, but it was donated years ago, and we use it as a shelter now."

I was astounded. Hmm…a mansion. Maybe this shelter thing wouldn't be too bad.

"I am going to live in a mansion!" I said aloud and smiled in elation. I undid my seatbelt then got out of the van. Suddenly, I felt right at home.

Miss improper English speaker, who I learned was named Tremica, bumped me and spat "Uppity ole high yella hussy, you sure are dumb as a rock!" before walking away.

I just smiled. I couldn't wait for the servants to bring me a hot meal and run my bath water.

Maybe being homeless wasn't going to be so bad!

~19~
You Know How You Get

But practicing the truth in love, we will in all things
grow up into Christ, who is the head. From him, the
whole body grows, fitted, and held together through
every supporting ligament. As each one does its
part, the body grows in love.
Ephesians 4:15-16 (NET)
***

Jnana

I fell asleep in Ashton's bed. I needed to feel
close to my son who was quickly growing into a
man. He was still my little boy, no matter how old
he got or how badly he thought he wanted to have
sex. I won't stand by and allow this kind of thing to
happen right under my nose and right in my house.
My son was not ready for sex, and I was not ready
to accept he is either. Tonight, all this mess will
come to a screeching halt!
I got out of bed and continued with my house
chores. I put the condom on the dinner table for
Ashton to remind my husband of his handiwork. I
also put the D graded paper on the table for Liana.
Today was judgment day in my house and I was
ready to be judge, jury and punishment executioner!
After I was done my chores, I worked on my
bookstore website. I had been open for five years
and it was time to bring my products to the mass
market. I was ready to expand my horizons
technologically too. I previously hired a website
builder, but I was dissatisfied with their vision. I

wanted my own vision to serenade my customers not someone else's idea of what my business brand should be. Although my main customer base was African Americans, I wanted my brand to be all inclusive. I was learning other ethnicities enjoy reading African American literature. Reading about other cultures was always a clever idea, in my opinion, so I carried different ethnic cultural literature.

I formatted my website with an easy-to-follow website building software I saw on a television commercial touting thousands of website templates and excellent customer service. I created a warm palate with several different shades of blue, yellow, and green. I wanted the visitors to my website to feel serene and open to spending a lot of time there. I uploaded a waterfall nature sound file as the background music for my website. I picked out an easy-to-read font that was both functional and classy. I added navigation buttons that went to the history of African American literature, excerpts from novels, and I included some of my favorite poems. Small business consignment items were included under the local tab. I picked out several of my customers' local favorites for the author spotlight. I took a survey of their favorite current local authors and asked them to nominate some up and coming authors. Through their nominations, I was truly educated about many authors I hadn't known about. The up and coming author and the author with the most votes were the author spotlight and their books were offered with a twenty-five percent discount. With each of the books purchased with this special, I was giving away a Namaste book bag and handmade book tag. Finally, I uploaded a recent picture of myself and the address, phone number, and private email for online orders for my store. After fixing a few random formatting issues, I put my website online. I was so excited when I closed out my internet browser then went back online and found my website active. I was seriously impressed with my handy work. All the navigation buttons worked, and all pull-down order windows were active. I still had some work to do on it but for now, I was done with my website. I sat and admired my site and smiled. I was really living my dream life with my small business.

I checked the time on my laptop, it read twelve fifteen. My two teenagers would be walking through the door in a few hours. My husband would not be far behind them at four. Tonight, was to be a day of reckoning for all three of them. Liana was going to get put in her place because she had really been running off at the mouth trying to act like the woman of the house. I needed to remind her there is only one queen in this house and the throne had my fat booty on it. Shandon was in hot water for a variety of issues, many of which we would talk about behind closed doors. Ashton was in hot water for the condom issue, but he also needed to convince me he knows what a clean room looks like. I just hope they could all deal with *how I get*! That really burned me up. How I get was what Shandon told me to humble me. Funny, all it did was to irritate me and set me on a tirade to set them all straight. I was the head of this household and yet it seemed as if my family needed a reminder. I guess my real talk was too much for my family too. Just when I was feeling comfortable in my own skin, my family made me feel as if I was less than. I was hurt but, I would get all this cleared up tonight and no one as leaving the dinner table until I felt better.

Shandon must have had second thoughts about our earlier conversation because he texted me four times since then. I ignored them all. Shandon could be a trip sometimes, even after all these years together. Though I loved him immensely, sometimes he got on my last nerve. I never knew he felt that way about educating our son and daughter differently when it came to sex. Then again, we really didn't talk about it before. I guess I just assumed he would tell me before he considered doing something as drastic as buying condoms for our sixteen-year-old son.

I realized how upset I was when I passed a mirror. My frown lines were in full effect and my eyes were blood shot from the stress. I needed to calm down, so I put in a mix CD Shandon made for me. Kem's music always calmed me. I sang *Heaven* and really got into it. Before I knew it, I was reminiscing about being back in my old high school days of performing in the talent show belting out old Aretha Franklin ballads. I played Kem's new CD, Promise to Love, and it reminded me of how much I truly loved my man. I thought about how blessed Shandon and I are to have such a responsible son. Even if he didn't come to me, he trusted his father enough to consult him. Even though I knew we were blessed, tonight would still be a day we opened the lines of communicating with our teens. I will do my part to make things better. Even if I must stand my ground against my husband.

I popped some popcorn and went downstairs into the movie room in the basement to spend my last couple of hours alone watching Tyler Perry's "Good Deeds." Tyler was a perfect example of someone starting small with big dreams and he now has national recognition as a consistent and inspirational force of nature. I could have bought the bootleg, but I wouldn't do that to Tyler, I support a dreamer. This movie impressed me on many various levels, Tyler's best yet. I pray everyone takes the lead to follow their dreams and to stay true to themselves, no matter what adversity stands before them. Faith means believing God's word even in the absence of things prayed for. Trusting God to reveal manifestation of His word builds patience and resilience. Faith…now that's what living a dream life is.

I watched the movie, but I must have dozed off afterward because I was awakened by Ashton kissing me on the cheek. He was still my little boy no matter how old he got. Our relationship was fundamentally a good one. I held in the pain of my disillusionment with my son. He smiled and I saw so much of Shandon in him. No wonder he felt a connection with his father. He was growing up to be just as handsome as his father. I sat up and patted the seat next to me. I needed to talk to my son alone. I wanted, with such tenderness, to convey my

263 | P a g e

heart desire for his life. Before I even opened my mouth, Ashton spoke.

"Mom, before you say anything, I saw the condom on the dinner table. I know you're hurt I didn't talk to you instead of Dad. But, well, you can be very direct sometimes. I didn't want to have a deep conversation about sex. I just wanted to talk to Dad because I know he must have gone through similar things regarding sex when he was my age."

I was taken aback by his maturity. But he must have been warned of this impending conversation by his father because he sounded coached, to the letter. Strike three for Shandon!

"Ashton, I understand, I really do. But I thought we were close, and we built a relationship where you were comfortable to talk to me about anything."

"Mom, I am comfortable to talk to you about almost everything. But this is *sex*. I know how you feel about teenagers having sex before they are married. So, I went to Dad because I know how open-minded he is. Not having sex until marriage is so old fashioned. I mean, lots of my friends have been having sex for a couple of years. They call me a late bloomer. That's not cool Ma."

"Ashton, I cannot believe you are saying to wait until marriage is ridiculous! Waiting until marriage is what the Bible says we should do. Now, I respect you care what your friends think. However, you shouldn't allow our thoughts to conform to that of the world. I raised you to respect yourself. You have known since infancy I am against teen sex and I think you really should be thinking about other things besides sex. Abstinence really is the way to

264 | P a g e

go for you. You know how I feel about this even though your Father got you condoms, in his misguided attempt to bond with you. What if it breaks or what if you get caught up in the mood and you forget to use a condom? A pregnancy or even worse, a lifelong disease like HIV or herpes, could be in your future. All these repercussions could occur over teen sex. Not to mention you would be sinning in the eyes of God."

"See Mom, listen to you. I didn't come to you because you aren't the best listener. You give me and Lili advice that's thinly veiled as law. If we, me, or Liana, sometimes even Dad, go against what you say, then you get mad at us. We all love you and we don't want to disappoint you, but Ma sometimes you make things so hard to deal with."

"Wow" Was all I could say. I feel like I got kicked in my gut.

"Ma, did you wait until you married Dad to have sex for the first time?"

"Ashton, what kind of question is that? How dare you ask me about my first time!"

"Ma, I really don't mean to be disrespectful. But you are worried about my first time and telling me I will be sinning. Aren't you being a hypocrite? Dad told me about his first time, and it wasn't when you and he got married."

Tears streamed down my face. Where was this all coming from? Ashton was usually the respectful, quiet one. He has never come at me like this before. I don't know what to say. First Trinity, now my son is telling me I am overbearing. I never viewed myself this way, but maybe how I see myself bore some re-evaluation. I thought I was ready to talk with my family, but I was knocked off my high horse. I had to regroup and pull myself together. I was the queen of this kingdom, but it seemed as if my children, with the guidance of my husband, were planning a sneak attack to overthrow me.

I dried my tears and turned my face from his, "Ashton, please go upstairs and get your room cleaned. When your sister and father get home, we will have dinner and finish this conversation later. I love you, my son."

He got up and hugged me tightly before kissing my cheek, "I love you too. Ma, please...don't cry." He said as he wiped falling tears from my face. He hugged me again and went upstairs.

After Ashton left, I was still reeling from our conversation. It seemed as if I alienated my son so much, he felt as if I would be judgmental about his wanting to have sex. I must admit he is correct. I felt at sixteen, he had his entire life ahead of him. The weird thing was too many teens had it in their heads sex was the way to seal the deal on their young love. It didn't work for grown folks so how in the heck could it work for young people still trying to find out who they are? Celeste was a nice girl, but I didn't believe she was going to be Ashton's wife one day. Nor did I want her to be the mother of my grandchild. She and Ashton had a lot of growing up to do. Bottom line was I wanted what's best for both, but I was unwaveringly against them having sex.

To answer Ashton's question, no, I didn't

wait until marriage for my first time. In a way, I wish I had. I remember my first-time having sex and though it hurt, a lot after the pain subsided, and I still wanted to get more of it. I remember I developed an unhealthy obsession to get more and more of it. I was amazed at the things I could do with my body and I was in awe of the power I wielded over boys. I got so caught up in sex it seemed to overtake my mind. The feeling, over time, robbed me of my common sense. I still had cravings night and day. The more I did it, the better it felt, and I learned other boys knew different tricks and positions; then I got hooked even more. I will not say I was a fast-tail young girl. Well…let's just say I was just a curious one. I always overthought things, but when it came to sex, I was the master of reading more and more about it. Back then, I was always up for some research. Just when I thought I felt the best, another part of my body would expose even more pleasure to experience. It was also a trip to see the look on boy's faces when I showed them a trick or two. Priceless.

With all my experimentation with sex, I was always careful not to get pregnant or to give the boy the key to my sexual health. I always had condoms and birth control. I insisted they protect my health first. The thing I didn't realize was while I was having sex, giving my all to boys that didn't really mean a thing to me, I never experienced a powerful orgasm. Not an earth shattering, toes curling one any ways. Then I met Shandon. I was so wrapped up in him emotionally sex was an extension of our relationship. He was the first boy to capture my

267 | P a g e

heart and soul way before he was blessed with a taste of my body. As we got to know each other, I realized he was just as sexually experienced as me. Over time, he taught me many tricks and I did the same for him. When I was introduced to the greatest sexual experience in life, love making. Sex was great, but the spirit touching, soul opening intimacy of love making was amazing. When there was emotion involved in love making and a spiritual connection exists, it took the experience to a deeper level. I learned a lot of sexual things while experimenting in my youth, but through love, I found a beautiful sensuality. In that sensuality, I found the intimacy that set my world on fire. That intimacy allowed for peace with each other outside of the bedroom. Even when Shandon and I weren't being sexual, intimacy allowed us to connect in many ways well beyond the joys of our bodies touching.

I wanted Ashton to wait to experience the intimacy that comes with love making. I didn't want him to settle for the hollow feeling of two bodies simply doing as nature equipped them. Right now, he thinks he is in love, but he doesn't realize as his body matures, so too does his mind. Love will be a completely different feeling to him at twenty, as opposed to what he feels right now at sixteen. It will mean much more if the love is within a committed, mature relationship. I didn't want to keep Ashton from having a girlfriend. I wanted to impart in him, the female perspective, my hard-learned lessons. He needs to wait! He is worth it and so is Celeste. I must convince him of all of this. I must get my husband to unite in this thinking so we could talk Ashton into abstaining from sex for a while longer. A united force is always a stronger force.

I breathed a sigh of relief. I was so glad my daughter was too young to go through this sex stuff. She hasn't even gotten her period yet. God is good for sparing me that conversation.

~20~
Reality Check

Then Jesus went to work on his disciples. "Anyone
who intends to come with me has to let me lead.
You're not in the driver's seat; I am. Don't run
from suffering; embrace it. Follow me and I'll show
you how. Self-help is no help at all. Self-sacrifice is
the way, my way, to finding yourself, your true self.
What kind of deal is it to get everything you want
but lose yourself? What could you ever trade your
soul for?
Matthew 16:24-26
***

Trinity

I walked into the mansion with my half-
filled thirty-gallon trash bag. I could smell the air
change from the crisp clean air outside to clogged
air. There was a mixture of food, perfumes, and
baby powder scents floating through the molecules
in the air. My nostrils were overwhelmed! It wasn't
that the shelter air stunk; it was just so many people
sharing it. I looked up at the ceilings which were
ten feet high with solar panels. The room in front of
me was huge and it appeared to be filled with lots
of women and their children. The women were all
shapes, shades, and ethnic backgrounds, just like
the women on the van. The children were in
strollers, toddling around, and running around
wildly. The room was full of toys and was noisy. I
scanned the room for the servants, but I found none.
I walked deeper into the house and looked in the

kitchen. It was huge. There were five women in it cooking. It smelled so good my tummy hummed a song of thanks. I was so ready to eat anything that smelled good. One of them made eye contact and spoke to me.

"Hey you, new girl. Go wash your hands and come help us. Today is Sunday, tonight we must make a big family style meal for twenty-five people. We need all the free hands we can get."

I was stunned. These women appeared to be the servants and they wanted me to help them cook. As if! It isn't my job to cook and serve, it was theirs. I rolled my eyes and kept walking. I heard her suck her teeth and sigh loudly for my benefit.

Whatever. Do your own job and make it quick. I'm hungry and I need a cold glass of lemonade, three cubes of ice, please.

I ventured further into the house. I saw lots of rooms with closed and locked doors. When I came to what appeared to be an office with an opened door. There sat Ms. Mabel with her beautiful energy.

She motioned for me to enter the room." Come on in, Trinity. I need to do your intake. We don't usually do an intake on the weekends but since this is an emergency, I've decided to make an exception for you."

I put down my belongings and sat in the chair next to her desk. I didn't know what to say, so I shrugged my shoulders and robotically replied, "Thanks."

She was sweet, but I didn't know why she was bothering me with normal intake protocol. This

271 | P a g e

was a temporary blip in my life plan. This would give me time to refocus and think of a way to dig myself out of this mess. Once I found another place to be, I would be out of there!

A few women walked by the office and peeped in. I heard a couple whispering about my appearance and how I could be such a hot mess yet still have such a funky elitist attitude. More haters. I brushed *both* of my shoulders off. Living here with all these catty women would be a challenge, for real.

I refocused my attention to the patiently awaiting eyes of Ms. Mabel then the woman from the kitchen came into the office.

"Ms. Mabel, I asked this woman to help us cook dinner and she just rolled her eyes and kept walking. Is she going to be staying? If she is, we need her either in the kitchen or helping to babysit the kids. You know how crazy it gets in here on Sunday."

I rolled my eyes again and sighed. This servant was coming out of pocket. I hoped Ms. Mabel fired her behind. That is…after she got done cooking. Ms. Mabel needed to check her because that servant was really stepping out of line.

Ms. Mabel was rustling through some papers but paused briefly to respond, "Bonnie, yes she is staying. However, I didn't do intake yet. Can you please give me a moment to get her papers signed and show her around before you start bombarding her with shelter responsibilities?"

"Okay, uh sure Ms. Mabel. I just don't want her to get in her head she is above cooking and babysitting duties. I heard about her thinking she is better than the rest of us *homeless* women. As if she isn't homeless and carless too!"

I sighed loudly. This heifer was talking about me like I was not sitting there. That time of year, I might have been light but dang, I was not invisible. How disrespectful!

"Bonnie, I will tell her about her duties as a resident here. Thank you for your concern, but, again, could you give me some time to do intake? Without waiting for a reply, Ms. Mabel ordered, "Thanks, now please shut the door behind you."

I smiled. Ms. Mabel handles hers…well!

Bonnie was the one to roll her eyes this time. "Yes Ma'am." She stomped out the room and shut the door.

"Trinity, as you heard, her name is Bonnie. She is the second person in charge here. She has control issues, but she's a good person. Now, let's begin your intake. First, I have some personal questions to ask you. Please feel free to be candid. Your answers will help me to better assess how we may help you during your stay here, no matter how temporary. Are we clear?"

I didn't know what to say. I didn't expect my stay to be very long before I got myself on my feet, but I played along, for now. "Okay."

"Now, what is your full name?"

"Trinity Marie Boussiant."

"Tell me why you are homeless Trinity and how long you think that you will be here."

I hesitated. Ms. Mabel was a church going woman. I didn't want her to think I was a jezebel for messing with other women's men.

273 | P a g e

"Trinity, look, I have heard it all. So, be frank with me. I will not think any less of you. However, if you lie to me, you will only hurt yourself. I am big on trust so please don't lie to me. Redeeming Hope is your opportunity to begin anew. Here you can be yourself and become the woman that God created you to be. You can now let go of the false image of yourself you created to survive in this world. I want to get to know the real you."

I was touched. Sheesh, maybe she could handle the truth.

"Well, I was having an affair with a married man and his wife found out about us and locked up the condo he told me he purchased for me and had my brand-new car repossessed," I said without taking a breath.

She was right. Ms. Mabel didn't flinch at my honesty about my lifestyle, "So, those material things were financed by him or his wife?"

"Well, I thought they were a reward from the husband for…uh…services rendered. Come to find out, it was his wife's money."

"Trinity, I don't mean to pry but are you a…working girl…a prostitute?"

Why does everyone keep asking me that?!

I was astonished she would even suggest such a thing to me. I sat up straight in my chair and swelled with pride, "No, why would you ask me such a thing?! I was just a woman getting paid for what most women give up for free. My time and body are valuable, why shouldn't they be well paid for? I'm worth all the money and things I accumulated."

Okay, I lied. But I couldn't tell Ms. Mabel I didn't think I was worthy of love, so I settled for material things to represent my worth. Still, I feigned acceptance to distract Ms. Mabel from my private truth about my lifestyle.

Ms. Mabel seemed unimpressed with my bravado. "Trinity, I believe my question is valid. You stated you are worthy of having your body and time paid for, but don't you see that self-worth is beyond the temporary pleasure you provide a man with your body? Don't you see no matter how much a man paid you for your time and your services rendered, as you put it, you were still selling your true self short? Matthew 16:26 says, *what good is a man to gain the entire world but lose himself? What will a man receive for his soul?* Tell me, how much does your soul cost Trinity?"

Whoa, she was really coming at me. What did I do to her?! "Huh? What does that mean?" I asked with unapologetic defensiveness.

She didn't seem fazed by my confrontational tone. Instead, she looked deeply into my eyes and spoke softly, "Look at you: you are a beautiful young lady with so much to offer. Even with your car and other valuables being taken from you, you are still standing in the light of God's glory. I saw you at church, you received Jesus as your personal Savior today and I could see you were instantly changed. Whatever you did before this morning, rest assured you are worthy of being exalted for your spirit, your mind, and your heart. You are more than the sexual nature of your body. When you give your body for the money you cheapen yourself. You also cheapen the emotional connection that should be a part of an intimate relationship. Do you understand?"

I sat in silence. In all the years I had been having sex, even as I opened my legs for countless men, I never had an emotional connection with anyone. If I closed my eyes and wished upon an orgasm it made me feel as if there was emotion. But when I looked into the man's eyes, all I saw was lust. I never saw pure emotion. They never really liked to kiss me. Many of them said it was too personal. They could do the most sexual things to me and taste my everybody part but kissing me was too personal, I never understood that until now. Ms. Mabel was really kicking some knowledge! The men wanted pleasure. Intimacy was not an option they wanted to share with me. *That* was too personal!

"Yes, I understand that now." As simplistic as it all sounded. Her words were sending a tidal wave of emotion into my soul. Why am I just hearing this information? Now I know the truth, what do I do with it?

"Good, I want you to know for the next relationship you get into. I want you to act worthy of being treated right. Simply because you are worthy of being loved and simply for whom you are. You are a beautiful flower and one day your scent will be emotionally intoxicating to the right man. You are worthy to be loved for all the beauty you hold, inside and out. Respect and unconditional love are the goal. A spiritual connection with a good man is paramount. A faithful man of integrity that will pray for and with you, who won't raise a hurtful hand to you. That is the kind of man for you. I challenge you to make today the first day in your love affair with yourself. To really grow, you must love who you are. To receive love, first, you need to find out who you are, that includes the African American side and the Caucasian side of you. Trinity, we can continue to talk about this later. For now, let me finish your intake and then I will show you around."

Ms. Mabel was really reading me. I never told her I had issues with my mixed race, or I didn't feel acceptance from my Caucasian side because my father abandoned my African American mother when I was a baby. I barely remember him or anyone on his side of the family.

"Okay," I said in response to Ms. Mabel being ready to end intake and show me around the shelter. She gave me more than enough to think about. A second longer and I would be in sensory overload.

I looked closely at Ms. Mabel. She had a caramel complexion with mahogany brown eyes, and many freckles all over her face. Her black hair was in a French roll with a bang across her forehead; she was thick like me. She was truly a beautiful black woman. She was loving yet stern like a mother. But what really got me was, though she was obviously a church going woman, she seemed to have street smarts. Not only knowledge gained from reading, but she looked like she spent some time in street life. From now on, I would watch Ms. Mabel. It seemed she wasn't as prim and proper as I previously thought. Even after knowing her for such a brief time, she grew on me. She believed I was worthy. Maybe it was about time I took a closer look at myself to see why I didn't see what she saw in me. Why was I worthy?

"So, Trinity, tell me a little about yourself. What do you enjoy doing? Who are you when you let down your guard and let someone see who you really are?"

I don't know what to say. Those are some heavy questions. What do I enjoy doing? Shopping. Who is the real me? I have no idea. But I knew when I looked into Ms. Mabel's eyes, she was anxiously awaiting my succinct answers.

"Well, I love to shop but I can't do that anymore because I don't have any money. Who is the real me? Well, I am Trinity Marie Boussiant and I just turned thirty-nine earlier this year. I used to be a Department Manager at an upscale department store. I have three years of college for art and design. I love to paint but I never really gave it much time. But I love to paint pictures of things in my head and make them come to life with my paint brush."

"Trinity, the person you just described is a beautiful reflection of God's love. I am impressed you are already showing some self-awareness. We mustn't waste our spiritual gifts."

I smiled, "Thank you, Ms. Mabel."

"Trinity, did you notice when you described yourself, not once did you mention anything about your sexual nature?"

I am stunned, I ran back what I said in my head and she was right. "Yes, I noticed that. I guess I am more than my body and how I use it to satisfy men. Imagine that."

"Yes Trinity, imagine that. Do you know why you are worthy?"

I tried to think of why someone like me, a sinner, would be worthy, but I found nothing. "Well, honestly, no, I don't. I have sinned with so many men and I just feel like Jesus is ashamed of me. That is until the beautiful moment at the pulpit at church today. God does love me, and He still sees beauty in me. Hold up…"

Ms. Mabel smiled. "That's a start. You are worthy because God says you are. Period. God loves you, completely and He accepts you have sinned. The blood of Jesus assured if you repent of your sins, you will be forgiven, and you are cleansed anew. When you gave your life over to God, you became a new person. A better version of yourself. Now, do you understand?"

Oh my, my heart skipped a beat. "Yes, I am worthy, *by faith*."

"That's it, Trinity! You got it. Now, from this moment on, walk in that faith. Don't question it. It just is. Just as the air we breathe, never asking where it comes from, so is the assurance of your worthiness. God loves you so much He wants to take care of you. He wants you to feel His love deep in your soul. Yes, take it all in. Now, there are some rules around here I need to tell you about. After we review them, I will need your signature at the bottom of the paper if you agree to them. By the way, agreeing to the house rules are a requirement for living here. So, let's see, number one: No violence, abusive language, and no gossiping.

Number two: No outside visitors, especially men. We have families here that are working through some sensitive personal issues that need to be dealt with in an unobtrusive, supportive, and compassionate environment. Number three: confidentiality. Each family living here is here for their own private situations. We must never take anyone's business out of these four walls. If there is ever a question about whether something is a confidential issue, simply ask yourself if you would want your business repeated. If the answer is no, don't repeat other people's business. Number four: You must volunteer at least ten hours a week at a social service facility you will be assigned to. If you get fired from there, you must leave here. Number five: You must cook, clean, and baby sit at least two days out of the week, for four hours each day in a group of other women you will be assigned to. Number Six and final requirement: You must keep your room cleaned. You must also make every effort to get along with your roommate. Your room assignment will be with Tremica. You already had a conversation with her on the van coming here. Her daughter comes to live here with her from time-to-time. Now are there any questions or are you ready to sign the paper agreeing to these terms?"

"Uh, Ms. Mabel, I do have a few concerns. Well, I can't cook, I don't have any experience being around children, I never have and don't know how to volunteer my time, and I don't get along with women, besides my best friend Jnana, at all. I do know how to clean though."

She smiled at me then patted my hand, "Well,

Trinity, Redeeming Hope is the perfect place to learn to do all of those things. Don't you think? We are loving and supportive of each other. So, are you willing to agree to these terms?"

I hesitated then shook my head. I was homeless and I was thinking of not signing this paper? I may be homeless, but I am not stupid. Snap out of it Trinity!

"Yes, Ms. Mabel I will sign the paper."

I signed the paper and wondered whether I was signing it in blood. I was too old to learn to do any of those things. Besides, my life was going good enough without adding new burdens to my existence. Right?

Ms. Mabel leafed through a big white binder wetting her finger when it got difficult to turn the pages. She continued to turn the pages until she came to one with a yellow tabbed space marker. She read some of the pages then turned her eyes back to me.

"Trinity, like I told you earlier, you are required to volunteer your time at a social service agency. Now, there is a nursing facility named Gentle Care which is in desperate need of volunteers. They have a patient named Paul Hanks that needs a volunteer to come read to him two days a week. From what you told me about yourself, I think this assignment would be perfect for you."

"Ms. Mabel, why does he need me to read to him? What's wrong that he can't do it himself?"

"Well, it says here he is legally blind, has been for at least thirty-eight years. He wasn't born blind, but a medical condition caused him to go blind. He doesn't have any family they know of, so the staff at Gentle Care figured if he had someone to interact with, he would come out of his shell. He hasn't talked much in years, although he still could speak. With no known family coming to see him, he has become a recluse. So, are you interested?"

Paul Hanks is an old, blind man that has stopped talking and has no family to visit him, how sad. I was touched by his story. But I was unsure how I could add any good to his life. I knew how to read, but they needed someone to really make a difference in this man's life. I didn't have anything in me that was good enough for that.

I looked up from my fiddling fingers to find Ms. Mabel's eyes staring right at me.

"Trinity, I wish you wouldn't doubt yourself so much. Yes, you have greatness in you. From what I see sitting in front of me, lots of it. You are worthy of giving your time to Mr. Hanks. I know it and it's time you find out on your own. Sometimes we must share our breath with those whose breath has become shallow. As I said, this would be a great assignment for you. You seem to believe your worth is a direct result of your sexual nature. There is nothing sexual in reading to someone. Volunteering time with someone else does remarkable things for your self-esteem, trust me. Are you willing to do something that's unfamiliar? Trinity, are you ready to step out on faith? Are you selfless enough to share your breath?"

I knew Ms. Mabel was challenging my character and just like I was her child, I didn't want to disappoint those loving eyes she smiled on me.

"Sure, Ms. Mabel, I would be honored to take this assignment."

She smiled so beautifully, and I knew she was proud of my decision, "Good Trinity, now sign this paper so I can show you around. Then we can go help in the kitchen. The women are really cooking up a storm tonight, let's hurry them along. I am famished."

I agreed wholeheartedly. I didn't know what Bonnie and the ladies were cooking but at any rate, I would sign anything if it would get me to the dinner table faster. On the way to the kitchen, Ms. Mabel showed me to my room. It was a small room with a desk, chair, two closets, a small concave television and two twin beds. I was disappointed. I figured since it was a mansion, I was going to have my own huge stately room. When I looked around, I saw I had another issue. The hater from the van was sitting on one of the beds. Oh great, I could not get away from that hating heifer!

"Trinity, this is your roommate Tremica. You met her on the van earlier. You two didn't get along too well then but I know going forward, things will be better. Correct?"

Ms. Mabel gave both of us the motherly tone and direct stern eye contact. We both begrudgingly agreed but slyly rolled our eyes at each other. Ms. Mabel smiled, then left the room. "Now, put your stuff down on the bed Trinity so I can introduce you to the rest of the house."

I didn't want to leave my bag on the bed. I didn't know that hating heifer. She might steal the last of my belongings.

Ms. Mabel turned back to me, "Put the bag down Trinity and come on!"

I did what I was told and followed her out of the room. Tremica better not steal a thing or it's on! We walked around the house towards the kitchen. Along the way, I met all twelve of the women living in the house, including the ten children. No wonder this is a mansion. A normal house couldn't fit all these people in it.

Arriving at the kitchen, Bonnie went to bossing me around after Ms. Mabel left to take a phone call. I was quickly thrown into my first cooking lesson which was to keep stirring the cheese sauce for the macaroni and cheese. I didn't stir as much as I should have, so some of the cheese and milk stuck to the bottom of the pot and burned. When Bonnie came to check on how the sauce was coming out, she was livid. She looked at me and rolled her eyes. She didn't blink like a regular person; her eyes only rolled? Angry heifer!

After dinner was done cooking, we all sat down at a huge dinner table. Ms. Mabel sat at the helm and said a prayer of thanks. Then we all, all twenty-six of us, ate an amazingly blessed meal. Bonnie was a hateful, eye roller, but under her supervision the southern fried chicken, collard greens, black eyed peas, baked macaroni, and cheese (with a sauce she had to remake), homemade yeast rolls, and sweet potato pie were delicious. It reminded me of the times when Momma used to cook for me. Besides the drama, cooking turned out to be fun.

Dinner was family style, so we passed the

bowls of food around to each other; I enjoyed myself. I ate everything on my plate. For the first time in my adult life, I didn't care about counting calories and gaining a pound. It felt lovely!

The shelter didn't allow me to have my own stately room without a hating roommate. Nor did it have servants to serve me lemonade. But it was home, for now. In the coming week, I was looking forward to meeting my volunteer client, Mr. Hanks. Now I had so much time on my hands, I could get back to my painting. I missed it a lot. Looking around the table at the women and children laughing and enjoying their meal, an old lost friend, solace, returned. I sure hoped she unpacked and stayed a while.

~21~
Facts of Life

Therefore, I exhort you, brothers, and sisters, by the mercies of God, to present your bodies as a sacrifice—alive, holy, and pleasing to God—which is your reasonable service.
Romans 12:1
***

Jnana

To rid my body of some nervous tension, I set the dinner table for my family. They were already sitting around me, guilty parties 1, 2, and 3. You could cut the nervous tension in the house with a dull butter knife. Still, I was determined to maintain my war path stance. Their little doe eyes couldn't even break my level of irritation. I was right and they were all wrong. Someone's head had to roll and if it had to be all three of them, well that's penance for their slipshod behaviors. I poked out my chest and was ready to be the worse person they knew. As I brought out the food from the kitchen, I made a big mistake when I looked into the sorrow filled eyes of the three most important people in my life. When I did this, I choked. They were all looking so pitiful. Nope, I must keep focused! I must set the tone. I lead, they follow. I run this family!

I went back into the kitchen to get the drinks. I returned to the table with the container of hot apple cider. I sat down at the table with my family and we passed the platters of food around the table. Each one was polite to the other. They even mustered a forced smile. When all plates were fixed, we bowed our heads in prayer.

"Dear Lord," I started, "Please bless this food and bless the people sitting around me. Jehovah Jireh, you are our provider, the reason for this bountiful offering and we all come in thanks to you. We all ask for your mercy tonight. Please give us the strength, to be honest with each other tonight and give us the courage to be open minded even if we don't hear what we think we need to. In Jesus name, we pray Father, Amen." Everyone said Amen and ate in uncomfortable silence.

My family seemed to enjoy their meal. A little too much. The silence was deafening. All I heard were forks hitting the plate and chewing. I was glad they were hungry because all I could do was move my food around on my plate. Stress made me lose my appetite. Disappointment made me ill. I willed my eyes off my plate and they were met with Shandon's eyes. He smiled wide then winked at me. My Baby get on my nerves sometimes, but I loved that chocolate man. I mouthed for him to say something to break the ice. He shook his head and looked down at his food. Dang, even my Baby was throwing me to the wolves. I finally put on my big girl panties then launched my solo mission of mass ignorance destruction, "So Liana, how was your day?"

She looked from Ashton to Shandon. My husband nodded then she answered, "Fine Mom. How was your day off?"

I looked at Shandon. Maybe he would give me the

cue to speak too, I thought sarcastically.

But my husband didn't make eye contact this time, "My day was fine Lili. So, Ashton, how was your day?"

"Ma, my day was good, but Mommy can we please stop all the small talk. We all know you are on a tirade so can we just get it over with? The suspense is killing me."

Shocked, I looked at Shandon again, this time he looked at me and smiled. Why is he grinning like a Cheshire cat!?

Liana said, "Ma, I agree with Ashton, can we get this over with? I saw you found my D grade paper."

"Yes, Liana, I did find the paper in your room. Would you like to explain the grade?" She wanted the flame first, alright, let it burn!

"Well, Mom, I'm not going to lie, I forgot about the test and I didn't study for it."

I was shut down…completely. I expected her to lie, then I could jump all over her case. But she told to truth. What is my next move? I was left without a plan b. Sheesh.

"So, are you going to be prepared for the next test Liana?"

"Yes, Ma. In fact, we had a pop quiz today and since we graded them as a class, I already have mine back. I earned an A. A lot of us failed the test, so the teacher told us he would drop the lowest test grade at the end of the marking period. So far, that D is the lowest grade."

"That's good Lili. Just make sure this is the only low grade and you will be fine. "

"Okay, Mom. Well, the paper is in my book bag.

Do you want me to go get it?"

I looked at Shandon, he smiled at her with pride. He must have forewarned Liana of my mood too. What was I going to do with my husband?

"No honey. That's fine. I'll look at it in the morning before I sign it."

"Okay, Ma. I'm done eating, may I be excused? I have homework to do."

I was done with her anyway. "Sure, you may be excused. Make sure that you rinse your plate and cup off and put them in the dishwasher."

"Yes, Mom."

Only my two men were left at the table. Now, we could really get down to business. I looked at Shandon, he was smiling at me. He gave me the thumbs up and I was relieved. I hoped the thumbs up meant he had my back. With Ashton, I really do need his support.

"Ashton, would you like to tell your Mom what we talked about earlier or would you like me to tell her?"

Ashton lowered his head in shame. I was afraid of what he had to say since we already begun the conversation about sex while we were in the basement.

My son sat up in his chair and poked out his chest. He seemed to morph into a grown man right before my eyes, "I'll tell her Dad."

I hurried him along, "Tell me what?"

"Mom, well, I wanted to tell you I have had sex already."

"What?!" I was flabbergasted. I started up to my feet so I could lay hands on him and shake some

289 | P a g e

sense into him.

Instinctively Shandon got up to hold me down in my seat. I am on the edge of being fit to be tied! My son and that fast behind girl Celeste already had sex? Oh my gosh! This has got to be the twilight zone. How could this be going down right under my nose and I not know this? How? "Ashton, you better continue before I get out of this chair! So, help me God, I am about to blow a fuse." Ashton tried to remain composed, but he was shaken by my uncharacteristic rage. He knew how I got, but this, he didn't expect. "As I said, Ma, I had sex but…hold on… I didn't have actual intercourse."

"What?! Ashton, what does that mean? You had sex but not intercourse? Tell me everything now and not in little bits and pieces." I let loose and yelled, "I mean it because I am quickly losing my patience with you!"

He scratched his head pensively. He thought about hedging and buying time but he looked at the anger on my burrowed forehead and reluctantly continued, "Mom, please promise me you won't tell Mr. Jenkins what I am about to tell you…Please."

He was in a world of trouble and he had the nerve to act chivalrous and try to protect that girl Celeste! What the heck was wrong with my son?

I shook my head violently, "Ashton, Jefferson Roberts, I will promise no such a thing. Now spit it out!"

"Okay, well, Mom and Dad, last week when I was over Mr. Jenkins' house, he and Mrs. Jenkins went to the store. Celeste and I were the only two at the house. We got to kissing and touching and I realized I didn't have my condoms with me. I left them in my jean jacket which I left at school. I told Celeste I didn't have protection. but she didn't care. I tried to stop her as she pulled my pants. Then she went down on me instead of us having actual intercourse."

Shandon and I looked at each other. I was sickened to my stomach, yet my husband had a grin stretched across his face. It was if it was a badge of honor his son had some girl suck on his teenage penis without him having to offer up anything in return. I ignored my husband. I would deal with him another time. If I let out my anger towards him, Ashton would be let off the hook. Nope, it was not going down like that. I shook off my husband's antics…for now!

"So, Ashton, let me get this straight, you were messing around at the Jenkins' house and you were going to have sex but instead Celeste performed oral sex on you? Is that it?"

"Well, she wanted me to do the same to her, but I said no, it looked so nasty."

I didn't know what to think about this. The thought of Celeste sucking on my son made me lightheaded. Where did she learn how to do that? At her age? I sat in silence trying to figure out how to react to all I heard. Shandon saved me when he spoke.

"Son, I think your Mom has a lot to take in at one time. You may clear your plate and go clean your room. We need some time to talk about this. We will talk to you later."

Ashton looked at me and I looked away. I

had never been more disappointed in my child than in that moment. Although he didn't have intercourse with Celeste, he allowed her to sexually fulfill him. I didn't know if I should be more concerned with his selfishness or the idea of him letting her do anything sexual to him at all. I needed help to sort all this information out. Thank God, I had Shandon to help me.

When Ashton remained seated, Shandon spoke sharply, "Ashton, while I applaud you for being honest with us, what you have done was very inappropriate. Not only did you violate the trust we have given you, but you also disrespected the Jenkins' house. I am disappointed in you. When you told me you were ready to have sex with Celeste, I never imagined things would go down like this. I can't put into words how I feel about you allowing her to satisfy your sixteen-year-old needs and you didn't think once about protecting her. I thought we talked about this, at length!"

"Well, yeah we did Dad, but we didn't have intercourse. She only performed oral sex on me. There was no need to protect her or me."

"Son, I wish you were correct, but you aren't. If Celeste went down on you, you were potentially exposed to bodily fluids that could have transmitted a disease. Now I have one question to ask you and I hope you will continue to be honest with us."

"Ask me anything Dad, I am embarrassed enough so I promise I won't start lying now."

"Good, now, is Celeste a virgin too?"

Ashton scratched his head in dismay.

I could see the veins in Shandon's neck

bulging. He is not the most patient person. So, I hurried Ashton's answer along. I was tame compared to Shandon once he got going.

"Ash, you can tell us what's on your mind. We love you and we can't think any worse of you than we do right this moment, so you might as well spit it out." I tried to quell any anger his father built up.

"Mom and Dad, no Celeste is not a virgin. She had intercourse with a couple of guys. She didn't tell me when she did it, but a few guys told me about it when they found out I was her boyfriend."

"Ash, are you saying she cheated on you a couple of times? You two have only been going out for six months." I am incredulous!

"Mom, yes, we were going together when she had sex with those guys. It wasn't twice she cheated on me. She had sex with those guys at the same time."

Shandon and I sat with our mouths wide open.

What kind of mess had my son gotten himself into!?

The silence was suffocating as me and my husband sat quiet and Ashton looked more embarrassed by the minute. I didn't know what to deal with first: my son claiming a fast behind girl as his girlfriend who was having a ménage 'a trios at sixteen! I didn't even know how to remedy the fact that he could have been exposed to a disease or the fact that my son had any form of sex with this girl. I thought Celeste was a nice girl, but I was seriously reassessing that judgment call. I needed more information about this girl because I was going to call her parents as soon as we got through talking to Ashton. Her parents had to know what kind of daughter they were raising. I'm sure they would

293 | P a g e

thank me for telling them the truth about their hot behind daughter. Yeah, right I thought as soon as the thought crossed my mind. The parents are always the last to know, including me.

"So, Ashton, since you go over to Mr. Jenkins' house darn near every day after school, is this the only sexual episode you have had with that nasty fast…I mean Celeste?" I asked hoping he responded with a definitive no.

"Mom we have kissed a lot and even felt each other up. but this is the first and only time we got close to being undressed. All I can say is I wanted to have sex with her. I mean, she always tells me about how good sex feels and how good it would be to have sex with me instead of other guys. I am still a virgin. That's why Celeste told me she wanted to be my first."

A pin dropping could be heard in the silence. We had to keep him away from this girl! She was hypnotizing our son with her body and manipulating his mind with her ignorant declarations.

Shandon broke the stale silence this time, "Alright Ashton, we have been talking for over an hour now. Why don't you…get out of our fac…? I mean, leave me and your Mom alone to talk. If we need to discuss this further, we will call you back down."

Ashton looked at the sadness on my face, his body slumped, and his head hung lower. He was naïve about this sort of thing but at least he still had a conscience.

"May I say something before I go?" Ashton asked in desperation.

We looked at each other. What more will he share? "Sure," we said in unison.

"Mom and Dad, I know I have disappointed you two, but I love you both."

I wanted to hold my son and comfort him like only a Mom can in a time like this. However, for now, I let him sulk in his own irresponsibility. There would be a time I could talk to him without it hurting so badly but now wasn't that time. My son was having sexual relations with a girl he knew was sleeping with other boys. I can't understand how he could have been so foolish.

When Ashton left the room, Shandon came over and hugged me tightly. I felt his strong arms squeezing a lot of built up tension from my body. I let my motherly tears of disappointment fall and he cried his fatherly tears too. I was proud of how my Baby had my back. Together, we presented a united front and that's so very important to me. I still had things to discuss with my husband about his earlier enabling behaviors, but I would let that go, for now. I could only deal with one problem at a time.

~22~
Am I My Sister's Keeper?

Do not be a witness against your neighbor without cause, and do not deceive with your words. Do not say, "I will do to him just as he has done to me; I will pay him back according to what he has done."
Proverbs 24:28-29
***

Trinity

I did not enjoy living at Redeeming Hope. The women had already formed their own opinions of me and that was okay with me. *I thought.* I don't need any of these women anyway. *Am I my sister's keeper?* I wished I could live in a men's shelter. *Yeah right! More men, more problems and more being led around by my carnal needs and not my spiritual desires.* Well, at least that would be so much easier than dealing with all these women with all their crazy issues. *Sheesh, I have too many of my own.* Living here made me appreciate my friendship with Jnana much more. She didn't have any of these issues. *Thank God!*

Since the day I turned twelve, I had issues with women. Before that, my life was a calm sea. But after my breasts started growing in, that calm sea got mighty rough. The day after my breasts starting to grow in, a button was pushed for the rest of my body to start maturing. The next month after my breast appearance, my booty got bigger and by my thirteenth birthday, I had wide hips, a big booty, and thirty-four B breasts. The more I developed, the more the boys noticed me. Conversely, the more the girls hated me. Before I developed, I had lots of female friends. Well, at least I thought they were my friends. The boys were my peers that teased me and called me names. I got so sick of being called names like pancake and fat girl. During those times, the girls always took up for me. They knew the struggles girls go through in puberty. I thought I would always have their support. After my pubescent blossoming began, my name was mud with most of the girls at school. I spent many nights crying myself to sleep and dreading that I would be subjected to the same nonsense the next day of school. After a bad episode with my ex-friends, I finally said to heck with the girls and made fast friends with the boys. Agreeably, most of the boys wanted to hang with me and get rep from their friends. But still some, amazingly, wanted to have sex with me. I didn't have sex on my mind back then. In fact, my fast blossoming body was the bane of my existence. I would have rather been fat and round all over. Over time I was no longer considered heavy. When I filled out in all the right places, I was considered thick. Secretly, I did miss all the sleepovers and the endless hours of fun shopping with my girlfriends. I missed the giggling times I had talking about boys with other girls.

Having boys as my only friends, changed my way of thinking and threw me into talking about cars and sports with the boys. I let a couple of more popular boys, who just happen to be boyfriends of two of my ex-friends, feel me up. I was invited to all the football parties and was often seen as a tomboy. I was lonely for female friends, but those times gave me a rarely seen insight into the male teenager brain. Though they are sex driven, they have issues too.

It was during those tenuous times I lost touch with the female population. Every single girlfriend I had since those hurtful times wrongfully thought I was interested in sleeping with her boyfriend. Ironically, every female since then ended up backstabbing me and gossiping about me. Every female friend, besides Jnana. She was the only female friend I had who had been honorable and trustworthy. She always had my back, even when I knew it caused a rift in her marriage. Admittedly, she had been more of a friend to me than I have to her. I never meant to hurt Jnana or Shandon. I care for them both deeply, but in my selfish emotional state, I didn't care about anyone but myself. When I got out of here, I will make it up to Jnana and Shandon.

I missed my best friend! I tried calling the house from a pay phone, but Jnana didn't pick up the phone. I wanted to tell her how much I appreciated her and how sorry I was for taking our friendship for granted all these years.

I hope our last conversation didn't hurt her too badly. I was venting at her and I regret many of the things I said to her. I even regret secretly hating how good she has things. I really needed to get my stuff together because the one female who had my back is the one I have hurt the most. Yeah, I must change some stuff about myself! I looked at the clock and shrieked. Oh my gush, I will be late!

Today was my first day babysitting the

children at the shelter. I was so afraid. I knew nothing about kids. Other than my love of watching Sponge Bob Square Pants and Doc McStuffins, I didn't know what kids enjoy. I had no experience with babies besides getting pregnant with them and aborting them for Greysan. I walked down the hall, but I stopped and lean up against the wall. The full realization hit me.

I aborted two babies for Greysan and all that time, he was having babies with his wife.

I cannot believe I was so foolish. In retrospect, if he loved me, truly loved me like I thought, he would have been proud I was carrying his children. But as soon as I told him I was pregnant he pushed money into my hand so I could abort the baby. At the time, he told me he didn't want me to have a child because he didn't want me to ruin my sexy body. Back then, I was so flattered he thought so much of me. Now I realized the truth, I felt so dirty and stupid. Stupid didn't even seem like a strong enough word to describe my ignorant mindset. I should have known each time I let Greysan into my body, raw, how he reveled in the feel of my wetness, I made myself an easy victim to his ploy. Each time I let him crawl into my body, he took up more and more mental space, corrupting my already shaky sense of self. He told me if he could refrain from using protection, he wouldn't get me pregnant. Each time he said he would use the rhythm method but when the time came to stop, he always got caught up in the feeling and corrupted my clean chasm. When I tried to force him off me, he held both of my arms down and kissed me hard

299 | P a g e

on the mouth. He did what he wanted to me and I allowed it, afraid of losing his favor. So much for me thinking I controlled anything!

The first time Greysan hit me was when I was pregnant with our first child. He accused me of sleeping with another man so my baby couldn't be his. I fervently denied I cheated on him and he hauled off and hit me. He knocked me down to the floor and beat me up like I was a man. As I look back, it was sad to say but I believe his intention was to try to beat the baby out of me. He never hit me in my face or pulled my hair, he only hit me in my stomach and my ribs. Greysan is just that evil. He would go to any cost to protect his secret.

Nonetheless, I didn't have any of the babies hence I have no experience with children. I was dumb enough to believe Greysan cared about me. I'm not blaming him. It was time for me take responsibility for my own bull crap.

Lost in my own memories, a group of women and children rushed down the hall past me. It snapped me back to earth and I put on a brave face. After getting myself together, I walked into the baby-sitting room and smiled. The first baby I saw had such beautifully big, brown eyes which sparkled back at me. When I smiled, so did she. Her eyes stayed on me as I walked over to her. She was so precious. I reached out my arms to take her from the crib. I was so eager to snuggle up next to those chubby cheeks. But as my hands reached out for her little body, someone pushed me out of the way. "Excuse me, new girl, this is my daughter Emily! I don't need you to take care of her since I am here."

What a surprise, "Tremica, I didn't know your daughter was here today. She wasn't in the room this morning."

"Well, Ms. Inmybizness, she was with my mother all this time. However, she is now here to stay. Do you have a problem with that? Well, if you do, we can talk to Ms. Mabel about you moving out of my room. I don't want you as my roommate anyway. You might leave Trick-O-Monous on the toilet seat!"

Looking at Emily's little brown eyes smiling at me, I said, "Nope, I don't have a problem. For your information, I got a shot for my STD, so you can keep your Stupid Trivial Drama. Tremica, you are not as high post as you may believe. So, chill out!"

I left her standing there in her own hateful pool of misery. Wow, how could someone so angry give birth to such a precious, beautiful spirited little girl like Emily? Desperate times make some men do the stupidest mess. Emily's eyes followed mine as her mother carried her across the room. Thank goodness, she didn't get any of her Mom's anger and unnecessary hostility through the umbilical cord. Oh, but for the grace of God.

I checked the list of things that still needed to be completed in the room. I asked for instructions on how to change a couple of diapers and I even fed one baby a bottle until he fell asleep. My heart was as calm as a lullaby when I held these babies in my arms. I smelled their clean scents of baby powder and diapers and became emotional because it was so beautiful. For the first time in a long time, I missed my two babies. I wish I never got those abortions. As I was striving to have a heart for Christ, sometimes the guilt and shame set me on a crying spell. I know God forgives me of all my sins, but I also know I needed to learn to forgive myself for being so foolish by having abortions for a man...my baby's father, at that.

There I was in a room full of reminders of my lost children. I stood there with an opportunity to run and hide or grow from the situation. I rested upon the knowledge of the Spirit to strengthen me during that test of character. I chose to grow. As I looked around and I saw a couple of children that would be the same age as my babies right now. I held back my tears as I thought about how one of my babies would be toddling around falling on their bottom. The other would be starting preschool, learning their ABC's. To ease my heavy heart, I spent the most time bonding with the children that were the same age my babies would be. I even helped a few to sing their ABC's. I and the little boy Jude laughed when we messed up on our LMNOP's. His little baby teeth were so cute, and he had the most loving green eyes I had ever seen. I just wanted to hold him and give him kisses. After the episode with Tremica, I just laughed and giggled with him. On the way to this room, I was sad. But being around those children was good for my spirit. It was not so bad.

As long as I can remember, I loved teaching children. I even taught a few how to paint while I was an intern in college. Being around the children did me some good. Before I knew it, my volunteer babysitting time was up. Tremica quickly took her daughter and left when it was time to go. I was on my way to the bedroom to lay down for a few when Bonnie called me into the kitchen.

"New girl! We will need you in the kitchen tonight since Sheila's son Isaiah is sick."

I was afraid to try cooking again after the macaroni and cheese incident. "Well, what are we going to cook tonight? If it's not microwaves, I can't help. Bonnie, you know I can't cook. You remember the macaroni and cheese sauce I made, uh burnt."

"Yes, I remember the cheese sauce, but no one learns how to cook the first time out. Dinner tonight will be turkey tacos, spring mix and spinach salad, and chocolate chip cookies. Does that sound simple enough for you to help us?"

"Umm, the salad part does. My salads are epic! But, let me go change my clothes. A baby threw up on me when I was burping her earlier. I'll be right back to help."

"Okay, we'll be here"

I was walking away when Bonnie called me.

"New girl, thank you. We appreciate your help." Her eyes stayed steady instead of rolling. Could it be I was making a friend? I hoped so. It was lonely being the outsider.

"You're welcome. You can call me Trinni instead of new girl."

"Okay Trinni," she smiled, "we'll be waiting on you. Don't be long."

"Okay, give me a couple of minutes."

"Okay."

I channeled my childhood days and skipped excitedly down the hall while humming a lullaby I learned while babysitting. I walked into the bedroom to find a new piece of furniture, a crib. Tremica was lying in her bed cuddled up with Emily and they were asleep under the covers. They both looked precious. Tremica had her mouth closed and her rolling eyes were closed. Perfect! This living arrangement might work out.

I moved around quietly and quickly to change my shirt before going back to the kitchen to cook with Bonnie and the other ladies. I was looking forward to making food in which preparation didn't require the use of a microwave. Go figure. I could not recognize myself. Before I felt uneasy, I rushed out of the room back to the kitchen.

I barely washed my hands before Bonnie started shooting off orders, "Trinni, we are going to need you to prepare the tacos. I know you wanted to help with the salad, but we are going to prepare that last. For now, I need you to cook the turkey meat. You *do* know how to cook turkey meat, right?"

I didn't want to embarrass myself again by guessing so I said no.

The three women snickered at my response. Bonnie turned to them and gave them the meanest look. Bonnie said, "Hush, you two. Neither of you were the best cooks when you got here either. How quickly you forget!" Turning to me with a gentle smile, she said, "Now Trinni, it's simple. Get the big frying pan from off the pot rack over there. Turn the stove on 5 which is medium heat. Take these five pounds of ground turkey. Break the turkey apart in the pan with a plastic spatula. You don't want to mess up the nonstick coating on the pan by using a metal spatula. Then fry the turkey up in the pan. When it starts turning brown, instead of being pink, it's cooking. After that…"

She looked up and saw the puzzled look on my face.

"Trinni, just do what I said so far. When you are done cooking the turkey in the pan let me know. Then I will help you to finish the tacos. Okay?"

I breathed a sigh of relief. I was glad she had mercy on me. She was giving me too many orders at one time. I was not a seasoned cook.

"Yes, thank you."

I followed the directions step-by-step and was amazed at how easy it really was. When I showed her the cooked ground turkey, she and the other three women looked surprised I could follow directions.

"So? Did I do it right?" I asked with bated breath. She chuckled, "Oh wow, y'all, Trinni knows how to cook ground turkey now!" She and the other ladies, Dana and Peggy excitedly gave me a high five. I was impressed with myself.

Bonnie ordered, "Now, take this colander and pour all the contents of the pot into it. Use the wooden spoon to move the meat around in the colander to make sure that you get all the liquid off the meat. Once you know all the oil is drained, pour the turkey meat back into the pan. Keep the stove on medium heat to finish preparing the seasoning part. Add the required amount of water from the directions on the taco seasoning packet then add the contents of the taco seasoning packets to the turkey meat. We used five pounds of meat so you will be using five of them, one packet for every pound of meat. Once you followed the directions for the seasoning, take these two bottles of salsa and add it to the meat. Mix the salsa into the turkey meat, when that's done, you are finished. Then I want you to cut up this cilantro, lettuce, and tomatoes for the taco toppings. The knives are in the drawer to the right of the stove. You do know how to use a cheese grater right?" Her eyebrows went up in anticipation of my answer. Gleefully, I could give her an excited, yes!

She smiled at me and giggled, "So you can take this block of Colby Jack Cheese to grate up the entire block. When you are done all of that, you are done."

I did as she instructed and took a sampling of my taco meat. It was darn good. I never made homemade tacos, so tonight's meal was going to be a treat. When I was done preparing the toppings for the tacos and grating the cheese, I helped the ladies make the salad by cutting up cucumbers, cilantro, carrots, and tomatoes. Then I made homemade Italian dressing, from the instructions on the packet, from scratch. I was excited; I even set the dinner table. Ms. Mabel snuck up behind me and gave me a hug. I knew she was proud of me by how long she hugged me.

"Trinity, I am hearing good things about you. You have been here a while now. Are you feeling any more comfortable in your surroundings?"

I looked at her body language and I knew she knew the answer. "Yes, I am Ms. Mabel. I love it here." I didn't tell her I sometimes feel suffocated by my loss of freedom or how being around all these women caused me to recollect where the root of my issues with women began.

"Aww, Trinni that's so good to hear. I know you were having issues with this not being a mansion with servants when you first came. How do you feel about that now?"

I was open and honest with my response, "Well, Ms. Mabel, I feel foolish for even thinking someone should have to wait on me. I am a grown woman and I should be helping around here. I had no right to expect anyone to serve me."

"Good...Trinity...good."

Ms. Mabel hugged me again and walked away without another word. I was left in the dining room alone to ponder whether she was happy with me living here or whether she was still unsure about whether I was going to change while living here. I went back into the kitchen just as Bonnie was telling the other ladies to call the family for dinner. Since I had been there, I realized the women didn't think of all the children as belonging to someone else. They thought of all the children as their own. The shelter was a family home and as such, we were the loving village that takes care of every child in the house. I had really grown to love many of those people, unconditionally.

Everyone there seemed to enjoy the family atmosphere. As I watched Tremica only interact with Emily, only looking up from her plate to feed Emily and pass the food bowls, I wondered, what's her deal? Why had she purposely separated herself from the family? And why had she distanced herself from me? Aren't we family now? I know from experience we all want to belong. I wonder why she appeared to be comfortable being alone.

~23~
Cultivation

"I am the good shepherd; I know my sheep and my sheep know me— just as the Father knows me and I know the Father—and I lay down my life for the sheep. I have other sheep that are not of this sheep pen. I must bring them also. They too will listen to my voice, and there shall be one flock and one shepherd. The reason my Father loves me is that I lay down my life—only to take it up again. No one takes it from me, but I lay it down of my own accord. I have the authority to lay it down and authority to take it up again. This command I received from my Father."
John 10:14-18
***

Jnana

It had been weeks since Ashton's revelation. As much as I tried to talk myself out of not telling Mr. and Mrs. Jenkins about Celeste, I felt like I had to tell them. It was my duty as a responsible parent. I would feel awful if something happened to Celeste and I knew she was having dangerous sexual liaisons with boys but didn't do anything about it. I know some would call me a busybody. Some would even say I'm only lashing out because of the potential harm this whole episode caused to my son. But I have prayed on it, so I am clear on my motivation. It was my duty to contact her parents. I know I already said it was my duty but, hey, just because I felt like it was my responsibility, didn't mean I was settled in my conscience. Don't judge!

As much as I rationalized, they would be okay with my truth concerning their fast and very sexually active daughter, I knew better. It goes back to the one fundamental truth concerning someone's children: they could talk about their child, but unless you wanted the winds of hell unleashed, you better not utter one disparaging word. I readied myself to make the difficult phone call to Mrs. Jenkins. I chose to specifically call Mrs. Jenkins because Mr. Jenkins might be like most fathers and think their little princess couldn't be out having sex with multiple partners at the tender age of sixteen. He might be in disbelief for a minute but when reality sets in, oh my, he will most definitely get angry and come after Ashton. I didn't want to be embroiled in the drama of destroying the precious illusion of daddy's little girl. I will leave that to Mrs. Jenkins. I took a deep breath then called her cell phone. After some small talk, we decided it would be nice to meet for coffee and catch up since we both were so busy.

I genuinely liked Mrs. Jenkins, Rebecca. She truly has a beautiful soul. I just hoped our friendship stands the test of this trial. I knew I was floored when I found out all I did. I still haven't been able to look Ashton in the face since that night. I know that sounds bad to not speak directly to your son for weeks but hey, I never said I was perfect. Shandon had the birds and bees talk with Ashton, but we never thought he would throw all he knew aside for the sexually power-driven wiles of some girl. I never thought to talk to him about what to do if he was confronted with this type of situation. In retrospect, I was amazed that even after the, in depth, talk Shandon had with Ashton, and the subsequent shopping trip for condoms, it still didn't sink in. He is usually the compliant child, so his recent behavior really had me confused. This is not my son. I am sitting here scratching my head trying to figure out how things got so out of whack. Hopefully, between me and Rebecca, we could figure out a resolution for how to deal with our wayward teenagers. Lord knows, if we accomplished this, we should write a book!

Today was going to be a busy one. I still had interviews to conduct for the replacement of Littia. I'm glad I bit the bullet and fired her. I wrote her up not once but twice since Shandon told me of her lack of good customer service. After I watched her cash register count closer, her drawer was coming up a little lighter too. I secretly put in a register cam and caught that heifer red handed stealing from me. The sad part was she would steal stupid amounts like five dollars and fifteen cents. I confronted her after watching her for a solid week. She didn't lie. I had to give that much to her. Even during crime, not only against the law but the bounds of our friendship, she was honest! Now isn't that ironic. Then again, maybe she genuinely didn't give a damn about me or my business enough to lie. Still, I would have given her money if she needed it, she didn't have to steal from me. Initially, I felt bad for her. She told me she was stealing such a specific amount because it costs her that amount to catch the bus with her kids for the day. However, stealing from me was stealing from my children. Five dollars and fifteen cents was a gallon of milk and a loaf of bread at the discount store. Business hadn't exactly been stellar around that time. In fact, it was declining steadily. In part, due to her poor customer service.

I hate that my hand was forced. As a business owner, I didn't want to mix business with friendship. However, over the years, it was hard not to learn to care for her and her family. On Saturdays she didn't work; she brought her kids in for a children's book reading and other times for face painting and coloring book hour. In the end, I had to make a decision that was right. She stole from my business and I could no longer trust her as my employee. Our friendship was still a work in progress.

To make effective use of my time, I checked in books that arrived in the shipment last week and rearrange things to make room. I am trying to find space for our new Christian literature section while I waited on the interviewees to arrive in four hours. I purchased some spirit enriching books to read for myself and my family as well. As I was growing in my spirituality, I expanded our special interest sections to offer more diversity for customers. After watching a TD Jakes video entitled *Touched* on You Tube last month, I didn't know what happened to me. But after I finished watching, I felt compelled to order more Christian literature books. I ordered books on intercessory prayer, Divine revelation and repairing broken Christian relationships. After ordering twenty new books, I pulled out my Message Bible and blew the dust off the leather cover. I didn't get into the Bible as often as I should. The truth was embarrassing since I had over ten different translations at my disposal. Asking for Divine guidance, I closed my eyes and let my Bible fall open in preparation for a Rhema Word. My Bible fell opened to reveal Colossians 2:2, I *want you woven into a tapestry of love, in touch with everything there is to know of God. Then you will have minds confident and at rest, focused on Christ, God's great mystery.*

I did not attend church regularly, but I knew there was a higher power greater than me. I had some unsavory dealings with religion in my life. When I was younger, we were bused to church on Sunday, but we only went to get the candy they gave us on the bus. After many months of hearing the sermon about a building fund and the backstabbing I saw the adults taking part in, I had a bad taste in my mouth about church folks. Even though I was only a child, I was sickened by how the people would sit and say Amen but as soon as they left their seats they were cutting their eyes at other people and gossiping like they weren't filled with the Holy Spirit. From then on, my dealings with religion had been minimal. After watching *Touched*, Shandon and I prayed more and we both agreed we should get serious about trying to find a church family for us to attend on a weekly basis for fellowship. As I got more serious in my faith, so did Shandon and my children. As a family, we sat and watched a television Bishop who had a wonderful grasp on the Word of God. I even watched multiple television broadcasts alone. For several Sundays, we visited different churches in hope of finding a church home. I just hadn't felt what everyone says I should feel when I walk into the churches we have visited. I may not be a church member or even have a church home, yet, but I knew my spirituality was growing deeper. I felt God pulling me closer to Him and I was lovingly accepting of this invitation.

****

Owning Namaste was my dream job. I always knew I wanted to be an entrepreneur. While in junior high school, I became obsessed with books. From the first book, I read as a child, *The Snowy Day* by Ezra Jack Keats, to reading *Of Mice and Men* wrote by John Steinbeck while in high school, I knew literature was my best friend. This area needed a bookstore for as long as I lived there. So, it seemed like a natural progression to pair my dream of running my own business and my desire to help other people to be bitten by the reading bug. But with all my passion, business hadn't been booming in a month. In fact, a couple of stores on the strip mall already closed. When the accountant came in last month, she questioned whether we should consider relocating. It was my dream business so to move to another location would mean I was abandoning that neighborhood. I was at a loss about what to do so I prayed and entered a covenant with El Shaddai for His help. I read in *The Names of God* by Dr. Kenneth Hemphill that El Shaddai, the God of more than enough, looks ahead and makes provisions for all our needs. So, I rest assured things would work out for us at Namaste. I thanked Father God ahead of time for the answer to my prayers.

When things get better financially, I wanted to build a digital media bar so customers could come in and read books and other media on digital readers in addition to reading hard copies of books. We live in a fast-paced world and there was no other area that advanced more quickly than technology. Long gone were the days when folks needed to carry their Bibles around. Now they could quickly pull up the many translations of the Bible with easily downloadable apps on their phones, tablets, or handheld digital readers. It was long overdue for me to catch up with the times. I was so far behind the times I still have a flip phone and old-fashioned land line phone at home. I will look into buying an I Phone 14 to upgrade.

I planned to have Trinity draw me a logo of a pretty girl in lotus pose with an open book in her lap when she returns. I wanted the color palate of my marketing literature to be warm and inviting. Like some soft greens, yellows, and browns. I had lots of work to do for my small business venture to begin to turn a profit again. I even ordered contemporary furniture for my customers. I recently put in double wide, high back reclining chairs. I also put in two comfortable and extra-long couches and three chaise loungers. I put a lot of work into creating an environment of peace and joy that is customer driven.

After a couple of hours, I was done shelving

books and straightening up. I looked at my watch. I still had an hour before the interviewees would arrive. After I posted some entries into my QuickBooks software, I returned some phone calls. With a few minutes to spare, I checked the phone messages. The first message was a hang-up. The second and third calls were from the same collection agency. The crooked book supplier had the nerve to threaten to sue me for breach of contract. Their brochure showed full-color books that appeared to be perfect bound. However, when I got the shipment, the books were black and white spiral bound copies. I will not be paying for photocopied books, no matter how cheaply priced they are! The nerve of them to send me those books in the first place. They initiated collection activity even after I shipped the bogus books back, at my expense! I hope they are holding their breath because they will never receive a red cent for that shipment! The final message on the machine was from Trinni. It had been a while since I heard from her. I missed my best friend so much!

"Hey Jnana! Lady, I just want to tell you that I miss you. I know I took our friendship for granted, but I miss you, so very much. I have some good news, I got saved last month and this week I received the Holy Spirit with evidence of speaking in tongues! Tell the kids I love them and give them both kisses. Love you my bestest friend in the world. I'll be in touch."

Then the message ended.

By the end of the message, tears were cascading down my cheeks. I have been worried about Trinni since she left, and I missed her something terrible. I didn't know where she was, but she sounded well. I checked my caller ID for a number. Sheesh, it was an unavailable number. I wondered where her cell phone was. Knowing Greysan, with his spiteful self, he turned it off. I hoped I could call her back so we could talk. Well, I will just have to wait until she calls me back. Either way, I can't wait to catch up with her. She won't believe all the mess that's been going on with Ashton. She always told me Celeste has this sneakiness and overtly sexual aura about her. When I think back, I used to take up for Celeste. Now I must eat my words because Trinity was dead on target about Celeste. That hussy would come over my house pretending to be a good girl when all the while she was anything but pure. Trinity warned me to get Ashton away from the situation but again, I ignored her. Now I have no choice, I am not trying to be a grandmother and I know for sure my son is not ready to be a father. I have so many plans for his future and no fast behind girl is going to derail them!

I had to shake off all my thoughts of going to find Celeste and shake some sense into her. I focused on good thoughts of Trinity. Though this breach in our friendship was a rare occurrence, I knew something big was happening for her. I felt bad about thinking she was out with some man. When she was growing closer to God. How beautiful. Now that's a love affair I could stand to engage in more often. What better reason to stay out of touch and to forget everything? In the past, whenever we argued, one or the other would call and apologize in a day or two. Never has a disagreement ever gone on this long. Yes, Trinity said some unnecessarily harsh things to me. For my part, I knew I took things too far this time. Still, we have been friends for far too long and helped each other through too much for this situation to continue unresolved. Trinity kept warning me that my real talk was too real for her. She was in a tender place emotionally and, as a friend, I was less than supportive. The next time I see Trinity I will apologize, profusely. I could only promise to try my best to pay more attention to my word choices. In the meantime, I will send up a prayer for my best friend's safety and for healing for our friendship. I'm so glad she got saved. I don't know anyone who speaks in tongues so I can't wait to hear Trinni do it when she comes back. It is amazing the way she was living when she left until now, being saved. I guess the rumors are true. God does heal and restore people the world may think are lost causes and too stuck in their own sinful patterns.

I looked at the clock, time sure flies. The first interviewee will arrive in less than fifteen minutes! I ran around and made a fresh cup of coffee and put out a tray of chocolate chip cookies. The interviews are timed perfectly. Each interview will be twenty minutes for each candidate, for two hours straight. After each interview, I will let each of the candidates walk around and set up one display each. It will give me a chance to see if they will go with the flow of my decorating style or step out the box and show their own individual creative imprint. I needed someone that will be responsible, ambitious, have good customer service skills and is honest. I also had a selective requirement for someone who was a self-starter. Specifically, I needed a self-starter who was ready to take on a modicum of responsibility. I didn't need someone waiting on me to order them around. I was not a micro manager at my business.

I heard the wood wind chimes ring out and I knew that must be the first of the interviewees arriving. I walked over and unlocked the door. I watched as he walked into the store. We shook hands, made direct eye contact, and smiled before we introduced ourselves. He had confident body language and a smile that was warm. So far so good. About twenty-five, black eyes, and freshly braided hair. Cocoa brown skin, thin long nose, and thin lips, he was fair on the eyes.

I offered him a seat. Before he arrived, I set up two chairs, one in front of the other. It's always very sterile and intimidating when an interviewer stays behind a desk. It makes them appear unapproachable and stern. I was determined to provide a unique perspective to the candidates. I was in authority, that much is clear, but Namaste was a relaxed work environment. With that being said, I didn't want to come off stuffy and off putting. I stood beside my chair to see how he would act. He was a gentleman and let me sit down first.

I smiled at him then took my seat. "Thank you for coming, I am Jnana the owner of Namaste. Did you bring your resume?"

He ruffled through many papers and looked up at

me. "I'm sorry but I forgot it at home."

The nerve of him to forget to bring his resume when he knew he was coming to a job interview. Next!

"Well, how do you expect me to interview you if you didn't bring your resume? I called to remind you to bring it last night."

"Well, I can tell you what jobs I held. Why are you making such a big deal lady?"

"Excuse me? You didn't remember to bring your resume to a *job interview*! Is there something wrong with this picture?"

"Nah, there's nothing wrong with it. Give me a minute to double check to see if I have it. Dang, you sure are uptight! Isn't that what Namaste means? Isn't it some oneness malarkey or something like that? Humph, you sure aren't making me feel at one with you right now! Did you forget to center yourself this morning or what?"

I got up from my seat and headed to the door. I didn't need the full twenty minutes to know this will not work out, for either of us.

"I found it so now we can do this here interview thing. Why are you over there by the door?"

Huh? Is he dense or what? "This interview is over Sir. You aren't a suitable candidate for this position. Thank you for your time."

He put his papers back into his folder and walked over to me. He stopped toe to toe with me, so close I could smell his breath burning my nostrils. His face was frowned up and his eyes weren't so warm anymore. I don't scare easy but darn if my legs weren't shaking. I would hold these interviews while the store was closed! No one would hear my screams if anything reckless went down. I stood still and tried not to breathe. You never know what will happen in this world today. He winked then moved closer to me.

He stood close to me then he licked his lips. I breathed a sigh of relief when he surprisingly stepped back giving me much needed breathing space from his unwelcome invasion of my personal space.

He looked me right in my eyes and spat, "Since I won't be getting the job, the least you can do is let me get some coffee and a few of those cookies. You aren't a very good host."

I was stunned when he walked away from the door and made his coffee, before grabbing a handful of cookies. The cookie crumbs seemed to crash loudly on to the floor as he had the nerve to sit down and get comfortable in one of the comfy recliners.

No, they aren't for you, I wanted to scream, *so get up and get out*!

My usually quick tongue knew to choose my words and actions wisely for the best resolution. I prayed my DVR security recorder was working properly to record the situation just in case anything went down. I looked up at the clock. Gratefully I realized the next candidate was set to arrive in ten minutes.

"Sir, the interview is over. It's time for you to go. I have other appointments to get to today."

He just shrugged his shoulders and smirked at me. See, I don't have time for this mess! I slyly looked at the clock on the wall. In the time, it takes the next candidate to get here, I could be a corpse! I hope they are diligent and arrive extra early.

I stood next to the door and watched him as he got up and walked behind the counter towards the cash register. I guess he didn't notice the closed sign on the door. There wouldn't be money in the register on the day it's closed. Right? Sheesh, talk about a stupid criminal. As he was distracted going through the desk, I took the opportunity to run out of the door. He could take whatever he wanted. My life was more valuable than anything he could rip off inside there. As I ran out the door, I ran into Shandon. Thank you, God!

"Jnana, what's going on? Why are you looking so frightened? He held me close to his chest, "And why is your heart beating so fast?"

I couldn't speak. All I could do was to point towards the store. After he looked in the window at the criminal, Shandon held me tight and told me everything would be okay. Since he was there, I knew it would be. I just wanted that crazy person out of my shop. Shandon was rough around the edges, so I was sure he could handle things very easily. My Baby took his job to protect me, at all costs, very seriously.

We reached for the door just as the interviewee was walking out. He was smugly humming a tune. His arms were full of books and CDs. Oh, no he was not trying to steal my new Anthony Hamilton and Kindred Family Soul CDs! Can you believe it? He was trying to steal one of the new Bibles that came in the shipment from yesterday. He even grabbed a few of my new spring scented Yankee Candles. He came for an interview, but he was trying to go shopping in my store. He done lost his darn mind!

"Where do you think that you are going with my wife's things?!" Shandon yelled as he grabbed the thief by the collar.

He tried to answer with arrogance thickly laced in his tone, "Look, man, she ran out so I figured since I didn't get the job, she could at least let me hold some stuff. Know what I mean?"

Without warning, Shandon punched the crook in his nose. My things flew up in the air as his body slid down onto the sidewalk like a rag doll. The books fell from his arms like there was an explosion under them. Glass sprayed everywhere and my CD's came crashing to the ground. As they crashed to the ground, I looked down and instantly my stomach churned. Darn if my CD's weren't broken in pieces! I didn't know my Baby had hands like that. I thought Shandon was just going to slap him hard across the face to save my stuff from breaking.

As he sat on top of the man, Shandon used his cell phone to call 911. Thank God for placing him here. I have never been so scared in my life. Lord only knows how things would have turned out otherwise. It sure was dangerous trying to find employees!

One interview down but I was over it. I will finish the rest of my scheduled interviews but if I didn't have any luck, I will use a temporary agency. That way they could weed out all the crazies before I even get involved.

The police arrived quickly. This fool had the nerve to lie and say I told him it was okay to take my things. It turned out he has been busy scamming other people. He has an outstanding warrant for pulling a similar scam across town last week. In that incident, someone was badly injured. Thank God for my Baby. Thank God for His mercy.

Shandon didn't have any more jobs for the day, so he ended up staying and interviewing with me. I got blessed and hired a mature lady that had ten years of sales experience and was very versed in marketing. Blessings abound!

After the afternoon I had, it was a welcomed pleasure Rebecca canceled. I was saved twice today. Maybe I'll follow Trinni's example and find my family a home church to attend. God knows I need to stop procrastinating! It is time for me to thank God for His protection by getting saved...spiritually.

~24~
Humility

Dear children, you belong to God. So, you have won the victory over these people because the one who is in you is greater than the one who is in the world. These people belong to the world. That's why they speak the thoughts of the world, and the world listens to them. We belong to God. The person who knows God listens to us. Whoever doesn't belong to God doesn't listen to us. That's how we can tell the Spirit of truth from the spirit of lies.
I John 4:4-6
***

Trinity

I was awakened by the feeling of soft little hands on my face. The fingers were on my eye lids trying to pull them apart. I opened my eyes and they were met by the cutest little eyes of Emily. Her black curly hair was up in a pink bow on her head. Her little baby nose and small cute lips puckered ready to kiss my cheek. She kissed me and slobbered all over my jaw. Then she giggled softly showing her tiny teeth. Her giggle was so cute. She was so precious. I instantly sat up and put her on my lap. She smelled like chamomile baby powder.

I looked over at Tremica's bed and she was still asleep. She must have fallen asleep with Emily on her chest again. Emily must have still been sleepy because she put her head on my shoulder and snuggled up next to me. I held her close and patted her back. In no time at all, she was fast asleep. Her little snoring was so soft and pure. I took the teddy bears out of the crib then I slowly lowered her into it, very careful not to wake her. Then I laid back down in my bed. I smiled as I drifted back off to sleep. Hmm, I could be a great Mom one day. I do have some good inside of me.

****

I was awakened by the sound of someone knocking on the bedroom door. The sun shining in the room stung my eyes. I looked into the crib and Emily was gone, I looked over to the bed on the other side of the room, Tremica was gone too. I must have been exhausted because I didn't hear either of them leave the room. I looked at the clock on the wall, it read twelve o'clock. Dang, I *was* tired! I heard knocking on the door again and Calesia came in the room after I ignored the more frantic knocking.

"Trinni, today is community fund raising day. We are be leaving in an hour. When you get up and dressed, please meet us downstairs in the living room."

"Thanks for coming to let me know Calesia. I will jump in the shower and be down in twenty minutes or so." I was irritated I had to get up but relented. If I were living right, I would be in my own bed right now and I could relax the day away if I wanted. But I wasn't living right. A hard head makes a soft behind. Still, what in the heck is community fund raising day?!

"Okay. Are you hungry?" She saw me mulling over

the answer, still half asleep. "If so, I can pack you a plate to eat on the way over to the shopping center. Bonnie and Latoiya made French toast and cheese eggs."

I hesitated no more, "Those two can really cook so I know it will be good. Yes, please, make me a plate while I get myself together. What is community fund raising day?"

"We're going to be out most of the day. We usually stay in groups of four women. Each group stands at different entrances of the shopping center. We stand out there selling until we sell the last chocolate bar. It usually takes until late afternoon. That's why I asked you if you were hungry. We don't want you to get out there and end up eating the chocolate bars we will be selling." She laughed.

I laughed too. God, I am happy I am making friends here.

Calesia smiled, "Alright Trinity, I will get back downstairs so you can get yourself ready. We are only waiting on you and Dana. Everyone else has been up for hours with our children."

She shut the door. I heard her rushing down the squeaky steps. I jumped into the shower and stood against the wall thinking heavy thoughts. I could feel a breakthrough coming, but I believe fear was holding me back. I was unsettled. As I washed my body, I realized I lost weight since arriving. I always lost weight in my stomach first. I could see it got flatter, but the curve of my hips was still very apparent. After many years of running from myself, I realized I was shaped the way a woman should be…I was voluptuous. As the suds ran down my naked body and flowed down the bottom of the tub, I thought back to one of the last showers at my old place. Oh, how I missed the sensually scented and moisturizing soap I used in my showers at home. I missed my rich honey hair conditioner and my body softening body washes. All the special amenities of home are what made me who I was. The Rosehip Moisturizer softened my skin and gave me a glow that created my beauty identity.

I missed my home, my solitude, and my peace of mind. I missed being in my own space. I shook those memories of who I used to be from my mind. I used to be a woman who would readily get into a relationship with a man solely for money. I used to be was an unapologetic sinner. Those days are gone. I must make new memories of the new, reborn, and saved me. It was amazing, of all the things money brought me, money sadly wouldn't secure my self-worth. Neither could it purchase my illusive self-love. With heavy thoughts, I washed up and made sure to scrub my body clean. I touch my body softly and realized it had been a very long time since a man touched me tenderly. In this moment, I was thrown into the realization that borrowed love was not real love. Sex with someone else's man was borrowed love. In that moment, I reinforced a promise to myself: The next time a man touched my body, he would be my man. The next time a man touched my body, he would be my husband and the last man to touch me. This personal declaration felt so good! I was ready for a faithful man who belonged to only me. Here in the shower, I made a promise to God too. Starting today, I would walk on the right path so I could be spiritually open to joy. I desired a man who not only loved me, for me, but one who would care about providing the security I need and craved. But first, I needed to learn to give those things to myself. I declared it to be, and so it was.

The water ran cold; I stepped out of the shower and meticulously dried my body off. I locked my door then stood in front of my mirror. The last time I stood in front of a mirror was on my birthday. Oh, what a horrible day that was for me. As I took in the vision before me and really looked closely at my naked body…I didn't see one solitary thing I found displeasing. I looked at my face which was thinning out. I took in every single inch, from my eyebrows, as bushy as they were from not getting them professionally threaded since I got there. I let my eyes run down my body and smile. I was amazing! I looked at the rest of my being in the full-length mirror. Yes, I was beautiful, sexy even. However, just a little hairier. Oh, how I missed my bikini waxes. Oh wow, I never thought I would hear myself say I missed that pain. Other than that, I loved how soft and supple my breasts were. I love my stomach; my stomach was not washer board flat, but it was mine. It was soft and feminine. The thickness of my thighs and the wideness of my hips made me a woman; hear me roar! I turned to the side, whoa, where did that high round booty come from?! I guess all the walking I was doing to and from the bus stop tightened my derriere real nice. I thought, maybe I would fit some squats and lunges in. I didn't want my booty fist tight. Soft, firm and round is how I liked my behind to be.

As I turned back to the mirror, I looked at my hair. I had thick, loosely curled hair that looked lovely. I ran my fingers through my hair and smiled, deep in introspection. I looked like a sexy lioness. When my eyes lit up, I saw them twinkle. Where had this beautiful, sexy woman been all my life? And why did I hide from my reflection for so long? Hmm, what a waste of time that self-destructive habit has been. I cannot believe I wasted so many years not loving the woman God created me to be. I stepped away from the mirror, so proud of myself. So proud of the self-love I was gaining. Two points for the growth.

I looked at the calendar. Today was Saturday. I wondered if this was the Saturday that Quintaria would be having a garage sale to get rid of my things. I was saddened she would go through all my things. My baby pictures and my other personal mementos were soon to be lost in what was assuredly a fit of rage. All my Mommy's things wouldn't be able to be replaced either. All I gained from my four plus years with Greysan was gone from my life. As I stood in the middle of the room, I cried. Not over losing Greysan, no, he was never mine. When I thought of all the things Greysan provided for me over the years, I knew it was without any true emotion or caring. Nothing he did should have conveyed love or commitment. Those feelings were manufactured in my mind and only in my mind.

As the tears fell down my face, I knew I would be okay. I didn't really adore Greysan. I loved what I thought he could give me, security. But even that was an illusion. With one phone call, his wife, Quintaria had someone put a pad lock on the door to my home and my car was repossessed. It is amazing what money can do when you really know how to wield the power that goes along with it. I thought being aligned with Greysan's money made me powerful too. However, I was anything but powerful. I was someone who was powerless because I desperately handed my personal power away every time, I opened my legs for money. Money, that even though I thought I had earned it, really wasn't mine. Oh, how foolish I have been. Somewhere along the way, I relinquished all my power. I handed it over to men who treated me like I was expendable. Thank God, I serve an Almighty Father who promises recompense. I receive...my Father...I receive.

I haven't felt God as powerfully as I did that day at the church, but I knew I was changed that day. I felt my Mom around me though. Her love shined all around me, especially now I am walking by faith and not by sight. Being at Redeeming Hope, helped me gain love for myself. However, there were moments when it felt like it wasn't coming fast enough for me. Even though I woke up this morning and looked in the mirror with some joy, I still felt as if there was something missing. I felt like something important and essential to my happiness was still missing. I remembered something the Pastor said at church Sunday and it hit me. I knew exactly what I needed to move on.... closure. On one side, I believed I showed Greysan all of me. I believed I showed him the real me. But on the other hand, I could say I haven't really gotten to know myself, so how could I have shown him the real me. Could I really have loved Greysan when I barely loved myself? No!

I glanced at the clock on the end table, oh no, I was running late. I have been up here over fifty minutes! I hurriedly got dressed the smell from the delicious breakfast waiting for me downstairs occupied my mind. When I got downstairs everyone was ready to go. Even Dana was downstairs. Half the residents in the shelter stayed to clean the house and babysit the children. The other half, the group I was in, went out to community fund raise.

With government cuts to social service agencies, the shelter residents went out and sold candy bars and popcorn to raise money for the daily needs of the residents. I was told that with the economy being so bad, the residents went out twice a month instead of once a month. I was spared the fund-raising duties when I first arrived so I could get settled in. But now I it was my turn to fundraise like the other ladies. I hoped it wasn't as bad as I thought it will be.

We loaded into the van and headed to the shopping center. I didn't want to upset anyone, so I didn't sit up front with Ms. Mabel this time. I sat in the back with the other ladies. Unlike my arrival many weeks ago, I could truly call these ladies my friends. I cared what they thought of me and them me. It was after one o'clock in the afternoon, so we figured it was the peak time to make some sells. We separated into four groups, each of which was assigned to the four entrances to the shopping mall. I was so glad the weather finally settled on warm seventy-degree spring weather. It went back and forth from warm to fall weather for two weeks now. The winter had been especially harsh.

Initially, I was ashamed to go up to the cars when they were stopped at a red light and ask them to buy our candy. Hustling to make sales, my reluctance disappeared. I quickly did a slight adjustment in my thinking and thought of how hard I would work if I were feeding my family. I watched the motivation of the other ladies and smiled, yes, they were a part of my family now. As a resident at Redeeming Hope, it was my responsibility to do my part to contribute. I put my foolish pride aside and sold the candy bars. Like Romans 12:2 says: *Do not conform to the pattern of this world but be transformed by the renewing of your mind. Then you will be able to test and approve what God's will is—his good, pleasing, and perfect will.*

I wasn't so high and mighty, filled with pride when I disrespected myself with other women's men. So, I will not allow foolishness to stop me from being supportive to my family. I was finally a part of a loving family and I had God's unconditional forgiveness. What else was there to live for? I prayed for the guidance to reach the hearts of people who were struggling to feed their own families let alone worry about buying chocolate to help support women and children at a shelter. After about thirty minutes, I got into the groove. A lot of people didn't buy a candy bar.

Some just wanted to donate money. One lady even wanted to donate her time. A few jerks wanted to get my phone number and take me out. Those jokers got a fake smile as I took their numbers plus the cash, they offered for the candy bars. As soon as they drove off, I crumbled up the paper holding their number and tossed it on the ground. I was better than they thought. I was no longer just a body. I was a whole being. Admittedly, some of them would have been my flavor if I were still going after married men. I prayed myself through that test because those men were looking nice and driving expensive cars. In a different mindset, they would have been good candidates for a new sponsor of my expensive lifestyle. Thank God for grace and mercy! I was indeed a changed Woman of God.

I am worthy of more than a temporary fantasy. I am more than a physical pleasure. I'm whole and I don't need a man to finance my lifestyle, God has got me. He has me well in His hands. I had to keep telling myself. *Get thee behind me Satan, get thee behind me!*

It was four o'clock when we got word that all the other three groups had sold out of their candy bars and popcorn. My group still had ten bars to sell. As the light turned yellow, I knew I had to make some quick moves to finish our sales so we wouldn't hold everyone else up. Me and two other girls ran towards the cars and made some sales before the light turned green. As the light turned green and the cars rushed through the intersection off to their lives, I strategized. How would I sell these two bars I had left? We walked up and down the median waiting for the light to turn from yellow to red again as the cars zoomed through the light. During those few seconds, I watched the nice cars drive by. Even the less than new cars looked good to me since I was on the bus line. The light turned green as I was daydreaming, so I ran up to the last car at the end of the line. They were so far back they would surely catch the next red light too. When I got to the window, it was heavily tinted. I softly knocked on the window. It was a shiny new 2017 Jaguar car. I knew this person would buy the last of my bars so we could get on back to the shelter. As I watched the window lowering, I caught a glimpse of some of the most beautiful gray eyes I had ever seen. Then my eyes fell upon the smooth complexion of a nicely tanned, creamy mocha latte man. I was in a trance as my eyes remembered the feeling of sweet soft lips that kissed my body and nibbled me so many times. Perversely, those lips were now curved up in a smirk. Time stood still as he looked at my hat which had the shelter's name on it, down to my t-shirt which also had Redeeming Hope on it. He laughed viciously before growling loudly at me like he was a possessed monster. Before I could muster the strength to move, he reached into his cup holder and threw a handful of change at me. Coins sprayed out in a barrage of stinging metal. Coins bounced off my forehead and some landed in my hair, others rolled down the street. As he drove off, I stood stunned, in pain, with the candy bars in my hands and change on the ground all around me. The other ladies ran up to me to make sure I was okay before grabbing the rest of the candy bars to sell. Embarrassed, I nodded I was okay. They knew something was up, but they went back to selling the candy so we could all get back to the shelter. They sold the candy bars at the next red light and we all walked to the back of the parking lot to load back into the van.

When we arrived back at the van, Ms. Mabel brought back a cooler of sodas and sandwiches for us. I had eaten a good breakfast this morning, but after four hours outdoors I was tired and famished. After we got into the van and got comfortable, the ladies didn't waste time chatting about the day's happenings between bites of their lunch. I searched through the stack of sandwiches for one that had my name on the aluminum foil. When I found two, I ripped open one of the sandwiches and took a big bite. I couldn't believe it. Ms. Mabel remembered my favorite sandwich is peanut butter and bananas with a sprinkle of cinnamon. I looked up at the rear-view mirror as she was driving. I was met by her loving eyes and she winked at me. My heart leaped; I felt so loved. My Mommy used to make these sandwiches for me when she was alive. In that instant, Ms. Mabel, quickly became the surrogate mother I longed for since Momma died. I teared up because I missed having a mother figure in my life so much. God knows that I need that connection and he has delivered Ms. Mabel. Thank you, Father.

I ate both sandwiches and gulped down the ice-cold cherry cola soda. I went from being famished to totally stuffed in ten minutes flat! I nodded off real heavy when someone tapped me on the shoulder. Dang, I sat way in the back for a reason! I was tired and I needed some undisturbed rest. What now? It was Dana who was tapping lightly on my shoulder, "Trinity, what was that all about? I mean that guy in the car really threw those coins at you. He threw them so hard they bounced back off your forehead. What did you say to make him mad like that?"

I didn't want to air my dirty laundry to her…to everyone on this van, but I had to vent to someone. How dare that sorry sack of crap treat me as if I were nothing! Why couldn't he look at me and see I was changing before he threw those coins at me?! Why did he think he could do anything to me and get away with it? Why was I a coward…I mean, I didn't even lash back at him. I just took his harsh treatment. Just like I always did.

"That was the married man I had an affair with. His wife is the reason why I am living here with y'all."

A hush fell over the van and I was once again uncomfortable with being the center of attention. Gone was the cheery atmosphere. I sucked all that out of the air with my revelation. I didn't want to get into my personal business, but I wasn't naïve enough to think that my past wasn't a topic of hushed conversations since I arrived at the church, a dripping rain-soaked mess. I knew they all had a laugh about watching my car being repossessed in front of a church.

"So, are you telling us that," Tremica's said in her annoying voice, "*You* had a fine man like that, driving a nice car like that, cheat on his wife…with you? What did his wife look like that he slummed

337 | P a g e

with the likes of you?"

She had the nerve to giggle and try to high five the girl sitting next to her. She was left hanging because Monica knew the main ingredient in Tremica's haterade was bitter and she didn't want a taste.

"Naw, see that was a low blow, even for you Mica. Why would you talk to Trinni like that? There are three sides to every story, the truth, his and hers. You act like you ain't never done nothing grimy before. Tell the truth, isn't that why you are living here?" Monica said as she shook her head at Tremica and changed seats.

Trying to save face, Tremica rolled her eyes and said, "Nah, that's not why I'm here. I mean, even if it was…and it wasn't…my circumstances are different. I tell you what, even if I cheated with a married man, I sure as heck wouldn't do dirt like that then get here thinking I am some perfect princess. Trinity thinks she is high post, when, she is a low life trick."

I only answer to what I really am, I am not a trick. I am God's child. Well-loved and cleansed, I am more than a conqueror. I am redeemed, renewed, saved, and sanctified. I told myself these truths and ended the conversation.

After I told myself those truths, I cleared the obvious pain out of my voice before I responded, "Tremica, yes that man did cheat with me. I don't need to respond to your ill estimation of my character but let me tell you one thing…last, I checked you were no better than me. I heard rumblings around of why you are here in this

338 | P a g e

shelter. You think you have kept your secrets secret? My business is gossiped about just like yours is. See, the only difference I see is that you had your child from a married man. I aborted my babies from my married lover. Your sin is no less than mine. You were also looking for love and acceptance in the wrong man, a married one at that. So, don't look so far down your nose at me. Let she who lives in a glass house throw the first brick."

Tremica sighed and said whatever before slinking down in her seat. For the rest of the ride back to Redeeming Hope she didn't say another word. A hit dog will holler, but she needs to recognize the mirror she aims my way also needs to point back at her. It was silent on the way to the shelter after my comment. Ms. Mabel played an Israel Houghton CD. *Moving Forward* came through the speakers and we all mellowed out. The universe provided solace at just the right time. I said a silent prayer for Tremica to find peace in her own skin. Just as I was trying to claim my own peace and accept my own harsh truths.

~25~
Flow

With many stories like these, he presented his
message to them, fitting the stories to their
experience and maturity. He was never without a
story when he spoke. When he was alone with his
disciples, he went over everything, sorting out the
tangles, untying the knots.
Mark 4:32-34
***

Jnana

Mom 911! :<(
Oh my gosh, why is Lili texting me with our
emergency text code?!
I texted right back,
Lili, wyd, what's the emergency?
She didn't skip a beat. My text tone went off
again. This type of communication frustrated me. I
hated being forced to communicate like this. She
was at school so I couldn't phone her. I had to get
bits and pieces through text.

I had to upgrade my family cell phone plan
from basic to an unlimited plan which gave us
endless data, text and voice calls for one price. I
finally ordered the I Phone 7. So glad I did, I loved
it! Although Lili and Ashton would rather text me
than have a live conversation, Shandon would
rather hear my voice. He loved me so much he
facetimed me several times a day and when he was
really busy, he sent heart emojis."

Even though most of my teenager's texts

contained few full words, they were still plentiful. To keep up, I had to purchase a text translation manual. Before I ordered the miracle book of text translation language, I spent way too much time asking what they meant by the letters and symbol faces. I was deep in thought about how technologically mature my teenagers were when my text tone went off again. Again, and again!

Mom, omg!

I won't stop bleeding. I soaked through my panties and there is a big stain on the back of my pink jeans. I think that I am dying! I told the nurse to call an ambulance, but she just giggled at me before putting the thermometer in my mouth. She told me that I have a slight temperature then told me that I should go lay down after she gave me a Tylenol. Mommy, please call her, she isn't taking me seriously. Helllp me! I'm too young to die. Mommmy!

Oh no, not my Lili. Please, not my baby girl! It seemed the infamous period had reared its ugly head into our lives. Flo, as some women affectionately called their monthly visitor, was an unwelcomed surprise, at first. Flo was the bane of many women's existence. She often arrived with her flunkies: cramps and maxi pads. Alas, she is missed when menopause brought hot flashes. It seemed like it was time for Lili to develop her love-hate relationship with Flo as well. Still, the cramps, unexplained anger flares and utterly ridiculous, unsettled behaviors made things interesting at our house already. How would I survive with another potential PMS sufferer in the house? The only

341 | P a g e

bright spot from when I got my period for the first time and today was there were now several types of maxi pads.

Gone were the days of having one option of the long pad made with bulky cotton that ran from front to back. Still, Flo was the bane of many women's existence. That was until she didn't show one month or even worse, came late. I remembered having to wear big bulky Stay Free pads when I first got my period; well over twenty years ago. I was sure people walking behind me could see the imprint of that pad.

When I was first introduced to Flo, it was the first day of summer and I finally got the okay from my Mom to wear my white cotton gauchos with matching baby blue ruffled top. That day I moisturized my body and feet well. Then I got dressed and put on my brown wooden Dr. Scholl's sandals. I was looking fly! Zadkiel Everett asked me to go get some ice cream and I couldn't go because of the unceremonious arrival of my period. Like Lili, I too thought I was dying. I had horrible cramps and clots of blood in my panties. I hid in the bathroom for hours. My Mom was working, and I was not talking to my Dad about this issue. When I heard my Mom come upstairs after work, I rushed from the bathroom and cried in her arms. She told me to get in the shower; after she made me a cup of hot lemon tea, she and I had our talk about Flo. Then my Mom gave me the pink Flo bag her mother and grandmother had passed down to her. When I received it, it was full of little tidbits like newspaper comics and antidotes to get me through the initial shock. Also enclosed were the letters from the women before me that had their periods. I held my stomach from laughter since the letter from my Great Grand Mom was hilarious. There was a candy cane for something sweet to suck on, a satchel of saltine crackers to eat when I wasn't quite up for a full meal, a Hershey Almond Chocolate bar for something sweet and salty, Tylenol for obvious reasons and a small journal with a pen. Per family tradition, I will proudly pass the bag down to my only daughter. That's right after I add in my journal entry and restock it. My text sound went off and I looked at the screen. As expected, Lili had texted me again. The message contained five sad faces.

I wish I could save her from this. But this is one of the many times I could not protect my child from life. My mind was on returning the text message when I clumsily dropped my phone. My phone bounced onto the floor with a thud. I held my breath hoping I didn't crack the front screen. I sighed a breath of relief when I remembered that I purchased a rocker case for my I Phone. That was money well spent. Thank God I didn't crack my screen! Shandon was already tripping that I spent so much on the phone so he would have had a fit if I had already broken the screen. I texted Lili back after getting my thoughts together.

I will be there to pick you up shortly. <3

I looked down at my phone and almost cried when I looked at Lili's text message.

☺ *Hurry*

I informed my employees I had an emergency and I would be taking off for the day. I asked my night shift person to come in earlier with the agreement that I would bless their paycheck with a bonus for bailing me out of this jam. Then I rushed out the door. I put my blue tooth on when I got in the car and phoned Shandon. The news devastated him. His young daughter was now becoming a young lady. I didn't know too many fathers that won't get emotional at this time in their daughter's life. As I sat on the phone, I could hear Shandon sniffling. He wouldn't admit it, but he was. Lili was a total Daddy's Girl, so I knew this was hurting him!

I made it to Lili's school in record time. I practically jogged into the nurse's office. When Lili walked out of the room she was lying down in, she burst into tears as soon as she saw me. She ran into my arms and I hugged her tightly before giving her a change of clothes, packet of feminine wipes and a small winged maxi pad. She walked back into the room to change her clothes. Poor thing, I could see from the back she was already wearing an industrial sized pad. We must make fast tracks to the supermarket to get her some maxi pads with wings. When she walked back out, she looked different, more mature. My eyes filled with tears right there in the nurse's office. If I were reacting to her like this, I knew Shandon would completely break down when he saw her. There definitely wouldn't be any denying things then.

I signed Lili out with the nurse after saying my thanks. As I walked down the hall, I felt a familiar vibrating in my purse and looked at the Caller ID. It was Rebecca. Sheesh, I forgot to phone her earlier!

"Hello?" I answered, half watching Lili holding her stomach discretely and trying not to walk into teenagers crowding the halls since the bell rang to change classes.

"Jnana, I'm driving up to the store now. I am so glad we rescheduled for today. The issues with Celeste have me needing to talk. I don't see your truck in front of the store. Are you around?"

Sheesh, I thought she canceled on me. I looked at my calendar and realized it was me that got the dates mixed up.

"Becca, actually, no. I got the dates mixed up. I was at the bookstore, but I got an urgent call from Lili earlier. I just picked her up from school. We are having a little crisis of our own."

"Raising girls…it is always drama! Okay, when you can talk let me know. The emergency with Celeste has me shaking my head."

My Mom radar clicked on and I got nervous. What's fast tail Celeste up to now? I quelled my unrest and put on my best calm voice, "What's going on with Celeste?"

I wasn't prepared to throw any more issues onto her plate, just yet, so I planned on staying quiet. For now.

"Jnana, please hold on, I forgot to put my Bluetooth on and there is a cop behind me. Give me a sec."

I waited patiently while she put on her Bluetooth. I looked over in the passenger at Lili who fell asleep. I must watch my tone and my words. Funny how kids could still hear things they aren't supposed to when they are *sleep*.

"Jnana, are you there? After I put it in, the cop decided to drive around me. Go figure."

"Yes, I'm here. I have Lili in the car with me, but I will arrive at home in five short minutes. We can talk but for now, you talk, I'll listen. You know how kids seem to *hear* things."

"Yeah, I understand. My kids hang on my every word when I am on the phone in the car with them. Sometimes, they even slip up and comment to me about my conversation! So, things have gotten hectic. Things at the school with Celeste have been a little tenuous lately, but now they are a steaming hot mess. I got a call from the school this morning. This morning, a girl told the bus driver she saw Celeste acting extremely inappropriate with a boy. When the bus driver pulled the bus over and walked to the back, he reported he didn't find anything suspicious. They called me after they called Celeste down to the office. Jnana, I can't believe there are so many spiteful girls that would lie on Celeste. My daughter is still a virgin. She would never do anything so low. I mean, on a school bus. It's just incredible how evil some girls can be. Celeste wants to transfer to another school, and I think it might be a good idea. I don't know why anyone has so much time on their hands to make this up."

I sighed happily. Whoever, the boy was, it couldn't be Ashton because Shandon took him to school after an early morning dentist appointment. If this story was true, Celeste was really spreading herself thin. I sure hoped Ashton finally came to his senses and broke up with her for good! At the very least he should stop claiming her.

346 | P a g e

"Becca, how are you holding up? I know this has to be a tough time for you."

"I'm not doing too good Jnana. Thanks for asking. I had to take time off from work for this mess! Celeste wouldn't do such a thing, she knows better. Besides, she won't even drink out of a cup after anyone. She is such a germaphobe!"

I stifled a giggled. Maybe, just maybe it's not someone else's germs she is afraid of. She doesn't want to spread the germs she has in *her* mouth.

"Give me a minute Becca"

I pulled up to the house and got Lili comfortable before I walked into my office to finish my conversation with Becca.

"I'm so sorry to hear you are having some issues with Celeste. However, I have some fuel to add to the fire. In fact, this is what I wanted to meet earlier to talk about."

~26~

Prelude to Joy

And now, dear lady, I am not writing you a new
command but one we have had from the beginning.
I ask that we love one another.
2 John 1:5
***

Trinity

I got up at 6 a.m., much earlier than my
usual 8 a.m. time. Inside of my pocketbook was part
of the sales from the fundraising I did for
Redeeming Hope last week. You may think I am
being a hot mess right now but hey, I gotta to do
what I gotta to do!

Since arriving at Redeeming Hope, I was
getting by on donated clothes that didn't fit as well
as my tailored clothes. I wore donated shoes that
were already worn repeatedly by someone else. I
was used to high fashion clothes with designer
labels. Yes, I was label obsessed, if you will, and I
was not making any apologies for it. As much as I
knew I had changed since living there, that fashion
maven part of me didn't budge much. I wanted my
stuff back! Quintaria had no right to sell my things.
She most definitely didn't have the right to sell
them at a $1-yard sale. I could remember the
moment when I read that ignorant mess in the
newspaper. I knew when I saw the garage sale signs
on Greysan's passenger seat that it must be going
down soon, so I watched the papers and I watched
the listings online. When I saw the listing for the

dollar sale, I knew Quintaria officially went stark raving mad. I was not greedy; I just wanted what was mine. The least she could do was let me keep the fruits of my labor. I fulfilled her husband's deepest, darkest fantasies. Not her! Now don't get me wrong, I was not a prude, some of those fantasies, I too shared, just under my control, not his. He didn't even acknowledge my safe word as I screamed that night, he violated me. After the way Greysan hurt me our last time together, he should be begging her to let me keep my things. I still can't get the echo of my own screams out of my ears. I could remember the aches in my stomach and most of my body from that episode of S & M. What a mess I got myself into that night. Greysan had some screws loose!

I shook off the mental violence, caused by negative memories of Greysan, and quickly got dressed. I put some mousse in my hair to plump up my curls and give it somebody. I was wearing my hair in a naturally curly bob nowadays. I even got my hair dyed back to my natural color, honey blond. A couple of area Christian owned beauty salons came to Redeeming Hope and gave all the ladies a makeover to increase our chances of getting a job and to help us to get a fresh start in life. When I came to the shelter, my hair was heat damaged and I had split ends. Those hair stylists really did some work on my hair. When I looked in the mirror afterward, I was shocked. I was stunning. I looked even more like my Mom. I'm not being vain when I tell you I felt so beautiful. They didn't put makeup on me, per my request, which made me even more amazed. I was naturally flawsome, awesome despite my flaws.

I finished my hair and rushed out of the house. I couldn't take the risk of someone finding out about me and asking about the money. Contrary to what you may think, I wasn't so happy to be doing it. My heart was convicting me! With that in mind, I couldn't readily look someone in the eyes and lie about the trifling mess I was doing. I felt guilty, but I hoped God understood my intentions and gave me a pass. Maybe?

I boarded the bus and paid with a small portion of the change from the candy sales. I got an all-day pass so I could go to the garage sale to rummage through my things before the garage sale regulars set out on the lookout for deals and steals. All of it would be steals! Afterward, I planned on catching the bus back to the shelter in time to mess my hair up and rip some of my clothes to make it look like I was robbed. Hey, don't judge me!

As I found a vacant seat on the bus, I was amazed that I got a couple interested smiles from the men on board. I couldn't figure it out; all I had on were low price retail jeans, a plain yellow buttoned up shirt, cheap canvas sneakers, and some dollar store glossy lip gloss! Gone was my classy look of high-priced designer clothes, handbags, sexy accessories, and calf defining five-inch heels. There was no designer tag going on with these clothes. I didn't even have on my luxuriously rich body butter or my bronzer which always gave me a healthy glow during that time of year when my skin was a tad pale. It was just little ole me, in my most natural state, yet I was still considered attractive to men. Go figure! I must do this more often!

It is always the same happenings when I rode the bus. Inevitably, it got crowded and most of the men wouldn't even get up to give a lady a seat. The loud cell phone talker gleefully aired her personal business for all to hear yet rolled her eyes at anyone brave enough to appear like they were listening. The frotteurism fetish guy thought I didn't notice that he kept rubbing his leg on mine. The selfish bus rider put their stuff on the seat next to them as if their stuff deserved a seat instead of a paying person. I especially hated when that happened because it was always when the bus was crazy crowded. Yup, same mess, different day! I put in my headphones to my mp3 player I got from donations to the shelter. I couldn't believe Ms. Mabel gave it to me. Since I rode the bus more than anyone else there, she knew I would put it to good use. I'm glad someone noticed I was putting considerable effort into establishing myself in this new world I found myself existing in.

I was enjoying the quiet of the nature music I had playing in my earphones when I spotted the nursing home up the street. I imagined seeing Mr. Hanks and it made me smile. He really was an amazing man. I didn't know why I just put my hand up to ding the bus driver I needed this stop! Today, Saturday was not my day to volunteer. But over the course of the last few weeks or so, Mr. Hanks and I became very close. I looked forward to seeing him and judging by the smile he graced me with every time he heard my voice; he enjoyed our time together too. He touched my life immeasurably. Since I had been volunteering, my self-awareness strengthened. Mr. Hanks led me to a place where I understood my value as a woman. I now understood my worth was separate from my sexual nature. I never had a man see me as a complete being before and it felt so lovely! I enjoyed his company and he enjoyed mine too. Imagine that, a man that enjoyed my company and he couldn't even see me! Often, he saw a much better me than I did. I remember hearing something at church about this. How God sees the best in us because He is the best in us. Mr. Hanks was such a wonderful reflection of God's love for me. He cared for me unconditionally and it was healing me, inside and out.

Shortly after I came to see Mr. Hanks, I stopped judging him by his disability. He didn't let his eyesight stop him from doing anything. He was simply a Child of God. When I came to see him, it was all about bonding with a human being who had quickly become someone I respected and deeply cared for. I felt like I was rewarded for giving so freely of my time. I learned to ride the bus because of volunteering with Mr. Hanks. Now I could shoot off what bus number goes to what part of town like it was second nature. I even listened to mostly gospel music and read my Bible daily. I always had confusion about organized religion. But when I saw Jesus and Momma on the church altar, it changed me. Now when I have questions, I get the answers from my Bible. Since I got saved, I have been so deep into my spirituality. I never knew I could be like this. What's the word I am looking for? It still felt unfamiliar, but I had it now. In one word, it was: serene.

I must admit I did have a tough time not judging Mr. Hanks by my father who abandoned me. I never had a positive, strong male in my life. I wish I could tell you how much it still hurts that I had to grow up fatherless because my father didn't care enough to stick around. Thank God for Mr. Hanks because having him in my life helped me to heal my need for a father figure. I couldn't even begin to thank him enough for taking me into his heart. In many ways, I got more out of volunteering than I realized I would.

As a woman that used to take two hours to get dressed before I could leave the house, I have stopped taking so long to get ready. Why bother? Mr. Hanks didn't care what I looked like. He only seemed to care about the core of me. I did have value that didn't have anything to do with my physical being, hmmm! Mr. Hanks even taught me to love and understand the Bible. Obadiah was my favorite chapter. I was confused by the King James Version, so Mr. Hanks gave me a copy of The Message Bible as a gift. Now when I read the Bible, I read the King James Version first then I went to The Message to get better clarification. Mr. Hanks changed me from a girl to a woman simply by loving me, unconditionally. He taught me that I should not only read the Bible, but I should strive to live the words contained in it. He taught me to expand my knowledge about life and how pivotal spirituality was in living a vibrant existence. Ms. Mabel told me this assignment was perfect for me, as if she had a Rhema Word from God; she was right. God used me even though I was still working on me. He used my brokenness to fix Mr. Hanks and in turn, we both experienced the feeling of completion. Who wouldn't want to serve a God like that?! God could cause spiritual connections to birth from a tiny seed of faith and bless it to grow from deep roots into a fruitful tree of life. God could move two broken people together to make His kingdom more powerful. I needed Mr. Hanks in my life, and I have a feeling he valued my existence in his life as well.

When I arrived one day, Mr. Hanks was listening to a gospel song, *Place of Worship,* sang with precious anointing by William McDowell. The song had us both in tears. I had no idea music could invoke such praise. That day in the room, Mr. Hanks and I praised God with such wild abandon that the nurses ran into his room to see what was going on. It didn't take long for them to get caught up in the Spirit either. They were in awe of seeing the soft-spoken, almost anti-social Mr. Hanks they had seen over the years avoid contact with others, allowing his heart for God to overflow in dancing and singing. It was such a wonderful moment to see God allow His children to be so intimate with Him through song. When the song went off, the nurses composed themselves and left with a wink and a smile. No doubt the rest of their shift would move about beautifully. As if nothing had happened, Mr. Hanks sat down and brought out his Braille Bible. He handed me one of his Bible's and asked me to turn to Job 14:7-9. *For there is hope of a tree, if it be cut down, that it will sprout again, and that the tender branch thereof will not cease. Though the root thereof wax old in the earth, and the stock thereof die in the ground; Yet through the scent of water it will bud and bring forth boughs like a plant.* "Trinity," he said, "if you don't learn anything from life, get this, we may not always have a clear and easy path to follow but if you allow God's Will to guide you, through the Holy Spirit, there is always hope. You are never too far from the good graces of God to be healed, restored, and finally realize that all you search for is inside of you already. You just have to allow your mind to remember you at your purest state of being."

Not wanting to ruin the moment, I smiled and nodded. But I was transfixed by his words. Has too much happened to me and have I sinned too much to begin again? No. How empowering this is to know!

I was so mesmerized by the wisdom Mr. Hanks always shared with me. He was so open with me. The rest of my visit, he shared personal stories with me. He told me stories of how his daughter's Mom used to bake him white sweet potato pie and how it made his mouth water every time he smelled it cooking. I could see his face light up when he talked about that pie. Then, I saw how his face saddened when he talked about how much he missed the mother of his daughter. I wanted him to be joyous again, like when he talked about that pie.

355 | P a g e

So, when I arrived back at the shelter, I talked to the ladies at the shelter. I was determined to recreate that glean I saw in his eyes when he took his walk down memory lane. The women at Redeeming Hope helped me make that pie. When I took it to Mr. Hanks, he cried. Then I cried. He opened his heart to me. He shared how he felt when his friend called to tell him about his daughter's first step and first tooth. His eyes filled with tears and I got up to hug him. But just as quickly as he began, he stopped talking and laid down before telling me it was time for me to leave. Each day, after that, I brought more pastries. Each time I got more tidbits about that little girl in the only picture in his room. I hoped I could give Mr. Hanks some of the joy he brought me by finding his daughter. So, from that day, I baked like I was birthed in the kitchen. When I went to see him, I brought him his favorite sweets: sweet potato pie and chocolate chunk cookies with cashews. I was so proud I taught myself how to make those goodies. Well, I learned by watching the Cooking Show Network that is. Everyone must start with baby steps!

    I didn't know why I was here. I was on my way to take stolen money to buy back my belongings and yet there I was at Mr. Hanks. Today, I decided to go tell him of my despicable plan. I was finally getting up the nerve to talk to him, at length, about the baby girl in the picture on his end table. He could try to tell me to leave if he wanted. I must know. With trepidation, I walked into the nursing home. I hoped they didn't look at me weird realizing I wasn't not supposed to be there that day. I was pleasantly surprised they waved at me when I walked in. They allowed me to sign in as usual.

****

When I walked into Mr. Hanks' room, he was still asleep. I looked at my watch and realized that it was too early to be coming by for a surprise visit. Still, I didn't want to leave. Being there gave me such peace. So, I slowly walked over to the chair by the side of his bed and watched him sleep. He was a handsome man, ruggedly handsome at that. I guess I never really noticed before now. His lips reminded me of someone. Now that I think of it, even the way he spoke reminded me of someone. But I couldn't put my finger on it. I reached over and picked up the picture of the little girl. I looked closely. Looking closely at the coloring of the picture, it must have been taken in the late sixties or early seventies. I looked even closer at the little girl in the picture then I looked at Mr. Hanks' sleeping face. There was indeed a strong resemblance. She had blond curly hair and a wide toothless smile. Her eyes glistened, and I was drawn into them. Dang, they look so familiar. Yes, this was his daughter. She was darker than he, with cappuccino coloring. My mind went to questions of where she was and what kind of person she could be to leave her father in a nursing home all alone. I enjoyed my time with Mr. Hanks, but his family should be reading him all his favorite poems and Bible verses. Some of which he knew by heart and recited them along with me.

What kind of woman would have a child with such a wonderful man and leave him? Not only leave him but leave him broken hearted and missing her and his child? If I knew where my father was, I would never leave him like this. I would give my all to him. Even though I didn't know him, even after all these years, I still loved my Daddy.   I must have been lost in thought with a heavy heart and head full of unanswered question because I didn't notice that Mr. Hanks was moving around in his bed. He threw his covers back and swung his feet onto the floor before moving towards the bathroom. I was afraid because I didn't know what he would say about me being there. He walked halfway to the bathroom before turning to face me. "Good morning Trinni. What a pleasant surprise it is to have you visit me today. You were on my mind last night before I went to sleep."

"I am so sorry to surprise you like this. I was on the way to a garage sale, but I was drawn to the nursing home for some reason. What a coincidence."
                    "Trinni, there are no coincidences in life. So called coincidences are only the universe working the way it's supposed to."
"You're right Mr. Hanks. You always know what to say."
"Trinity, you said you were going to a garage sale. Were you looking to purchase something specific?"

"No Mr. Hanks, I was going to buy my own stuff back."

"What does that mean Trinity, why would you have to buy your own stuff back at a garage sale?

"Well, it is a long story, Mr. Hanks."

"Give me a minute Trinity."

He walked to the bathroom and as I heard the water turn on for him to wash his hands, I contemplated sharing my story with him. I didn't want to risk him judging me. He would surely think differently of me if he knew the mess I had been doing to my life. He walked back into the room and sat down in the recliner.

"Come sit over here with me Trinity. It's obvious that you need someone to talk to."

I ignored his plea and changed the subject. I couldn't mess things up. He liked me. I couldn't do anything to change his mind. I couldn't risk it.

.

"Mr. Hanks, how did you know that I was here?"

"Trinity it's always nice to have you here, but please don't tell me that you brought more sweets with you. I tried to get into my favorite slacks yesterday and I couldn't zipper them without holding my breath. I have a little pudgy stomach now thanks to you and that pie, oh and those luscious cookies. Please tell me that you haven't bought anymore today, please."

"No, Mr. Hanks, I didn't bring any sweets. As I said, I was on the way to a garage sale."

Mr. Hanks giggled roughly, "Thank God. Now, Trinni, I am legally blind, that doesn't mean I can't see shading and movement. Besides…you have on that perfume you always wear. It reminds me of the scent my daughter's mother used to wear when I first met her."

"Oh really? This is the perfume I wear when I start missing my Mom. I found it in her things after she died. This was my Momma's signature scent. She wouldn't be caught dead without it on."

Mr. Hanks shrugged, "Oh well, I believe it was a popular fragrance back then, so I am sure many women wore it. That perfume was as common as people naming their daughter Trinity in our group of friends. The group of friends me and my ex ran with was a hippie crew that were also Jesus lovers. Everyone was on a kick to find their spirituality." He shook his head to clear away memories that caused a lone tear to start down his face. "Anyway, whenever I smell that scent on you, it invokes lots of memories."

I smiled. I didn't bring sweets but today would be the day I learned some information that would help me to find Mr. Hanks' family. He stared off into the corner of the room and whispered, "Oh, how I loved that woman. She was the reason why I lived. I loved her with every fiber of my being. In fact, it was that strong love that made me leave her and my daughter."

"Mr. Hanks, I don't understand, love doesn't make you leave your family. Love makes you *stay*."

"Trinni, I left her because I didn't want her to feel

obligated to take care of me. When I went to the doctor, I was told my eyesight would worsen over time until one day I would have minimum vision. I just couldn't bear to be a burden for her, so I left. Our daughter was a toddler and very dependent on her already. I couldn't add to her already heavy load. As an interracial couple in the sixties, we were already getting backward glances and vile hatred spewed our way. I just couldn't bear to be the blind white man with the beautiful capable black woman. Without me being able to support my family, my pride wouldn't allow me to stay. I could never bear it if she ever resented me, I loved her so much. So much so that when I looked at her, it felt like my heart would explode from joy. That last month, I stared at her and etched her every feature into my memory. The night before I planned on leaving, I made love to her so deep and slow, I was sure we touched souls like never before. I hope I'm not sharing too much, but that night, we were both in tears. It was that beautiful. I wanted to be assured that I took a precious part of her with me. From that day on, our souls have been one. Because of the scent you are wearing, she still owns my heart. The next morning, I waited for her to leave to go drop our daughter off at daycare before she drove to work. I packed through tears and grief. A couple of times I talked myself out of leaving. I told myself that our love was strong enough to get us through anything. But in the end, I had to force myself not to be selfish. I had to leave to make things easier for them. I cursed God for this dagger in my heart then I prayed for forgiveness. I had to at least be thankful for knowing what a love like that felt like. For her, I thank God. Through tears, I wrote a note that I left on the bed with two pink roses. As I prepared to leave, I stood at the door and inhaled the scent of my home. It smelled just like that perfume you have on. That's the scent I draw upon every lonely day here. Those days which were abundant until you came here to volunteer Trinity. Thank you, Trinity…for…being you." He paused then smiled at me with a familiar twinkle of dimples around his mouth.

"You're welcome Mr. Hanks. I am the only me I can be."

"Trinity, I need to tell you something. I have never shared this story with anyone before. I just need to talk this out. I have grown to trust you and I want to share with you who I really am and what has shaped my existence since then. Since I left my family, every so often I would call our mutual friend to see how my daughter and Lady were doing. I heard that my woman was doing okay but she had eventually met and married a street thug who got her addicted to drugs. When I heard that she was prostituting out in the streets to feed the habits and obsession of her husband, I stopped calling to check up on her. My heart couldn't bear it. She was so beautiful, but she was painfully naïve about people. She was so trusting; she never thought anyone was out to hurt her. One day that same friend called to tell me that my lovely soul mate had died. I hung up before he could tell me how she had died. Oh, the agony and guilt I felt that day! I was so focused on her resenting me. But in that moment, having her resent me but still living, would have been well worth it. That day I regretted leaving. I felt like a failure that I left my love to drown in the world. It is my fault she died since I had abandoned her."

Mr. Hanks paused to wipe his face and get himself together. He was falling apart right in front of me and I couldn't do anything to help him. In that moment, I felt so very hopeless and helpless! "Trinity, I can't express to you how my heart was broken into a million pieces that day. I called on God like never before to save me from the guilt I felt. Like a faithful Father, he healed me of my deep guilt. I didn't go back for her funeral. I just sent a kiss out into the universe. Our spirits are bound for eternity so I know one day I will see her again. Over the years, I haven't heard much about my daughter. I did hear, however, that she is beautiful and has a strong resemblance to her mother, only lighter. It has been thirty-eight years since I saw my daughter. I have had many regrets about leaving that day but regretfully I can't turn back the time to make it all right. My Father has forgiven me, so I have learned to forgive myself."

I sat silently and looked at Mr. Hanks. I know this sounds horrible but for the first time, I was glad he was blind. I couldn't stand to have him look at me and see the tears streaming down my face. Mr. Hanks was assuredly *my father*. I longed to finally meet my father but Lord Almighty, not like this! "Mr. Hanks, I have lost track of the time, I must get going. Bye." I didn't wait for him to say anything; I made fast tracks out of there. My Dad didn't leave because he didn't want me. He left because he was going blind! Oh, what a revelation.

****

I practically ran to the bus stop in hopes of catching a connecting bus to get to the garage sale at the condo. I still have time to at least buy some of my stuff back. At that point, with all the mental violence going on in my head because of Mr. Hanks, my Father, shopping was just the medicine I needed. As I walked to the bus stop, my name was called from behind. I didn't usually answer just anybody calling my name, but this voice sounded so familiar. So familiar, it chilled my bones. That voice belonged to a man with beautifully familiar yet mysterious eyes. Officer Micah called my name again as I turned to stand face-to-face with him. My eyes squinted in recognition but just as quickly warmed under the glow of his sweet smile. My eyes moved up and down his muscular body which is visible in his civilian clothes. He looked even more handsome out of his police uniform. The surprising thing was he was smiling back at me. Hold up, before I get too sappy, it hit me, was I under arrest? Under the vindictive puppetry of Quintaria, anything was possible! Was he on to my plan to steal nonprofit monies and use them to purchase my ill-gotten material things? Whatever his deal was, it couldn't be good. I sat down on the bus stop bench and pulled my pocketbook, full of stolen cash, closer to me. I already proved to y'all that I am not jail material! I am not ashamed to admit I am not even built like that.

364 | P a g e

Still intoxicating me with his beautiful smile, he asked me if I wanted a ride. Officer Micah was double parked in the slow lane and didn't seem to care. When I ignored him, he walked back to his car and my heart sank. I didn't want to give in to him too easily. When he reached his car, he was met with honking horns. He flashed his police badge to the road rage drivers then quietly drove around him. Darn, his powerful aura was so attractive! He asked me if I wanted a ride again. Before I could answer, he walked around to the passenger side and opened the door. Wow, chivalry wasn't dead! I sat still on the park bench and played hard to get. He was looking so sexy! I loved handsome, aggressive men. His smile got wider, and my body betrayed me. I smiled back at him. I could not believe I was allowing myself to get caught under the spell of his warmth. I was fighting to maintain my sexy, but this man's aura was magnetizing. I kept trying to remind myself of the sermon from Sunday. Focus Trinity focus, what was it again? Okay, uhh, that's it: "Look not on the exterior, yet look deeper to the spirit." Yeah, that's what the Pastor preached. I half squinted my eyes and looked deeper. I was distracted by Micah and his beautiful skin and that toned body. Then I looked at him closer and really listened to my spirit. I was obedient to what I heard. In the past, I got so infatuated with the exterior and superficial aspects of a man. I asked myself, is this man's spiritual core pure? Is he saved? Will he wait for me? As if he could feel my questions in his spirit, his eyes spoke, an undeniable, yes to all the above. Suddenly a lady sitting next to me on the bus stop bench got up.

"Gurrrrl, if you don't go with this gorgeous man, I will!" This heifer walked towards the car.

Officer Micah looked at me with doe eyes and pleaded, "Come on, Trinity, please give me a break. Please, come get in the car." I smiled. He must be attracted to a natural woman like me because he was sure giving me shade when I was all made up and wearing high-priced clothes. We're not even going to mention that I was in handcuffs! I was on the verge of an emotional crisis. Stay or go? I smiled serenely since I was honestly leaning towards, Oh God yes! Then it hit me, according to his pictures on his desk at the police department, this handsome, sexy, chivalrous man was s-i-n-g-l-e! I gathered my stuff and truthfully, I ran to his car trying hard not to trip. This single, gainfully employed, and honorable man was being nice to me. For now, that was good enough for me. Stop tripping, I was not settling, I was being realistic. You got to crawl before you walk, right?   He helped me into the car, shut the door and walked around to the driver's side. I leaned over and opened the door for him. He got in and smiled at me. He was driving an old beat up hooptie but with him now seated beside me, I felt like I was riding shotgun in a Bentley. Normally, I loved riding shotgun with a sexy man in the driver seat, but this was different. This man set my soul on fire and only the touch of his lips upon mine would put that raging fire out. I quieted my flesh. I will let this beautiful man be the welcome distraction from the

366 | P a g e

initially hurtful yet wonderful revelation that Mr. Hanks was my father. Don't get it twisted. I was not getting faded already. This man will earn my favor. If you didn't already know, let me hip you to the truth: Trinity is worthy…by faith!

~27~

Dishonor

What about me? Where could I get rid of my disgrace?
And what about you? You would be like one of the
wicked fools in Israel. Please speak to the king; he
will not keep me from being married to you." But
he refused to listen to her, and since he was stronger
than she, he raped her.

2 Samuel 13:13-14

***

Jnana

I pulled out of my driveway and headed to the expressway. Traffic was at a near standstill. No matter how many times I got off the exit and hit the highway, I got instantly stressed. I hated driving in traffic! You could say I am not the most patient person. It never failed, either I have someone around me putting on makeup, drinking coffee to start their day or eating their messy breakfast, which they end up cleaning up while driving above the speed limit. Add to all that craziness, there are yet still others changing the radio station, talking without a blue tooth, or carrying on an intense conversation with their passengers. The worse inattentive driver I have seen was reading a book! I remember wondering how good that book had to be to risk life and limb of every single person out here.

When Ashton told me he would be taking drivers education classes this year, I was terrified. Foolishly, he figured all he had to do was to be a good driver and everything would work out great. Honestly, you need to drive for you and everyone around you and, you must drive defensively. The road is a dangerous place to be, especially in the rain. You know, what is it about bad drivers that make them wait until the first drop of snow, sleet, or rain to fall before they get out there and test out their driving skills? It boggles my mind. But it never fails!

Thank God, I only have twenty minutes to drive until I could get off the expressway. Then I had only five lights, two stop signs, and a right turn until I got in front of the store. To help de-stress, I turned on my favorite morning radio show, Steve Harvey in the Morning. I was wrapped up in listening to the reactions to the Strawberry Letter when I pulled up in front of the store. What I saw in front of me could be drama. I did not expect Rebecca to have arrived this early! I figured I had time at least to make coffee and get my thoughts together before we talked. She must be extremely eager to talk, much more eager than I. I cringed when I noticed another body in the car with her. It was Celeste. I didn't know how this meeting could end up being as peaceful as I expected. I still wanted to smack some sense into her for sullying Ashton's innocence. I was sure with her mother there, she would play little Miss Innocent to gain sympathy and make me look like I was crazy and only on a witch hunt. With this plan, she was sure to look like a victim. This could either turn out with both of us mothers wanting to slap her, or Celeste might be able to mind meld Becca into thinking that I am crazy. With trepidation, I walked up to their car and we exchanged pleasantries. I looked at

Celeste and she had her head down. She mumbled a barely audible response to my extremely syrupy sweet good morning greeting. I unlocked the door to Namaste and quickly began making coffee. I barely plugged in the coffee maker before Becca started. Sheesh, could I at least get a cup of coffee in me first? Why is she in such a hurry?

"So, Jnana, I want to apologize for my outburst the last time we talked. I was under the assumption that my daughter was innocent. Well after I got the call from the school, I got a hold of Celeste's cell phone and broke into her email. My assumptions have changed regarding my *shy and innocent* daughter. My daughter has been with multiple boys! In fact, I would read you some of the conversations she had with several boys, including much older boys who are out of high school. But Jnana, her conversations are nowhere near Christian conversations! Celeste knows better." She looked over at Celeste who was trying her best to act invisible in the chair. If Becca's looks could kill, I would be calling 911! "I cannot begin to tell you how disappointed I am in my child. A child I thought was growing into a virtuous young lady. However, she is growing into a jezebel, right before my naive eyes. Last night, I even walked in on her having simulated sex with someone via webcam. I cannot tell you how embarrassed I was by that."

I looked over at Celeste and had to shake off any sympathy for the tears that were flowing down her face. I wanted to hate her; I really did. I didn't know what she was going through, but I knew all the sexual activity had to be a call for help. No! I had to tell myself, this was not an innocent child. This was a child who was caught in her own mess. She deserved that wake-up call and I wasn't going to stop it. This was no longer the cute little girl who I met for the first time when she and her mother came to Namaste for story time when she was just 2. No, that little girl was gone, never to be seen again. This young lady probably had more sexual partners than most of the grown women I knew. With that said, how to heal and move forward was the quandary we found ourselves in.

"Becca, I accept your apology and believe me, I totally understand your anger." She smiled and seemed to relax a little. "When I heard Celeste performed oral sex on Ashton, I was livid!"

Smack!

Becca smacked her so hard Celeste fell out of the chair and landed into a display of books. Celeste didn't bother getting up off the floor. At least she had some semblance of sense to know how serious this was.

"What!? Oh my God and where?!" Becca yelled at me.

"At your home." I got up just in time to stop her from going after Celeste again. I held her while Celeste scooted out of her mother's reach. She had a fear in her eyes that was tugging at my heart strings. Becca was gritting her teeth and she was fit to be tied!

"Jnana, not Ashton too."

Those words burnt in my chest and broke my heart even more than when I first found out. I was incredibly disappointed in both Ashton and Celeste.

371 | P a g e

"Unfortunately, yes it was with Ashton too." I bent down and picked up the books, more to steady my thoughts and prevent me from smacking Celeste too.

"So, it is all true Jnana. Oh my God."

"Becca, yes, I have known for weeks. I know how hard this is to take in. I know I sound like a horrible mother, but I have yet to talk to Ashton since I found out. My heart is just so betrayed. I willingly sent him to your house every day and to find out this has been happening right under my nose gets me."

"Jnana, I get it. This is ripping my heart apart! I mean they both know better. I haven't even figured out how to tell my husband. He'll be horrified when I tell him everything that's been going on."

From the back of the bookstore, I heard a wail.

"No! Ma, you can't tell Dad. Please!"

The rage in Becca's eyes called me to say something, anything to try to stop her temperature from hitting a boiling point and bubbling over.

I took a chance and called Celeste back over to her chair. "Celeste, please come over here and tell us what has gotten into you!" I half ordered and tried to appease Becca.

Celeste walked over and sat quietly in the chair. I said a silent prayer. I didn't know how long Becca can restrain herself.

"Start talking young lady, now!" Becca spewed at Celeste. No joke, a picture fell off the wall from the pure bass in her voice.

"Mommy, I don't know what to say." She looked at the anger in her mother's eyes and changed course, smart choice. "I mean, everything you found out is true. Everything Ms. Jnana and the girl on the bus said are true. But the way it's coming out is Ashton or the other boys didn't want to be with me. That's not true. The other boys were just to make Ashton jealous. I mean, I love Ashton and he loves me. I didn't want to be with all those other boys, they just showed me attention. Ma, I don't know, I guess I just got addicted to the attention all the boys showed me. Boys that didn't pay me any attention before. But when they found out what I did with other boys, they wanted me to be with them too. I really wanted Ashton but when he found out about the other boys. I told him I only loved him. We wanted to be together, but Ashton wouldn't have sex with me, so I guess he didn't really love me. But I think he does. Well, I don't know, I'm so confused. Still, I never forced anyone to let me do anything to them. They wanted it! They wanted *m*e."

Celeste stared off into the room as if she were under a spell. I wanted to shake her back to reality! Tears seemed to pool in her eyes, almost afraid of falling. Becca and I exchanged glances and shook our heads. How ridiculously delusional. Still, we were speechless. Celeste sounded like she enjoyed manipulating the mind of boys. But she was so clueless to the reality that it was she who was being manipulated by what she perceived was acceptance. Where did she get such demented thinking? She appears so lost. I shook myself back to nonjudgmental thoughts. I tried to understand how she could want to be accepted. But what I could not figure out was how she didn't see those boys were not accepting *her*. The boys were only accepting her sexual favors. That's what some teenage boys and, sadly, grown men do. They take what they are given. Those sexual favors they perceive come with no strings. I tried to have an understanding mindset. I mean I was once a needy teenage girl. Still, the thought of Ashton battling himself under the pressure of Celeste infuriates me. What could he have been thinking? He wasn't thinking with the right head. I really wished Shandon was there because he was the only one who could reach me when I was on the brink of exploding.

"So, Celeste, what's going on with you? I mean this is some ridiculous mess you have going on. You are acting and saying some really grown up things. I just don't get it. What is your motivation for having sex with all these boys? I taught you better than this!" Becca was on the brink of exploding too. But still, I was waiting with bated breath for the answers.

Celeste sighed then looked down. Wrong move! She knew this situation was one that was going to test her mother's constitution. As such, she would want to choose her words wisely. Still, she had better quicken her pace of responding to her mother's direct inquiries. She looked to me for help. She could see that this was an inopportune good cop, bad cop situation and she figured I was the good cop. Her eyes pleaded with me to help her dig out of this mess she dug for herself. Not a chance!

"Celeste, you can cut out those crocodile tears! You

weren't crying when you were out in the street acting all loose with all these boys. Now I want to hear the answers to my questions, now! I've been patient enough. This is your first and last warning. Trust me."

Celeste dried her tears and sat up in the chair. Something shifted behind her eyes and she got this grown woman look upon her face. Whoa, this is going to be a trip, I can feel it!

"Mommy, I have been having sex since last year. Do you remember Bilal?"

"Celeste, what does he have to do with anything? Of course, I remember Bilal! I couldn't stand his sneaky behind."

"Well, he raped me."

"What?! When did all of this happen?"

"That night you came home from work. Do you remember that night when he was over the house tutoring me and when you came in, he rushed out the door? Mommy, do you remember how I was crying? Do you?"

"Yes, and? You told me you were crying because you got a bad grade on your math test. Since it wasn't a day for you to be tutored, I was upset he was even at the house."

"Well, I let him in when he acted like he left a book at my house. I was already in my pajamas and I just thought he was going to come over to get something. I searched for his book, but I didn't find it downstairs. When I went upstairs to check my room, he followed me up there. When I turned around to go back downstairs to tell him I couldn't find it, he was standing behind me."

375 | P a g e

Celeste started crying again and I wanted to hold her so bad. My heart was bleeding for her.

"Did he leave a book at the house?"

"No, he told me he waited for you to leave for work before he came over to see me. That he had a crush on me. I trusted him so I let him in. He told me he wanted me to be his first and I was nervous. I told him I didn't like him like that. I thought everything was over then he took some alcohol out of his bookbag. He poured us both a cup of alcohol and we watched a movie together. When a kissing scene came on the screen, he leaned over and kissed me. I tried to push him off, but he pinned me down and pulled my pajama pants off. Then he raped me. Afterward, he told me that he wasn't really a virgin. But, Mommy, *I* was!"

Celeste seemed to go back to that moment she was raped and stared off into space. She began to shake and pulled her legs up to her chest. I was overwhelmed and my tears started to fall. I looked over at Becca; she was in pieces. I knew how I felt when what happened with Ashton came out. However, I never want to go through having to learn my daughter was raped! Whoa, that's too deep. Finally, Becca got up and hugged Celeste. She held her so tight. I know she was trying to overcompensate for not protecting her daughter from being raped by someone she trusted enough to have in her home. Someone she even paid for tutoring services. There was an uncomfortable silence in the room. No one said a thing as Mother and Daughter embraced each other. I sat quietly thinking…so this was why Celeste was acting out.

There was silence but finally, there was peace. From there we could move forward, and we could all begin to heal. Now we could see where all the promiscuity was rooted. It also explains why she was the aggressor in those sexual acts. Those times were her attempt at trying to regain control over her own body. She was trying to steal away from those boys something she saw as important. Her self-respect was what she was trying to take back. As well as her power that she felt she lost when she was raped. Sadly, in her effort, she was losing something way more valuable. She was losing herself in each act. Only God could lose her from the violent act. She needed to pray. Right this moment, it was time. It was the perfect time to pray. I tapped Becca on her shoulder and held her hand. She gently reached out to hold Celeste's hand. Then we three got down on our knees and we prayed. We cried then we prayed and cried some more. When we were done, we got up and talked a little more. Then there was silence again. There wasn't awkward silence, just peace. We all were in our thoughts. Finally, I broke the silence. I eyed the clock and knew we all needed time to heal and really begin to move forward.

"Well, ladies, this meeting was like a roller coaster ride. It dipped and dived into a discussion I had no idea it would go into. How about we stop our meeting right here and I order breakfast from the deli next door? They make a delicious mushroom and spinach egg white sandwich on homemade sourdough bread. They even have some Pike Creek Bananas Foster Coffee. How about I order us some food for the soul?"

They nodded yes and I went to make the phone call. I placed the order then busied myself until it was done. When the food was done, I went over to pick it up. They had a special dessert, so I also bought each of us a piece of their famous sweet potato cheesecake. When I came back, mother and daughter were laughing and enjoying each other's space. I knew though the journey to healing would be bumpy, their faith had already begun. We had an enjoyable time as we ate our brunch. We even put on some music and got our praise on. Then we prayed some more. Between me and Becca, we will help Celeste through this. When I get home, I will have a discussion with Ashton. It is past due for me to reconnect with my son. I miss my son. I am his mother and he is my son. It's time I love on him like a mother should. Maybe there are some things he has gone through that I know nothing about. Maybe, just maybe, this messiness with Celeste was just a symptom of something bigger going on with him. My family was always my focus. But I will admit I loved on them less as they got older. As for Becca and Celeste, they have bigger issues to tackle. No doubt Becca will have the cops pick up Bilal for statutory rape. Let's hope the cops get him before Celeste's father catches up to him!

~28~

Abstain

Don't withhold yourselves from each other unless
you agree to do so for a set time to devote
yourselves to prayer. Then you should get back
together so that Satan doesn't use your lack of self-
control to tempt you.
1 Corinthians 7:5
***

Trinity

I knew I was feigning. I woke up and my
entire body seemed to be on fire. It had been three
months since my last sexual encounter. It was with
Greysan, no less. Though it wasn't about me getting
my satisfaction, at least I got some pleasure out of
being touched by a man. Even if it was from
Greysan. I know some of you are shaking your head
but hey, this was me. I was a highly sexual woman.
I don't know who started the myth that Christian
women don't have desires. *This* one did! Some of
you may not mind cobwebs gathering in your
Queen, but I did. I felt like I was losing my mind
and I was way past delirious. It felt like I was
coming undone. I knew I should be moving from
my spirit but let me admit this to you, I desperately
needed some physical activity!

I know some of you are wondering about
Micah, but I think he was too good for me. If you
were reading closely, you would already know that
I have this bad habit of messing things up before
they fall apart so it's best that I do this now. I might

as well sabotage things before I get my heart mixed up to a point where I couldn't salvage myself. Settling for married men is what I knew, so maybe, just maybe that's all I deserved. Anyways, I'm sure there are other women better suited for Micah. He might even be with one right now! I've heard rumors about all the women cops have come on to them every day. Maybe he was a cheater like all the other men I know. Maybe. My low, if not nonexistent standards, for men have gotten me by for years. Why change things now?

For the first time ever, I have the phone in my hand about to call a man for sex. I will tell you; I was not proud of this. I was not usually the caller, I was the callee. Yes, I just made up that word, sue me!

Ok, I've got to clear my head and seriously contemplate which of my past married lovers to call. This isn't about money, another first. This was about my desire for pure animalistic satisfaction. Let me be honest about my intentions! I got warm when Alpha male number #1 came to mind. This man was an Omega Psi Phi. He's a sexy Que Dawg with long thick uhh…let's just say he is tall. This man has body parts that speak my name in three different languages, and he has another attribute that made the ocean jealous. I breathed and recalled his number as if my life depended on it. Right now, there was a serious urgency. My sexual life depended on this very call! So, as I dialed each digit, my heart quickened, and my palms got sweaty. My knees started knocking against each other with every recollection of this sexy brown man. Five feet eight, soft brown skin and a bald head I remember grab…well anyways, this man was just perfect for what I needed that very minute. His big hands seemed to know my every desire and his soft lips kissed me numerous places better than I ever felt. His body was made for pleasure: sexy smile and strong muscular thighs. Oh, did I mention his body was made like he was carved out of clay? This man is in no way a selfish lover. He listened to my breathing from which he could tell some very personal things about me. No man had ever taken the time to care when I was experiencing pleasure. So, with all his great attributes, what was his one negative? I bet you want to know why he wasn't my one and only man. Hmm, well, let's just say he was a married father of five crumb snatchers with a lawyer wife who would divorce him and take him for every dime he has. As a successful fortune 500 stockbroker, she would clean him out! She was such a legal panther that she would sue me for alienation of affections. I only wanted a piece of his loving. I didn't want to keep him. He never wanted to keep me either. That's why he was the best affair I ever had. We understood each other so well. When we see each other, it's all good. Then we kiss until the next time.

As I dialed his phone number I thought of Micah. I had to shake that thought off. Guilt was overwhelming me, big time! I was about to hang up when he answered. When I heard his voice, my heart stopped, and the guilt tugged at me even more. Did I mention that his voice is as deep as a late-night quiet storm radio host? So, I said, hey

Baby and right away he recognized my voice. So, we make small talk then we get to the meat of the conversation.

"So, hey Baby, I really need you. I'm in the middle of a drought. I need rain only you can provide." I purred seductively.

"Ahh…Trinity…Baby. You know I never say no to you. Umm, I would really love to come see you, but I can't."

Umm, this isn't sounding too good, "What's going on Zachary?"

"Uhh, I would really like to run to your rescue, but this isn't a good time for me. I am packing the kids up for the weekend. Wifey and I are going on a second honeymoon to the Tropics." He sighed then I heard him rustling around. I heard a woman's voice in the background, and he spoke so low I was having such a tough time hearing him. I had to press the dirty pay phone receiver to my ear. "Can I deal with this as soon as I get back?"

I didn't respond. I just hung up. What a waste of fifty cents! His wife must have been standing right next to him because he was acting like I was his secretary calling from his office. What was I doing? While I was determined to get some stress relief, I was not going backward. I couldn't ever get used to the feeling of being last on a man's list of priorities. This feeling made me feel so worthless. The tears fell and I wanted to kick myself. Dammit, I was not going backward again. That's it. I will not do this anymore! I settled long enough for some man putting me second or third. Zachary was telling me he was going to call me when he got back from a second honeymoon. What's wrong with this picture? To think I put up with such disrespect for so long disturbs me. Why was I so weak? Why was I available to be used and abused and thrown aside when a man's true love calls on him? I needed to make a change, today! When I felt too much guilt, I was brought to remembrance of I Corinthians 10:13, *anything you face will be nothing new. But God is faithful, and He will not let you be tempted beyond what you can handle. But He always provides a way of escape so that you will be able to endure and keep moving forward.*

I said a prayer and I felt better. I am tired of being comfortable feeling uncomfortable!

I know you want to punch me, hell, I wanted to punch myself. I could not believe I gave in to the urge to sabotage myself. I was scared, there I admit it! I was afraid of those feelings I felt growing in my heart for Micah. I figured if I slept with another man I would know for sure if it was something deep I felt or infatuation. Don't tell me you never heard the quote, "to get over a man, get under another." Well, as you can see me following that advice has backfired! As Mr. Hanks told me, things work out as the universe desires them. This was my sign to keep moving forward. This was the true moment when I needed to learn how to trust. I was scared, but in that moment, I trusted the journey and was still. Micah was the man I was willing to be focused on. Micah tried to spend more time with me. But I denied him full access. It was time to put the past behind me and look towards being available to a single man that really wanted me all to himself. It was time for me to allow Micah to be a good man to me. I tried to put my trust in a man, the first time ever. I allowed him to treat me the way I always dreamed of. I worked through the fear of being abandoned again and submitted to the feeling of falling in love. Micah was worthy of me. I just needed to get to a secure place so I could get out of my own way. I trust God, completely. By faith, I know He knows what is best for me. I dried my tears and smiled. I was finally ready. Peace be still.

~29~
Un-Faith-full

Have nothing to do with foolish, ignorant
controversies; you know that they breed quarrels.
And the Lord's servant must not be quarrelsome but
kind to everyone, able to teach, patiently enduring
evil, correcting his opponents with gentleness. God
may perhaps grant them repentance leading to a
knowledge of the truth,
2 Timothy 2:23-25
***

Jnana

I tossed and turned most of the night. I just
could not get comfortable! Things have not been so
blissful at my home. I have not even had a quiet
moment to talk to Ashton yet. Plus, Shandon and I
were at odds for several reasons. Looking at the
bedside clock I saw it was 6:07 in the morning.
Though I usually hated getting up this early on a
Saturday morning, I really didn't want to lay in bed
with my husband and risk having him wake-up
trying to touch me. I was just not feeling him like
that right now. So, before anyone got up, I went
downstairs to have breakfast by myself. I walked
down the steps in the dark and smiled. There was
something so beautiful about a still house. As I let
the peace settle me, a sudden thud on the door
scared me. I ran to the window and looked out the
curtain. The newspaper! Closing my bathrobe
tightly I opened the door and picked up a wet blue
bag. As I did this, cool rain splashed upon my face.

Now, I was fully awake!

Looking into the fridge I spied the last of my spinach and mushroom white pizza. Yummy! I am too lazy to even heat it up, so I sat down and pull the newspaper out of the blue plastic bag. I opened the newspaper to my favorite section, the local section, and what I saw made darn sure I was at full attention. There splashed on the cover page was a headline that read *Banked out*! Underneath the headline is the words, Hextlers Bank, Acting Director, Greysan Lobes, reluctantly steps down amid sexual harassment claims. There was a huge picture of Greysan walking with his trademark swagger next to his very attractive female lawyer. They appeared to be walking way too close. My mind reeled. Could it be? *His lawyer*? Nah, there was no way she would be so foolish! I was going to call Trinni, but I had no way of getting in touch with her! Instantly a scripture, Psalm 105:15, came to mind, *you shall not touch my anointed thus saith the Lord.* I thanked the Holy Spirit. This scripture is a Word, indeed!

As I read the rest of the article, I prayed for Greysan, he was in a lot of trouble. There were several women, including Lisa, the secretary Trinity told me about, who have come forward with claims of sexual harassment. They all had the same story of being fired once they spurned his, very aggressive advances while they worked as his secretary at the bank. Greysan was really a piece of …work!

I was so engrossed in the article I didn't even hear Shandon coming down the stairs. From the frown on his face, as he walked into the kitchen, I knew this was not going to be the quiet, serene way I wanted to start my morning. Things had been really tense between us since the whole condom incident. But he was wrong, I was right, what more is there to say? Once he apologized, I would think of forgiving him. It seemed that he never heard the very relevant phrase, happy wife, happy life. I should've Googled it then printed it off for him because he was tripping!

I walked to the stove and made Shandon his favorite breakfast, a mushroom, tomato, and spinach omelet with hollandaise sauce and wheat toast, lightly browned, while he read my newspaper. Then I made him a plate along with a cup of black coffee. I placed it in front of him and kissed him on his cheek.

"Good Morning Shandon."

"Good Morning Jnana. Thank you for breakfast." He replied without looking up at me.

"You're welcome," I replied tersely. Oh boy, here we go!

It was early morning and the kids were off at their prospective best friends' houses. You would think we would be taking advantage of the empty house. But as we both sat, tensely at the table, in our bathrobes, I realized this was odd. Usually, we would be in bed making love as soon each of us opened our eyes. This was for the birds! It had been a long time since we were this disconnected. I break the ice, oh here I go again, spoon feeding him conversation, "Uhh, so, what's got you up so early?" I ask nicely but honestly, I was so tired of humbling myself while Shandon gets to pout.

"Nothing" Shandon replied simply. He left me hanging. I won't be doing this too many times, trust.

I cleared my throat. How many times did I have to feel foolish before he got a clue? Then again, maybe I should get a clue! "Do you care to expound upon that answer, just a little *Shandon*?"

"No." Really? Just a simple no?

"Fine." Two can play this game! He wants to be childish, I can too. Just watch me!

I pushed back my chair and stomped upstairs. I packed a bag and gathered my toiletries without a word sideway. I grabbed my purse and went out to the car without saying goodbye. I needed a break from this nonsense. As I drove down the street, my cell phone rang. Surprise, surprise, it's Shandon. I rejected the phone call and when he called back again, I rejected that too. Just as I was about to turn up the music to sing along with Jill Scott's *Hate on me,* he called back again. I finally relented and put in my Bluetooth before answering.

With attitude, I shout, "What!"

Shandon tried to match my bravado but missed the mark when his voice cracked, letting tenderness show, "Where are you going?"

I stifled a giggle, "Why?"

"Don't play games with me Jnana!"

"No." I gave him back his foolish; two letter answer. Judging by his silence, it was clear to me his medicine tasted *bitter*. Let's see how he deals with it.

"Look Jnana, stop playing with me, I am not a

child! I am your husband and you will tell me where you are going!"

This time I couldn't stop myself from giggling out loud, "Oh so now you want to assert some authority? Were you my husband when you betrayed me? You did not discuss going to get Ashton condoms with me. You went against our agreement, which we both made early on in our marriage. Instead, you chose to be sneaky and blindly support Ashton having sex with that girl. How dare you!"

"Betrayed you, oh those are strong words. I betrayed you by helping *my* son out? You didn't have him alone woman! And what about when you betrayed me by putting your friendship with her before me? Numerous times! Ashton is my son Jnana!"

"Shandon, I am your wife and you will not talk to me like that! Now, you betrayed our covenant. You know - three cords? How could you? We have been together far too long for this to have gone the way it has. Why couldn't you trust me? Why? I apologized for the whole putting Trinity before you mess. I haven't even spoken to her. Babe, you are my best friend now. I choose to put you first. Yet still, all this is not enough! I thought we…you…forgave me and wouldn't bring it up again."

He was silent and I began to cry. This hurt! I have never been so willfully hateful to my husband, under any circumstances! I finally manage, "I cannot do this anymore."

I heard him sniffling and I knew he was crying. My heart ached for him, but I tried hard to

389 | P a g e

keep being strong. He must know how this made me feel. He could cry if he wants.

"What are you saying, Babe? Do you want a divorce?" Then he completely broke down.

I didn't respond as I listened to my husband cry. I wanted to turn around and drive back home, but I couldn't give in that easily. As I sat at the kitchen table this morning, I was eager to talk things out and finally put it behind us. He was the one playing mind games. I wasn't! So now he had the nerve to cry. Where was his emotion when I was sitting in front of him, my heart aching, crying out to him? He didn't save me! Why should I save him now?

"Jnana, what are you saying?" He whispered into the phone.

"Look, I need a break. Honestly, I need a break from *you*. When the kids come home, just tell them that I am over at Momma and Poppa's."

"So, it's that easy? Do you want a divorce after all these years? I thought that we…you were happy just like I am."

I shrugged. He was breaking me down with the tenderness in his voice. Hold on I had to tell myself.

"Yea, I thought we were too."

"So, do you?"

"I need some time to myself, to think. Ok?" I have got to get off this phone, this is killing me.

"Jnana look this has gotten out of hand. Can we pray? Please?"

Whoa, Shandon is really pulling out the stops. Pray? He sure blindsided me with this. How can I say no to prayer?

"Look Shandon, I am not in the mood to pray. So, no, I won't pray."

"Wildflower, come on, let's pray. Let God make this right between us. You know He will restore our marriage to the way it used to be. Only God can heal us and stop this madness."

"Shandon, why are you calling me Wildflower? You haven't called me that in a long time."

"Wildflower, I'm trying to get to the heart of you. I am simply trying to reach deep in you to that beautiful woman that I love. Right now, you are being so guarded and cold."

Then he sang *Wildflower* by New Birth to me. I was choked up. I always loved when my husband sang to me. Oh, how I love this man! "Shandon, this is tough on both of us. Look, all I want you to see is that I feel betrayed. We were supposed to stand as a united force, yet you talked to Lili and Ashton before I even got a chance to discuss my feelings with them. You made me feel abandoned."

"Jnana, I'm so sorry I made you feel abandoned and betrayed. You are my wife and I always want to be your husband. I love you, completely. When you get an attitude, you don't hear much of what I or the kids say. It's like we are burdens you don't want. It's like we have no choice, what Jnana wants, she gets. I couldn't really see things going any differently that day either. I had to protect my kids. Even with all these issues, I feel like we have, as a family, how can you be so bold to act like you want a divorce? How could you Jnana...after all these years?"

"Protect your kids?" Shots fired! Thank gosh for

small favors, my fire was back! "Oh no buddy, you will not push this off on me, "I tried to talk to you, Shandon, numerous times. Each time you were prideful, and you refused to give in. You shut me out and walked around ignoring me with all your negative energy. I will not live like that a day longer. As for, what I want and nothing else matters, I bend, just not enough to get walked on by you and the kids. You ask me, how I could want a divorce after all these years but *after all these years* you should know that I hate being ignored! I hate it! I could not continue to live like that, I won't!"

"Babe calm down. Just come back to the house. I'm sorry. Please, don't leave me, please? I will talk to you now, I promise."

I was not impressed by his outpouring of emotion. It's a little too late.

"Jnana?"

"Shandon, we both need a break from each other. Listening to you, it appears as if you aren't too happy with me either. I am feeling uneasy for the first time in our marriage. Maybe we should try a trial separation. Maybe get individual counseling and see how that goes. I have to go Shandon."

"Are you really getting off after saying those things to me? You act like you just told me to pick up some eggs on the way home from work. We really need to pray, this has me really bothered. Your tone tells me that something else is going on here."

"I have to go Shandon."

"You cannot go…please. You are my light."

I smirked, "No, God is your light."

"Ouch! That's cold, you know what I meant."

"Humph, yea, I knew what you meant. Look I got to go, Namaste is calling on the other line. I'll be in touch."

"I love…"

I interrupted him before he could finish, "Goodbye Shandon."

"Oh wow, I don't get an I love you back?"

Dang, this man is relentless, "No, not right now. I don't know how I feel about you. With my head, all messed up like this Shandon I can't say anything I might not mean. Anymore." Dang, that hurts me to say.

"Fine, goodbye," Shandon whispered, defeated.

I took the call and explained to Paulina that the sound system was on a timer. All she had to do was press reset to clear out the old timing so she could commence with an event with the live band without our music overshadowing it.

As soon as I hung up the phone, I broke down in tears. I hoped no one called 911. From the outside looking in, I was sure I would appear to be having a mental breakdown. After I felt as if I had cried my soul out, I pulled myself together and pulled off. I never expected it to hurt this badly. Was I really leaving the love of my life? I didn't want to lose my husband. Still, how do I compromise when Shandon takes things into his hands and expects me to fall in line? I didn't think I was even built to deal with this kind of thing happening in my marriage. I ran things and Shandon politely followed along. How could I, after all these years, expect my household to run smoothly with my husband leading it? I trusted God and I trusted my husband. But how do I step back and let God work through my husband to lead my family? As I asked myself all these questions, a final one rose to my throat and choked me like bile…where is my faith?

~30~
Soul's Core

My beloved has gone down to his garden, to the
beds of spices, to browse in the gardens and to
gather Lilies. I am my beloveds and my beloved are
mine; he browses among the Lilies.
Song of Songs 6:2-3
***

Trinity

As I stood in the arms of the most beautiful
man I have ever seen, I melt. Not in the way I
previously did in this position. No, within these
arms, there is peace. There is lots of passion within
this embrace but there is also trust. I trust this man
with my tenderness, and I feel so safe that I let out
all the pent-up pain in one breath. Previously, when
I had the arms of a man wrapped around me, in
those times, there was no peace. There was always
pain. In those arms, there were times that my soul
was at war with my carnal side. During those times,
the man holding me only wanted my naked body
while, but I ached to have the hole in my soul
healed. The man holding me always craved my
sexual pleasure, wherein, I always craved his
acceptance of me as my true self. The war in my
mind always started off that way with me damaging
my soul with each self-disparaging thought. Then,
in one last futile effort to exact revenge upon my
already weak self-image, I would step back and
look into that man's eyes. I wanted ever so dearly to
see caring and love. As I leaned in and looked

closely, during those times, and with such glee at maybe that time would be that one genuine and beautiful moment I dreamed about all my life, I tried to find something real. But that glee would quickly turn into a mental train wreck as the man standing before me was not interested in allowing me to see the true him. That man was only interested in ripping off my clothes and undressing the sexually expressive part of me. He was neither concerned with my soul nor my respect. He just wanted sex and lots of it. As a war within mind raged on, that man would be grunting and groaning over me, even as I tried to enjoy the pleasure, my carnal side taunted me about the many other men that took every fantasy I created and unwittingly turned them into my own personal hell. With every sexual episode that came as an unfair end to my personal war, I took snapshots in my head. I have many thumbprints within my mental pictorial diary that provide evidence that sex takes no prisoners. There were no guts and no glory when one hoped for a spiritual connection when a sexual encounter is the only consolation being offered. In the past, the only thing sex offered me was a soul damaging pain. I had many memories of me feeling less than a woman each time I unclothed myself for one man after another. None of the men ever offered anything that matched my soul imprint. They only offered physical pleasure. Honestly, some hit the mark, and some missed the mark altogether! After he got dressed and left, I felt worthless, dirty and I absolutely hated myself.

I held my breath so I could feel Micah's

heart beating against mine. This feeling of intimate is so deep, tears rise in my eyes. My heart hurts. I care deeply for this man. More than I ever imagined I could. Still, I need to know. Before I go any further, I must know. As I inhaled his masculine scent, it invigorates my mental warfare. I steadied myself to step back and look into his eyes. Those beautiful, deep brown soul filled eyes seem to speak to an inner part of me that has never been caressed so lovingly. Oh, how I adored this man. Hold up, focus! As if on cue, I was thrown into a vicious battle between my carnal side and my soul again.

Trinity, you cannot let his outward beauty distract you from his inner beauty. But he is so sexy! I just want to see if he can make me feel loved, even if temporarily. *Yes, temporary, like a band-aid! We must love ourselves, first. Stop this right now, Trinity, this is always our downfall, we lead from our carnal desires, not our soul, focus Trinity, focus! This man's value is deep, he is worthy of letting down our wall, he won't hurt us. Promise. Look deeper!* Whatever.

I ended the conversation with myself and I hold back my tears. I didn't want to be wrong again, especially not this time. I couldn't be. I didn't think that my heart can stand another disappointment. As I press back and prepare myself to look into his eyes, he pulls me tighter.

See, my carnal side further taunts me, he wants to press up harder against us to show off what he is working with. This is just about sex. Trinity, yet again, you are wrong about him. You aren't worthy of this beautiful man, get a grip! You met him when he was arresting you. Gurl you better get you a life! I have several seats. The first is one with a reality check. Cash it!

I quelled my inner volcano and relax. I focused in on what Micah says as he cuddled up closer to me. He held my hand then whispers, "Trinity, please don't move. I could feel your soul stirring and I can't bear it. You can trust me. Let me in. Please, I promise that I will unclothe my soul for you too."

This had to be a fantasy. With those words, this man has unearthed some things in me that I never knew needed digging out. I never felt like this before. This man has his arms around me, and he is holding me so tight that I can feel his heart beating in sync with mine. This feeling, this peace, feels beautiful. Even my inner carnal voice is silent. This is the first time, ever, my soul wins the argument. Still, I must know. I rest into him for a second longer and allow this moment to live in my dreams. His breathing has calmed against mine. He has relaxed his body into mine and I laid my head upon his strong chest. I hate to interrupt this beautiful moment, but before I go any further, I must know. I pushed back and looked into his eyes. As I gazed deeply into his soul filled eyes, I waited for him to ruin the moment by ripping at my clothes. However, as I rested beautifully in the vision of joy in his eyes and saw no remnants of sexual desire in his physical, my carnal voice awakens and questions me. Why won't she just leave me alone?!

Ooh, gurl, he is gay or maybe just maybe he didn't like a thick mocha shake like us. Maybe he has a woman, you know that we are only worthy of jump off status. Look, he wasn't even aroused after holding us that tight, he doesn't want us. Major Fail!

I shook those thoughts away; my carnal side is just afraid of this unfamiliar feeling of peace. I put my fear in check and embrace this moment. This moment may be my moment of breakthrough. I will push ahead. I will fear not! He looked deeply into my eyes and I didn't even try to hide my uneasiness from him. I am open to this experience, to him. To joy.

"Trinity, may I be honest with you? I mean *really* honest?"

Ooh gurl, this is it. He is going to tell us that he isn't digging us after all! *Hush, this is love.*

My carnal side is getting on my last nerves. She is about to die a quick violent mental death!

Micah stood totally transparent before me. I fight not to get distracted by his luminous smile or that dimple on his left cheek that seems to be winking at me. I looked into his eyes and for the first time, my heart barometer stops in glee. He has that look that I have craved all my life. It is serious, deep and oh so very loving. His hands are beside him, relaxed. Usually by this point, the man has his hands on my blouse ripping at my buttons. Usually by this point, the man standing before me has his mouth pressed perversely on mine trying to suck my breath out with his tongue. Usually by this point, the man is pressing his hands on my shoulders so that I could fall violently to my knees. Usually by this point, I am undoing his zipper as if under a spell. Usually by this point, I am acting like a carnal robot, eager and ready to please. But this isn't the usual, so I don't know what to do. I wonder what other women do at this point. I am trying to be brave, but this is too much for my feeble heart to bear. Father God help me. I quickly pull him close to me and lay my head softly on his chest. I count his heartbeats, trying feverishly to gain some courage to proceed forward. Then, I do something I know will cure my uncertainty, I close my eyes and I pray. I pray this look in his eyes is what God has intended for me. I pray, if this is the man for me, God will give me the words to express my feelings without leading first from my past hurts. I pray for understanding in an unfamiliar situation. Lastly, I pray I had love in my eyes, and not shown him that I don't trust him. Because I truly want to. I asked all those things in Jesus' name.

This time he pulled back and looked at me. He had no rushed desire for sex in his eyes. He cupped my chin and looked into my eyes. I was afraid of what he would see in them, so I smiled serenely. Peace. He returned my smile and kissed me softly on my lips. Now, I have another mental picture of peace. I will now have two pictures in my peace photo album. The one with Momma and Jesus holding me at the church was already filed there permanently.

"Trinity, trust me. I won't hurt you. Please let me look at you. Babe, you are so beautiful.

"Micah, tell me what you see when you look into my eyes"

"Well, Trin, I can tell that you are a caring woman with a heart so big. You are sweet, and you have such a unique way of seeing the world, I find myself questioning the way that I view things. As a police officer, I can be jaded with the cold realities of life. But since spending time with you, I see a lot of joy in this world. You have truly enriched my life."

"Wow, you see all that in these eyes?"

"Yes, I see all that in those beautiful eyes of yours. I do and I see much more than that too. But I'm not going to tell you all that right now. See, I don't want you floating around with your head gassed up like a balloon."

I smiled. This man really sees me. Finally, a man sees all of me. *Thank you, Lord.*

"Micah, earlier you asked me if you can be really honest with me. Well, yes, please do." I took his hands in mine and felt the connection between us heighten.

He smiles and says, "Now Trinity, I like you, I really do." He sees my face fall a little then says, "Patience…let me finish. I was attracted to you when I first saw you, but I had my job to do. I mean, I *was* the officer there to arrest you. I couldn't allow my personal feelings to get involved. Even as I looked at you across the board table at the department store, I couldn't help but be taken in by your magnificent beauty. I couldn't help but notice that even though you were overly adorned with artificial physical enhancements, there was an undeniable beautiful spiritual essence all around you. I know you saw my eyes locked on yours

401 | P a g e

when you were in the back of the police car. Tell me I am wrong."

"Well, I can't say that I was paying much attention to anything in the boardroom besides the fraudulent charges being spoken against me. At the time, I was completely mortified to have so many witnesses to one of the lowest points in my life. I have done some messy things in my life but stealing some married woman's identity is not one of them."

"Trinity, I could see you weren't a hardened criminal. I could also see there were many holes in the police report but again, I had a job to do. I had to execute the warrant signed against you. I saw you weren't someone looking for a come up when you asked to be made up for the mug shot. Yes, I did hear when you asked that," He rubbed my hand so gently, "Ever so often I would check up on your case with a friend of mine in the D.A.'s office. One day she called me to tell me the charges were dropped because the complainant refused to cooperate with the prosecution. They said all letters updating you on the case were returned to their office by the Postmaster. When did you begin living at the shelter?"

"I'm so relieved that the case has been dropped! Even though they were trumped up charges anyway, I am ecstatic. Micah, this is what really happened: after the man that I was having an affair with broke up with me to pursue his secretary, I was cut off my monthly living allowance. When, his wife, realized that I was living in a condo and driving a brand-new vehicle purchased by her husband, she padlocked the condo and had the car repossessed. She got me fired and arrested for those fake charges of identity theft. Shortly thereafter I moved into Redeeming Hope."

"Hmm, that's all pretty interesting. But it doesn't change what I feel for you. Not a single bit. Now, sweetheart, I know you are trying to keep yourself emotionally distant from me but you still haven't answered my question: did you realize that some energy transferred between us when our eyes locked in the police vehicle?"

I smiled. This man was persistent. Though I found the determination sexy, it was disarming "Yes, I did feel an intense attraction to you. But see, as I remember it, the only look in your eyes was pure hatred. Micah, you looked at me like I was trash! I surely didn't sense any underlying attraction coming from you. None."

"Trinity, I never looked at you as trash. That's not how I view anyone…especially not you. Babe, you know that I had a job to do. Please understand that I needed to stay professional. However, I will admit that it became harder to keep my focus when I realized that the attraction my partner had for you wasn't being kept under wraps. He was blatantly pursuing a physical situation with you. I must admit that I was torn between jealousy and outrage. Trin, he had no right to touch you like he did. I had a tough time not cursing out my partner for being so aggressive and beyond disrespectful with you. I made sure he didn't cross the line at the door or there would have been a serious conflict for me. Rest assured, he and I had it out in the station after we transferred you for fingerprinting. His behavior was unusual, so I told him how I felt about his unprofessional and disrespectful behavior and left it at that. I apologize that I made you feel that I didn't respect you. Please know that was not my intention."

I smiled as he rubbed my hand softly, "Babe, I understand, and I forgive you. That's water under the bridge."

He smiled widely and his eyes warmed even more, "Trinity, as I look at you now, I see that you have made some positive personal changes, these last few months. Your spirit is aglow. I have heard through the rumor mill at the nursing home about a young lady volunteering with a blind man. I have been visiting a relative who was recuperating from hip surgery so I visited regularly and each time I have been here, I must have just missed you. I heard how that person's presence has moved the man to open and be kinder and more loving to the staff. He even went out of his way to being less isolated from the rest of the population. I had no idea the young lady was you until I saw you coming out of Mr. Hanks' room and put two and two together. Sweetheart, I can't deny my attraction to you any longer. I cannot deny that even in the police car your eyes saw deep inside my soul and I had a difficult time keeping a hard face. Let me be up front, I want to court you."

"Court me? What do you mean by that? You want to play some basketball?" I joked trying to cut the tension between us.

He was having none of that. He moved closer to me and his eyes looked into my soul, "Trinity, I'm an old-fashioned boy at heart. Please allow me to treat you as you deserve to be treated. Please. Now, I know that we haven't spent a lot of time together, but I want you to know me very well. So, are you ready for this type of relationship?"

"Micah, yes, I am. Are you ready?"

"Without a doubt! Look, I have been a player most of my life, that I can tell you without pretense. I have bedded women simply out of sexual need and had no ill feelings about it. I have been unapologetically wayward in my thoughts and actions toward women and I have few regrets about it. I was a single man doing single man things. However, with you, I want it to be different. Normally when I hold a woman in my arms, I am ready to go in to seal the deal, straight up get the sex. When you were in my arms, how you rested your body softly upon mine, I know you trust me. I wanted to hold you tighter and feel the connection between us. I mean I am attracted to you sexually; I mean look at you. I hope that I am not being too honest with you right now."

I smiled and he got this nervous look on his face. I rubbed his hands to reassure him.

"No, you are being perfect right now. Yes, I am a little taken aback by your honesty. However, your directness is refreshing. There is something about you that makes me trust you without question. Here is my honesty: I warred with myself about what your intentions were when you pulled me into a friendly hug that quickly turned into a passionate embrace. I want you to want me. But for the first time in my life, I am ready to want a man to want

405 | P a g e

all of me, not just my body. I believe that I am worthy of that and no less."

"Trinity, look, I do want you, very much. But my carnal needs aren't important right now. Hold up, I am looking at your face frowned up. You are staring at me in disbelief and your body language, with your hand on your hip, doesn't give off the best vibe of open-minded communication. Give me a chance to explain, please?"

"Micah, there is no need to explain. Look, I am far from perfect. I don't have a flawless past when it comes to men and relationships. I can bet my past has as many muddy footprints as yours. So please stop feeling the need to explain your past. I understand and I accept you as you are. Completely."

"Trin, I find you very attractive, extremely attractive. Your body make up is just so sexy. I mean your proportions are very appealing. And I would like to touch you all over and live out my fantasies with you. But and this is a first for me too, I am requiring that we do this the right way or not at all. I want the day we make love to be special. When we make love, I want us to blend souls, not just connect bodies. I don't want to ruin anything deep that we could find by rushing things. I think you deserve all I can offer. As a man, I have not always been honorable in the way I feel compelled to be with you. And this is not me explaining myself. It's just that there is something in me that tells me that you are so special. I won't risk being a lesser man to you than you deserve. You are worthy of all that you dreamed of. I want to be well beyond

406 | P a g e

all the desires of your heart, mind, and soul." He took my hands in his and looked deeply into my eyes. No lie, I felt my soul leap, "Trinity, Babe, if you will allow me the pleasure."

I didn't know what to say, this man was all I wanted. All I needed and all I ever yearned for. But I must be cautious. Even though no man has ever said all this to me, this may be some new 2017 reverse psychology game. I breathed in and out and looked into his eyes. I looked deep into his soul. Beautifully, in it, I saw sincerity and honor. I didn't see game playing in the reflection in his eyes. I saw a grown man who was ready to let down his guard and dive into love's deep waters. I'm glad! I'm taking off my life jacket because the water looks mighty pleasant.

I smiled serenely, "I am ready for something real…with you Micah" was all I could muster.

From that day, a month ago, Micah called me from his cell phone, home phone and office phone. He even busted out of his self-professed comfort zone and called me from his Momma's home phone. He exceeded all my expectations at building trust in him. He learned very quickly that I need to trust to love. Still, this was a scary journey. When I looked back on my romantic life, I realized I had never truly been in love. It's sad but I had to be honest. Learning to love a man is in line with my journey of learning to love myself. Micah's pursuit of making me happy went leaps and bounds and levels higher than I ever thought a man would go for me. I felt secure in his dedication to pursuing a committed relationship with me. I was happy for the first time in my romantic life. More importantly, I was at peace. I had deep feelings for Micah and quite possibly loved him. But I still had issues with me feeling as if I was not worthy of him. This man, this beautiful man of God, could have any woman he wanted, but he wants me. Why? When I was confused about a man, I usually had sex with him to figure out if it was lust or infatuation. With Micah, it was different. I didn't want to consummate this relationship until I knew I was good enough to belong exclusively to him. I was not confused about his intentions, nor was I confused about my feelings for him. I will fall hard for him, I'm sure of it. Amazingly, I knew he was already falling hard for me. It's not in the things he gives me, no, it is in the respectful words he uses when he talks to me, the softness of his touch and the passionate way he courts me. I want to be that, 'When a man findeth a wife, he findeth a good thing,' type woman. I watched the I Am Woman Conference 2016 on Daystar and I watched a sermon by Pastor named John Gray. He said that "a wife is not the presence of a ring, it's the presence of your character. Too many women want to be married but are walking in the spirit of girlfriend." I want to be a woman with the character of a wife. I no longer want to walk in the character of girlfriend. And not the character of jump off. I want to be the woman I always desired to be. I want to be a confident and assured Woman of God. I want to see the woman that Micah sees when he looks at me. He sees something so beautiful in me, I want to see it.

Though we both wanted to make love, we

were waiting. This was a test of will for both of us because we both were highly sexual people. However, we entered into an agreement that we would be highly spiritual people and put our Lord before our flesh. Micah asked me to move out of the shelter and move into his house with him. I've refused, repeatedly. I won't ever again be kept by another man. I have been looking for a job, but it has been difficult. Still, I have some irons in the fire, so I am just waiting on some calls to start coming in. I wish I still had my belongings from the condo so I could paint some paintings I know would sell. The window to my creative self is wide open. Just like my nose for Micah. Ahh, true love makes me want to create some beautiful pictures that will illustrate just how joyous I am. For now, don't judge me, I'm calling Micah to break up. I love him, I really do. However, I couldn't risk getting wrapped up in a relationship, yet another, where I love the man more than I love myself.

~31~
Kindred Spirits

"Be ye not unequally yoked together with
unbelievers: for what fellowship hath righteousness
with unrighteousness? And what communion hath
light with darkness?"
2 Corinthians. 6:14

***

Jnana

I drove around aimlessly until I came to the
park where I met Shandon for the first time. I, a
self-professed bookworm, was having a picnic in
the park with a delightful book. I was deeply
engrossed in the storyline and fashioned myself to
be the heroine who was being courted by a
handsome hero of war returning to pursue my favor.
I remember Shandon was stretching right next to
my blanket, even though other runners stretched
way across the other side of the grassy knoll. When
I finally looked up, because he was blocking my
sun, we locked eyes. I shook it off and went back to
reading my book but whoa, I thought I caught a
glimpse of Heaven there in his beautiful eyes. That
day, he must have run a million miles because he
ran past my blanket two times and walked by it two
times. The course is two and a half miles! The last
lap, stretched from his run, again, right next to my
blanket. He had run so long that he had drunk all
the water in his water bottle. He looked a little
parched. As he stretched, he smacked his dry lips,
loudly and repeatedly. I looked up and he smiled at

me. To mess with him, I went into my cooler of ice-cold bottled water and took one out. I opened it up and gulped it loudly. Then, I looked over at him and smacked my lips before making an ahh sound. I didn't care about his numerous, barely subtle, hints for some water. He was going to be a man and ask me for a drink! Finally, after he appeared to stretch enough to cool off all the muscle in his body and mine, he asked if I had any cold water inside of my cooler for him.

"Sure," I smiled, "I know you must be exhausted from your million-mile run. Not to mention thirsty as all get out."

We shared a giggle. "Yes, on both points. I am not sure what got into me today. I had this unforeseen motivation to…" He smiled beautifully, "work out harder than usual. Every time I got back to this spot on the course, something pushed me to sprint faster."

"Hmmm" was all I offered. I need him to be more direct. Come on, I cannot spoon feed him this. He has got to work for my time.

"Hmmm," He rubbed his chin and his eyes ran up and down my face, "Since you appear to appreciate directness, here it is I want to take you out. Would you allow me the pleasure?"

"Yes, I would love to accompany you on an outing. I enjoy being in the company of a man who knows what he wants and goes after it, I mean, me. If and only if…"

He looked deeply into my eyes and smiled, "Anything."

"I agree to you taking me out if you would have

lunch with me right now. That is…if it is okay for you to eat so soon after working out so hard."

Shandon didn't waste any time sitting down on my blanket with me. He politely took my CD out of my CD player and put his in. On the CD Shandon had a jazz play list that set my heart on fire. Out of my speakers smoothed the most romantic jazz music I had ever heard. The sexy saxophone sang out and the trumpet matched the beat of my heart. All I could do was close my eyes and enjoy the musical flow. This man really had some amazing taste in music. He is incredibly sweet to share this beautiful music with me. He had the old greats like Nina Simone and artists like Al Jarreau and Ella Fitzgerald.

Shandon tapped me on the shoulder and whispered in my ear, "Do you like?"

I looked at his beautiful smile and I tried to stay in the moment of bliss, "Uh huh. This music was so lovely. It has completely changed my mood."

He put his fingers softly upon my lips and looked deeply into my eyes, "Shhh, this is my favorite song. It's called Enchantress by Lonnie Liston Smith."

I melted as he removed his hand from my lips. I pulled my eyes from his and closed my eyes to fully enjoy this song. It was beyond beautiful! This man was really winning points by sharing his favorite song with me.

"This song is so beautiful…uhh, what's your name?"

It suddenly hit me that I was having lunch with a total stranger and I hadn't even bothered to get his name! I was really slipping. Suddenly, I sat up and looked around to make sure there were people that saw me with him. I couldn't believe that I let down my guard this easily. I never do this! Shandon noticed my body tense up and me looking around at the people around us.

"Is everything okay?" He asked surprised by my sudden change in behavior.

"Not really," I answered quickly and not caring if his feeling got hurt.

"Look, I'm sorry that I neglected to introduce myself to you. I mean, we just got so comfortable with each other, so easily. It feels as if I know you already."

"So, what's going on?"

He moved closer to me and took my hand, "My name is Shandon. Which means man of God, deep spiritual wisdom. I didn't mean to weird you out. Please, accept my apology. Btw, I was glad you liked my playlist because I made it especially for you."

I was getting soothed by his warm, strong hands wrapped around mine. His voice was deep, and his cologne smelled quite amazing, even after all the exercising he had done.

"Wait…what? Why would you do that? For me? We just met."

"Give me a chance to explain. I realize that this won't make things sound any less strange, but I have seen you here before. Several times in fact. Since that first time, I made it my business to block out time to be in your space. I love the way your beautiful caramel skin glows under the sun. I have

wanted to talk to you for a while now. I just wanted a chance to hear what your voice sounds like."
Dang, this man really knows how to lay it on thick! "Why were you so focused on me?"
"Well, first off, your name is Jnana, which means knowledge. Every time I saw you here at the park, you were seeking knowledge. Whether during people watching or reading a book, you cause me to be in awe of your essence. My Momma always said for me to look for the woman that doesn't need a gang of girlfriends to enjoy herself. Look for the girl with a book in her hand instead of her studying men. Look for the girl that is humble yet beautiful. And you fit the blueprint for all those things. So, my Momma was right."
I smiled widely, no wonder he knows how to treat a lady. His Momma had mad wisdom, "Hmm, that's really some good advice that your Momma gave you. So, with that very powerful knowledge, are you single?"
"Yes…yes, I am" He answered barely allowing me to get out my entire question.
"Okay, so tell me, when did all this caramel skin stuff start? I mean I just started noticing you recently. Have you been stalking me? Nowadays, a girl can't be too careful."
He got really serious, "No…no, nothing like that. Please, don't take it like that. Look, maybe I should…" And he got up and began getting his stuff packed up.
I looked at him in disbelief. Sheesh, things were going well. When did the tide change? I started to take his CD out so that he could leave. I

was disappointed, but my Momma gave me some knowledge too. Never run after a man. Ciao!

I looked up to hand him his CD and noticed the widest smile across his face. Then, laughed. "Come on, smile, you know that I got you."

I couldn't help myself, I smiled. I was in awe of him now because he got me. But it was too early to let him know I was getting some good vibes from him. My heart didn't want him to leave. Pulling myself out of my thoughts, I realized he was sitting on the blanket with a sad look on his face.

"What's wrong?" I asked. Oh my gosh, I hurt his feelings.

"It just hit me. We were connecting and you were going to let me leave. Dang, you were acting as if this is nothing. Aren't you feeling the sparks between us? I am. I mean your energy is so beautiful and I just want to get to know you better." He expressed as he put his CD back in the player. The smooth groove relaxed me once more.

I blushed. This man should write a book on how to romance a lady. "Yes…yes, I am."

He got comfortable on the blanket and I took our food out of the cooler. Neither one of us said a word while we enjoyed our meal. I packed turkey and cheese sandwiches, strawberries with white chocolate sauce and some apple cider. I made sure not to look at him for too long. His handsome face might distract me from really digging into my sandwich like I wanted to. I was hungrier than I thought. I kept looking up and he was playing eye peek-a-boo with me too. Every so often, when I looked up, he would be looking at me too. His eyes seemed to drink me in. I must have put too much mayo on my second sandwich because a big wad squeezed out of the sandwich onto the side of my mouth and dripped down on my shirt. Without skipping a beat, he reached for the napkins and cleaned up my shirt. When he leaned in and kissed the mayo off my mouth, we shared our first kiss. It was soft and sensual. He took my heart right here in the park. After a couple of seconds, we moved back and looked into each other's eyes. Breathless, we were both at a loss for oxygen. Whoa, it was magnetic! After the kiss, he moved back over to his side of the blanket and I ate small bites. I was not taking the chance of sharing another kiss like that would surely lead to something else. Hey, we are grown! But, neither one of us was down for doing grown stuff in the park, nonetheless. The dam broke and we were no longer tense with each other. The conversation flowed easily as he told me stories that made us both laugh. I love a funny man. I told him stories about my dreams. He seemed to buy into every one of them. Then, our legs got tired of being bunched up. We stretched out and played leg tag. The first time our legs touched, we shared sensual energy. Something is in the air. We could have sat out in the park all day, playing our little game of emotional tag. Until the rain came pouring down on us. All my things and both of us got soaked. Shandon grabbed my books and stuffed them under his shirt. That gesture, his appreciation for what means the world to me, literature, made me fall instantly in love with him. How chivalrous.

 As we ran for cover, Shandon held my hand.

I tightened my grip and prayed that he is my spiritual partner, sent especially from God, for me. When we finally reached the pavilion, in the middle of the park, Shandon set up the music and asked me if he could have this dance. Here? My eyes asked with a smile. He reached out for my hand. Pensively, I let him take me into his arms as the first strike of lightning lit up the darkening sky. He turned up the volume, just a tad, as to not compete with the beautiful sounds of thunder in the air. He walked back towards me and I put on a brave face. I never felt like this for any man before, especially not this quickly. *I've learned to respect the power of love* by Stephanie Mills rang sweetly out of the still dripping wet speakers. I felt so safe that I laid my head down on his chest. I closed my eyes and listened closely to the words. I never trusted a man as I do Shandon right now. Our dance continued as he held me closer when Isley Brothers' *Summer Breeze* came on. The rain beat down upon the pavilion and the atmosphere at the now deserted park was perfect. I couldn't have dreamed of a more perfect first…date. When Switch's *There'll never be a better love* came on, Shandon got brave. He leaned back, cupped my chin, and kissed me. That kiss was better than the first one. The kiss deepened quickly. It may have been the rainstorm, but the heat got turned up so high, we could have blown up a thermometer! We both pulled back and I swear that smoke flowed from both of our mouths!

****

417 | P a g e

My phone rang and forced me from reminiscing about me and Shandon's initial meeting.

"Yes!" I answered, suddenly draw back into anger.

"Jnana, can you please take the edge off of your voice?"

Oh no he didn't! "Can you please apologize?"

He offered in consolation, "Well…"

I sat in silence, my eyes scanning the park in which something so beautiful began. But, right this moment, pride was killing it. I knew it but I didn't know how to stop it. Lord, help me. I tried to be vulnerable earlier and Shandon shot me down. Now it's his turn to give in.

"Are you there?" Shandon asked, obviously hearing me huffing and puffing into the phone like a crazy person. I couldn't help it. This is my husband and he should give in to me! Haven't all our years together taught him anything about the way that I roll?

"Yes"

"Well?"

"Well what, Shandon?"

"Well, aren't you going to say something, Jnana?"

"No, there is a question on the table. Until I get an appropriate answer to it, I have nothing more to say."

"Okay."

"Okay."

We sat on the phone for another minute in silence. Then, I hung up. I was over my husband's games. I had an unlimited calling plan but right now, I didn't have unlimited patience. He better not call me back again or he will get the reject button.

Of course, I heard my phone vibrating. It was him calling again. Not! I will let him sulk. Before I allowed myself to get angrier, my phone vibrated again. I rejected his call. I too rejected the subsequent four other calls he made to me. Looking around to make sure that no one was around, I put my hands up to my ears and screamed, loud and long until I felt better. When I was done, I pulled myself together and turned up the volume on my radio. I pulled out of the parking lot and sang along with Mali Music's *Yahweh* song. The flow of the words relaxed me all over again. So, I put it on repeat! My husband may not always act like he knows how to treat me, but my God *always* knows how to treat me.

My stomach grumbled and beat box on my back. It was that empty feeling that reminded me I was hungry. I just realized that after Shandon came downstairs, I made him breakfast, but I didn't get a chance to finish *m*y breakfast. I pulled into a restaurant parking lot and prepared to get out. But as if paralyzed, I couldn't get myself together to get out of the car. My marriage may be over. Just the thought caused me to break down. I put my head onto the steering wheel and cried until my lap was soaked with tears. I lifted my head and looked at my beautiful wedding rings. Lovely diamonds and rubies set in white gold with a band engraved with both of our names was designed by both Shandon and me. I hate to think that one day my finger would stand empty and my home would be void of my husband. My husband is the love of my life. My heart ached. I picked up my phone and looked at the

419 | P a g e

display. Shandon called another four times. I could not do this. I felt myself coming undone. I could not do this alone. I needed a reality check!

I knew there was always one person I could count on to be a real talk fan. More so than I will ever be. She is one who would immediately set me straight and make me put on my big girl panties. I pulled out of the restaurant parking lot and headed to Hardees. I loved their cinnamon raisin biscuits. I grabbed a cup of coffee too. Then, I drove to the place to get my reality check that I was so sure I needed.

I didn't hesitate to use my door key. Just as expected, dinner was cooking on the stove. My tummy was already full of biscuits. Still, it flip flopped at the scent of my Ma's sweet potato pie. There was no place like my Ma's house. None! I said a silent prayer for my spirit to strengthen me through the raw honesty I was in for.

~32~
Worth Risking All

Brothers, I do not consider that I have made it my
own. But one thing I do: forgetting what lies behind
and straining forward to what lies ahead, I press on
toward the goal for the prize of the upward call of
God in Christ Jesus.
Philippians 3:13-14
***

Trinity

"Babes, can we talk?"

Courage Trinity, courage.

"Sure, my love, what's going on?"

"I'm so sorry, I really am but I need to break up
with you."

"Trin, what's going on?! What do you mean that
you are breaking up with me?"

"I'm sorry, I'm really sorry."

"I love you, Babe, I do."

"I love you too Babes. The issue is I don't really
love myself yet. Even though I am still a mess, I
thank God for His omnipotent mercy because I am
not as much of a mess as I used to be. I just feel a
little unclear about a lot of things in my life. I
haven't been able to get a job yet. And my bank
account is closed. I need to get my finances in
order."

"Trin, relax, I got you. I am working. I can help you
with a bank account and money to put in that
account. You do know that, right?"

"Uhh, Babes, you don't understand. I love you so
much, Micah. But, Babes, I need to get *myself*

together. I refuse to let another man carry me. And another thing…well…I don't love myself. I love you way more than I love myself. That's wrong. That's so out of order. You deserve a woman that is confident and assured of her worth. Please give me time to work on me, please."

"Look Trin, I love you. I knew if you gave me a shot that we would be in love like this. I also feared you would get to the point where you would question yourself. Okay, I won't try to carry you. How about allowing me to support you while you find yourself? Please don't push me away. And please don't try to destroy our connection. Please stay, don't doubt yourself. Please. Trin, you deserve this love. You deserve to have someone stay instead of abandoning you. You deserve to be loved like I love you. I will love you through this. I want you to be my wife. Please stay. Please."

I cried. You know that kind of crying where your eyes burn because the emotion is so heavy. I loved this man, to my soul's core. I breathe his air. He is that deep in my spirit. I want to stay. Really, I do. I let the quiet soothe my thoughts for a second. Then it hit me… no! Here we sit, his legs intertwined with mine. His hands were holding mine and his eyes were looking deeply into my soul. And here I let the feeling sink in. This feeling right here is my bliss. This is my harmony in the key to love.

I wiped the tears falling down his handsome face. "Babes, I love you, I do. And one day I will be able to give myself fully to you. However, I couldn't do this. Not like this. Babes, I couldn't stay. I need to take this time…for me. My self-worth is important to me. It is worth me risking everything with you. Now I don't want to lose you. Understand me, I don't want you to walk away from me. However, with God's grace, you will wait for me. I must do this on my own. Know that I am still yours, we are still committed and exclusive, but I need to find myself. Micah, my love, will you wait?"

Without skipping a beat, he whispered, "Yes, I will wait for you. I have waited all my life to find you. I will wait, for as long as you need. I am still committed to you. But I want you to know that when you return to me, you will be my wife."

"I will be honored to be your wife. I love you."

"I love you too, my sweets."

I smiled. I had a man who loved me, for me. Thank you, Father God. I was reminded of a scripture that spoke beautifully to this situation: Philippians 4:8-9. In the Message Bible, it reads: *Summing it all up, friends, I'd say you'll do best by filling your minds and meditating on things true, noble, reputable, authentic, compelling, gracious— the best, not the worst; the beautiful, not the ugly; things to praise, not things to curse. Put into practice what you learned from me, what you heard and saw and realized. Do that, and God, who makes everything work together, will work you into his most excellent harmonies.*

Though Micah didn't fully understand my reasons for such a sudden decision, especially since things have been going so well, he is here to support me. I wouldn't allow my guilt from hurting him to sway my decision. I will follow God's Word, to the syllable. I wanted to do what was

423 | P a g e

right, and I wanted to praise God through this trial of faith. I had full faith. I desired harmony with my flesh and my spirit. When I found that harmony, I would know it was time to contact Micah and move forward with our life together. This was the way it had to be! Micah is a good man. The perfect one created for me. I was willing to bet that I'm a good woman. I needed to learn to trust that this is what God wants for me. I made some strides toward being secure in myself and loving myself. On this journey, I will throw myself deeper into prayer, meditation, and spirit building reading. I needed to answer one fundamental question: what makes Trinity happy? What makes Trinity feel in harmony with the universe? Where do I begin to answer these questions was no more a surprise to God than it was for me. That place was within the lovely world of painting. I did not have my art supplies at the shelter. But I could always sketch on plain white paper and use a regular pencil. *Thy Grace is sufficient, Father.*

My mantra scriptures for this time of self-reflection will be Philippians 4:8-9 and Psalm 27:14, *Trust in the Lord. Have faith, do not despair. Trust in the Lord.*

~33~
Submit

For this is the way the holy women of the past who
put their hope in God used to make themselves
beautiful. They were submissive to their own
husbands, like Sarah, who obeyed Abraham and
called him her master. You are her daughters if you
do what is right and do not give way to fear.
I Peter 3:5-6
***

Jnana

"Ma, you just don't understand. I mean, I really
don't think that you get it. I am really going through
dealing with Shandon."
"Really?" She asked glibly without even pausing.
"And what don't I understand Jnana, please tell
me."
"Well, for one," I made a big mistake and looked at
her face. Upon it was the same look she used to
give me when I was a little girl. "Sorry, Ma, I didn't
mean to be disrespectful. I am just so frustrated
with my husband right now."
She came over to hug me and I relaxed like I used
to when I was a little girl. There is something about
a Mother's love.
"I know that you're frustrated. Calm down and tell
me what I don't get."
I breathed in and out a couple of times. "Well, Ma,
Shandon can be so stubborn sometimes. And he can
be selfish too. I could not tell you how often I had
to tell him to put his clothes in the hamper down in

the basement or put his shoes out on the porch so his boots don't soil the carpet. Uhh, that man drove me crazy!"

"Is that all?"

"Ma, what do you mean, is that all?"

"Baby, do you know how long your father and I have been married?"

"Ma, it's been so long, I cannot even remember."

"Jnana, let me say this, in all the years that I have been married to your father, I would never think of telling him, the man that paid this mortgage, on time, every single month, who paid you and your brother's private school tuition from kindergarten to graduation, and has been a good husband to me for over 47 years, to put his boots outside so that he didn't soil the carpet that he paid for."

"But Ma, we have plush carpet in the living room, I don't want it ruined."

She shook her head and I held my breath. "Jnana, you can choose your petty demands or your husband. Shandon is a good man. He is a good provider *and* a good father. Most of all, he is a good husband to you!"

"I know Ma, but you just don't know. Sometimes Shandon's little habits really grate on my last nerves. He lets the kids get away with so much. I still can't get over how badly he handled the situation with Ashton. Ma, he didn't even consult me. That hurt me so much."

"Those kids are *his* too. You are talking like they aren't. Besides, why would he consult you when he knows what kind of support his son needs? Now, I know that think of yourself as a superwoman, but you cannot handle everything. Shandon was once a young teenage boy with raging hormones. Why would his solution to an issue with his teenage son *not* be good enough for you? What expertise do you have in that department? Huh?"

"Ma, I just thought that…"

"Jnana," she held her hand up, "Shhh"

"Ma, what's wrong? Why are you telling me to shhh?"

Ma giggled then she got serious. "Do you realize that you haven't taken the time to think before you responded to anything I've said? Your mouth was always open when I was talking, and it looked like you were thinking of a reply. While I was still talking, nonetheless. Now *that* can really grate on someone's nerves!"

"But Ma…"

"Hush! You are still acting like an all knowing, selfish, tunnel vision teenager. Dang, be quiet sometimes! Do you understand?"

I wanted so much not to reply but I knew that, even as an adult woman, it would not end well. "Yes Ma'am."

"Now that I have your full attention, let me tell you a story. Is that okay?"

I decided to test her. I sat quietly.

Wrong decision.

"If you don't answer me now. So, help me God! Jnana, don't you dare get fresh with me!"

"Yes, Ma'am. I'm sorry for being disrespectful. But you are talking to me like I am still a little girl. I am a grown woman with my own husband and family. I'm not a kid anymore Ma."

"Fair enough, so Mrs. Grown Woman, have you ever heard of proverbs 14:1?"

"Of course, I have Ma."

"The wise woman builds her house, but with her own hands the foolish one tears hers down. Which one are you?"

"I have wisdom Ma. You taught me that."

"Well, that wisdom has not afforded you the fortitude to submit to your husband now has it? You are tearing down your home with *how you get* and your assertion that if you are not happy, no one should be happy. Where did you learn such nonsense? Surely not from me! Do I have your attention now, Mrs. Grown Woman?"

"Yes, you do have my full attention." I slumped down in my chair. This is going to be a long talk. I felt the familiar buzzing in my pocket. It was Lili. I pushed send and answered the call.

Before I said a word, she started talking, sheesh, she inherited that from me!

"Mommy, do you know where Daddy is? About an hour ago, he left the house looking for you. Where are you?"

"No, Lili, I am at Nana's house. Is there something wrong?"

"No, I just wanted to know where my parents are."

Well, we are both okay. Thank you for checking in on us. I'll call Daddy and see where he is and I'll ask him to call you, okay?"

"Okay. I love you, Mommy."

"I love you too, Lili."

I hung up the phone after my call with Lili. Before I could even make the call to Shandon, I looked up to find my Ma's eyes burning through my skull. Sheesh, what now? Did I just give her more evidence to chastise me for? I ignored her stare and called Shandon.

He answered on the first ring, "Shandon," I didn't let him say a thing. "Lili just called me worrying about you. She said you left a while ago looking for me. Can you please call her so that she won't be worried about you?"

He sighed, "I will Jnana. I am out here looking for you. But I ended up stopping off at Home Depot. They are having a sale on ladders." He giggled the way I love. "I guess I got sidetracked. I left there a minute ago though"

I still love my husband, very much. "Shandon, I love you, I do Babes."

I could see his smile through the phone, "I love you too my wife. Where are you?"

"I am at Ma's house. I needed to break away for a few. Where are you now?"

"Well, I left Home Depot and then I decided to drive by Namaste to check on things. Once I noticed you weren't here, I made sure everyone was doing what they get paid to do. I don't want you to have a repeat of the Littia situation. I already checked in the deliveries and straightened up a little. I am about to pull away, now I am on my way to get some Wawa coffee before heading home to my worrisome daughter. I miss you my runaway wife."

"I did not run-away Shandon. I just needed a break." I looked up at Ma and I felt embarrassed. "Jnana, do you remember all those years ago in the park when we first spoke? Do you remember how long we danced in the pavilion while we waited for the rain to clear up?"

"Do I? Who knew that it was going to be a torrential thunderstorm?! I remember being totally soaked by the time we finally gave up and ran to our cars. We had to have been out there an hour or so. Why?"

"Well, that day, I vowed, while I held you so tightly in my arms, that if you would be mine that I would make sure that you were always happy. I want you to be happy whether I am happy or not. I have made you happy, all these years, haven't I? Jnana, have I ever purposefully made you sad?"

"Shandon, you have made me happy. You have made me very happy most of our marriage. However, I realize I cannot say the same thing. Babe, I am coming home soon. We can talk much more later. Okay?"

"Okay, hurry home, my love."

"I will."

When I hung up the phone, Ma had two plates of warm sweet potato pie and two cups of hazelnut coffee set out. Boy, this will be a *long* visit! She patted the chair at the dining room table to signal me to sit down. I obliged.

"Jnana, baby, now I support you in all you do. I am proud of the woman you have grown into but…"

My phone vibrated again. I looked at the screen, Becca, nah, I could not talk to her right now. I rejected her phone call. I was in the midst of my own drama right now. When I looked at Ma's face and how impatient she appeared to be getting, I turned off my phone. I sipped on my coffee and dug into my pie. Ma's pie was the best. She got up from the table and freshened our coffee from a coffee pot that was as old as I am.

"Ma? But what? What were you going to say? Have I disappointed you?"

"Jnana, now I don't see you that often, although we talk every night before bed. I figured that we could have an uninterrupted conversation, but I see that you have a lot going on. I really wanted to deal with the subject at hand."

"What subject at hand?" Now *I'm* getting impatient. I hoped she would get to the point. Now I knew how Shandon felt when I gave him a blow by blow of my day and how I felt about this or that. Sheesh, this is torture!

"Since you want to rush me along, young lady," she giggled and I breathed a sigh of relief, "Like I don't know what you're doing. So, here it is in brief, your attitude could use some adjusting."

"That was brief? That was huge! What about my attitude? What's wrong with *my attitude*?"

"Do you even hear your tone? That right there is what I'm talking about. That's how you talk to your husband. You talk to him like you are the man. You are not! You are the wife, not the husband. You are a wife, that never submitted to her husband."

"I thought we were past the submit conversation Ma. I *have* submitted to my husband."

"Have you really? So why did you come over here to get a reality check because as your kids say, that you were tripping? Why did you feel the need to put your two cents into the situation with Ashton that your, very capable husband, already handled? For the record, both I and your Daddy stand behind Shandon. If you truly submitted to your husband and didn't feel the need to have your hands in everything, it would have been water off your back. You would have supported your husband and been proud to have a good man who knows how to guide his children. If you submitted, you wouldn't be such a busy body trying to find a way to control everyone in your household. Let me be clear Jnana, you already have Lili's period to deal with. Tell me, did you consult Shandon on how to deal with that? Did you happen to consult Shandon on wings or no wings maxi pads? Did you Jnana?"

"Ma…no…I sure didn't." Whoa, that hit me straight in my forehead! I was so distracted that I did not even ask Shandon how he felt about it.

"Yes, let that revelation marinate Jnana! Now, let's deal with your attitude. It's not your words. It's your tone that really burns my biscuits. You even get that frown in between your eyebrows and your mouth frowns up. Predictably, that's how your face looking right now! I know you so well I can tell that you are getting an attitude by the way that you cock your head to the side, just so."

"See, Ma, now it seems like you are just trying to pick a fight. Besides, Shandon has always said he loves that I am a strong woman."

"He says strong, not overpowering. You wear the pants in your household. This is as backward as the day is long. That man loves you so much that he has put aside his happiness…for yours…for years! How long do you think it will take before he starts feeling resentful that you never let him live the dream, he has had about being the man of his house? You do remember your wedding vows, right?"

"Of course, I do, Ma."

"Oh, so you remember him saying to you that he can't wait to lead his family?"

"Well, yeah, I do remember him saying that. But I didn't think that he *really* wanted to be the leader of his household. I mean it was just his wedding vows. People say things in their vows they don't necessarily mean." I regretted those words as soon as they crossed my lips. I cringed. Oh boy, here we go! I sat silently and waited for the downfall.

"Oh, is that the trend nowadays? So, when you said your vows and declared to your husband-to-be that you would allow him to be the head of the household it was just words to you? And when you quoted a Bible verse and promised to submit, fully, to him, it was also just words? Could it be that you were standing before the Preacher with Shandon and lying to him *and* to God?"

"Well…" I whispered.

"Speak up young lady. I didn't hear you."

"I didn't mean that Ma."

"Oh, I hoped you had more sense than to admit that foolishness to me Jnana! Now I just want to remind you that you were created from his rib. He was created from dust. The man was created before woman. Now, Shandon is a strong man. He is your match in every way. Let him be the leader of your household. Do the correct thing and move back to your God created the role of support to your husband. Become a virtuous, abiding and submitted wife. You should submit to your husband as you both submit to God, just as your children should submit to their parents. You wouldn't want your children to obey Shandon and not you, right?"

"Of course not."

"So, why should your husband expect you to submit to God, but you have not submitted to him as the Word of God requires? But then we *know how you get*. You are a rebel. You make your own rules."

"Oh boy, not you too with this *you know how I get* stuff! The kids, Shandon and even Trinity have said those words to me. Now I sit here, and my own Ma is saying those words to me too. Is there a conspiracy or something going on? I am officially over those words! If I hear those words again, I'm just…I am just going to scream!"

"Now, Jnana, don't forget your place. You will not disrespect my home. Nor will you disrespect me. Chile, don't forget that I *am* your Mother!"

"Ma, I am so sorry, I didn't mean to disrespect you, again. There I go with my tone. Ma, I just don't know what you want from me. Help me, please." I slumped in my seat when she cut her eyes at me before walking into the living room. I sat quietly at the table and finished my pie and coffee. Humph, I am frustrated but I am not foolish. This stuff is so good! I ate with measured speed. This method of buying time gave me a chance to calm down before I walked into the living room. I feel like a little girl running after my Mommy. Sheesh, I didn't even do anything wrong. She is the one, clearly, acting out. After I ate the last bite of pie and drank the last taste of coffee, I sucked up my pride and I humbled myself. This was my heart, my Ma, needed me to get off my high horse. For her, I would do anything. I walked into the living room and where she was waiting on me. She patted the cushion next to her. I sat down and hugged her tightly.

"Ma, I don't want to fight anymore. Tell me what to do to fix my marriage and rebuild my house. I want everyone to be happy and I know they must not be. Tell me what to do Mommy. Mommy, help me, you know that you want to." I leaned my head down on her shoulder and waited on her wisdom. I never take my Ma for granted. Her wisdom is mostly raw to the bone, but it has never steered me wrong. It could be harsh, but it is always real. I do not always receive it in the right mindset but when I got out of my feelings to really hear it, it always worked out for the better.

"Submit."

"Ma! Submit? That's it? I mean, this isn't the olden days. I am done with walking around barefoot and pregnant. There are women like me that make as much money as their husband and buy the bacon and can fry it up in the pan. A couple of my customers at Namaste are even women that work outside of the home and their husband are happy being at home Dads. This is a new era Ma. Nobody really submits, not anymore. There are lots of Mothers running their households. Those women aren't submitting. They are handling their business!"

"Jnana, I know that you think that submitting to your husband is an old school notion but that's not true. I submitted when I got married. I did happily for your Daddy. Now you came over here for advice. You said that you would do what I told you. I gave you what you should do. Yet you are still running your mouth."

"Ma, I respect your advice. I really do. I will give it some thought. But, honestly, Ma, it's just that you didn't seem to be submitted to Daddy. I remember being a little girl and watching you run Daddy ragged. You were the Queen of our household. At times, it seemed as if you could run the household with your eyes closed. Daddy did whatever you wanted when you wanted so that you would be happy."

She giggled softly, "Your Daddy is an amazing man. He loves me and he has always known how to treat me well. However, he only made me think that I was in charge. I know you rarely remember us arguing or disagreeing, especially in front of you children. I was his wife and I fully submitted to his authority. He was the leader of the house, not me. I submitted to him as a Man of God's helpmate."

I sat in silence for a minute or two while I delved into memories of my childhood like a slideshow. I had clarity. My childhood appeared differently to me when I reviewed it through the eyes of my Ma in the role of a submitted wife.

"Now that I think about it, Daddy *did* discipline us, and he handled paying the bills. I don't remember you and Daddy arguing much. Those disagreements I did remember stopped when Daddy put his foot down. It was during those times that you simply kissed him and walked off to leave him to his thoughts."

"That's a splendid example of a woman submitted. Let me be clear, I was never afraid of your Daddy. In all our years together, he never laid a hand on me. I knew how to submit as a woman of God. I knew how to abide in His word. You women today are so strong. However, there is a serious lack of faith."

"Wow, why haven't we had this conversation before?"

"Because I figured you were going to be like these worldly women stubborn enough to believe they can reinvent the wheel. You don't run red lights or steal or otherwise break the law. So why is it so hard for you to keep God's law?"

"Well, I never thought about it like that."

"Please give it some thought. We should love our husbands with agape love. Self-sacrifice is a pure show of agape love. A wife submits to her husband, not because he deserves it, she simply submits because that's the law of God."

"Ma, I have been reading the Bible for years and I never read that scripture like you are explaining it. I just figured submitting was a way for a man to keep his boot on a woman's neck and keep her barefoot and pregnant."

"Jnana, a good, God-fearing man will never run over an abiding woman nor abuse her. Why would you, an abiding woman, want to marry a man like that anyway? You know that the scripture says believers should not be unequally yoked with unbelievers."

"I don't know, Ma, I don't know."

"Does Shandon run all over you?"

"No, he is a good man. He loves me even when I am not acting lovable to him. He is a great father. He supports me in all my dreams. He has integrity and would never hurt me. I never felt so safe with any other man."

"But, even with the man of your dreams, you still feel the need to run your household. Hmmm."

I slumped down and wanted to disappear into the couch. Ma gently placed her hand on my chin and made me look into her eyes. "Jnana go on home to your good man. He loves you and you should submit to your husband."

"Thank you so much Ma, I needed this."

"Don't thank me, Honey. Just go home to your family. Today, stop using your mouth to tear down your own home. You are the wife. Know your role. Step down and give the rightful place of leadership to your husband. It is his birthright."

"I will Ma, I promise."

I barely got out the door before I burst into tears. My heart felt like it was breaking into pieces. I almost lost my husband because of my foolish, selfish attitude and strong woman tactics.

As I drove away from Ma's house, I had a lot on my mind. I turned on my radio and Wildflower by New Birth came on. The thought of Shandon singing to me brought a smile to my face. My Man really knows how to love me. He may work my nerves, sometimes, but he sure knows me well. He is the only one who could get me from angry to soft and tender in no time. He, instinctively, knew singing my favorite song would

438 | P a g e

get me back to my core. I could play hard with everyone but Shandon. With him, I could really be me and feel safe. As I was humming along with the song, a huge revelation hits me: Shandon did something on his own with no direction from me. Humph, imagine that! When I met Shandon, it was his outgoing and very strong personality that set him apart from all the other men I had known. It was extremely attractive to me to find a self-assured, yet far from an arrogant man who was still sweet and loving. One who did not need to stand behind being a man to pronounce how strong he is. I loved that he had his own friends and he was not defined by his job title. He was truly ready to give himself to a committed relationship without having wild oats to sow. He was autonomous from his mother and had no exes that would sully our relationship with drama. His strength of character and intelligence was very appealing. Still, somewhere along the line, his strength and self-assured personality took a back seat to my overly aggressive, slightly narcissistic personality. Some time ago, I assumed he would be at my beck and call and serve me. He was simply to be an extension of me. Unfortunately, as I see myself today, I became the precise women I despised seeing out in public with their husbands. Those women were domineering and unapologetically in control. Those men that let their wives get away with that behavior were quickly dubbed by me as henpecked. I always wondered where they had lost themselves and taken on their wife's slave persona. It seemed as if those women were pulling their husband's around on a leash. Yet, that appeared to be the state of my relationship with Shandon. Oh, how clueless I had been. Why do I feel as if I have the right to place such stipulations on my husband? I love him and see him as my equal, yet my behavior does not reflect it. Who am I to have tried to destroy the most attractive trait my husband had…has? Who in the heck do I think that I am?!

I yawned to clear the tightness in my chest. It was so tight with guilt and shame. Earlier, I would not pray with my husband but in my car, I prayed. I threw myself on the mercy of God and I plead my case. I have been so wrong! I did not mean to go against God's law. I did not mean to sin against my husband.

I raced home and found Shandon's truck in the driveway. I sat in the car planning my words for a few minutes. I am clueless. This has got to be a monumental occasion. How do you go about telling your husband, the man that you never submitted to, that you are now ready to submit? I wonder if he will think that I think he was weak. That I do not respect him. I wonder if he will feel disrespected by any insinuation of my lack of faith in him as a man or his ability to lead our household. I could not take that risk. I love, honor, respect and have full faith in my husband. I trusted him since that first day in the park. It is not like I intentionally mistreated him. I mean I figured submitting to my husband meant that I was being weak. I saw submission to my husband as something entirely negative. The way that Ma described it, it is like the scripture, he who finds a wife, finds a good thing. I could see now things will be better now that I have a mind, body, spirit, and soul of a submitted wife. I was ready to, fully, submit to my man. I was the rib of his rib and loving wife of a good, God fearing man. It was the righteous thing to do.

      I walked into my front door and there was music playing. It made me smile. The negative energy shifted, and it felt lovely! There was life going on around here that was positive. Ashton and Lili were standing in front of the television in the living room playing Xbox 360 Kinect, *Just Dance* game. I walked to my children and hugged Lili. I hugged Ashton and he held on longer than his usual teenage boy hug. He whispered in my ear that he loves me, and he apologized. His beautiful eyes filled with tears and I told him that I forgive him. I prayed that he forgave me too. I never realized how much my approval means to my son. I will not take our relationship for granted, ever again. I will do better in my service to rebuild my household, in the wife's place, with my husband's support. I walked into the kitchen to find my husband dancing with a mop. Yes, a mop! He was singing *My Darling, Darling* by The O'Jays. I stifled a giggle as he tried to do a spin then dip it down low before pulling it back up to lay it close to his chest. He even pretended to brush a curl out of the mop's eye. I could not hold it in anymore. I burst out laughing at that gesture. Shandon dropped the mop when he realized that I had been watching him. He dropped the mop so quickly it fell on his foot with a thud.

"Jnana, how long have you been standing there," He asked as he jumped around on one foot.

His eyes went to something straight behind me. There stood our children who were laughing at their father too. For a dark-skinned man, I could see that Shandon was turning red from embarrassment. I went to my, romancing a mop, husband and pulled him in for a kiss. He wrapped his arms lovingly around my body.

Our children quickly retreated to the living room, "Eww, that's gross!" They said in unison.

I snuggled up close to my husband and smelled his cologne. Oh wow, he has on his *it is time for some good loving*- cologne. Mmm, he smells good enough to eat!

"So, Jnana, what is this all about? You have been ignoring me all day long but now you walk in here and come snuggle up to me like it's nothing? What gives?"

Oh, he is mad!

You said that you are sorry, that is what I have been waiting on. That is what gives. Dang, this submission thing is not so easy. I shook that thought off. "Babe, I was tripping. You are my husband. The way you handled things with Ashton was your call. You made the decision and I should have supported you, but I didn't. I am so sorry. I won't question your judgment again. You are the leader of this household and I have been stepping out of pocket and it won't happen again. I trust your judgment and I honor you. Babe, I have all faith in you, and I love you."

"Yes, you were tripping. But then I started it all when I tripped and fell in love with you that day in the park" He said as he nuzzled my neck and pulled me closer.

"Babes, I was very wrong, I am so sorry. I love you." I said as I laid my head on his strong chest.

"Jnana, yes, you were very wrong. Very, very wrong. And I love you too. So, what are you going to do to remedy that?"

I stepped back, "what do you mean what I am going…" I softened my tone and smiled gracefully, "to do about that, my love?"

"Well, we still have that silk scarf. How about you show me how you like to submit?"

I frowned up my face.

"Your Dad called." He smiled and kissed me softly. "Thank you."

I wasted no time running upstairs to get ready for our night together. It is time for me to show my husband how loyal I can really be.

I have been a very, very bad girl!

~34~
Puzzle Piece

Likewise, you who are younger, be subject to the
elders. Clothe yourselves, all of you, with humility
toward one another, for "God opposes the proud but
gives grace to the humble." Humble yourselves,
therefore, under the mighty hand of God so that at
the proper time he may exalt you...
Peter 5:5-6
***

Trinity

"Would you like me to go with you?"
"No, thanks for asking but this is something I need
to do alone."
"Well, okay. I guess that you're right. But Trin, I
just want to shield you from pain. You have had to
endure a lot in your life and now that I am here, I
feel like it is my job to protect you. Now is a time
of joy."
"I do. I really appreciate you caring for me, I really
do. However, no matter how this turns out, I will be
okay. I put my big girl panties on."
Rubbing his strong hands on my hips, he smiled,
"No you don't." Then he kissed my neck. "You
have on those silk and lacy panties that I brought
you when we went shopping last week. Good thing
we vowed to be celibate or else I would be taking
them off with my teeth."
I smiled, this man was such a catch, "Yes, it is a
good thing. I have never done this type of thing the
right way, which is why it never turned out right.

But with you, Babes, we are going to wait until our wedding night."

He held me closer and pulled me into a kiss. I blushed. A man that loved me completely yet would wait to consummate our relationship until our wedding night. Thank God for His grace and mercy!

"Trin, we are both struggling with keeping the vow, but I have full faith that we can carry it through."

"Well, I figure that we have a long way to go Micah. I mean, my second finger from the left, remains bare. So, I'm not sure if you are keeping your options open or not."

Dang, there goes that pang of insecurity! Just as quickly as those words came out, I cringed. I looked at his face and I instantly felt horrible. You thought I ripped his heart clear out of his chest and squeezed it in my palm.

"Ouch, Trin, that was harsh. I have been here to support you as you unpacked your baggage from past relationships. I have been your friend, your confidante and someone that you can trust. Is it possible that just because we haven't had sex, you believe that I am keeping my options open? Is that really how you view me?"

I did not know what to say, especially with him looking so deeply inside of me. His words were pulling at my heart strings and I really did not have a reply that wasn't going to hurt him even more.

"I don't know what you want me to say, Micah. You know this is new to me. Stop acting like this is so easy for you to deal with."

"Trin, I've been trying so hard to protect my heart, I

445 | P a g e

apologize. This is not easy for me. You are the only woman for me, of this I am certain. My rib, you possess it. Your oxygen is in my blood and we are one. Can I be clearer than that? There are no options, you are my one choice!"

All I could do was to kiss him. He was so passionate in his declaration of how much I meant to him. How could I let him down and throw my insecurities in his face? I loved this man. This is the only union, wherein, I have ever felt as if God has blessed it. When I was done kissing him with a passion that matched his. I stepped back and walked away. I was seriously tripping! I needed to get some space.

****

Micah wanted me to drive his car to the nursing home to see Mr. Hanks, my Dad. But I refused the very generous offer. I figured the two buses I would have to take to get there would give me more than enough time to get my mind together. It has been tough still volunteering at the nursing home since I realized that he is my father. Every single week I went to read to him; I kept the secret. The only difference I made when I went to see him was, I listened more intently than I did before. Now, I allow my thoughts to flow on the very real fact that he was my father, the man I have been longing to meet all my life. Yet, I found him while living at a homeless shelter during a volunteer opportunity. Yes, God really does have a sense of humor because this was pure comedy!

I prayed many a prayer for my father to come back into my life and when I was not even looking, he dropped right into my lap. Since the fateful day, I realized Mr. Hanks is my father, I asked God to impart a spirit of forgiveness inside of me. I knew I needed to let go of the anger of him leaving me and causing the heartbreak death of my Mom. He left us to fend for ourselves when it was his job to protect us. If he did not leave, my Mom might still be alive.

I allowed my thoughts to run wild like a runaway train. I knew I was angry and resentful. But allowing those negative feelings I developed for my father to erase the positive feelings I have grown to have for Mr. Hanks is killing me right now. I allowed those negative thoughts to take hold until I switched my playlist on the I Phone that Micah had brought for me. I had to clear away all the negative thoughts, so I put on my favorite song to clear away the depressive mood. *Chances* by Isaac Care is my reality check. The song always gets me back to a clear mind and forgiving heart. It forced me to refocus my thoughts on me being a flawed woman that should not be so lofty in thought to judge anyone. Especially how much I despise being judged. *Who am I to judge anyone?*

I looked out the window and noticed a young woman with a baby in her arms, carrying a stroller, running beside the bus. The ignorant bus driver kept right on driving as if he did not see her. But, from the smirk on his face, he saw her. Oh, how I miss my car. Public transportation could be a hot mess sometimes! I figured since I was at the door to my victory the devil was playing games with my mind. Ahead, are my Dad and Micah but behind me was a quick way to get off this bus and call one of my married ex-lovers to get a ride. Without a thought, I shook my head. Ahead, I am moving! Whoever said Christians did not battle with their flesh was not telling the truth! For this war going on inside me was really testing me. Where there is a test, there shall surely be a testimony! During a spiritual test, the devil really stirs things up. He throws doubt and anger in the way of progress. All his mess is meant to distract me off course. I tell you this, I did not have to work to sin, but it sure takes a lot of work to stay on this side of change. I must work hard to walk the straight and narrow road of righteousness. Trust me, I was not complaining. This was the life worth fighting for. *I* was worth fighting for. I took off the mask of lies and excitedly stepped into shoes of faith. I only have one question to face. Will Mr. Hanks, my Dad, still be an active part of my life when I tell him the truth?

      I looked out the window and saw that we were approaching the nursing home. My stomach got queasy and I was suddenly filled with nervous energy. I reached my hand up to pull the string to signal the driver that I am ready to get off the bus. I grabbed my things and prepared to depart the bus. I walked into the nursing home and signed myself in. I practiced what I was going to say as I walked down the long hall. I leaned up against the wall and silently said a prayer. I prayed that God was with me as I finally told my Daddy who I was, his long-lost daughter. I barely made it through the door before I noticed he was sitting up in the bed reading his Bible. In the background, I could hear *Pray* by Ceca Winans playing softly. He looked very relaxed. Sadly, I was going to disrupt that relaxation. A tear fell down my cheek and my heart felt heavy. I walked quietly into the room and walked over to his bed. I sat softly onto the bed and said it, "Mr. Hanks…uhh, Daddy…you are my Daddy."

He instantly closed his Bible and sat up in his bed. "Trinity, I haven't seen my daughter since she was little. How are you so sure that I am your Daddy?"

I got nervous. Oh no, I pray this is not going to be a *you are not the father* moment. I reached out and grabbed his hand. It was warm to my touch and he reached out and rubbed my other hand with his. I relaxed.

"Well, the first time I came here, there was an instant connection to you. I couldn't put my finger on it. Then as you opened to me, your stories of your long-lost family began to sound like me and my Mom. I went back into old photo albums that my Grandma kept after my Mother died, and I found a couple of pictures of my father. The man looked exactly like you. My Grandma told me the story of the day my Dad left me and my Mom. It was identical to the story you told me. Because it was from my mother's perspective, she also told me of how destroyed my Mom was when you packed up and left while she was at work. She ended up having to sell most of the furniture to pay bills and make the rent the next few months. So, your story couldn't have illustrated the financial, emotional and physical downfall of my Mom after you left." He squeezed my hand and I looked up to his face. It was wet with tears. I moved the Bible off his lap and moved more onto the bed. I helped him into his recliner by the side of the bed. He did not stop crying the entire time. I felt horrible tearing his heart out of his chest. I know that I was confronting him with his ill deed even though he did it with the best of intentions.

"So…you are my beautiful little girl. I felt a connection with you when I first met you. But I have learned over the years to be cantankerous to keep people at bay. I never want to lose anyone as I had you and your mother. I pushed that pain so deep inside of my soul. It killed me to miss my family so much. Then…then you bounced in here that day smelling just like the love of my life, your Mother."

"Daddy, that got me thinking when you reacted so strongly to my perfume too. But I didn't know what to think. I mean of all people for me to have to volunteer to read to, who would have thought that it would be you, my Daddy? God really does have a sense of humor!"

"Yes, God sure does! Trinity, my beautiful daughter…may I ask you one favor?"

"Yes, Daddy, anything."

"Can you say, Daddy, one more time?"

I smiled, "Yes, Daddy. I am so happy you turned out to be my Daddy. I love you, Daddy."

"Trinity, daughter," He beamed, and I knew that it made him very happy to have me back in his life.

"Wow, *daughter,* that word really sounds good to speak again. If you haven't noticed, I am so happy to have you back in my life."

"I'm happy to have you back in my life too Daddy." He smiled again and my heart melted. "Daddy, I really am. I had begun to care deeply for you when you were simply someone I was volunteering to read to. But as I brought you sweet treats, you opened up to me and I could finally get to know you as a person. I never realized how much I missed having my Dad in my life until I saw myself through your accepting eyes that didn't want anything from me. I learned to love myself for who I am and not what I could do for a man. You did that for me, Daddy. I will never be able to repay that selfless gift. Thank you."

"Trinity, my daughter you are a very caring and loving person. I won't take credit for you finally embracing the whole of who you are. I know you have changed. Your conversation has changed and you're learning to be an abiding woman that is very separate from the worldly woman that used to come visit me in the beginning. Your energy has even changed. You seemed like you were being forced to come here before. But, lately, you bounce through here so happy that you get me excited to begin my day right along with you!"

"Aww, Daddy that's sweet. You grew on me, what more can I say."

We shared each other's company. For the first time, he laughed, genuinely. No more polite pretense and no forced uncomfortable conversation between strangers. We were now Father and

Daughter beginning the wonderful journey of bonding all over again.

"Trinity, so tell me, why don't you have a boyfriend? Or a husband? I have never heard you talk about a man in your life."

"Daddy, I have a good man. But God is still working on me. I took a break from him so that I could really get right with God and myself. I must admit I had trust issues and I haven't chosen the best men in my past. Micah is such a good guy, but I didn't want to hurt him by not being ready to give him my all."

"Trinity, how do you take a break from a good man? Don't you realize that some men come to restore you? Don't you know that God sends men to help you to unpack your baggage, just as you help them to unpack theirs?'

"Daddy, no, I didn't see it like that. In fact, when I really think about it, since I took my break from Micah, he has still supported me, from afar."

"See, that's a good man. He can still want you to be happy and whole, no matter what."

I pulled my Daddy into a hug and he held me tightly. "Yes, Daddy, some men do come to restore."

We did not say another word before I sat him back on his bed and gathered my things to leave. I gave him a soft kiss on his cheek which was still damp from his tears. I gathered my things and said goodbye.

As I walked down the hall, I gave all the praise to God. For my, God is my redeemer and He is my hope. God is also my restorer. Though I was imparting a revelation to my Daddy, I knew I was also changed. I have no words to even describe how my soul felt. All I could say was that now I was whole…complete and honored to be so blessed.

~35~

Meek Isn't Weak

But [let it be] the hidden man of the heart, in that
which is not corruptible, [even the ornament] of a
meek and quiet spirit, which is in the sight of God
of great price.
I Peter 3:4
***

Jnana

I got up early and snuck into the bathroom. I
jumped in the shower and got dressed. I glanced at
my husband as I quietly put on his bathrobe. I had
no idea why I had been so short-sighted. I have a
good man. I always thought Shandon was attracted
to strong women, so a strong woman I showed him.
Even though I believed he accepted me as I was,
somewhere along the line, I acted out. I got lost. I
became worldly when, as a wife, I was supposed to
be thinking of my marriage in terms of how Christ
created wives to be. It is amazing the domino effect
that occurred in every area of my life when I
became a lukewarm Christian. My employees
started acting out, my friendship with Trinity
experienced a lapse and my family unit became
fractured. Unbreakable, unshakable faith was our
glue. Yet, when mine began to frazzle, so did theirs.
I was the wife and mother, so I needed to do a
better job of creating a home filled with praise. I
needed to restore my family to the full existence of

unwavering faith in God and the Son who came to provide us salvation and a second chance.

I must make sure that my tone of voice is respectful, and I do not let my words reflect disrespect for my husband. When Ma asked me if I would want the children to submit to Shandon and not me, it hit home. Shandon and I are partners as parents but as a wife, I have always reserved the right to overrule his decisions if need be. I just figured I made as much as he does and work just as hard as he does so why not run things? He wanted me happy and being in control made me happy. Do not get me wrong, I was not a control freak. I just like things in order, and I like things to be the way I like them. All these years Shandon did not seem to have a problem with it, so I kept doing things my way. But now I have a new perspective. Now I could submit to my husband. Initially, I was going to have a huge conversation with Shandon, but I decided against it. Why did I have to discuss how I was going to go about being a better wife? I sure did not discuss my choice to do what I wanted or how I wanted and yet Shandon had to roll with my agenda. I decided in favor of allowing my actions to reflect my new state of mind and supportive heart. I am a Woman of Faith. It is high time I let my life reflects this truth.

I have been reading up on submission as a wife and the first thing that hit me was that submission is to be freely given and voluntary. Although it feels a little uncomfortable making this change, it *is* freely given and voluntary on my part. The other day, I was drawn to Philippians 2:6-7 which states: *Who being in very nature of God, did not consider equality with God something to be grasped, but made himself nothing, taking the very nature of a servant, being made in human likeness.* Even more resonated with me in II Corinthians 10:4-6: *We use our powerful God tools for smashing warped philosophies, tearing down barriers erected against the truth of God, fitting every loose thought and emotion and impulse into the structure of life shaped by Christ. Our tools are ready at hand for cleaning the ground of every obstruction to building lives of obedience into maturity.*

It is amazing what happens when we truly live righteously and see scripture through new eyes and with a pure heart for Christ. God's Amazing grace is changing me from the inside out and without a doubt, I can say that I feel *so* good!

To fortify myself during this time of spiritual transformation, I attended the Wednesday Bible study and first Friday of the month women's group meetings at our new home church. From attending those events, I really learned a lot. By faith, I was confident in my ability to submit, fully, to Shandon. He is my husband and the leader of my family. By faith, I was doing my work to change my negative thoughts about submitting.

If there are two words I always thought held purely negative connotations, they would have to be submitted and meek. Through reading books I ordered at Namaste, *Marriage Covenant* by Derek Prince and *Power of a Praying Parent* by Stormie Omartian, I fully stepped into the knowledge that my previous negative attitude regarding organized religion allowed me to be held spiritually captive for most of my adult life. I was raised in a church, yet I was not a spiritual person. Now, by faith, I want to build a deeper relationship with Christ. Meek no longer means weak to me. I am not a doormat for my husband simply because I am submitting to him as I submit to Christ. In my heart, it means dying to self so that Christ can live fully in me. Without any ego or pride to hinder my evolution as a Christian, I could see me flying like an eagle. No longer will there be a spiritual disconnect. No longer will there exist a feeling in me of being held spiritually captive by the devil. Submit no longer means that Shandon gets to order me around. He never did such a thing to me anyway, so I do not know why I ever used that as an excuse in the first place. In my present state of mind, I was the support for my husband while he took on the position of leading our family. I fully supported his decisions and I no longer needed to have the last word nor be disobedient to the Law of God. I knew I made a good decision when I married and had a family with Shandon. He is a strong, highly intelligent Husband and Father. His unwavering integrity is how I knew I could trust him completely. He has and never will lead me astray. I was ready to be a better woman and a better wife. A fully submitted wife. Now I see, I *am* worthy, by faith.

****

Today is our wedding anniversary! I have so many fabulous activities planned for Shandon and me. By the end of the weekend getaway, I am sure we would both be too tired to stand up. For now, I will start our day off beautifully, while we both have lots of energy. I prepared breakfast in bed for my husband. The same breakfast we woofed down the first morning of our honeymoon, all those years ago: toast with grape jelly, a swig of orange juice and some fresh fruit. Anything heavier on our stomachs might have held us back from all the love we gave to each other for an entire day of lovemaking then sleep then waking up to make love some more. In between, we nibbled on some sustenance and a little fluid. We wanted to wear each other out but we did not want to end up in double beds sharing a hospital room because we were dehydrated!

As I put the tray of food on the end table, I got back into bed. I wanted to sneak under the cover and begin waking up my husband the best way I know how. However, he pulled me close to his body and I snuggled my back into his chest. As Shandon held me in tightly, the cocoon of our love caused us both to flow into a beautiful sleep. In the safety of his arms, our hearts beat in sync and created an angelic lullaby.

It was only when awakened by a sweet kiss upon my lips did, I realize that Shandon had already gotten up out of the bed. I must have been more exhausted than I realized. As I opened my eyes, my eyes beheld the deep and full of love eyes of the most beautiful man I have ever seen.

"Happy Anniversary, Mrs. Jnana Jael Roberts. You are looking quite tasty this morning."

I smiled, after all these years, he still thinks I got it.

"Happy Anniversary, Mr. Shandon Donovan Roberts. You are welcome to taste as often as you please."

He blushed and I watched him. This handsome man before me…is all mine. Oh, how blessed I have been! A sudden urge overtook me. As Shandon stood over me, I got warm inside. I felt like showing my husband some love and that is just what I did. There is nothing more packed with vitamins and minerals than some morning protein. It truly does a body good!

Shandon pulled me off the bed and lifted me into his arms. As I wrapped my legs around his waist, I could feel that he is just as excited as I am. Shandon held my chin and kissed me with a passionate intensity of a blue flame. He held me in mid-air as we loved as husband and wife. I rested my head on his shoulder and let him set our groove. We made love right there in the middle of our bedroom floor and it was so beautiful, I wanted to cry. I cried out at least three times before Shandon laid me on the bed and held me close. We kissed passionately as Shandon gave in to his occasional love of deeply spontaneous loving. It was soon after that we collapsed in each other's arms. Then he carried me into the shower where we washed each other tenderly. Then we made love some more there under the water. We were still heady from our love making when we got out of the shower and began to dress for the day ahead of us.

"Do we have plans for today, our eighteenth anniversary, or should we order in and stay in bed all day just like we did on our wedding day?" I waited with bated breath for his response.

I watched Shandon as he rubbed his chin and pondered my question. After much introspection and a mass amount of patience on my side, he finally answered, "No. We won't be staying in bed all day. I…we have plans for today."

He went into his closet and walked out holding a blindfold. Then he gently laid the lovely piece of yellow fabric on the bed next to me.

"Jnana, Baby, after you finish getting dressed, I want to take you out for a day of celebrating our wedding anniversary."

I was stunned. That is it? No further explanation and no other instructions other than get dressed? Shandon is usually a man of few yet powerful words but even this is strange. My worldly side wanted to cause a ruckus and force him to tell me more about our plans. Sheesh, I already planned our day, myself. I must find out if his plans are at least as fabulous as mine, right? But the submitted wife in me rose and allowed me to keep my mouth shut. As I basked in the glow of peace, I felt good. Shandon, however, seemed uneasy. He was so, painfully, used to the worldly, strong, stubborn, and opinionated side of me that he anticipated…expected…messiness from me. As I allowed stillness to rule my being, He watched me and was surprised I did not give him my usual reactive response to his simple request.

I met him face-to-face and smiled. "Alright Shandon, I am up for whatever you have planned." His face revealed a look of utter shock. He did not even try to hide it. Hmmm, I guess we are both learning how to deal with my transformation.

"So, Jnana, you are just going to go along with my plans? No back talk and no issues with nitpicking very detail? No twenty questions and rants about how you haven't liked surprises since your tenth birthday party? No drama at all?"

Without hesitating and surprising even myself, I replied, "Shandon, you are my husband. Where you lead, I follow. I am down for whatever you have planned."

I turned on some music and continued getting dressed and doing my hair. I made sure not to make direct eye contact with Shandon. He was watching me, a meek woman, like a hawk and waiting for me to show any weakness in my countenance. He did not seem to recognize the wife who submitted to what his words are without a lot of discord or manipulations. Honestly, I do not recognize myself either. I had planned our day too. So, why was I not upset or arguing with my husband about why he would think that his plans are more important than mine? Simply. Because the will of my husband is more important than the plans of my ego. Let that marinate…yup, it is that deep!

When we were both dressed, we walked downstairs and ate breakfast. There was peace. As if for the first time, I realized our children were watching the way we interact. When we are happy, they seem happier too. This revelation makes me even more focused on maintaining my new heart for Christ. My desire is to be supportive of my husband and to be a consistent place of comfort and peace.

"Ma, I bet you don't know what today is." Lili sang to me.

"I bet you that I do. It's me and your Dad's eighteenth wedding anniversary."

I smiled at Shandon and his eyes lit up. How foolish I have been to risk losing this wonderful man of mine.

"Yup, it sure is! Ma, was your wedding day all that you ever dreamed of?" Lili pried.

She looked at Shandon and he made a strange face at her.

"Uhh, let me see, not exactly." I quickly sipped on my orange juice hoping she didn't ask for further details. We all sat in uncomfortable silence, our forks hitting plates was the only sound.

Shandon's work cell phone rang, and his ringtone interrupted the uncomfortable tension.

"Currents, Shandon speaking. I thought we handled this last week. Additions? Oh, okay, give me twenty minutes and I will be right there."

He muttered something quickly before grabbing his toolbox and rushing out the door. Not even skipping a beat Lili took advantage of her Dad's absence.

"So, Ma, now that Daddy is gone, can you tell me about your wedding day? Why it wasn't all you dreamed of?"

She smiled and I felt boxed in. How convenient. I assessed her for a minute and pondered whether I wanted to share such a private pain of mine with my teenage daughter. Ashton felt my discomfort and excused himself from the table.

"Ma…I uhh, I have some homework to do." Ashton said oddly rushing out of the room.

What is going on with the men in this family?

Lili smiled wider, "Now?"

Sheesh, "Okay…okay." I relented seemingly against my will.

She sat with her legs beneath her and put her chin in her little hands. She was so eager for the story. How could I disappoint her?

"Well, first, the hairdresser, Donna, was late! The make-up artist, Louise, a woman that I had met at a wedding merchant expo, had made me look like a clown so I had to do my own make up. While I was doing that, I spilled foundation on my dress! Lili, it was a hot mess getting myself ready. Your Grandma and TiTi Loz tried to help me as much as they could. But I was so intent on it being my day, my way that I was so stressed out. I didn't even allow myself to enjoy the bonding moment with them. I wish I had because your TiTi Loz passed a couple of years later."

"Ma, that's a lot! So, was there anything that went right?" She asked, almost taking mental notes.

I lamented and the deep love for Shandon filled me to the brim, "Yes…one beautiful thing. I married the man of my dreams. I married your Dad. Of that, I have no regrets."

"Aww, Ma, that's beautiful. I am so glad that you and Dad are still together. A lot of my friends' parents are divorced."

I sat quietly and thought of how close I could have come to being divorced because of my own selfishness and short sightedness.

"I am so glad too, Lili. Your Dad was created especially for me. I have been so blessed to have had him in my life."

"You're going to make me cry Ma."

I hugged her close to me, "Why?"

"Well, when I grow up, I want to marry a man just like Dad. You look so happy lately." She looked off into space as if in a daze "I wonder what it feels like to be in love."

I cringed. Lord help me, this child of mine is way too young for all those shenanigans. Give me strength!

"Lili, falling in love is easy. Staying there is quite difficult. It can be downright scary sometimes!"

"But Ma doesn't I John 4:18 say that *perfect love casts out all fear*?"

Sitting in front of me, Lili asked the question proudly, almost patting herself on the back. She had memorized and presented on that scripture for Bible school last Sunday.

"Yes, Lili, it does."

We sat in silence as she watched me revel in the glow of a fearless love with Shandon. The idea of my innocent teenage daughter colliding with young love scared the wits out of me.

My cell phone rang from an unknown number and I rejected it. They called back three more times before I finally picked up the call.

"Hello?"

"Jnana, come outside and take ten steps to the left then sit down on the porch bench. I'll be there in three minutes." Then the call disconnected.

"Ma, who was that? Your face is as white as a ghost. Is there something wrong?"

As I processed Shandon's instructions, I did not answer Lili. She sat quietly as I robotically did as I was instructed. I waited patiently on the porch swing. Do not ask me why. It is against my nature to be so compliant, but my curiosity has me excited by the mystery. Of all the anniversary surprises, this one is the most unique Shandon has ever done. I rocked back and forth, giddy at the prospect of the day ahead of me. Shandon pulled up in front of the house and walked up to the porch. He pulled me to my feet and kissed me passionately. Then he walked behind me. Tenderly he put the yellow scarf over my eyes then led me down the steps. His breath was all I heard. I was holding mine. What is this all about? What is going on around me? I wanted so badly to ask all types of questions but did not. I had to quiet my mind. I trust my husband completely; this must be something special and I am on board for anything he has in mind. Shandon opened the car door and gently placed me into the seat. Before he closed the door, he put on my seat belt, stealing a feel of one of his favorite parts of me. I giggled like a schoolgirl. After all these years, Shandon still thinks that I am sexy. What a blessed woman I am.

"Jnana…"

"Yes, Shandon."

"I love you" He reached over and held my hand. I heard a familiar song playing and my eyes filled up with tears.

"I love you too. Shandon… Babe…it's our CD."

"Yes, it is Jnana."

         We rode in silence as we sang *There will Never Be* by Switch. Then, the car stopped. Just as gently as he put me in the car, he took me out of it. I used my senses to tell me where I was. I heard children's laughter and smelled the salt water. We were not driving long enough to have arrived at the beach. I searched my mind for parks around our house with a pond. I came up blank.

"Are you okay Babe? Is the scarf too tight?" Shandon asked me sweetly in my ear, nibbling on my lobe.

"Yes, Babe, I am just enjoying having you lead me. This is a wonderful anniversary surprise. Where you lead, I shall follow."

"Shandon kissed me on my neck, biting gently. "Hmmm, I love how that sounds. I cannot wait to get you back home tonight. I have one more surprise you are sure to be excited by."

I just smiled. My husband sure knows how to romance me.

"We're here. Now, when I take off your blindfold, I want you to go into the room and get dressed. Everything is laid out for you. There are some very special women waiting to help you to get ready."

"Okay."

He removed the blindfold and I did as I was asked. I walked into the room, even more, curious about what was going on.

"Ma! Lili! What are you two doing here?"

Ma giggled and hugged me tightly. I am here for you, that's what I am doing here."

Lili hugged me and her eyes filled with tears. "Ma, Uncle Jasper brought me and Ashton here after Dad picked you up."

"Hmm, you all are so sneaky. I had no idea! You know that it's hard to surprise me, but I must say that I am totally surprised by your Dad pulling all this off."

Ma walked into a closet and came out with the most beautiful ivory, mermaid cut, cap sleeved wedding dress ever! There were even a diamond studded tiara and some sexy three-inch teal heels. Before I could process the lovely sight before me, Donna and Louise from my first wedding walked in. The only one missing now is my sister Loz, but I knew that on such a glorious day such as this, she is smiling down from Heaven. I looked around at the most important women in my life and my breath caught. My heart cannot handle anymore joy. I forced myself to breathe. I will not allow my stress to ruin this day. I will allow the bliss to flow into me. Not only did I marry the man of my dreams, once, but he wants to marry me again. Oh, how blessed I am.

Ma walked over to me and smiled at me. She took my hands and kissed my cheek. "Jnana, thank you. You have made me so proud. You submitted to Shandon. As you can see by his surprise, he is beyond pleased to finally be able to lead his family with you as his helpmate."

"Ma, I cannot thank you enough. I am built to be an abiding woman who submits fully to her husband. I cannot be happier. Your brand of real talk finally got through my thick skull. Thank you for not giving up on me."

"Jnana, I would never give up on you. You are my daughter and I love you. Just continue the path that you are on and God will continue to bless you. Now, I have something old to give to you."

Ma handed me a beautiful box with a pink ribbon enclosure. My heart about exploded in my chest when I opened the box. "It was a beautiful sterling silver cross that my sister Loz had worn every day for the last few years of her life before she passed from heart disease. "Oh, Ma, it's so beautiful."

"Ma," Lili said, "I have something blue." She handed me a blue circular box. Inside it was a blue handwritten card from Shandon. Inside the card, he wrote how much he was pleased with having my hand in marriage, for the second time. Lili handed me a diamond bracelet that Shandon's Mom had worn at her wedding. "Mommy, this is your something borrowed."

The makeup artist walked over and handed me a make-up case which held beautiful mineral make up in all different natural shades. I guess she knew I would not trust her to make up my face and ruin this day. "This is your something new. I really wanted to give this gift to you for you to do your own make up. But really...I would be honored if you would trust me to make you even more beautiful than you already are. I promise you that I will do a better job today. Please?"

I remembered my mantra, no stress or mess so I relented. "Okay," I said a prayer then left it alone. I will enjoy this day, yes, I will!

"Now Ma, we have one more surprise for you. Close your eyes."

I did as she requested. What else could it be?

"Now, open your eyes, Ma."

As soon as I opened my eyes, I recognized the box. Our vows box. I opened it and inside was Shandon and my original vows and a new gift. Shandon had placed a beautiful bracelet with his, mine and our children's birthstone on it. I cannot lie. I got teary-eyed when Lili put it around my trembling wrist. I never dreamed of being treated like a princess, but that is precisely how I feel today. For the next hour or two, I sat quietly and got my hair and make-up done according to Shandon's very specific orders. Then, they helped into my wedding gown by Ma and Lili. We got misty eyed as Lili gently placed the tiara upon my head of tendril curls. This was the lovely wedding day I always wanted. Having my daughter here to share it with me is even better.

I was led into a room which was decorated with purple and silver accents. Here and Now by Luther Vandross was playing softly. Lili handed me my bouquet of lavender and purple flowers. She opened the door to the church and all our family and friends were seated before me. Ashton came from behind and took one arm and my Daddy took the other arm. Now, this is icing on the cake! My son looks so handsome and Daddy is wearing the same suit from my first wedding. Oh, God is so good! I had to work hard not to cry and ruin every single drop of make-up.

When I got close enough to the front of the altar, Shandon and I locked eyes. He had on a white suit with a purple tie. He was smiling so wide; you would think that I was not already his wife. Lili was standing at the front of the church, now dressed in a beautiful lilac dress. I walked closer and I could see Shandon's face glistening with tears. I stood in front of Shandon and he gently took my hand in his. I am not going to lie, the energy surging between us made me tremble. He felt me and rubbed my hand gently. I smiled. He always knew what I needed, at the right time. The Preacher stood quietly as Shandon and I romanced each other with our eyes. This man is all mine! We have come a long way! Oh, how God restores.

"Welcome everyone," the Preacher said, "today we are gathered here to witness the second marriage of Shandon and Jnana. I had the pleasure of officiating their first ceremony as well. As I look before me, I can see that both Shandon and Jnana have amassed a wealth of family and friends, all of whom love and support them. I thank you all for attending such a glorious day before the Lord. Now, we can get started. Are you two ready?"

As if rehearsed, Shandon and I both answered together and we both were just as excited and animated. "Yes!"

"Well, we can take that as a fervent yes! Now, as God has surely blessed you both, I want to say that I can see the maturity in both of you. You lost the naivety that most couples possess as they stand at

470 | P a g e

this altar. Now, you have a maturity that's very apparent. With that in mind, I applaud you both for sticking it out, through thick and thin. Many couples hear their vows and happily say, for better but seem to mumble for worse. However, to be successful at marriage, you must take the better with the worse. Times won't always be happy and joyous. Sometimes, you will have to put on your boxing gloves and fight for your relationship. Even if some moments look bleak, with God on your side, nothing will knock you down without the two of you fighting together to get back up. I commend you two. I can see the battle scars, yet you two are still standing. To God be all the glory! To the crowd, what you don't know is that this ceremony is a total surprise to Jnana. She didn't know a thing about today up until a few hours ago."

The crowd roared with excitement and glee. They all know that it is not easy to surprise me, so they are attendants at a truly miraculous event. I am usually the one planning surprise parties for everyone.

"Well, Shandon and Jnana wrote their own vows last time and it's a surprise to me how they will proceed today. He looked to Shandon for guidance. Shandon took the microphone and held my hands in his. "Jnana Jael Roberts, my beautiful wife, I have loved you since the first time I saw you outside at this very park. You have supported me as I built my business and been my helpmate. You and I planned this life we are living but here is one thing that we couldn't have planned for, struggles. I am so blessed that you stuck it out with me and never stopped loving me. We have had our share of lack and times where we both might have thought to throw in the towel, but God has restored our relationship. You are my helpmate. You are the one woman who truly wanted me to give myself totally to a God that never stopped wanting the very best for our marriage and our family. I love you to the deepest depths of my soul."

He handed me the microphone and I was so emotional; I could not find the words to speak. There was silence as I got myself together. Shandon hugged me and I felt so loved.

"Well, I don't even know how to follow those beautiful vows. Seeing as though this day is a total surprise, I haven't prepared any appropriate vows. But…on a whim…I guess that I can come up with something heartfelt."

The crowd roared with laughter.

"Thank you, everyone, for coming to support Shandon and I. Shandon Donovan Roberts, my love, I honor you today for allowing God to use you as a vessel. You came and rescued me from such a doldrum life. I was a slave to my career and my education. You came and restored me. You are the love of my life and I feel so blessed to have you. You loved me, even when I wasn't acting lovable. Where you lead, I shall follow. I love you from the deepest depths of my soul. Oh, and I have a surprise for you too. Ashton, can you help your sister to get the surprise for your Dad?"

As our children went to get the surprise, I felt so filled up with love. This will be quite the surprise for Shandon!

I gently sat Shandon down into the seat that Ashton had brought up to the altar. With my own spin on I Samuel 25:41, *she got up and then bowed down, face to the ground saying, "I'm your servant ready to do anything you want. I will even wash the feet of my master's servants!"* I placed a towel on the ground then kneeled on it. Then, I lovingly took off both of Shandon's shoes and placed his feet in the basin of warm lavender water that Lili brought to the altar. I carefully looked Shandon in the eyes to show him how serious I was about being a submitted wife and helpmate. I rolled up his pants legs and did the one thing he wanted me to do since our first night together. I touched his feet.

"Shandon, I am your helpmate and I vow to serve you for the rest of my life. I wash your feet to show you that there is no part of me that I will ever hold back from you. I want to please you in every way, and I am your wife, in every way. As I look you in your eyes, look deeply into mine and see my heart. Shandon, my love, I am honored to submit to your will."

Shandon began to cry, and I knew he could feel my dedication to him and our family, more than ever. I dried off his feet and put his shoes back on. Tears still in his eyes, he pulled me into a kiss.

"Hold up you two, we haven't gotten to that part yet!" The Preacher said half laughing. Shandon and I pulled back and restrained ourselves.

"After those beautiful, love filled words, and Jnana's declaration of true submission, I have nothing that can follow the vows or the ceremony.

473 | P a g e

Shandon, you may now kiss your truly submitted bride."

Shandon and I barely waited until he finished his sentence before we passionately kissed. I know that our children were extremely embarrassed. They just need to get over it! Hey, my husband still got it too! And all that he has trust, that is all that I want!

~36~
Funny Valentine

I, therefore, a prisoner for the Lord, urge you to
walk in a manner worthy of the calling to which
you have been called, with all humility and
gentleness, with patience, bearing with one another
in love,
Ephesians 4:1-2
***

Trinity

I am feeling free from the Reiki chakra
nature music I listened to on YouTube.com as part
of my morning ritual. I made it a habit to meditate
on the Word of God and repeat daily mantras of joy
the last few weeks. This awakening was at the
bequest of a counselor at the shelter. Such a small
addition to my daily schedule has helped me to
evolve into a whole woman.

When I moved into Redeeming Hope, I
thought that it was just a place for me to solve my
housing situation. However, in many ways, I was
helped along on my spiritual journey. I attended
individual counseling and weekly groups. I learned
coping strategies for dealing with real life situations
in workshops. Initially, I was required to attend
Bible study and Sunday church service. But I
decided to go with an attitude of needing God
instead of feeling obligated to attend church. As a
result of that decision, not only is the outside of me
being transformed but the inner part of me is being
renewed. Jeremiah 1:9-10 says, *I have put my hand*

upon your mouth, put my words in your mouth, for you to tear down, pull up, demolish, and take apart start over building and planting. I took that scripture to heart as I pulled myself away from the destructive behaviors that kept me in bondage. I want to live free in the flow of life. I desire a life full of joy and one with purposeful intention of personal growth. I am sick of being a hamster running on the wheel of life, never getting ahead. I realized my constant frustration has been when I forced myself into the same situations. Those situations with married men may have carried a certain comfort because they did not require me to look inside myself for happiness. If I kept looking outside to find peace, I was in a constant holding pattern. No man has ever completed me. It is time that I learn to complete myself.

****

I paid my ten-dollar fee to get in and then I sat in a dark corner of the small yet quaint jazz joint with my bag. The ambiance was warm browns and creams and it has a groove all its own. The band members, whose ages ranged from late teens to late sixties, had an aura full of positive energy. My eyes scanned the creative beings so engrossed in their love until my eyes rested upon the deep soulful eyes of the very attractive keyboardist. He had a bald head, smooth brown skin, graying goatee, beautiful lips, and a smile that lit up the dark club. Dang, he was attractive! I loved me a creative man. I looked deeply into his longing eyes and I smiled back at him. He mouthed hi to me and I waved. Instinctively, I looked at his ring finger, I knew it, married. From that moment, I ignored his eye advances. No more married men. Period! Looking into his eyes did not come close to staring into Micah's eyes. Yeah, we had a moment there, but it was fleeting. Besides, that man has nothing on my Micah. Micah has my heart. Trust!

The songstress was belting out Funny Valentine like no one's business! I closed my eyes and let myself fall into a state of bliss. Her scats, high notes, and falsetto mesmerized the crowd. We all knew the words by heart but with her interpretation of the lyrics, she was tugging at our heart strings. I was so glad I came out tonight, this will be a night of wonder. There was something in the air, I could just feel it!

I took out my drawing pad and sketched a few pictures while listening to the live jazz. My body grooved and my eyes lowered, this vibe is lovely! Although I have tried to shut out any thought of him, I cannot push away the strong feelings I have for Micah. I believe I have found the love of my life in Micah. But I must be sure that I am at a place in my life where I can truly compliment his beauty. Until then, I will not commit myself to a situation that I will, in time, sabotage. Whenever I feel as if I am losing myself or that a man is getting too close, I get scared and ruin things. Feeling unworthy of happiness does that to me. Sometimes, I do wonder if he is missing me as I am missing him. I shake away those thoughts. Sure, he is! I am a good woman, he knows it and if he truly loves me as he professed, I was in his thoughts. There will be a time when he and I will reconnect, but that time is not anytime soon. I was in the flow of things, waiting on God to do his best work in Micah and me. For now, I will send a sweet kiss into the universe. Until then, my love.

Tonight, I am on my India Arie flow. Airy white broomstick skirt, soft yellow midriff top, flat cream colored open toed sandals, handmade jewelry and my hair is in two strand twists. Unable to afford the expensive perfumes I used to wear, I asked Micah to take me to a natural foods store where I purchased jasmine, lavender, and chamomile essential oils. Tonight, I do not have any makeup on and my scent for tonight is a homemade perfume I made from a mixture of the essential oils and with witch hazel. To make my own cologne is cheaper than buying those expensive perfumes I used to crave.

The M.C. strolled confidently up to the microphone and spouted out a few jokes. As expected, he homed in on the front row and proceeded to embarrass a few of the people that were foolish enough to make themselves an easy target. The woman with the weave she was wearing way too long. The man wearing the long fur when it was hot as all get out in here. And, of course, there is always the inevitable couple that arrives right in the middle of his set looking for their seat in the dimly lit room. They all got jokes that seemed to be his best rapid-fire jokes. After his reckless jokes got less play, he signaled to be handed the open mic stand up list.

I was the guest artist who would be painting while the poets did their word play. All my original art was to be put on sale immediately after each set. I was introduced and asked to come up on the stage to set up. The stagehand helped me set up my easel, then I placed the paints onto the table provided and put the brushes in the cup of water to soften up.

The first poet, Sistah Zeetia, was called up first. She did a piece on radical love as a metaphor for domestic abuse. She had women in the audience on their feet waving their fists in solidarity. This sistah, small in stature but big in presence, had her hair in flame red locs twisted up in a knot on top of her head, the long orange sun dress and matching five-inch heels completed her outfit filled with badness and attitude. When she was done, I stood up and showed the crowd my painting. The painting featured a cocoon with flowing red locs surrounding it with five different hued butterflies. The M.C. inopportunely rushed back onto the stage to purchase my painting for his teenage daughter's upcoming sweet 16 birthday. I tried to hide my glee as moans of displeasure fell from the mouths of other people that wanted to purchase it. Sistah Zeetia was extra heated because she was supposed to have first dibs on the painting. After all, her poem inspired the piece. The next performer up was a singer who wrote a song he dedicated to his new wife. His wife beamed with pride from the front row. The song was 5000 miles, a Johnny Gill ballad which spoke of the deep spiritual connection

479 | P a g e

between a couple in love. I could not get Micah off of my mind enough to paint one stroke. Tears streamed down my face as I witnessed the man serenading his wife up to the stage and proceeded to make love to her thoughts with every note. There were several couples caught up in the melee of love, kissing and snuggling up to each other. The crowd was so into the performer that the M.C. let him sing another selection. He switched the mood and sweetly began singing Jill Scott's *Hear My Call*. This song inspires me like no one's business! I began painting purple and blue mountains on the yellow background. I inserted a man meditating on a green blanket, his arms extended to God in total submission. I drew a funnel cloud of ash grey above his head and a light of bright yellow to signify the Heavens. As the last note was sung I completed the last stroke. The singer turned around and in quick order placed a one-hundred-dollar bill down for the painting.

"God bless you Sistah. You are a blessing from God," he said before descending the stage steps.

My next painting was in response to a request for a blind painting. It seemed that someone decided it would be fun for me to do my rendition of the silence in the universe. To add intrigue, I donned a blindfold. This would be my initial foray into soul painting, painting from the core of being. For five minutes, I painted like my artistic life depended on it. I dipped my brush back and forth in pots of paint, quickly washing then drying the brush in between strokes. The first stroke sparked a distinct newness, yet the second brought me alive. I

480 | P a g e

was just as excited to see the masterpiece that I was painting from listening only to the still small voice of the universe. The M.C. came out after five minutes to take off my blindfold. I fell instantly in love with my painting. Applause erupted inside the small club. Both the crowd and I got to see my creation at the same time. We were all impressed at the result. I had blue overcast skies, fiery orange suns, castaway sands and a black body of water that seemed to spill off the edges of the canvas. All I could do was take a bow in reverence. However, inside I was bursting at the seams with joy. This is what I am created for! I said a silent and deeply felt thanks to my Creator for this generous spiritual gift. This art represented who I am at my soul's core, beautiful, serene, deep, and spiritually awake.

The night went on like this for another hour. Each of my paintings sold quickly. I slyly glanced at the clock on the wall over the bar and realized that the last bus would be leaving soon. I began to clean up my supplies so that I could make it to the bus stop on time.

Leaving the jazz club brought tears to my eyes. In there, I felt one with the other creative beings. I felt like I belonged. The accolades I received for my painting was heartwarming. The fact that I sold all my paintings is a plus! I did not realize that inside the audience, there was a gallery owner who brought my last two pieces of art. She is holding a women's empowerment art show and wants me to headline. Me! Headline! Get that! Words cannot describe how great it feels to be growing spiritually, mentally, and how wonderful it feels to finally give in to the thrill of painting.

I rushed to the bus stop and my legs were moving so quickly, I was half jogging. I am in great shape! Physically, I am beginning to enjoy walking. I am even in a comfortable place with myself physically. Wow, I put those words out into the universe. Comfort…with self…this is a monumental occasion!

There was only one thing missing in my life puzzle, Micah. It has been many weeks since I last talked to him. I am a little surprised because I figured by now, he would have called me, begging me to change my mind. He texts me and sends me scripture every morning. Occasionally, he even sends me a cute selfie of himself. As if I can forget how gorgeous he is. As much as I wanted to feel upset that he has not shown up in places he knows that I will be, I loved that he is giving me the space that I need to figure myself out. I know that if he had forced me to stay, I would only resent him. His understanding shows me that he trusts in what we feel enough to back off and let me come to him. That meant so much to me. If he and I would have continued, I would have hurt him because I did not think that I was worthy of happiness. Oh, it is so different now. I know that I deserve him. I know that I deserve to be happy. And soon I will rush back into Micah's life and never leave again. I have a few more loose ends to tie up. When I go back to Micah, he will be my one choice, not an option. God knows that I will not have it any other way.

I left the club with enough time to jump on the last bus back to the shelter. Ms. Mabel had given me special permission to be out after the eight o'clock curfew for residents. I have never been out this late without having a vehicle. Still, I am prepared. I have my mace and personal alarm at the ready. It is no joke to be a female out by myself after dark. Each car that whizzed by, I prayed that they kept driving by me. The light in the bus shelter was out, of course. I watched endless cars keep going, then my heart stopped when one stopped! Desperately I checked to make sure that the mace sprayer was facing away from me and was intact to spray someone's eyes out. The car pulled off abruptly, then, and only then did I begin breathing again. Whew, that was a close call! A few more cars drove by then that same car pulled back up to the bus stop. This time they opened the car door and got out. In my brain, I was running but my body was not cooperating. So, there I stood frightened to death.

"Trinity, can we talk?"

Whodini sang that freaks come out at night but who would have guessed that Greysan would be out here asking me, politely, to talk. After all these months! They say that exes know when you have moved on because they often come creeping back into your life to try to get their hooks back in. I am so in love with Micah, he treats me like a lady and loves me completely. He is patient, loving, and kindhearted. When we have had disagreements, not once did he even come close to raising a hand to hit me. He and Grey are solar opposites. But am I over

483 | P a g e

Greysan? As I sit here, in the dark no less, I do not know. As I am pondering that thought the bus drives right around Grey's car. Great! Now, I am stuck. He smiles at me and reaches out his hand. I missed the last bus of the night, so I have no choice.

I gathered my things and got into his car. He did not bother to open my door for me. What a gentleman! Strike one. I barely got into the car before he leaned over the console and tried to kiss me. I do not know how to react to this unexpected affection, especially since the last time I saw him he refused to kiss me. I purse my lips together and keep my lips tight. He tried hard to push his tongue through my lips until I pulled away. I let him put his hands all over my body. What a surprise, he did not notice that I wasn't reciprocating his amorous advances. When he began to put his hand up my dress I pulled away and stopped him. Micah has my heart and when we are married, he and only he will have my body. Still…I cannot believe how perfectly this situation has fallen into my lap. I was laying awake this morning wondering how I could lore Grey to spend time with me. Do not get me wrong, this isn't revenge, this is closure. I am sure about how well I am progressing in my self-awareness journey. I am in love with myself for the first time ever in my life. I even stood, naked, in front of the mirror! I found so many beautiful things about myself. I am fierce! I even love wearing my hair natural. I never saw myself as a fist raising soul sistah before but truly that is who I am. There is nothing wrong with being strong in spirit, voluptuous in the body and peaceful in the soul.

I have prayed and meditated to gain control over my mind. My mind has always been my downfall. The thoughts of fear and mistrust always come up when my worth was questioned. It is funny that the very feeling I despised, one of feeling unworthy, was perpetuated over and over when I dealt with married men who were never going to find worth in me. How could they? I was lowering my standards and allowing them to sleep with me without a commitment. What man would respect a woman who went against the natural order of things? A woman who would allow a spoken for man to take benefit from something that is supposed to be special in a committed monogamous relationship. Every time I excused married cheaters, I went against what I truly believe and what I truly want. I want a man all my own, I deserve no less! In the midst of mind warfare, I came across this life changing, thought healing book, *Tree of Life: Thought Pruning Through Mindful Christian Meditation* by Stacy C. Brown. That book has helped me tremendously! Prayer is not a fix all, however it's essential in my journey towards wholeness. As Marvin Sapp sang beautifully, *He saw the best in me.* How could I think less of myself when my Creator thinks so highly of me that he allowed the bloodshed of our Lord Jesus Christ? When I put all that in perspective, I straightened up!

So, with all this growth, why am I sitting in the car with the most lecherous man I know? As I said before, closure. There is no longer any illusion about his money. Ha, that is laughable! I mean his wife's money. And there is not a stitch of love for him in my heart. I finally saw him for who he really was. Hindsight is 20-20. I am pretending to go along with his plan to seduce me. I wanted to see how desperate he gets before I put a stop to things. I know that I am playing with fire, but hey I have my mace with me. If he does not get too out of control, things will be okay. I said a silent prayer for the angels to encamp around me, just in case. Trust me, I knew this is a dangerous game, but unless Grey wants me to do him like Tina did Ike in that limo, he better keep his distance!

****

At my bequest, Greysan had driven to Spoons so that we could have a late dinner. Sweet honey dripped down my chin. I moved my tongue to slowly lick it up. When I raised my eyes to his, the desire was still there. I watched him as he rubbed his chin. A smile moved across his face. That smile once warmed me from the inside out. He reached up and caressed my hand. Then he got up and moved to my side of the booth. At my bequest, he drove to my favorite restaurant, Spoons, for a late dinner. He leaned over and seductively nibbled on my neck. He blew softly. He still remembers. When he pulled me in for a kiss, I screamed, louder than intended, "No!"

His eyes got big and he slumped down in his seat. It is late, but for some reason, he thinks that people know him.

Abruptly I said, "I have to go to the bathroom!"

Suddenly, I pushed past him, and he fell out of the booth onto the floor. I nearly ran over his body to get to the bathroom. I stood in front of the dirty mirror and looked at my reflection. The joy that I experienced so abundantly at the jazz joint has been so easily overshadowed by such a vile man. I reached down and splashed cold water on my face. I must regroup. I was losing control over this situation. I took out my cell phone to call Micah but decided against it. I must deal with my loose ends before I contact him again. I splashed more water on my face. When I looked into the mirror this time, in my eyes I saw sorrow. Why am I here? The closure is not worth this much backtracking with Grey. I was startled when I heard the squeaky door opening then the lights went out. Then, I heard the door lock.

"Trinity, I heard the water running. Baby, you don't have to fresh up for me. I missed you. I know that you missed me too."

"Grey, why did you turn the lights out? We can talk with them on."

I heard his voice moving throughout the room, "Come on, Trinity, and stop this nonsense. You don't have to play all these games with me. Let's get down to business."

"Grey, please turn on the lights, please. You know that I'm afraid of the dark."

My heart was racing out of my chest. I fumbled around in my pocketbook and tried to concentrate on the sound of his feet. I could hear his voice moaning next to mine. Oh my gosh! No, he could not be doing that to himself. With him preoccupied with stroking himself and trying to find me, I finally reached the lights. When I turned the lights on, I got quite a sight. Grey was totally naked and touching himself.

"Come help me, Trinity. I know this is what you always wanted me to do for you. Remember you always wanted to watch?"

"Grey that was then, this is now. Can we go now?"

"Why? Don't act shy now Trin. Come on, I missed you. Don't you care that I missed you?"

Desperation is not a good look for Grey. I cannot stand weak men. How could I have not seen this before? He is broken and he only wanted to make me feel lower than he already felt about himself. Why am I just seeing that he did not feel strong enough in his marriage, so he used women to feel like a man? The money was hers; the house was hers. He was just the seed planter. She got pregnant to keep him and he got her pregnant so she would feel she needed him to stay.

"Come on, Grey, please pull your pants up. Let's go finish dinner. I was enjoying your company before. As you realize, this is the first time we had a meal out in public together. That makes me happy but, honestly, I don't have time for this nonsense! It's getting late, I really must get back to the shelter."

"We can go back to eating when you come over here and get on your knees and finish what I already started for you."

"I'm out of here! I'll be waiting at the table."

Tonight, things between Greysan and I could still end peacefully. As if I have never seen it before, I now see the vulnerability in Grey. I can finally say that I do not love him…probably never loved him. Now I have closure.

"You aren't going anywhere! He growled as he reached up and turned out the light again. He angrily grabbed the back of my neck and pushed me to my knees. I scratched and tried to claw myself out of his grasp. I reached into my purse and found my mace. I sprayed until the canister was empty. Back draft hit me, and my eyes began to burn. He yelled then hit the floor. I moved quickly out of his reach.

"Trinity, why did you mace me? I wasn't going to hurt you. I only wanted to remind you of how good it felt when we were together. Uhh, my eyes are burning so bad!"

"Oh, so you were going to have sex with me in a dirty restaurant bathroom to remind me of how much you missed me? Really?! All this reminds me of is how little you really think of me. You never cared about our babies and you never cared about me being homeless and carless. I will never forget listening to you making love to your secretary. I will never forget the feeling of the cold metal of the handcuffs on my wrists when I got arrested. You could have stopped your wife from doing all those things by telling her the truth about your whorish ways. But no, you would rather throw me to the wolves!"

"Trinity, you don't understand. I didn't know that she was going to do all that stuff to you. Please believe me. Come kiss me, we can make up for all those wrong things. Just give me a chance. I really did love you, please believe me. I left her and got

489 | P a g e

my own place after all the mess she did to you. I promise you that I got my own apartment."

For some sick reason, I really wanted to believe I meant something to him. There was something in me that needed to know that I did not give up so much and gotten so little.

"Okay, Grey, well, let's go to your place. We can make up there and maybe even spend the night together for the first time."

"Well, uhhh, Trinity, it's kind of late. Umm, my kids are there, and you know, some other time. Okay? How about we finish this right now? Right here is okay. Look I can lock the door. Why leave when we were practically the only ones in the place this time of night?"

"Grey, please take me home. It is kind of late." I said glibly.

"Only, if you will do what I ask. Here you want some money? I have five hundred just for you."

I had heard enough. I earned that much tonight at the jazz bar by doing what I love. Touching Grey is no longer something I love to do, nor do I want to suffer through it for money.

"No thanks, Grey. I don't want your money, but I do have to go. Good night, I'll just walk."

Predictably, he had to throw one last jab.

"You run on off to that shelter. You might as well come back to me. No other man will want you. You are ugly, fat. Your own father didn't want you!"

I smiled, yes *Mr. Hanks...my Daddy does.*

I turned back around to face him. I stared him down with the power of Jesus Christ behind me, "So you say, Greysan. My God sees that I am beautiful, perfectly shaped and one man does love me. I'll keep you in my prayers, Grey. Goodbye."

I walked towards the door with my head held high. I am neither fat, ugly nor unwanted. His last dig was weak at best.

"So, you think that you can just walk away from me? I made you, without my money you wouldn't be anything!"

I chuckled. This come back is weaker still. I looked him into his eyes, I was not afraid of the evil look on his face. This is how he executes control over me. God has not given me a spirit of fear, so I turned back around and put my hand on the door to leave.

I had to tell him how I really feel; I must get it all off my chest. "Btw, I never loved you, Grey. You were a cheating man, someone I never truly respected. How could I trust you? Don't answer, you don't even trust yourself."

I know my truth was rough, but I am fed up with worthless men thinking that all they must do is throw me empty promises and I will fall into their bed. I was tired of feeling weak. I wanted my power back and I am taking it by force! I no longer wanted to be emotionally manipulated by words that only serve to diminish my womanhood. I am whole, and with this episode of closure, I am so ready to move on with my life. I am beautiful and I do not need to clamor greedily for a man to tell me this undeniable truth. I already feel it in my bones. So, I took a bow. Greysan's once handsome face and the sweet smile faded before me. He looked confused yet was not done being desperate.

491 | P a g e

"Honestly, Trinity, Lisa is gone. I'm done with her. Can you believe that that trick is trying to sue me for sexual harassment? Oh, the lies she told everyone at that bank!"

I shook my head in disgust. Karma, karma, karma! "Thank you, Grey, for the life lessons you forced me to see. Thank you even for the punches. I forgive you for the lies you told me and the pain you inflicted upon me. It took me a long time to see it but now I see the truth. Now our babies can finally rest in peace. You forced me to see myself for the first time in a long time. Goodbye."

"Nasty hussy! You will be crawling back on your knees to me. Give it time. Money hoes always return to the bank! You ain't nothing but that sexy body of yours. Nothing!"

I am not going to lie. That last one hurt. The sad part is that it used to be who I claimed, with pride. The woman in me now is claiming honor. That was then, this is now. The blood cleanses me. I have a renewed spirit.

"Greysan, I don't receive those words. I rebuke you. I am Trinity Marie Boussiant, a woman of virtue."

"Oh, this is rich! A real-life jezebel is quoting the Bible now. That's laughable. You are a tramp and always will be."

I chuckled loudly, "Actually, I am no longer a tramp. I made a choice to change my life. Through faith, and a lot of prayers, I have been abstinent, and I am living life vibrantly. As for my Father, I found him, and he loves me very much. He believes

I am beautiful and smart. He tells me that I am special every single day."

I walked out of the bathroom to claim my life back. I did not even stop when I heard a bottle fly over my head. If it would have hit me, I would have unleashed the winds of hell on him. I may be saved and sanctified, but by the blood of Jesus, I was no longer weak. You better know, Greysan got lucky!

~37~
S.T.D. (Save The Drama)

If some enemies broke in and seized your goods,
you let them go with a smile, knowing they couldn't
touch your real treasure. Nothing they did bothered
you, nothing set you back. So, don't throw it all
away now. You were sure of yourselves then. It still
is a sure thing! But you need to stick it out, staying
with God's plan so you'll be there for the promised
completion.
Hebrews 10:34-36
***

Jnana

"Jnana, you may have a problem!" Becca rushed
into Namaste without even greeting me. Oh, the
drama of it all!
I inhaled than exhaled, oh Lord, what now?
"What's going on Becca? Is Celeste okay?"
"Well, no, she is not okay. I took her to a doctor's
appointment yesterday. I have been through a lot
with Celeste. But this latest news is just too much
for me to handle!"
Sheesh, she sure can be dramatic. Why haven't I
noticed that before? I am exhausted and she just got
here.
"So, why do we have a problem? What did you take
Celeste to the doctor for? Is she okay? Stop being
so evasive Becca, darn, just spit it out!"
"Oh, I am so sorry Jnana. I am just beside myself.
Well, two weeks ago Celeste started having
stomach cramps and had painful urination. When

494 | P a g e

she told me this, I figured that she might just have a urinary tract infection, so I gave her some cranberry juice to drink. Well, it was then that she told me about the unusual discharge too. I called her doctor and made her their first available appointment. Jnana, Celeste, has Chlamydia!"

"What?! You have got to be kidding me, she has an STD?! How, where, why?"

Becca gave me this look, "I know right! When we talked with her, I really thought that we got through to her. Honestly, I did."

"So, what did she say after the doctor told you the result? Is she still alive? I mean you had to have had a fit in that doctor's office, right?"

Becca breathed in deeply and she got this angry look on her face. "Yes, I went off. But I didn't go hard until we got home. I will admit that I slapped her across her face. Of this, I am not proud. Jnana, I just feel like such a fool. How could I have raised a daughter like that? She knows better! I know she does!"

"Look, Becca, I'm not going to let you blame yourself! You did the best you could with what parental skill you had. It's natural for parents to blame themselves. But our children will do whatever they want. They feel immortal. Celeste is no different. I'm just surprised that she's not using protection. In this day and age, why isn't she?"

"Jnana hold on to your hat for the new development. My daughter, as irresponsible as she is, wants to get pregnant! Can you imagine that? No job and no place of her own, yet she actually thinks that getting pregnant is a good plan."

"Oh, Becca, I am so sorry. I know this is taking you through! I don't even want to imagine what stress you have been under. Have you prayed about this?"

"To be honest, I haven't even ventured a thought to pray. I have been so stressed out and I am ashamed to admit that my faith is shaken. I just don't know what to do. I never expected any of this from Celeste."

"Look, I get it. Sometimes we get in such an emotional state that we forget to pray. We even lose faith, but we can't stay there Becca, we can't!"

"I know, Jnana. But I don't know what to do. I am at the end of my rope."

"No, you are not! Don't you dare speak all that negativity into the universe. You need to get yourself together and put on your spiritual big girl panties. It's way past time to fight! You are on the battlefield of spiritual warfare right now. You need to straighten your spine and draw on your faith! There is no other way around how you get your family back on track. If you lie down and die now, the devil wins. She is your daughter and you need to pray her back. Are you willing to do that? Do you have faith or not?!"

She looked me in my eyes and tears cascaded down her cheeks. "Yes," She finally replied in a whisper. "I am willing to take back my daughter and do it boldly, by faith."

I hugged her tightly and we prayed. As the tears continued to fall, I realized that I had won a soul back for God. I felt courageous and I felt like I had finally shown God that I am more for Him than I will ever be for myself. And the feeling felt

496 | P a g e

beyond beautiful! I felt free. I looked to the skies and smiled. Inside I felt pure. In many ways, I finally allowed the voice of the Holy Spirit to speak louder than my negative thoughts that kept me from being faithful to God's will. As Becca and I parted, I handed her *Prayers that avail much*, the commemorative edition by Germaine Copeland and I book marked page 212. That book has been an invaluable resource to me as I gave into the desire to pray myself in and out of every day. Becca hugged me and held on tight. I could feel her spirit was light and easy.

"Thank you, you are a God send, Jnana. I love you my Sista." Becca said as we stepped away from each other.

"Becca, you are welcome. Trust me, I know what you are going through. I had been through this with Ashton and best believe I put my own mother through some of these teenage girl issues when I was Celeste's age. Thank God, my mother knew how to pray me out of my messy phase instead of giving up on me. Believe me, having prayer warriors for parents kept me out of harms way in many situations I should have been in a world of trouble. Celeste will grow out of this too. You just have to keep praying and make sure she adheres to the rules of your household."

"I grew up in a strict household, so I didn't want to be untrusting and strict with my kids. But now I see that I should be making sure they stay within set boundaries of behavior. I cannot thank you enough, Jnana."

"You're welcome. Now, I must go, I have a staff meeting in thirty minutes, so I must prepare for it and order out some food. I'm glad you stopped by Lady."

She held her book tight. "Me too, Jnana, me too."

As I watched her leave and drive off in her car, I said a silent prayer. "God be with her."

As a mother of two teenagers, I always knew she needed to keep angels encamped .

Redemption

And through him to reconcile to himself all things,
whether on earth or in heaven, making peace by the
blood of his cross. And you, who once were
alienated and hostile in mind, doing evil deeds, he
has now reconciled in his body of flesh by his
death, in order to present you holy and blameless
and above reproach before him,
Colossians 1:20-22
***

Trinity

I was jostled awake. Dang, I was having a good
dream too! I opened my heavy eyelids to find Ms.
Mabel stood over me holding one black thirty-
gallon trash bag. There were lots of other bags on
the floor around her feet. I finally sat up. I rubbed
the sleep out of my eyes and wiped the slobber off
my cheek. Finally, wide awake, I asked her what
was going on.

She had such a big smile, she was showing all of
her partials, "Trinity, do you remember when we
read in the scripture, that you must seek first the
kingdom of God and all His righteousness, and all
these things shall be added unto you?"

"Uhh yes Ma'am, Matthew 6:33 right? Ms. Mabel,
I mean no disrespect but can you please just me tell
me what's going on instead of playing this guessing
game? I was up late last night, and I want to rest up
before I go to see Mr. Hanks...my Dad, this
afternoon."

"Well, Trinity, an angel of mercy delivered your

stuff here this morning. She also sent her apologies for the misunderstanding."

"My stuff?!"

I jumped off the bed and ripped open every single bag, one bag after the other. In the bags, I found my art canvases and my art supplies. My watercolors, pastels and charcoal were all here. The only thing missing was my finished paintings. I did not want to get caught up in what I did not have so I celebrated what seemed like the impossible gift. My stuff, my wonderfully beautiful stuff! I cannot believe this, God restored me. Then it hit me, I threw everything back into the bags and sat on my bed like I saw a mouse. I wrapped my legs up to my chest and my breath caught in my chest. What is going on here? Is someone playing a sick joke on me? Tremica came to mind as the jokester sick enough to play such a mean prank. I will just continue to pray for her peace! But then how could she know how to get my things?

Ms. Mabel was watching me in disbelief, "Ms. Mabel, please tell me how you got my stuff. Tell me how they got here and who dropped them off. Please!"

"Trinity, your stuff was delivered here with the other donations this morning. The person who delivered the stuff told me that these things belong to you. I knew that this was your stuff because there were personal pictures and other personal effects that have your name on them. I went through all the bags and boxes and separated yours. Some of the things, like sexual aids and such, are contraband so I threw them away. This is a Christian facility so we

500 | P a g e

can't have those types of things here," She shook her head at me, "Sorry."

"Ms. Mabel are you sure that there are no bombs tucked neatly in a pant pocket or itching powder in the crotch of the clothes?"

She giggled gleefully while I sat screw faced on my bed. I do not see one thing funny!

"No Trinity, there are no hidden bombs or itching powder sprinkled anywhere on the clothes. In fact, they smell like they are freshly washed. Some of the nicer things even have dry cleaning tags on them. Here, this is the note that was attached to the bags."

I quickly snatched the note from Ms. Mabel's hand. I did not care about being rude. I needed proof that this was a blessing and not a curse, "A note? For me?"

"Yes, Trinity, there is a note attached to the bags and an attached envelope for you. I read the note, you know, just to be assured that everything was on the up and up. I know you don't mind. I will leave the envelope for you to look inside for yourself. So, I am going to leave you alone to get reacquainted with your things and to read your letter. I'm sure that you will find the note interesting reading material. I know that I did!"

When Ms. Mabel left the room all I could do was cry. I do not know why I got my stuff back. I do not even know what is included in this stuff. No matter about these things, just yet. I have been living right. This is my blessing that I have been praying for. It is confirmation that I am on the right path to how God wants me to live. I am tired of mopping up the muddy footprints I let man after

501 | P a g e

man track in and out of my life. Yes, this is a huge confirmation that I am on the right track.

The day I was on the way to the garage sale; Micah had taken me to lunch. I forgot all about my things once we started talking and laughing. There is nothing like a man that knows how to make me laugh. The day I saw him, he did not care about my lack of weave down my back or whether I had on high priced designer clothes. He only cared about the woman inside. I cannot tell you how this has happened, but I am starting to feel this flutter in my stomach when he looks at me. The soft smile that he greets me with and the welcoming peace he has in his eyes when he speaks to me has created a special vessel in my soul. With each passing day, Micah is filling my heart up with acceptance, joy and yes, even real love. Thank you, Father God, I am so blessed.

I shook beautiful thoughts of Micah out of my head. I shook myself back to reality: you cannot truly move on to the future unless you have tied up loose ends of the past. As I began to go through my things I got up and modeled a few. The tight dresses did not feel right anymore. As I modeled a piece of lingerie I had worn for Greysan, a mandarin orange lace cami top and black thong set with conveniently placed cut outs, I began to reminisce on those times when I gave my body to a man that wouldn't give me his heart. I was good for sex but not good enough for anything deeper. It wrong to offer only sex when I got something just as empty back. It wrong to take the money he willingly offered. As the burning reality of those answers rose like reflux in my throat, I relented. I refused to hold the men to high standards because it allowed me to excuse my own sinful behavior. Never again.

As I looked in the full-length door mirror, as sexy as I looked, I realized something. The freak in me is alive and well. I was afraid that my self-imposed celibacy had killed her off. The goddess freak in me just needs to wait for the man, her husband, to let her out again. All my tricks and even my eagerness to experience sexual highs until I am spent, tell me that the sexually expressive side of me will never die. In fact, finding one man to experience those highs with will make the experience even better. Now, that is what I am waiting on! Sexual chemistry within a monogamous relationship will be pure satisfaction. Micah and I have so much built up sexual energy, we will have to take a vacation!

I changed back into my sweats and I began to look through my things, I focused on dealing with the remnants of my past: good, bad, and ugly. These things represent the old Trinity. The person that I am today enjoys living in the now. My past has passed me. It is time to look into the glorious future.

I giggled at the pictures and I cried. I rubbed and smelled some of Momma's brooches trying to imagine her wearing them. Momma squeezed a lot of living in her short years by the looks of the colorful jewelry she has accumulated. I only wished that she could have lived to see the woman I have grown into. Once spiritually mute, now I was ready to sing aloud. I was changed! I am redeemed! I am not a woman who runs herself through the mud for married men anymore. I am a beautiful, well-loved child of God. I am wonderfully fulfilled Trinity Marie Boussiant, worthy woman of grace.

I looked at the letter and envelope then put them back down. What peace can come from this? *Keep me, Lord, hold me tight.* First, I pick up the envelope. Inside was ten thousand dollars! But why? I read the letter in hope that it gave some direction as to how my stuff found its way here and what this money is payment for.

Dear Trinity,

This is Quintaria, Greysan's wife. In good conscious, I could not keep your personal effects. I did however keep your household things. I will be selling the condo as a furnished unit. Please understand. Let me say, I know how charismatic my husband can be, so I figured that fair is fair. I forgive you. My husband is another thing altogether. If you did not already realize, this is my money that he is spending like water. As were those credit cards he let you and his other mistress use. The job he holds, held, was a wedding present from my father. Greysan is broke without me. I also kept your paintings. The payment for them is enclosed in the envelope. I have a friend who is a curator at a gallery. She was the one that priced the paintings for me. Btw, she is extremely interested in holding a show for you at her gallery, her card is enclosed. She is eagerly awaiting your call. You are extremely talented. How did you end up with such a leech like my husband? I do not get it. Anyways, please do not stop creating. I bet that you are

504 | P a g e

wondering why I am doing things this way instead
of burning your stuff. Well, Trinity, I know about
the abortions. I am so sorry that you had to
experience such loss when I was giving life. I figure
I was as wrong in all this if I do not right this
wrong as much as I can. I figure that this erases
some of my bad karma for marrying such a loser
like Greysan. Btw, sorry for getting you fired. I took
my anger out on you when I should have dealt
solely with my husband, the snake. My fault.
God bless you.

"I am restored!" I yelled.

As those beautiful thoughts flowed easily in my mind, ugly spirited Tremica came into the room. I tensed up from the negative flow of energy that always accompanied her. Without a word, she sat down on the floor with me and watched me cry. I could not get myself together. Tremica started crying too. Wow, she has a heart! Without saying a word, she dried her eyes and began to help me to sort through my stuff. We sat there for what seemed like hours and did not say a thing. When she saw me looking at my baby albums with pictures of my Momma inside them, she spoke.

"You know Trinity, I really like you. I know that we didn't hit it off when you first came here, but I just want to apologize. I was upset because you were so gracious and everyone that seemed to avoid me took so easily to you. I was afraid of how you often forced me to see the angry feelings I harbored about having a child with a married man. See we both settled for the likes of a man who didn't honor us, but you were lucky. You were smart enough to

505 | P a g e

abort your babies. I decided to have Emily so now I am attached to this man for life. At least now you can go on with your life, unattached."

I looked at her and dried my eyes. I am so joyous that she finally told me why she felt so distanced from me. I finally know that it was not from the energy that I was giving out to her. I feel better now that she has revealed that she is battling her own demons. Now that the truth is out, we can move on with a mutual understanding. Even become friends. But, before we can move forward, I must tell her my truth.

"Tremica, I am not lucky. You are. I wish I wasn't so foolish to abort my babies. You still don't see that you are blessed to have such a beautiful child. It doesn't matter who her father is. Emily is God's child. I wish that I had my babies to hold and love. Don't you see that you hated me from the beginning because, in your mind, I was stronger than you? The truth is that I was weak to give a man, someone else's husband at that, my power! You truly are stronger than you realize, Tremica. You put the love of your child and protecting her life before your feelings for a man, whereas I didn't. In retrospect, I was looking for someone to love me. To be totally honest, any man would have done the job. But having a married man to love me and give me time and money made me feel even more special. Back then, I couldn't see the truth. What he did to her, he would eventually do to me, especially since I didn't have the money that his wife has. It didn't take him long to prove that he would go out and sniff up someone else's skirt either."

"Trinity, I never looked at things like that. My married man lied to me when he said that he would treat Emily like his other kids. The truth was that he never planned on leaving his wife or as I foolishly believed, introducing Emily to his other kids. I believed all his lies and even believed him when he said that he loved me and wanted me to have more of his babies. He said that I was a better woman than his wife. I have been too busy being angry that he abandoned me and Emily. Now, I wish that I could have loved myself enough, back then, to stay away from someone way below my standards. Isn't it funny that I lowered my standards for a married man when I would never have done so for a single man? Before my married man, I had a good-looking successful man who treated me well. But this married man said all the right things and it stroked my ego that some other woman's man wanted me. I guess that it didn't help that I was mad at my best friend when her man came on to me. I only wanted to hurt her. I didn't expect to fall in love, let alone have a baby. Once she found out, I had to move out of our apartment."

"Tremica, yes that is funny. In search of love, we make some crazy choices in men. I never messed with my best friend's husband, but I won't judge how you could have made such a choice when you were feeling low. Both of us are here, in this place in our lives, for a reason. Both of us fell for someone else's husband. Both of us are out of that situation and have a fabulous chance to begin anew. Going forward, why don't we empower each other to grow into being whole women? I'd rather be your friend than your enemy."

"Trinity, I agree. I am so sorry for all the hateful things I said to you. You really are an amazing woman. I remember when you came here, you were so funny thinking that Redeeming Hope was going to house you in a mansion and that we were going to take care of you as your servants. Oh, the look on your face when you learned the truth! It was hilarious! But gurl, you have grown so much since that day. Now, you see the benefits of taking care of yourself. You can cook a little, but your baking is off the hook! I still can't get the taste of your strawberry cheesecake out of my mind, it was bananas!"

"Yes, Tremica, I have grown. We both have. I watch you with Emily and it warms my heart. You may have been hateful to all the women here, but you are a good mother. When I first came here, I was so lost and out of balance. Spiritually, I have grown a lot. As result, I have become a better person. I never thought that I would be able to be celibate for this long. One week was my limit, now it's been months."

"Yes, I am a good Mom. I feel like I can be myself around children. The women, I believe, judge me too harshly. When I feel attacked, I am rude, and I do what I need to protect myself from being hurt. I guess that I should lighten up, huh?

We both laughed, "Ya think?!" I picked at her and she took it in playful fun.

"Yes, I do. I am sick of looking for love but settling for sex! I still have a lot of work to do on myself, but I can say that being celibate has helped me a lot.

Now I can choose a man without allowing sex to cloud my mind."

"Trust me, I get it. God does a mighty work in His children. God is so good."

"All the time."

By the time our conversation was over, our faces were flowing with tears of greater appreciation for each other. The girl that rolled her eyes and abused my efforts to become friends with these women is now a woman that I respect. Not all women who cheat with married men are stupid bimbos. Many of us are just lost on the road to being found within ourselves. We just want to be loved. Now, Tremica and I are ready to move from being a married man's jump off to jumping into a life filled with loving self-first. An open spacious life without lying cheating, married men!

We hugged and went back to going through my things. I came across several of my Mom's photo albums. I put them aside. I am going to see Mr. Hanks, my Dad, later, today so I will take the books with me. I took the other things downstairs and let the ladies choose whatever they wanted. All besides my art supplies. Oh, and my shoes, do not judge me!

~39~
Soul Real

"I see what you've done. Now see what I've done. I've opened a door before you that no one can slam shut. You don't have much strength. I know that; you used what you had to keep my Word. You didn't deny me when times were rough. And watch as I take those who call themselves true believers but are nothing of the kind, pretenders whose true membership is in the club of Satan—watch as I strip off their pretensions and they're forced to acknowledge it's you that I've loved. Because you kept my Word in passionate patience, I'll keep you safe in the time of testing that will be here soon, and all over the earth, every man, woman, and child put to the test. I'm on my way; I'll be there soon. Keep a tight grip on what you have so no one distracts you and steals your crown.
Revelation 3:8-11

***

Trinity

As I opened my eyes, a smile spread across my lips. I quickly put my feet onto the floor and looked outside. What a day The Lord has made. The warm air of summer was blowing through the window. Today is a day of restoration. It will be the glorious day that I will finally contact Micah. I am so excited!

I looked to the other side of the room and Tremica was sitting up reading a book to Emily. It is lovely watching her with her daughter. I look forward to being a mother one day. Tremica and I have gotten close since our talk. We talk about everything and I can honestly call her my friend. She and I cooked the big Sunday dinner together last week. She shared her family recipe for jerk chicken, cabbage, and steamed broccoli. I taught her how to make a homemade apple pie from scratch. It had a flaky crust and all. Everyone raved about the meal for days. I remember Micah telling me of his love of Caribbean food. I have already planned to make that meal as the first meal I will cook for Micah when we are husband and wife.

I got out of my bed and walked over to Tremica's bed. "Good Morning Mica. And…" I bent down and kissed Emily on the cheek. I took her from Tremica, and she giggled. Spittle dripped out of her little mouth and she showed her cute little teeth. "Emilllly!" Then I blew on her little jaw making a funny noise.

"Morning Trinni. Gurl, you sure rested well last night. You hugged up on that teddy bear with Micah's picture on it the entire night. You even said his name a couple of times."

"I did not, Mica." I looked at the goofy look on her face. "Stop playing…did I?"

"Uhh, yea! You must be sprung out because you sure never said Greysan's name in your sleep. Although you probably wanted to punch him instead of hug and kiss him like you want to do with Micah." She giggled and I had to agree. Micah has my heart. Big time I am s-p-r-u-n-g out.

"Mica, gurl, I don't have time for you today. I must get myself together. I'm going to call Micah today after church. I miss him like crazy."

"I can tell. I am so happy for you Trinni. How do you think things will go when you contact him?"

"I know how he feels about me. I feel him in my soul, Mica. I have lusted before and I have even been infatuated before. But this is the first time I can say that I am in love. It's positively no mistake that I am finally in love when I love myself totally too."

"Trinni, do you think it's that simple? That you have to love yourself first before you can love another?"

"Yes, I do Mica. In fact, I'll go another step further. I realize that God loves me completely. No matter how many married men I sinned with. No matter how much money I spent on frivolous things. But, once I prayed for forgiveness and asked God into my heart when I did that, everything changed. I mean, it was still very tough not reverting to my old patterns. However, when I realized that I was already complete in God's eyes, everything else was simple. I asked God to help me, but I had to move from my faith as well. You know that scripture says that faith without works is dead."

"Whoa Trinni, that's profound! I must get to work on loving myself too so I can get me a good, single man. Did I tell you that Emily's father is coming back around? He wants to be with me now. Says that his wife is cheating on him and he wants to leave her to be with me."

"Wow, what did you say to him?"

"I know that you'll understand this Trinni but…it's so hard. I mean, I want Emily to be with her father and me in a true family. I just don't know if I can trust his intentions, you know."

"Yes, I do know. Have you prayed about it?"

"Yes, I have. I'm still waiting for an answer. But I must say that the Holy Spirit has already convicted my heart. I have trust issues already. I told Hollarin he must give me time and he must show me divorce papers before I will try anything with him. I mean, I can't say that all men are cheaters, right?"

"No, you can't assume that because he cheated with you that he will cheat on you. Sometimes, people look for someone to make them feel whole, needed, and desired. Their spouse can't fill that void. Especially if the cheater doesn't know what's missing inside. So, cheaters seek out people who won't force them to find that wholeness within themselves. Mica, do you think that he really loves you? I mean *really* loves you?"

She got this soft look upon her face, "Yes Trinni, I do. He has waited on me to be intimate and I'm not giving in anytime soon. I believe that he has learned his lesson. He sees now that he has got to be a father to Emily, no matter what happens between us."

"Good for you. Stand up for what you deserve and take no prisoners. God loves you as you are. He wants you to begin living like the true Christian He created you to be. Sheesh, listen to me dishing out all this advice like I'm not still a work in progression myself. I need to take some advice of my own."

"No disrespect Trinni, but you do. Funny how we can see everyone else's circumstances so easily but it's so tough to stay grounded on our own. But I respect your opinion, I really do. I can't talk about this to other women. They get all judgmental on me. You are a good friend. Thank you."

"Remember, that as it states in John 16:14 says: *we must not be self-conscious, we must strive to be Jesus-conscious and the rest will follow suit.*"

"Let me write that down, I need to put that in my phone so that I can be reminded of that scripture, every hour on the hour. With Hollarin around, my flesh is constantly being tested. I mean, we used to make love like rabbits and he always loved me. He just acted like a fool most of the time. But that scripture really spoke to me." She looked at her cell phone and smiled, "You know that he just texted me Good Morning Beautiful. He's so sweet when he wants to be. Oh, my gosh, Trinni, you better get going, the van will be leaving soon."

"Mica, sitting here looking at the glow that that man has put on your face has caused me to lose track of the time. Why didn't we have talks like this before? We have wasted so much time"

"Because we were both healing. Oh, and I hated you!"

"Oh yea, that! I had completely forgotten that little thing."

I got up and sat on the edge of her bed. Mica, I and Emily got in on the group hug. My life is coming together beautifully. God said, and he will make your enemies your friends. Oh, how that is true!

I moved around the room gathering the things I needed then sat on my bed.

"Trinity, may I ask you a question?"

I pulled my shower shoes on and sat on my bathrobe, "Sure."

"How are you so sure that Micah loves you? I mean *really* loves you?"

"Well, Micah saw me at my worse and still stuck around to see the best. He doesn't pressure me to have sex and Mica, it's been months! We are both getting antsy but neither of us will give in to lust, no matter what. When we disagree, he may raise his voice and get passionate about his point, but he will never make me feel like I need to worry about him hitting me. I feel safe with him. Micah lets me be my own person. I don't have to pretend to think or believe something to make him like me. He accepts me as I am. The most important way that I know Micah loves me is this: he prays with me and for me. See like this, he texted me that he loves me a trillion times along with a cute little picture of him blowing a kiss to me. Mica, he is not afraid to be silly with me!"

"Aww, Trinni, he does love you! So, do you trust him? I mean we know that when you deal with cheaters, every single, solitary man is suspect."

"Do I trust, Micah? Without hesitation, I will say this, yes. I know that I am a good woman and I know that he and I complement each other so beautifully. I am unique and I know that he loves that about me. He doesn't laugh and joke with other women like he does me. There is something sacred in the way that we deal with each other. He,

515 | P a g e

respectfully, wouldn't want other people to have a chance to create a scenario that he is cheating on me. He has very firm boundaries of behavior. Because of that, I never have to question his intentions with other women. He can talk to them, but he has been in this world long enough not to let the wiles of random women turn his head."

"Dang, that's really commendable. Most men are so hell bent on getting their egos stroked. They laugh and joke with women and know that the woman wants them, yet they still get involved in situations where their behavior can be called into question. Those men, I will never respect. Those men, under the right circumstances, will always cheat. They have no respect for themselves or women. They are always on the prowl! Subtlety but still on the prowl!"

"Exactly! Thank God Micah isn't like those men. He has integrity."

"Well, as Pastor said last week at church, from I John 4:11: *If we love one another, God dwells deeply within us, and His love becomes complete in us-perfect love!*"

"I pray that you will find the answer to your questions regarding Emily's father. She is such a precious little girl. She deserves a full-time daddy. But don't settle Tremica. You are a good woman and you deserve a good man."

"Aww, thanks, Trinni. Now you really better get going!"

I jumped into the shower and put on my favorite song; Kari Jobe's *You are for me*. I do not care what mood I am in when I listen to this song, my mood lightens, and I feel so blessed. There is something so surreal about this song. It is beautiful and it hits me in my core. By the hook, I am always in tears. How lovely it feels that God loves me so deeply and completely. I had secretly dreamed of having a personal relationship with Him. Now that I have it, I will not do anything to push it aside. I know that He is for me. As I sing it over and over, feelings of spiritual wholeness flow over me as the warm water cascades upon my cleansed being.

      As I brushed my teeth, I smiled. I missed Micah *so* much. I did not know why the feeling flowed on me real hard. It was amazing, I started out my birthday year alone and crying. Now, I had a relationship with my Creator, my earthly Father and now Micah. My desire to have positive men in my life has come full circle. All three beings loved me unconditionally and completely. I was beyond blessed. I know that finding Micah is my reward for being obedient and breaking my stronghold of dependence on sex to make me feel wanted. I have broken through the notion that my body is nothing to be valued or respected. Now, I know that my body is sacred and should only be shared with the man that values me as a woman, not just a temporary fix for his desires. I may not be perfect, but I am no longer a hot mess. I was progressing. I was a masterpiece from birth. I was blinded to the one fact: my faith would bring me to the door of my spiritual break through. I was like a seed, full of promise and life, but I had to reach for the living water, I had to ask Jesus into my life for that seed to sprout. It was only for the asking that I am now a beautiful flower. I invited Jesus into my soul and now He will live there for eternity. I expect that our connection will deepen with each arriving season.

To think that I spent thirty-eight years searching for acceptance of a man when completion was all in the hands of God. I had read so many self-help books and was convinced that I was a love addict, an obsessive-compulsive lover, and a needy fatherless child. The only book I needed to crack open was the Bible. I had believed the books that told me that I had some mental deficiency that allowed me to repeat an endless cycle of dysfunction with men that only used me. I spent many years feeling empty after sex because I felt dirty. I knew that sex with married men was wrong. I have known since day one that I was corrupting my own soul with low self-esteem. To this day, I can list every single man I allowed in my bed. I could tell you names of even more that I had allowed to take up space between my ears too. I know that even today, I can write a list of each man and how much money he gave me. What I cannot account for is what things I brought with that money. I know that my past behaviors could identify me as a prostitute, but it is all perspective. I had convinced myself that I should get paid for my time, other women do. I know that I may be misunderstood. But women like me are not whole. We have been raped, molested, and abused in many ways. Women like me have lost our link to our spiritual chain. We keep looking, feeling, and even praying for the perfect sized link, in the world, to make us feel whole. I can see now that that is a futile effort. Drugs, alcohol, stripping, money, and using sex to repair a broken heart are indicators of the devalued, unloved, and unseen. Broken women, like I used to be, feel lonely even in a crowded room. But you would never know it because often we are the life of the party, the outgoing women or even the shy, scared types. The outward appearance gives you the illusion that we are happy. But, if you take a moment, you can see the pain behind the eyes. The insurmountable tears bursting at the well of the soul. Broken women, like myself, have brought into the lies that the devil keeps perpetuating. The battle in the mind is often won by cunning and deviousness of the devil. Negative thoughts get blown out of proportion. Emotions lead to a skewed view of reality. The ironic thing is that broken women will attack at the very insinuation of disrespect from others. Yet, we disrespect ourselves daily. Broken women like Tremica and me have been this way for so long that it takes perseverance and lots of prayers to heal our broken hearts and injured spirits. For now, throwing myself into times of solitude, prayer, and meditation will help me to stay focused on growth and to not back track.

I quickly got dressed, then I opened the door to our room and rushed down the steps. I do not want to miss today's service. The pastor is starting a series on abundance. Hmm, just call me an abundant child of God. I came downstairs to find the women sitting around waiting for the van to arrive. They looked so bored; way too bored to be on the way to church! On a whim, I put my Mary

Mary CD into the audio player. I played the track God in Me and turned the volume up high. By the hook, everyone was dancing and singing along with the song. What began as a quiet praise turned out to be giving all thanks and praise to Our Lord and Savior. God is good. All the time.

Humph, women that have deep hurt can be fixed. By faith! And a little music. By faith, there is joy in the future. Most of all, there are many blessings in the Now. We just must stop pretending to be comfortable being broken and afraid. And instead, we must allow the world to see the light, the God in us. The fearlessness through brokenness in us.

On the ride to church, all I thought about was Micah. I rehearsed in my mind all the things I wanted to talk to him about. All too often when we talk, I get sidetracked and the conversation always ends up in a different place than either of us expected. He makes me laugh and he makes my heart sing. As soon as I get back to the shelter, after church, I am going to call him. I sure miss that man!

****

As I walked into the sanctuary, I waved at many of the people I saw. There sure is a lot of natural sistahs here. I feel in good company. My naturally curly hair is flowing down to my shoulders and I feel beautiful. It seemed as if I was flowing on air when I was tapped from behind. I turned to look into a set of beautiful eyes. *Thank you, Jesus.*

"Hi"

"Hi, yourself."

"I didn't expect to see you here." I smiled angelically.

"I didn't expect to see you here either. But it is a welcome surprise. You look beautiful Trin." He sighed softly. "You really do."

I am breathless. No man has ever told me that I am beautiful without wanting anything from me. This man has got me so twisted! I love the way he says my name, so slow and smooth. He says that I am beautiful but, wow, this man looks carved out of stone.

"Thank you. Humph, Micah, you clean up quite well yourself." *Grey who?!*

He took my hand and held it gently, rubbing it softly. We stood quietly and looked into each other's eyes.

"May I sit beside you?" He asked breaking the beautifully comfortable silence.

"Yes, I would love it if you would."

"Thank you."

We walked, us holding hands, to where the Usher guided us. I felt like I belonged to him and it suited me just fine. He was polite and helped me out of my coat. I watched him as his eyes ran up and down my body. He smiled and was pleased with what he saw. I watched him take off his blazer and I did not remember him looking so cut. He must have been working out hard because his shoulders were wider, stomach was just the right size (I cannot stand men with a six pack, I need a thicker man.), and his chest was firm. I had to tear my eyes off this fine man. I looked around trying to compose myself. Many other women could not tear their eyes off…my man…either. Le Sigh. Corporate prayer began and I was a little shy about letting myself go, but watching him pray, I quickly became comfortable. He was not shy about speaking in tongues or raising his arms in praise. This is what an honorable, God fearing man praises like. I had previously watched other men praising like this, but I did not think that any man like that, God filled, would want someone like me. Today, I realize that my worst enemy was me. I allowed foolish thoughts to invade what I always felt in my spirit, I am loved. And I am worthy of a good, God fearing man like Micah. And he is worthy of me too.

Micah has such a beautiful singing voice. As *Something Beautiful* by Anthony Evans began, he held my hips close to him and sang sweetly in my ear. Nervously, I looked around. Some of the women from the church were cutting their eyes at me. Yes, I have a man and he looked just like this and he is not married. Do not be jealous ladies! What God has for you, is for you. But this man is m-i-n-e. Moving forward by Israel Houghton came on next, one of my favs. I sang out loud and Micah smiled lovingly at me. Yes, I know, I cannot carry a tune with a bucket. But, for the Lord, I will praise along with the most sanctified. As the faster songs came on, we played around and danced. Micah sure has rhythm. Hmmm. I forced my thoughts off the flesh and focused on the words to the songs. I could not stop feeling so proud that this man was as happy to be with me as I am he. *He saw the best in me* sang with powerful anointing by Marvin Sapp came on and I got lost in the spirit. Tears started falling down my face and I let myself give in. I totally forgot Micah was standing next to me. The words tore me up. Micah wiped the tears from my eyes and helped me sit down when praise and worship ended. When the announcements were given, Micah put his arm on the back of the pew, and I got caught up in his scent. This single man smells heavenly. I have me a single man! God sure is good. When visitors were asked to stand and the members were asked to welcome them, it was a stampede of women trying to push past me to get a hug from Micah. Respectfully, he held out an outstretched hand. Screech, in your face thirsty women! When he sat back down next to me, I snuggled up next to him. This man is the business!

During service, he said Amen and clapped when Pastor made good points. He is not shy, not by a long shot. He breezed through the Bible to the correct chapter when a scripture was given as a point of reference. So, he reads his Bible often, goodness, grace, and mercy. When it was tithes and offering time, he wrote out one envelope for us both. Mr. and Mrs. at that!

After service was over Micah held my hand as he walked me up to the front to meet Pastor and First Lady. Then he proceeded to knock me off my feet. Right in front of everyone, he asked Pastor if he would perform our wedding ceremony. He told him that he had already planned out every single detail and that the event would take place exactly seventeen days from now. Pastor politely accepted, pending any schedule conflicts. As we walked away, he asked me if he could take me out to lunch. He said that he had wanted to go to Warm Daddy's in Philadelphia for their gospel brunch and thought I would enjoy it. I gratefully accepted. I found Ms. Mabel in the crowd and introduced Micah to her. She smiled that wide, partial showing smile, and I beamed. Her motherly eyes twinkled, and she said aloud, "Thank you, Jesus."

 Micah pulled me closer and looked into my eyes with pride.

"Ms. Mabel, Micah would like to take me to brunch in Philly. Do you have anything planned for us women at the shelter today?"

She shook her head, "Chile, this man is asking to take you out on a date. Bless your heart for asking, but I wouldn't dare stand in the way of you keeping company with someone who clearly loves you."

"Thank you for understanding my love for this beautiful woman, Ms. Mabel." Micah pulled her hand up and kissed it politely.

"Uh huh, and does that mean I have an invite to the nuptials?" Ms. Mabel smiled widely.

I spoke up, "I'm so sorry, I just heard about it when everyone else did. I would be honored if you would stand in for my Mother on my wedding day. Please Ms. Mabel, will you please accept?"

She hugged me tightly and tears streamed down our faces, "Trinity Marie, I would be honored."

We parted ways and again, Micah held me closely and smiled proudly. When we were finally at the car, he pulled me in for a kiss. We rode to Philadelphia in silence. I, to reflect on the joy at finding true love, twice over. First, with my Lord and Savior and then with my earthly King, Micah. I know that I could not have loved Micah with such vulnerability had I not first given in to my love of Jesus. Micah, unbeknownst to me, was quiet most of the drive, planning his next move.

When we arrived at Warm Daddy's I got the surprise of my life. My Daddy, Grand Momma, Poppa, Micah's family, and Jnana was there with her family. As I went about hugging everyone, Micah went up on the stage. He politely asked us all to sit down. With tears in my eyes, I watched my man stand in front of the microphone and sing Love Ballad from LTD. After he sang the last words, he called me up to the stage and smiled.

"Trinity, it feels like I have loved you a million years. Every moment since we became committed has been beyond my wildest dreams. I love you, completely. Will you be my wife?"

"Yes, yes, yes!" My voice echoed throughout the place.

Applause erupted and everyone rushed the stage to congratulate us. Then we got our plates and ate lots of tasty food while the band performed.

Looking across our table I mouthed, I love you. Micah put his hand on his heart and said, I love you more.

I felt a tap on my shoulder, and I knew instantly who it was. Jnana! I locked eyes with her when I came in the door but did not walk towards her. It has been a minute since we last talked.

Judging from the bigger rock on her finger and the warm smile on her face, things have changed with her just as much as they have changed with me. No matter the time apart, I missed my bestest friend in the whole wide world!

I spun around and greeted her the only way I know how. With love and glee.

"Jnana!"

"Trinity!"

We hugged for what seemed like eons. Then we stepped back to access each other. The last time she saw me, I was looking a hot mess and my mental was even messier.

"You clean up real nice Boussiant."

"As do you, Roberts."

We looked at each other to see who would burst out laughing at the other. It is a trip that neither of us could last much more than a few seconds before we fell out laughing. Nope, time apart has not changed the true friendship bond we share. *But God!*

"So, what's been going on with you Trin? Well, besides that huge rock you have weighing your hand down." She smiled and love shown upon her face. Jnana always knew how to support me like a loyal friend should.

"Well…" Micah came and wrapped his arms around my waist. "I'm getting married!"

"Ohmygosh, that's so fabulous Trin! I'm so happy for you. And who is this? I don't believe that I've met you before."

"Jnana, this is Micah, my fiancé. Micah, this is my best friend Jnana."

They said their pleasantries then, in true Jnana fashion, she started to interrogate Micah. Hmmm, this should be interesting. As a police officer, I am sure he has interrogated his share of folk too.

"So, how did you meet Trinity?" She rubbed her chin and waited patiently for his reply.

"Well…Babe, would you like to answer that question?" He held me tighter and smirked.

"Jnana, I already told you about Micah. Remember the day that I got arrested? Remember the police officer I told you about? Well, this is he. God works in mysterious ways. Micah is now the love of my life."

"Whoa, Trinity, you have got to be kidding me. I do remember you talking about him. But, sadly, I also remember being very judgmental and doubting that a police officer would want you, especially one that was arresting you. I'm so sorry Trin."

"It's okay Jnana. I know I was acting really foolish back then."

I put my head down and felt embarrassed. Micah pulled me closer to him and kissed me tenderly on my cheek.

"As you can see, she has made a lot of changes since that day. What Trinni couldn't know back then was that I was very attracted to her too. Aside from being a police officer, I am a man first. A man that likes the finer things in life. Trinni is the finest woman I have ever laid eyes on. I saw beauty in her that I was sure she hadn't quite realized. Still, I was drawn to the beautiful woman inside of her."

Jnana was surprised that such words were being aimed my way. In all our years as friends, she had

527 | P a g e

never seen a man love on me so genuinely. She was in awe.

"Trin, you have caught you a good one. This man really loves you. I can tell. I am so happy for you." Before I could speak, Micah spoke up. "It's nice to meet you Jnana. I see an old school friend that I haven't seen in years walking into the restaurant. Trin, Babes, I'll bring him over here so that you can meet him."

Jnana was speechless, again. "Alright Babe, I'll be right here."

He smiled and headed across the room. Jnana and I watched as he made a beeline to Greysan and his arm candy. What the…

We both stood with our mouths open as Micah brought Greysan over to us.

"Patches, I would like you to meet my fiancée Trinity Boussiant and her best friend Jnana." Micah had to hold me up because I nearly fell out onto the floor! "Hi, Trinity, nice to meet you," Greysan smirked at me and I cuddled up closer to Micah.

Bless Your Soul Reading Group Guide
Worthy, by Faith

1. In the beginning of the novel, Trinity waits all day for Greysan to pick her up for their date. If Greysan had not been honest with Trinity, do you believe that she would have found out that he was married with children? Knowing her relationship history, did it make a difference that he was married?

2. Jnana is very outgoing and outspoken during the story. What other personality traits of hers caused problems in her marriage? If she had not submitted, would her marriage have survived?

3. Trinity was a kept woman for married men with money. How had her mother's relationship choices negatively affected her? Do you believe that the abandonment of her Father emotionally affected her?

4. Trinity allows Greysan to treat her horribly. How could she have taken control over her desire for Greysan to love her? What could she have done when he threatened to put her out of the condo? Was her plot to blow up his spot appropriate?

5. Jnana appears to have a perfect marriage and perfect teenage children. Is that really the

true picture of her family? Do you know anyone that has this same kind of situation in their family?

6. Jnana and Trinity appear at different spectrums of faith. Are they more religious or spiritual? Do people of faith allow sex to be prominent in their relationships or is the perception that Christians have a little sex?

7. When Trinity became homeless, she had a challenging time getting along with the females in the shelter. Why is it that some females have a challenging time creating and maintaining positive uplifting relationships with another female? Are most of your friends, male or female? Why?

8. When Shandon counseled Ashton about sex, Jnana got really upset and felt left out and betrayed. Did she have a reason to react so emotionally? When Lili came on her period, Jnana did not consult Shandon. Why do you think that she had to control every aspect of her family?

9. Trinity was arrested for identity theft. During her arrest, she felt intensely attracted to Micah. Is it realistic that a relationship that started out from an arrest would culminate into the blissful relationship Trinity and Micah formed?

10. Trinity and Jnana searched for balance within themselves. When they both found an intimate

relationship with God for themselves, they found peace. How do you feel about women who pull away from a relationship to find God for themselves? Would you believe a relationship would be a distraction or a help?

11. When Greysan finally caught up with Trinity, were you afraid of her trying to find closure? Do people try so desperately to find closure that they refuse to let go of the past?

12. Jnana was shocked to find that Ashton was sexually active with Celeste. How would you have dealt with the situation? Would you have insisted on getting him tested for STDs when you found out the amount of sexual activity Celeste was in to?

13. When Trinity received her things back from Quintaria, were you surprised? Would you have given Trinity her things back considering she was aborting babies from an affair? Do you think that she has truly changed?

14. Jnana has a great relationship with her mother. And Trinity finds her father. Is a good relationship with parents essential for adults to get real talk and emotional support?

15. Throughout the book, being worthy is a prominent theme. What ideas do you have

about faith and being worthy? What empowering names found in the Bible do you call yourself when your faith is being tested? Does a positive body image affect how worthy a woman feels about herself?

16. Is it possible to love someone else when you do not love yourself? Would such a relationship be unequally yoked if the other person is already fully confident in who they are in Christ?

Stacy is also author of Speak It! Learning to speak the word of God over your life. And as an educator, she has created over ten inclusive children's learning workbooks that will inspire all children to strive in their educational journey.

www.ingramcontent.com/pod-product-compliance
Lightning Source LLC
Chambersburg PA
CBHW060447090426
42735CB00011B/1939